International Economics

Global Markets and Competition

2nd Edition

Henry Thompson

Auburn University

International Economics

Global Markets and Competition

2nd Edition

World Scientific

NEW JERSEY · LONDON · SINGAPORE · BEIJING · SHANGHAI · HONG KONG · TAIPEI · CHENNAI

Published by

World Scientific Publishing Co. Pte. Ltd.

5 Toh Tuck Link, Singapore 596224

USA office: 27 Warren Street, Suite 401-402, Hackensack, NJ 07601

UK office: 57 Shelton Street, Covent Garden, London WC2H 9HE

British Library Cataloguing-in-Publication Data
A catalogue record for this book is available from the British Library.

ISBN   981-256-346-6 (pbk)

Printed by FuIsland Offset Printing (S) Pte Ltd, Singapore

Preface for the Student

International economics will affect your private and business life. International economics has moved center stage as countries become more integrated with trade, foreign investment, and migration. The world is shrinking with better transportation and telecommunication.

The foreign exchange market is simply the largest market in the world. Industries expand and collapse in the face of international markets and competition. The World Trade Organization (WTO), North American Free Trade Agreement (NAFTA), and European Union (EU) have become a fundamental form of government.

Protection eases pressures of international competition. Industries seek the protection of tariffs and quotas, securing their own profit at your expense. Governments hinder international trade and investment. Government central banks interfere with the foreign exchange market. Such maneuvers impede international commerce and lower income.

This text focuses on international markets. An economy is a collection of interdependent markets, and in international economies are linked across borders. Comparative advantage is the most important tool for predicting international production and trade. International supply is based on underlying production capacity.

International trade is the arbitrage of products from countries where prices are low and products unique. Arbitrage makes traders profit and distributes products more economically. The interaction of international supply and demand determines production and trade. The effects of trade depend on the types of industries, from competition to monopoly.

Trade policy is designed to redistribute income toward favored industries and groups. Costs of protection outweigh benefits but industry and labor groups lobby for protection because they gain at everyone's expense and politicians respond to political support.

The graphs, examples, applications, and problems in the text are essential. There are hints for even numbered problems. Good luck. I think you will enjoy *International Economics: Global Markets and Competition*. Visit the website at *www.auburn.edu/~thomph1* where you can find analysis of current events and links. Contact me at *thomph1@auburn.edu*.

Preface for the Instructor

International Economics: Global Markets and Competition is unique:

- a one-term text for students with principles background
- microeconomic models stress positive theory
- advocates free trade, skeptical about government trade policy
- theory advances through partial and general equilibrium
- over 250 boxed examples from the literature
- problems lead students through theory

This text applies the tools of microeconomics and general equilibrium. The foreign exchange market and balance of payments are integrated throughout the text. Open economy macroeconomic models are included in the final chapter stressing micro foundations.

The text does not assume intermediate theory or calculus. Numerous boxed examples are a central component, introducing tools and concepts.

Technical points are made with examples and graphs, avoiding "formulas" and algebraic symbols. Classroom presentations should be more general, using diagrams and algebra.

Problems are designed for learning and were developed in the classroom. Hints for even numbered problems are in an appendix. Students can be called on to work problems at the board, increasing their capacity to absorb the material.

You will be surprised at how well your students learn using *International Economics: Global Markets and Competition*. The website at *www.auburn.edu/~thomph1* can be integrated into classwork. There is analysis of current events and links to resources. Contact me at *thomph1@auburn.edu*.

Thanks

Numerous students and colleagues have provided suggestions and comments. Sonja Langby uncovered logical slips, Lijun Chen carefully rechecked Problems, and Mostafa Malki updated Examples. The excellent staff at World Scientific Publishing made putting the text together a pleasure.

Contents

MARKETS AND TRADE

CHAPTER I

Markets, Trade, and Comparative Advantage

Preview

This chapter introduces some fundamental concepts of international economics:
- *International markets*, supply and demand across countries
- *Excess supply* and *excess demand* in international markets
- *Comparative advantage*, the foundation of trade
- *Balance of trade*, net receipts from trade

INTRODUCTION

The most important tools of economics are supply and demand. Goods and services are traded in markets that determine prices in nominal currency terms. Markets include the stock market, the foreign exchange market, and the international market for steel. In market transactions, money changes hands between buyer and seller at an agreed price.

An international transaction occurs when the buyer and seller are in different countries. Two currencies are involved in an international transaction when the buyer's currency is traded for the seller's currency.

International economics is different since governments can tax transactions with tariffs at the border or limit transactions with quotas or nontariff barriers. International economics is characterized by a lack of labor mobility between countries. International migration is difficult and typically restricted by law. Investment is also inhibited across national boundaries.

Comparative advantage, a cornerstone of economics, is a relative advantage in production efficiency based on opportunity cost, the value of the next best alternative. When a country produces a particular good or service, it gives up producing alternatives. Resources are limited and it is important to use them efficiently.

The balance of trade regularly makes headlines. The balance of trade is a country's export revenue minus import spending on manufactured goods. Trade deficits occur if import expenditure is greater than export revenue.

A.   INTERNATIONAL MARKETS

Everyone is involved in international markets every day. Almost everything we buy has some foreign element or component. Virtually every job contributes to exports and uses imports. International markets provide the basis of international economics, and this section presents international markets.

Domestic Demand

The law of demand states that as the price of a good rises, the quantity demanded falls. As an example, car dealers offer discounts and rebates when inventories are too high.

Figure 1.1 shows domestic market demand D for rugs. This demand curve represents the quantity of a particular quality of rug that would be demanded at various prices by domestic consumers. If the price of a rug is $15, 100 units are demanded per month.

Demand curves slope downward for two reasons:

- *substitution effect* — a higher price induces consumers to look for substitutes
- *income effect* — a higher price, especially for a good that has a large budget share, lowers real income and consumption of all goods.

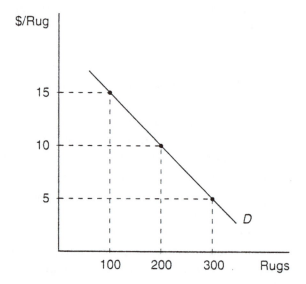

Figure 1.1
The Domestic Demand (D) for Rugs
Quantity demanded is inversely related to price. When price goes up, the quantity demanded falls.

Some goods have readily available substitutes. If the price of beef rises with a quota on imported beef, consumers switch to pork, chicken, lamb, or fish. If the price of Japanese cars rises with a voluntary export restraint, consumers switch to European or US cars. If the price of Dutch cheese rises with a tariff, consumers switch to Wisconsin cheese.

Embargoes of the Organization of Petroleum Exporting Countries (OPEC) during the 1970s significantly raised the price of crude oil. The price of gasoline rose relative to other products. Consumers began to substitute away from gasoline, but real incomes fell. The higher relative price of gas lowered the purchasing power of consumer income, lowering the consumption of all products.

The world of international economics must be simplified to understand what is going on. The process of abstracting and simplifying is a crucial step in the scientific method. Scientists build and test simple models that reflect the real world. If a model proves useful in predicting what happens, it becomes accepted. The demand curve in Figure 1.1 is the first step of economic model building.

Demand curves slope downward due to substitution and income effects.

Demand curves are different across nations. Various factors determine the position of a demand curve:

- consumer tastes
- number of consumers
- price expectations of consumers
- consumer income
- prices of related products

As tastes for a product become stronger, the demand curve shifts right. Consumers are willing to pay a higher price for the same quantity of the product and demand more at any price. Only 40 years ago, US consumers had little taste for Japanese cars or electronics. Imported beer, beverages, food, bicycles, and clothes were rare.

More consumers in a market increase demand. As nations grow, there is increased demand for goods and services. When a country enters international trade, the number of potential buyers of its products expands. The North American Free Trade Area (NAFTA) increases the demand for some products produced in Canada, Mexico, or the US. The US government outlaws trade with Cuba, a loss of potential consumers for US exports. If Europe opens its protected agricultural industry to free trade, the demand for US agricultural products will increase.

Expectations of higher prices induce consumers to buy now in order to avoid higher prices later, increasing current demand. With news that the Ukrainian wheat harvest will be poor, buyers of wheat expect higher prices in the future, increase their current demand, and push up prices. The expectation of lower prices in the future lowered present demand.

Higher income raises demand for *normal* goods and lowers demand for *inferior* goods. Income limits what consumers can spend on all goods and services. As incomes rise in newly industrialized countries such as South Korea, Mexico, and Brazil, their demand for normal goods rises, increasing the demand for US exports. Demand for public transport, an inferior good, may decline in these growing countries as people switch to cars.

Many goods are related in consumption. Demand for a good is positively related to the price of its substitutes. Coffee and tea are substitutes. When the price of coffee rose in the early 1970s as the international coffee cartels restricted output, demand for tea and the price of tea increased. Coffee and sugar are complements and the two are used together. If the price of coffee tripled, demand for sugar and its price would fall. Demand for a good is negatively related to the price of its complements.

If the demand curve in Figure 1.1 increases because of these nonprice influences, it shifts right. A decrease in demand would be represented as a shift to the left of *D*.

> *Demand curves shift to the right (increase) or left (decrease) because of nonprice influences.*

EXAMPLE 1.1   *International Trade Growth*

Since World War II there has been steadily increasing international trade. Growth in trade has outstripped output growth, which itself has steadily grown. US firms are becoming more involved in international trade and US consumers enjoy products from around the world. The same is true worldwide.

Domestic Supply

Supply curves are the marginal costs of production of firms in an industry. Marginal cost is the additional or extra cost of producing one more unit of output. Marginal cost slopes upward for two reasons:

- *Diminishing marginal productivity* of labor, natural resource, and capital inputs
- Increasing output may bid up prices of inputs

The law of diminishing marginal productivity says that the additional output per unit of input declines as the input increases, holding other inputs constant. For a given physical plant, the marginal product of an additional worker declines after some point. For some large industries, increasing output may also raise labor demand enough that wages rise.

The marginal cost curve of a typical firm slopes upward. When output in an industry rises, firms within the industry are producing more or new firms are

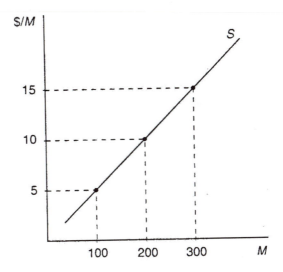

Figure 1.2
The Domestic Supply (S) of Manufactures (M)
The quantity supplied is positively associated with price. When price goes up, the quantity supplied rises. When price goes down, the quantity supplied falls.

entering the industry. Output in an industry will generally rise when the price of output in the industry rises. There is a positive relationship between price and output.

Figure 1.2 shows the upward sloping domestic supply of a manufactured good. It might represent cars, apparel, or computers. Supply curves are likely to differ across nations. Differences in the supply curve are due to

- technology
- the number of firms
- prices of productive inputs
- price expectations of firms

With improved technology firms can produce more output with the same inputs. More efficient jet engines have lowered the cost of international air travel. With the same amount of labor, fuel, and other inputs, airlines lower their costs. Improved technology is represented by a shift in the supply of air travel to the right.

An increase in the number of firms in an industry increases supply. A good example occurred in the personal computer (PC) market. Original PCs were made by a few companies that enjoyed high prices and profits. Other firms began to enter the industry, many of them foreign firms or domestic firms using foreign components. As firms entered, supply rose and the price of PCs fell.

Lower input prices also increase supply. Many US manufacturing firms import intermediate inputs. A tariff on imported television components is a tax that must be paid at the border. If the tariff is eliminated, the cost of making televisions inside the US falls. Immigration lowers wages, which increases the supply of manufactured goods.

Price expectations shift supply. If firms expect lower prices, they will sell inventories and increase current supply. The international oil market provides an example of how price expectations affect current supply. International oil dealers and brokers stockpile oil, buying it from oil producers and selling it to refineries or other dealers and brokers. If an OPEC meeting ends in agreement, dealers expect oil prices to increase. An OPEC agreement keeps oil prices high by restricting the output of member countries. Higher oil prices mean the stockpiles held by brokers and dealers will be worth more in the future. Supply decreases immediately and price rises right away. If OPEC is not able to reach an agreement, dealers expect falling prices and sell their inventories causing current supply and price to fall right away.

Supply curves slope upward, reflecting the higher marginal cost associated with higher output. Domestic supply curves shift because of nonprice influences, which can be international in origin.

Shifts in supply or demand must be distinguished from movements along the curves. A change in price causes a change in the quantity supplied or demanded along the curve. A change in a nonprice influence shifts the entire curve.

EXAMPLE 1.2 *Relatively Large and Closed*

Relative to other countries, the US economy is a closed giant, producing about 20% of world output. The US leads all countries in its share of world trade but trade is a small share of US output. The ratio of export revenue plus import spending to output has grown to about 20% for the US, about the same for Japan, and about 50% for Europe. For many small countries, $(x + m)/$GDP is much higher.

Markets and Market Clearing

The domestic market for manufactures is shown in Figure 1.3. The domestic *equilibrium price* is determined where the quantity domestic buyers are willing to consume just equals the quantity domestic suppliers are willing to produce. In this example the domestic equilibrium price is $10/unit. Firms produce 200 units, which are exactly consumed at the equilibrium price.

At any other price the quantities supplied and demanded would not be equal. At a price of $15, production is 300 and consumption 100, and inventories

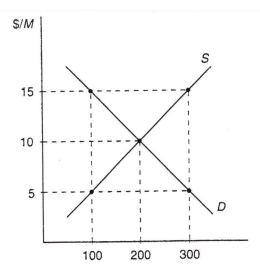

Figure 1.3
The Domestic Market for Manufacturers (M)
Domestic supply (*S*) and demand (*D*) interact to determine the domestic equilibrium price
$10 and the domestic equilibrium quantity 200. The equilibrium price equates quantity
supplied with quantity demanded.

increase by 200. Suppliers would lower price to keep their inventories from
accumulating. At a price of $5, desired consumption at 300 is greater than
production at 100 and consumers bid up the price in competition.

This market clearing mechanism explains why government policymakers
cannot arbitrarily set prices and expect the economy to respond with desired
production and consumption. Suppose a politician thinks a $5 price of this
manufactured product is desirable. A price ceiling is put into effect, a law that
will not allow the price to go above $5. Buyers want 300 units. Suppliers will
produce only 100 since they have no incentive to make more than 100 units
given their cost of production.

At the other extreme, a government policy maker may decide that a $15
floor price would benefit the manufacturing industry. Firms respond to the high
price by expanding output, but consumers will not buy the 300 units produced.
The government may purchase the surplus, as happens with some agricultural
products.

*Markets clear at equilibrium prices equating quantity demanded with quantity
supplied.*

EXAMPLE 1.3   *Origins of US Merchandise Exports*

The top 7 states in the US are listed below by merchandise export revenue in
1997 in $billion (Department of Commerce). Exports are based on port location.

Production may not occur in these states but exports reflect regional production. California, Texas, and New York account for over one third of exports. California and Washington are located on the Pacific Rim and trade heavily with Asia. Texas trades heavily with Latin America. New York is on the Atlantic and exports to the EU. Michigan and Illinois have ports on the Great Lakes and export to Canada.

	total	% Americas	% EU	% Asia
US	$595 bil	10%	27%	36%
CA	17%	4%	19%	48%
TX	9%	11%	11%	20%
NY	8%	15%	37%	24%
MI	6%	5%	13%	8%
IL	6%	9%	26%	24%
WA	5%	3%	28%	47%

International Markets

In an international market, there are producers and customers at home and in other countries. Suppose there are only two nations. Figure 1.4 shows the home

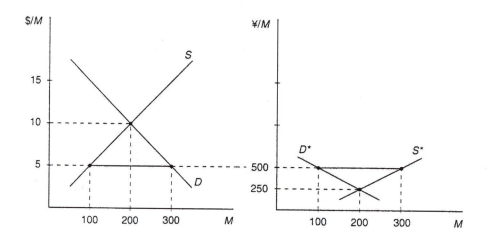

Figure 1.4
The International Market for Manufactures (M)
Free trade takes place where the excess demand from one country equals the excess supply from the other country. At a price of $5/M, excess demand of 200 from the home country equals excess supply of 200 from the foreign country. the foreign country will export 200 units of manufactures to the home country.

and foreign markets for a manufactured good M. Asterisks are used for the foreign country. Neither supply nor demand is identical across countries, and price is almost always different. In Figure 1.4 the equilibrium price in the home market is $10 and the equilibrium price in the foreign market is 250 yen.

When comparing price in the foreign country with the price at home, traders must convert to a common currency. This conversion determines where the good is cheaper. This is the role of the foreign exchange market, where the *exchange rate* is expressed as the dollar value of the yen ($/yen). The exchange rate is the price of one currency in terms of another. In Figure 1.4, the exchange rate is $/yen = 0.01, each yen worth one cent.

This international market offers an opportunity for trade or *arbitrage*. Traders can buy the goods in the foreign country at a price of 250 yen or $2.50 = 250 × 0.01, which is less than the $10 domestic price. It is profitable to buy the good in the yen country and sell it in the dollar country. Arbitrage across national markets is the foundation of international trade.

International trade seeks the price where excess demand from one country equals excess supply from the other. At any other price the amount one country is willing to export will not equal the amount the other country wants to import.

A price of $5 clears the international market in Figure 1.4. The home country imports 200 = 300 = 100 units at a price of $5 or 500 yen. Domestic firms produce 100 units at the international price. Domestic production falls from 200 to 100 with the opening of trade. Domestic consumers enjoy lower prices with international trade and increase the quantity demand from 200 to 300. On the foreign side, production rises from 200 to 300 with the increase in price from 250 yen to 500 yen. Foreign consumers suffer higher prices, cutting their level of consumption from 200 to 100.

International trade creates winners and losers. In an export market, domestic firms are better off but consumers suffer. In an import market, domestic industry suffers while consumers enjoy benefits. Efficiency is improved through international trade. Global benefits outweigh costs and there are overall gains from trade.

International markets arise when prices vary across nations and clear at prices where the excess demand in importing nations matches the excess supply from exporting nations.

In practice, international traders are concerned with *transport costs*, including the costs of shipping, storage, insurance, and delivery. If each unit of *M* in Figure 1.4 cost $6 to transport from the foreign country, imported goods would cost $5 + $6 = $11, more than the domestic price. An importer who disregards transport costs would soon be out of business. For simplicity transport costs are assumed to be zero in Figure 1.4.

The model of international markets has been repeatedly tested in international markets. International economists rely on the scientific method to build, test, and revise trade theory.

EXAMPLE 1.4   *Trade in Business Services*

World trade in business services totals about 1/4 of merchandise trade. The US is a major service exporter and increased specialization can be expected in the future. Shares of world business services in total trade from the WTO are listed.

	exports	imports
US	18%	13%
UK	8%	6%
Germany	6%	10%
Japan	5%	9%

Problems for Section A

A1. Draw the shift in the demand curve for the manufactured good in the home country if the quantity demanded at every price in Figure 1.1 increases by 200. Find the new domestic market equilibrium price and quantity in a market diagram similar to Figure 1.3.

A2. Predict what happen to the international price and quantity traded of the manufactured good in Figure 1.4 with an improvement in technology in the domestic market.

A3. Suppose the domestic wage of manufacturing labor rises with a new labor contract. Draw a new domestic supply curve and show what happens in the international market of Figure 1.4.

A4. Create a diagram similar to Figure 1.4 in which demand in both countries is identical and trade arises because of differences in supply. Do another diagram in which supply is identical across nations but differences in demand lead to trade.

EXAMPLE 1.5   *Trade Index*

Countries vary in their involvement in international trade. The sum of export revenue plus import expenditure relative to output $(X + M)/\text{GDP}$ is a gauge of "openness". In 1992 Singapore was the most open economy and Brazil was the least open according to the IMF. Singapore and Hong Kong are commercial centers. The top 3 and bottom 3 countries are listed along with major US trading partners. The US remains a relatively closed economy.

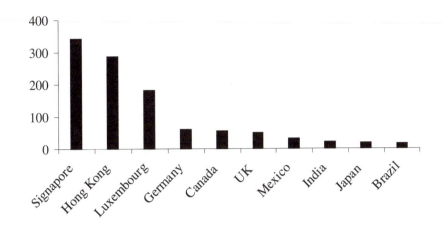

B.   *EXCESS SUPPLY AND DEMAND*

Excess supply and excess demand are tools that simplify the analysis of international markets. The difference between quantity demanded and supplied in a
country at any price is *excess demand*. The difference between quantity supplied
and quantity demanded at any price is *excess supply*. Using these concepts, the
international market in Figure 1.4 can be reduced to a simpler diagram.

Excess Demand

The excess demand in Figure 1.5 is derived from the home market diagram in
Figure 1.4. At the domestic market clearing price of $10, excess demand *XD* at
home is zero. At lower prices, excess demand is positive. At $5, *XD* is 200 with
home firms producing 100 units and home consumers buying 300 units. The
home country is willing to import 200 units at an international price of $5.

An increase in domestic demand shifts the home *XD* curve. Suppose an
increase in demand drives the domestic price up to $12.50. Excess demand
increases as in Figure 1.6, making the home country more willing to import the
good. At $10 the quantity imported jumps from 0 to 100. Decreased supply
would also cause *XD* to rise.

An increase in domestic supply has the opposite effect on *XD*. The home
country becomes less willing to import the manufactured good. At any price,
XD falls, a shift from *XD′* to *XD* in Figure 1.6. At $5, home imports would drop
from 200 to 100. The increased domestic supply and falling *XD* move the
economy away from importing. Decreased demand or increased supply causes
XD to fall.

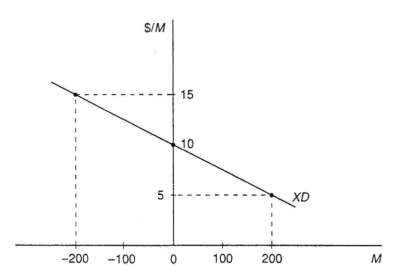

Figure 1.5
Home Excess Demand for Manufactures
Excess demand (*XD*) is inversely related to price. When price rises, *XD* falls. At *P* (price) = $10, *XD* = 0. When *P* < $10, the quantity demanded is greater than quantity supplied, and *XD* > 0. At prices above $10, there is negative excess demand or positive excess supply.

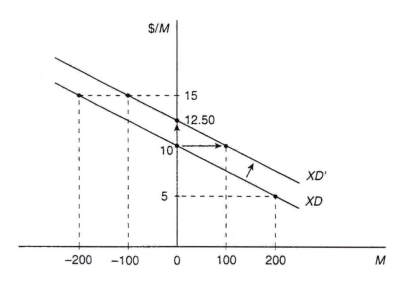

Figure 1.6
An Increase in Excess Demand
Increased demand for manufactures in the home country has the effect of shifting the excess demand (*XD*) for manufactures (*M*) to the right. Decreased supply of manufactures in the home country has the same effect. The difference between the quantity demanded and quantity supplied rises at every price.

Excess demand shows the quantity of a good a country wants to import at every price. International excess demand shifts when the underlying supply or demand shifts.

EXAMPLE 1.6   *Trade between DCs and LDCs*

Most exports come from industrial countries and most is exported to other industrial countries. LDCs account for about a quarter of exports, shipped mostly to industrial countries. Remaining shipments go to newly industrial countries (NICs).

		From	
		DCs	LDCs
To	DCs	72%	65%
	LDCs	23%	26%

Excess Supply

Excess supply of the foreign country can be derived from the foreign demand and supply curves in Figure 1.4. Foreign excess supply *XS** in Figure 1.7 is

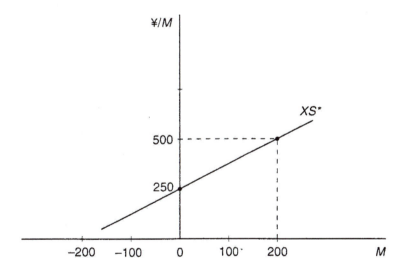

Figure 1.7
The Foreign Excess Supply of Manufactures
Excess supply (*XS*) is positively related to price. As price rises, quantity supplied by the foreign country rises and the quantity demanded falls. When $P > 250$ yen, $XS^* > 0$. At prices below 250 yen, there is negative excess supply or positive excess demand from the foreign country.

zero at the foreign market clearing price of 250 yen ($2.50 by the exchange rate). At 500 yen, XS^* is 200. Changes in foreign supply and demand shift foreign excess supply, similar to the shifts in excess demand. A good exercise is to draw shifts in XS^* resulting from increases and decreases in foreign supply and demand.

> *International excess supply shows the quantity of a good a country wants to export at every price. Excess supply shifts whenever the nation's underlying supply or demand shifts.*

EXAMPLE 1.7   *Largest US Ports*

The largest US ports by exports are listed below with their two largest categories of exports, from *Foreign Trade of the United States* published by Bernan Press. Total export in 1997 was $595 billion. The most frequent large categories are transportation equipment, industrial machinery and computers, and electric and electronic equipment. Seattle and Detroit ship mostly transportation equipment. San Jose and Houston ship machinery.

	exports	largest categories	
New York	$29 bil	14% prim metals	10% machinery
San Jose	$29	45% machinery	41% elec equip
Seattle	$27	74% transp equip	7% lumber
Detroit	$26	69% transp equip	12% machinery
Los Angeles	$26	31% transp equip	12% machinery
Chicago	$23	26% elec equip	16% machinery
Houston	$19	37% machinery	5% chemicals

International Markets Again

In a viable international market, there is a price where excess demand from one country equals excess supply from the other at the current exchange rate. The interaction of international excess supply and excess demand determines the quantity traded and the *international equilibrium price* of the traded good. In the international market of Figure 1.8, the international price of the manufactured good is $5. The excess supply in the foreign country is just matched by the excess demand at home at the international price of $5. The market for this manufactured good clears internationally.

At an international price below $5, $XD > XS^*$ and there is a shortage of the manufactured good on the international market. Exporters in the foreign country will notice they cannot meet demand as inventories decline. Importers want to

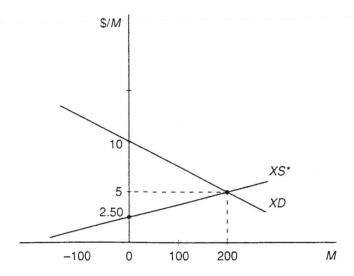

Figure 1.8
International Excess Supply and Demand
In this international market for manufactures, the foreign country exports 200 units of M to the home country. The international equilibrium price of \$5 equates excess demand (XD) from the home country with excess supply (XS^*) from the foreign country. In this example, the exchange rate is yen/\$ = 100.

buy more than exporters are willing to produce, a clear signal for foreign producers and exporters to raise price.

If the international price is above \$5, $XS^* > XD$. Producers are making more than they can sell, and inventories accumulate. The way to eliminate the surplus is to lower price.

The international price balances supply and demand across countries. An automatic adjustment process pushes the international market toward the international equilibrium price of \$5 with the quantity of goods traded at 200 in Figure 1.8.

International markets clear at the price where excess demand from importing countries equals excess supply from exporting countries.

Transport costs can be crucial in determining whether a good is traded internationally. Gravel and cement are heavy relative to value and cost too much to ship very far. At the other extreme, the ratio of weight to value is low for electronic components and drugs, goods that are heavily traded.

National borders impose costs also. Customs procedures, paperwork and grappling with bureaucrats, have to be cleared. Foreign exchange transactions, cross border insurance, and border delays make international commerce costly. Charles Engel and John Rogers (1994) find that national borders add as much cost as

2500 miles between US and Canadian cities, and these two countries have relatively open borders.

EXAMPLE 1.8   *US Agriculture Trade*

US agricultural trade is categorized for 1997 when the US exported $57 billion and imported $36 billion. The US has trade surpluses in agriculture.

export revenue		import expenditure	
animal products	21%	animal products	19%
oil seeds	19%	fruits and vegetables	19%
grains	19%	coffee	10%
other	30%	other	46%

Shifts in Excess Supply and Demand

The exchange rate can influence international prices and the trade level. An exchange rate of $/yen = 0.01 results in the international price of $5 and trade level of 200 units of *M* in Figure 1.8. If the dollar depreciates in the foreign exchange market, its value falls and the value of the yen rises. Dollar *depreciation* means the exchange rate $/yen rises. The same yen price for the manufactured good from Japan translates into a higher dollar price.

Foreign manufacturers do business in yen and they are concerned with the yen price. Foreign producers supply less at every dollar price when the dollar depreciates. A dollar depreciation creates a reduction of *XS** as in Figure 1.9. The international dollar price rises and the volume of trade falls. The price of imports in the home country rises and the quantity imported falls.

A reduction in foreign supply of the manufactured good will also cause *XS** to fall as in Figure 1.9. An increase in foreign demand, perhaps due to higher income, will cause a similar decline in *XS**. On the other hand, a depreciating yen, an increase in foreign supply, or a decrease in foreign demand cause an increase in *XS**, a lower international dollar price of the manufactured good, and an increase in the quantity traded.

Suppose the home country is specializing away from the manufactured good, producing more services for international trade. As the number of domestic manufacturing firms declines, domestic supply falls, resulting in an increase in excess demand. There is an increase in the international price and a higher volume of trade. In Figure 1.10 the international price rises to $6.25 and the quantity traded rises to 300. The increase in *XD* could be caused by an increase in domestic demand.

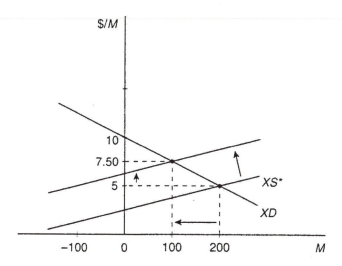

Figure 1.9
The Effect of a Depreciating Home Currency on Imports
When $/yen rises, foreign excess supply (*XS**) falls. Dollar prices translate into lower yen prices for foreign producers. The decline in foreign excess supply pushes up the international dollar price of manufactures and lowers the level of trade. A depreciation raises the price of imports and lowers the level of imports. *XD* is excess demand from the home country.

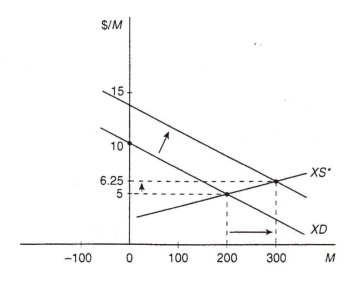

Figure 1.10
An Increase in Excess Demand
Rising excess demand (*XD*) for manufactures (*M*) from the home country increases the international price of manufactures from $5 to $6.25 and raises the level of trade from 200 to 300. *XS** is excess supply in the foreign country.

Trading partners may be involved in a free trade agreement to lower protection against imports. Tariffs are taxes on imports and are one form of protection. Quotas are quantitative limits on imports. Current examples of trade agreements are NAFTA (North American Free Trade Area) between the US, Canada, and Mexico, the EU (European Union), and Mercosur. Domestic producers competing with foreign exporters expect lower prices and falling profit when trade is liberalized. The anticipation of falling prices causes relatively inefficient domestic producers to exit the industry. Domestic supply falls and *XD* rises. A higher international price and more trade occur, as in Figure 1.10.

Anything that affects the underlying supply or demand in a trading country shifts its excess supply or excess demand, changing the international price and quantity traded.

EXAMPLE 1.9   *Trade and War*

A common political belief is that democracies do not have wars with each other, but closer to the truth countries do not go to war with their trading partners. Solomon Polachek (1997) examines the history of wars from 1800 to 1986 and finds a higher degree of democracy does not decrease conflict but a higher level of trade does. Countries do not want to fight with their trading partners. Free trade decreases wars because countries want to protect their income, supplies, and customers.

Problems for Section B

B1. Show what happens in the international market for manufactures in Figure 1.8 if the dollar appreciates above yen/\$ = 100.

B2. Illustrate the effects of a simultaneous decrease in domestic demand and increase in domestic supply on excess demand. Predict what will happen to the international price and quantity traded.

B3. Suppose Japan imports wood and the Japanese supply of lumber rises when a forest matures. Show the effect on the international market for lumber, assuming excess supply comes from the US.

EXAMPLE 1.10   *How to Export*

The Department of Commerce has a Trade Promotion Association with data on countries looking for products. The Small Business Administration has an Office of International Trade (OIT) with training conferences and counseling. The SBA has a group of retired business people SCORE (Service Corps of Retired Executives). Importers have to wrestle with customs and red tape and the exporters may have to provide transportation.

C. THE BALANCE OF TRADE

Trade involves exchanging one thing for another. Imports are goods that we enjoy consuming without having to produce. Exports are goods that we have to go to the trouble of producing but cannot enjoy consuming. Importing firms and ultimately consumers in the home country must pay firms in the foreign country for imports. With millions of products traded internationally among hundreds of nations, how is a balance struck? This section begins to look at this issue by introducing the balance of trade.

International Transactions

A country pays for imports with the foreign currency it collects through exports. In every economy, each firm or consumer makes optimal choices given available information, prices, budgets, and so on. A wheat broker looks for the best deals in buying and selling wheat. Car buyers look for the best deal for their money.

> *The balance of trade reports the difference between revenue from exports and spending on imports. The BOT is the international net inflow of cash from trade.*

When a good is exported, the foreign importer must convert its currency to pay the exporter. This transaction involves a bank or foreign exchange dealer willing to trade currencies. The foreign importer trades local for foreign currency. When an importer buys foreign goods, foreign currency is bought to pay the foreign exporter. Some traders keep bank accounts in foreign currency to avoid frequent foreign exchange transactions.

EXAMPLE 1.11 *Snapshot of the US BOT*

The US has BOT deficits with NAFTA, Japan, and the EU. The services surplus comes mostly from these major trading partners. BOT deficits are offset somewhat by surpluses in services, TS. These 2004 figures are from the *Survey of Current Business.*

	BOT	TS
NAFTA	−$29 billion	$3 billion
EU	−$25	$6
Japan	−$24	$3
total	−$82	$13

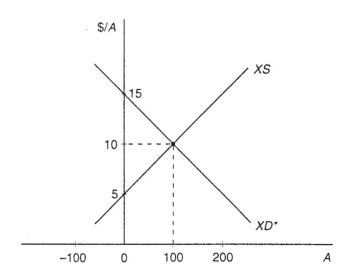

Figure I.II
The International Market for Agricultural Goods
Excess supply (*XS*) from the home country and excess demand (*XD**) from the foreign country meet at an international equilibrium price of $10, with 100 units of agricultural goods (*A*) exported from the home country to the foreign country.

Calculating the Balance of Trade

The *balance of trade* equals the difference between *export revenue X* and *import expenditure M*:

$$BOT = X - M = (P_{exp} \times Q_{exp}) - (P_{imp} \times Q_{imp})$$

The *BOT* regularly makes the front page and the evening news. It is a *trade deficit* when negative, and a *trade surplus* when positive.

A typical country exports many types of goods. For simplicity, suppose only agricultural goods are exported. The international market for agricultural goods, with domestic excess supply and foreign excess demand, is shown in Figure 1.11. The exchange rate is yen/$ = 100. In the foreign country the price is 1500 yen ($15) per unit of the agricultural good without trade. The price without trade is the foreign *autarky* price, an ancient Greek word for self-sufficient.

Excess supply comes from the home country, where the autarky price would be $5. The international market clears at $10 (1000 yen) with 100 units of agricultural goods traded. Export revenue is $10 × 100 = $1000. Suppose import expenditure on manufacturers for the home country is also $1000, as in Figure 1.8. The balance of trade for the home country equals zero and trade is balanced.

EXAMPLE 1.12 *Merchandise Exports by US State*

The top 5 merchandise exporting states in the US are reported by the Census in *US Merchandise Trade*. California and Texas are the largest exporters but Washington is the most involved in export production.

	% total	exp/output
California	14%	9%
Texas	11%	12%
New York	6%	6%
Washington	5%	19%
Michigan	5%	12%

Balanced trade almost never occurs in the real world with international markets for thousands of different goods. Suppose a bumper crop of agricultural goods is enjoyed in the importing country in Figure 1.11. Foreign supply increases, lowering XD^*. The world price of agricultural goods falls below $10 and the level of home exports falls below 100. Export revenue X for the home country falls below $1000, creating a BOT deficit.

A deficit in the balance of trade occurs when the country spends more on imports than it receives from exports. A trade surplus occurs if export revenue is greater than import expenditure.

Chart 1.1 shows the merchandise balance of trade for the US in dollars per household, based on 90 million households. Manufacturing firms in the US like to suggest that a trade deficit is a cause of economic ills. Their suggested remedy is protection, which would allow their relatively inefficient manufacturing production to continue. Both exports and imports are growing as

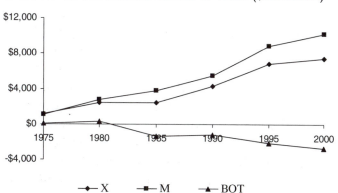

Chart 1.1 US Merchandise Balance of Trade ($/household)

the US economy becomes more open. Before 1970 the US had regular BOT surpluses. The BOT deficits in recent years are offset in part by surpluses in service trade. Furthermore, the quantity of exports is underestimated because there is no mandatory reporting or taxing of exports. At any rate, there are automatic forces that create a tendency for an economy to move toward balanced trade in the long run.

EXAMPLE 1.13 *The Big 3*

NAFTA, the EU, and Japan account for about half of world output and over half of world trade in these shares of merchandise trade from the World Bank. Growth has been highest in NAFTA. Japan has not entered into any trading blocs and is more protected than NAFTA and the EU.

	% exp	% imp
NAFTA	24%	29%
EU	20%	18%
Japan	10%	8%

Trade Deficits

If a country spends more on imports than it receives from exports, the opposite must be true for some other country. A deficit in one country is mirrored by surpluses in others. A country with a deficit may:

- Borrow internationally and go into debt
- Spend its wealth

Debt is essential for economic growth. Firms borrow to invest in the capital equipment to increase future productivity. Consumers assume the debt of a mortgage to buy a house, buy a car, or go to college. Debt creates the means to grow and increase productivity. Nations as a whole assume debt in order to grow.

Mercantilism is the mistaken belief that deficits are bad. Scrooge was a devout mercantilist, bent on hoarding gold. As Adam Smith wrote 200 years ago in *The Wealth of Nations*, wealth is not measured by the amount of money or gold amassed. Productivity is the measure of wealth. It is rational to go into debt or sell assets to acquire capital to increase productivity. As a college student, you are acquiring human capital. Growing nations typically experience BOT deficits, importing the capital machinery and equipment to raise productivity.

There is another good reason not to become too excited over the reported BOT deficits. They are not very reliable. Reported data are accumulated through surveys of the Department of Commerce. Nations keep better records of imports that are subject to tariffs and quotas. The US underestimates its merchandise exports. Using Canadian data on imports from the US, it is not clear whether the US had trade deficits at all during the past 20 years. The sum of trade balances for all nations should be zero, but it is a large negative number proving exports are underestimated.

A *USA Today* headline on April 18, 1997 was "Error Good News for Trade Deficit". Due to errors overestimating oil imports, the trade deficit in February 1997 was overestimated by 18% or $1.2 billion. Why less of a deficit is good news is not explained in the article.

Another mistake to avoid regarding trade deficits is to concentrate on bilateral trade. The US has recently had BOT deficits with Japan. Figure 1.12 includes trade with the rest of the world (ROW). The US has a trade deficit with Japan. Japan has a deficit with the ROW, and the ROW has a deficit with the US. Bilateral deficits can be totally offset by other bilateral surpluses. Trade may be persistently unbalanced between any pair of countries, yet remain balanced overall. US manufacturers competing with Japanese exporters publicize the bilateral trade deficit with Japan as though it were a problem.

Even in the face of a trade deficit, no government policy should be undertaken to remedy it. Automatic adjustment processes lead to balanced trade. A trade deficit involves an excess supply of domestic currency and depreciation. Imports become more expensive. Also, money leaves the economy with a trade deficit, lowering the purchasing power of domestic consumers. The deficit adjusts itself.

Economists believe markets work as efficiently as anything could. To be successful, government policy to remedy an economic problem must recognize the problem and act in a timely fashion. Government policymakers have historically not been able to do either.

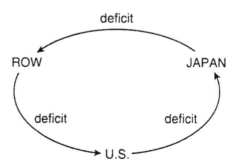

Figure 1.12
Multilateral Trade Balance
Trade in this example can be balanced for each nation — the United States (U.S.), Japan, and the rest of the world (ROW) — while bilateral deficits persist. The United States has a bilateral deficit with Japan; Japan has a bilateral deficit with the rest of the world; and the rest of the world has a bilateral deficit with the United States. Still, multilateral or global trade is balanced.

EXAMPLE 1.14 *Confusing Trade News*

Trade makes the monthly news when trade figures are released. The story below is edited from *USA Today*, 19 November 1999. Journalists, not economists, write the news. These monthly spot checks contain bits and pieces of information but they mislead by depicting deficits as bad and exports as good. It is a mistake to focus on any bilateral deficit such as the one with China. The "world currency crisis" refers to the depreciation of some overvalued fixed exchange rates. China is joining the WTO after decades of closed controlled inefficiency. The US cannot expect a surplus with OPEC anytime soon. This story is confusing and unfocused.

* * * * * * * * * * * *

WASHINGTON (edited from AP) The US trade deficit widened to $24 billion in September even though beleaguered American farmers saw their exports climb to the highest level in 19 months. America's deficits with China and Japan rose with China setting an all-time high for any country. The latest deterioration in trade left the overall deficit running at an annual rate of $255 billion, 56% above last year's record. Exports edged back 0.9%, reflecting declines in exports of airliners and autos. Imports hit a new high, rising 0.1% as the price of foreign crude oil shot up to the highest level in 31 months. American manufacturers have lost a half-million jobs since early 1998 as the world currency crisis has cut sharply into exports and contributed to a flood of cheaper-priced imports. Administration negotiators reached a major agreement with China in which the world's most populous nation agreed to dismantle its high trade barriers in return for U.S. support for its bid to join the World Trade Organization. But opponents of closer engagement with China have vowed to defeat the measure in Congress contending it does too little to level the playing field for American exports or deal with their complaints about China's record on human rights, religious freedom, weapons proliferation, and allegations of nuclear espionage. America's deficit with the Organization of Petroleum Exporting Countries also set a record, rising to $3 billion as the U.S. foreign oil bill climbed $6.8 billion, reflecting higher volume and price.

Problems for Section C

C1. Find the revised import expenditure given increased excess demand for manufactures in Figure 1.8. Suppose the international price rises to $6.25 and quantity traded rises to 300. Find the BOT using the export revenue in Figure 1.11.

C2. Predict what will happen to the BOT if excess supply of agricultural goods in Figure 1.11 increases with improved technology in the exporting home country.

EXAMPLE 1.15 *Recent US BGS*

> The two parts of the BGS are shown below since 1960 in billions of constant 2004 dollars. The BOT was positive through the 1960s and 1970s but turned negative in the 1980s with increased oil imports and international competition in labor intensive manufactures. The BOT fell substantially following 1995. The TS has been positive but much smaller in magnitude. The 2004 BGS deficit of −$617 billion is over 5% of GDP, no small potatoes. The trade deficit is financed by net foreign purchases of US assets, and 20% of those are government bonds that will be financed by future taxes. The other 80% involves foreign asset holders buying US stocks, bonds, and other assets. The margin of error in the estimate is over 8% of the BGS.

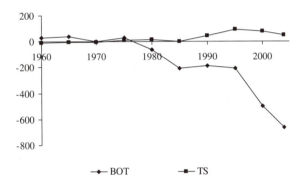

EXAMPLE 1.16 *"Battle in Seattle"*

> The WTO has 135 member countries and held a meeting in Seattle in December 1999. *Time* magazine ran a story (29 November 1999) prior to the meeting. Major issues were agricultural protection and subsidies in the EU and Japan, labor issues in the LDCs, global environmental agreements to avoid pollution havens, protection of local business services from US multinational firms, and dumping in the US. There were protests in Seattle from anti-globalists, protectionist reactionaries, US steelworkers, French farmers, clergy demonstrating for third world debt relief, radical political groups, Industrial Workers of the World, forest activists, and environmentalists. The WTO has become the most powerful and influential international organization and has usurped the power of governments to tax and regulate trade. The Seattle meeting collapsed but negotiations continue since there is simply too much to gain from trade.

D.   COMPARATIVE ADVANTAGE AND SPECIALIZATION

A slogan of international economics is *specialize and trade*. International economics is constantly sharpened on the arguments of domestic industries seeking protection through government tariffs, quotas, and nontariff barriers. Free trade leads to increased international specialization with relatively inefficient domestic firms failing in the face of foreign competition. This section introduces the principles of opportunity cost and comparative advantage. Gains from specialization and trade arise because of comparative advantage.

EXAMPLE 1.17 *Increased US Trade*

The US economy has become steadily more open to international trade since the 1950s with lower tariffs, more efficient international transport, and improved telecommunication. Trade accelerated during the 1990s with NAFTA. The index of total trade $[(X + M)/\text{GDP}] \times 100$ is a percentage that gauges export revenue plus import spending relative to national income. With increased trade, the US has become more dependent on international markets for both import supplies and export revenue. Almost all countries have similar rising trade indices over these decades with increased global trade.

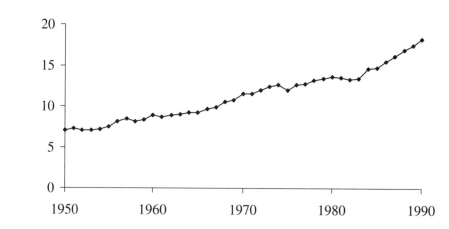

Opportunity Cost and Comparative Advantage

When you sit down to read this text, you are giving up an alternative activity. The value of your best alternative is the opportunity cost of reading international economics. Opportunity cost is the best alternative when a choice is made.

Consider the example of you and your roommate and the two tasks of vacuuming and making beds. Your roommate might be better at both, taking less time than you to finish either task in the same manner. Suppose you are relatively quicker at vacuuming. Your *opportunity cost* of vacuuming is lower. If you vacuum while your roommate makes beds, you both will gain. The two of you could specialize and trade, each spending less time on these routine tasks.

EXAMPLE 1.18 *World Merchandise Trade*

Merchandise trade grew in value during the 1990s although growth in Japan and the Asian NICs declined during the Asian crisis of the late 1990s. The groupings below account for about 2/3 of world merchandise trade. The Asian NICs are Taiwan, Hong Kong, Malaysia, Korea, Singapore, and Thailand. World trade grew 6% annually during the 1990s. Trade in business services accounts for about 20% of total trade. NAFTA has had the highest growth in trade followed by the EU. The Asian NICs have had very high growth rates for most of the 1990s but declines during the late 1990s. Data are from the WTO.

	exports		imports	
	% world	% growth	% world	% growth
NAFTA	17%	7%	21%	8%
EU	42%	6%	40%	6%
Japan	7%	2%	5%	0%
Asian NICs	10%	9%	8%	3%

Absolute versus Comparative Advantage

In these examples, an *absolute advantage* in producing a good means a lower unit labor input. In the example of vacuuming and making beds, your roommate takes less time to finish either task and has an absolute advantage in each activity.

An absolute advantage in a good means fewer resources such as labor and energy are used to produce a unit of the good. Suppose a country has an absolute advantage relative in producing both manufactured goods (cars, appliances, clothing) and services (banking, telecommunications, education, entertainment). Perhaps it has more capital machinery and equipment or more highly trained labor. Does this mean it should be totally self-sufficient, consuming only the goods it produces and not trading at all?

Comparative advantage is based on a lower opportunity cost in a particular activity. When comparing labor inputs across goods, Mexico uses *relatively* less labor in manufacturing than does the US. The opportunity cost of lost service output when the US produces manufactures is higher. Mexico gives up more manufactures when it produces services. Both nations can end up consuming more of both goods if each specializes in producing the type of good in which it has a comparative advantage and trades with the other.

No trickery is at work. Each country is simply spending its time and resources on the activity in which it has lower opportunity cost. Total output for the world will increase when each country specializes. Countries may have absolute advantages in most goods, some goods, or no goods at all. Still, each country should specialize according to its comparative advantage.

Nations can potentially consume more of all goods when they specialize and trade because the world's ability to produce is increased.

Looking for comparative advantage means looking for activities with low opportunity costs. This relative efficiency advantage explains why specialization and trade are beneficial.

EXAMPLE 1.19 *Regional vs Global Trade*

Most trade occurs between countries located close together. The US trades heavily with NAFTA, Latin Americas, and the Pacific Rim is growing. About 2% of world trade occurs between the Americas and Japan, and 3% between the Americas and the oil exporters. Another 3% occurs between Europe and Africa. The rest of world trade takes place between neighboring countries. Transport costs are lower, cultural ties make trade easier, and regional free trade agreements lower protection.

Labor Inputs and Comparative Advantage

Suppose the hours of labor it takes to produce a unit of manufactured goods (M) or services (S) in the US and Mexico are:

	US	MX
S	2	3
M	3	4

The US has an absolute advantage in producing both products since less time is required to produce a unit of either.

Nevertheless, the relative price of services is lower in the US. In the time it takes to produce 1 unit of S, only 2/3 of an M could be produced. It requires 3 hours to produce an M in the US, and 2/3 of an M would be produced in 2 hours. In Mexico, M could be produced in the time it takes to produce 1 unit of S. The opportunity cost of producing S is higher in Mexico than in the US. Mexico gives up more M when its resources produce a unit of S. The US has the comparative advantage in services.

In the time it takes to produce one M, 3/2 units of S could be produced in the US but only 4/3 units of S could be produced in Mexico. The opportunity cost of producing M is higher in the US than in Mexico because the US gives up more *S* when it produces a unit of *M*. Mexico has the comparative advantage in producing manufactures.

Comparative advantage is found by comparing opportunity costs or relative prices across nations.

Nations tend to specialize according to comparative advantage. Competitive forces lead nations toward specialization according to comparative advantage. Global resources are used more efficiently, and total world output increases with specialization according to comparative advantage. This idea is one of the oldest in economics and remains one of the most important. With specialization and trade, the value of consumption increases in every country.

Comparative advantage abstracts from details of market supply and demand. Prices of goods in the domestic and foreign markets and the exchange rate take on secondary importance when it is understood that comparative advantage offers a more fundamental explanation of trade.

The original example of comparative advantage created by David Ricardo more than 200 years ago involves the labor to produce wine (*W*) and cloth (*C*) by Portugal and England,

	PORT	ENG
W	80	120
C	90	100

Portugal has the absolute advantage in both goods. With the labor it takes to produce one *W*, 80/90 *C* can be produced in Portugal and $120/100 = 6/5$ *C* can be produced in England. The opportunity cost of wine is lower in Portugal. Portugal gives up less *C* to produce *W*. Portugal has the comparative advantage in wine and England has the comparative advantage in cloth.

EXAMPLE 1.20 *The China Trade*

China is entering the WTO and opening to international trade and finance after decades of suffering as a closed planned economy. China is an LDC but foreign investment is increasing income as production and export of assembly line manufactures increase. Main categories of Chinese exports and imports in 1997 from the UN are below listed in $billion. Exports of labor intensive apparel and textiles have increased. Imports of textiles are yarns used to make cloth, and cloth is imported for apparel manufacturing. Imports of machinery are used in production. China had a trade surplus in food products and a deficit in crude materials, each $7 billion. With the entry of China, the Pacific Rim will become a major stage for world production.

exports		imports	
clothing	$32 billion	chemicals	$19 billion
textiles	$14	elec machinery	$14
elec machinery	$13	textiles	$12
telecom equip	$10	machinery	$10
chemicals	$10	oil	$10

The Power of Comparative Advantage

Comparative advantage can predict trends in the pattern of trade between countries. The economic agents (producers, exporters, importers, and consumers) do not have to worry about comparative advantage. Firms are looking for profit opportunities and consumers are seeking better goods and services at lower prices. International trade arises because these agents act in their own self interest. You do not need to know the principle of comparative advantage to run a successful international business but the principle offers a unifying principle for understanding economic decisions.

Comparative advantage is perhaps the one true principle in the social sciences. No matter how inefficient a country might be in an absolute sense, it must have a comparative advantage in some activities. Comparative advantage works for nations, regions, states, cities, neighborhoods, or individual firms. Specialization between people can also be understood with comparative advantage. Lawyers do not do their own typing, no matter how good they type.

EXAMPLE 1.21 *Infrastructure & Trade*

Infrastructure facilitates commerce and trade. Infrastructure includes roads, bridges, utilities, telecommunication, airports, ports, water, sewer, and so on. Spiros Bougheas, Panicos Demetriades, and Edgar Morgenroth (1999) uncover evidence that better infrastructure lowers transport costs and increases the level of trade among European countries.

Problems for Section D

D1. You are a whiz and can clean the bathroom in 15 minutes and the kitchen in 30, while your roommate takes 20 and 45 minutes for the two tasks. Find who has the absolute and comparative advantages in each activity.

D2. Determine the absolute and comparative advantage in this hypothetical situation of hours of labor input between the US and Canada:

	US	CN
S	2	3
M	3	2

Does one country have the absolute advantage in both goods? Find the opportunity costs and relative prices of S in each country. Which country will specialize in which good?

EXAMPLE 1.22 *DCs and LDCs*

The US and the EU account for most of world output and exports. Asia is a major producing area but less oriented toward exports and with a much larger population. LDCs have almost 80% of the world's population but produce only 40% of world output and 2% of exports. These percentages from the World Bank illustrate vastly different productivity in DCs and LDCs. The last column shows *GDP/capita* relative to the US.

		% Output	% exp	% pop	% US GDP/capita
DCs		55%	78%	16%	81%
	Japan	7%	7%	2%	83%
	US	21%	14%	5%	–
	EU	20%	40%	6%	79%
LDCs		40%	18%	78%	12%
	Asia	23%	8%	52%	10%
	Africa	3%	2%	12%	7%

EXAMPLE 1.23 *US Fresh Tomato Import Market*

Isolating changes in international markets is a challenge as this data on the US fresh tomato import market suggests. Quantity demanded QD has risen over the last few decades. The quantity unit is millions of pounds. Domestic quantity supplied QS kept up until the start of NAFTA in the early 1990s when imports from Mexico began to increase. The difference between QD and QS is the quantity of imports QM and most come from Mexico. Tomato prices have generally been steady over the period. With rising population and income, tomato demand increased and domestic supply kept pace until the onset of NAFTA. Import competition discourage domestic production, and supply fell during NAFTA. Most US tomatoes are grown in California, Florida, and Texas, where the workers are typically migrant Mexicans or Mexican-Americans. Tariffs would limit imports of tomatoes but encourage more migration from Mexico.

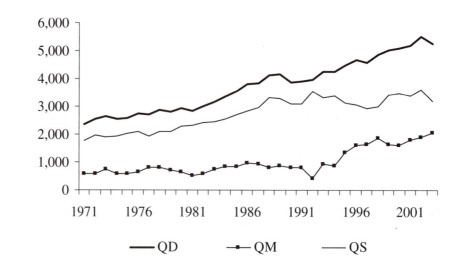

CONCLUSION

International markets constantly adjusting to grind out relative prices of traded products. The fundamentals of every market are the same. With application you can recognize and predict adjustment patterns. You are a consumer and will be involved in the production of goods and services. Your firm and industry will be exporting or facing import competition. It is important to become familiar with the fundamentals that determine international prices and trade.

Terms

Absolute and comparative advantage
Arbitrage
Autarky price
BOT surplus and deficit
Currency depreciation
Diminishing marginal productivity
Excess demand
Excess supply
Exchange rates
Expectations

Export revenue
Import expenditure
International equilibrium price
Mercantilism
Normal and inferior goods
Opportunity cost
Relative cost
Specialization
Substitution and income effects
Transport costs

MAIN POINTS

- International markets clear at prices where excess demand from the importer equals excess supply from the exporter.

- Excess demand is the difference between quantity demanded and quantity supplied, and excess supply is the difference between quantities supplied and demanded.
- Changes in the demand or supply for a traded product affect its international excess demand or supply, international price, and level of trade.
- The balance of trade is export revenue minus import expenditure. A trade deficit (surplus) occurs if import expenditure is greater (less) than export revenue.
- A country has a comparative advantage in producing a good if its opportunity cost of the good is relatively low.

REVIEW PROBLEMS

1. Diagram what will happen to the price and quantity of oil traded when OPEC restricts supply with a diagram based on Figure 1.4.

2. By tradition, Japanese businesses deal only with Japanese banks. Japan is a net importer of banking services. As Japanese businesses begin dealing more with foreign banks, show what will happen in the market for banking services.

3. Illustrate what will happen in the international market for cars as income rises in China.

4. Diagram what will happen in the market for wheat between the US and Russia when a forecast says Russia will have a long winter and a spring drought. Russia is the importer of wheat.

5. Illustrate what will happen in the international market if the Buy American campaign aimed at US consumers decreases domestic tastes for imported apparel.

6. The US is an exporter of business services and is trying to get other nations to lower their protection. Show what will happen in the international market for business services if foreign nations increase their demand for US business services. Will domestic consumers of services enjoy the change?

7. Diagram what will happen in the international market for cars if the US announces a lower tariff on imports that will take effect in one year. (Hint: This announcement affects both the excess demand in the US and the excess supply from Japan.)

8. Show what will happen in the international market for cars if technology for auto production improves in the importing countries.

9. Illustrate what will happen in the international market for gold if news of war causes buyers and sellers to expect higher gold prices.

10. Suppose US and Venezuelan demands for steel are approximately the same. The domestic and foreign autarky prices are $500 and 22,500 bolivars respectively, and the exchange rate is bol/$ = 45. Determine the likely exporter. Illustrate international excess supply and demand when the international price is $475, the volume of trade 100, US production 100, and Venezuelan production 300. Find consumption in each nation.

11. In Problem 10, find US import spending on steel. How many bushels of wheat would the US have to export at $2.50/bu to balance trade? At $2/bu?

12. Explain whether you think a BOT surplus or deficit should be preferred. Would any governmental policy help attain this goal?

13. Consider the following pattern of labor inputs between the US and the EU. Who has the absolute and comparative advantage in each good? Predict the pattern of trade.

	US	EU
S	2	3
M	3	4.5

14. Justify your opinion about the goods in this list in which the US has a comparative advantage: oil, insurance, new cars, thread, accounting, textiles, engineering, clothing, olive oil, economic forecasting, chemicals, wheat, telecommunications, warm winter vacations, cool summer vacations, citrus fruits, fast food, architectural design, education, internet service.

READINGS

Jeffrey Schott (1996) *WTO 2000: Setting the Course for World Trade*, Washington: Institute for International Economics. Framework of the WTO.

Kenneth Pomeranz and Steven Topik (1995) *The World that Trade Created: Society, Culture, and the World Economy, 1400 — The Present*, New York: M.E. Sharpe. Lively history, an excellent book.

Khosrow Fatemi, ed. (1996) *International Trade in the 21st Century*, New York: Pergamon. Academic articles on trade issues.

Lynden Moore (1985) *The Growth and Structure of International Trade since the Second World War*, Sussex: Wheatsheaf Books. Descriptive study.

John Adams (1979) *International Economics: A Self-Teaching Introduction to the Basic Concepts*, Wellesley Hills: Riverdale. Drills on international economics.

Joseph McKinney and Keith Rowley, eds. (1989) *Readings in International Economic Relations*, Champaign: Stipes. Academic readings on trade policy, international finance, and multinational firms.

CHAPTER 2

Trade with Constant Costs

Preview

The principle of comparative advantage was formulated over 200 years ago by David Ricardo as he sought scientific causes of international trade. He developed a constant cost model of production with fixed inputs per unit of output. Applications and extensions of the constant cost model remain useful in economic research. This chapter covers:

- *Constant cost model* of production and trade
- *Gains from trade* with constant cost
- *Labor productivity* and *international wages*
- *Applications* of the constant cost model

INTRODUCTION

David Ricardo systematically investigated the fundamental causes and effects of international trade. According to mercantilism, a popular economic doctrine in the 1700s, wealth is equivalent to the stockpile of gold and other assets. Mercantilists believe exports create wealth but imports squander it, and government policy should restrict imports. Mercantilists in Ricardo's day were industrialists, and some industrialists and labor unions share a similar view today.

Adam Smith had argued against mercantilism in *The Wealth of Nations* (1776) pointing out that national wealth is more accurately the nation's capacity to produce goods and services. To increase wealth, Smith argued, a country should increase productivity. Smith argued for producing goods in which the country has a cost advantage, and trading for cheap goods on international markets. Smith believed the *invisible hand* of international competition would lead a country and government protection should be kept out of the way. He presented sensible arguments against government intervention.

Ricardo took Smith's idea a step farther, realizing that gains could be made from trade even by a country that had higher costs than every other country in producing every good. To enjoy returns from specialization and trade, *comparative advantage* is sufficient. Every country must have this relative efficiency edge in some activities.

Ricardo constructed one of the first and most enduring scientific models. His model of specialization in production and trade has offered generations of economists a solid foundation for understanding trade.

Production must lie at the heart of trade. In Ricardo's economy, one input (labor) is used in fixed amounts per unit of output. The fixed inputs create constant opportunity cost. In the simplest model, two goods are produced by two nations. Both countries gain through specialization according to comparative advantage.

Fundamental relationships among international wages, international labor productivity, and exchange rates are developed in the constant cost model. The model has been extended to include many products. Current applications and tests of the constant cost theory of production and trade support Ricardo's basic insight. Comparative advantage and the gains from specialization and trade have proven profound and lasting principles for social science.

A. CONSTANT OPPORTUNITY COSTS OF PRODUCTION

Firms hire inputs to produce for consumption or trade. Ricardo used a production process with one input to uncover the principles of production and trade. The first step in the scientific method is to construct a testable model or theory. Ricardo's effort was one of the first to approach the understanding of very complicated subject with an abstract testable model.

Labor in the Constant Cost Model

Assume that there is only one input, labor. Other inputs such as capital machinery and equipment, natural resources, and entrepreneurship are implicit, and Ricardo understood their importance. The other inputs embody the labor used in their production, and in the *labor theory of value* the source of all value rests in labor. The assumption of the single input labor simplifies the model. With *fixed input proportions* the amount of labor required to produce each unit of output does not vary as the level of output varies.

> *Constant cost theory assumes inputs are used in fixed proportions in production processes.*

Suppose the amount of labor it takes to produce a unit of services is 2 and the amount of labor it takes to produce a unit of manufactures is 3. These labor units could be person-years. It takes 3 people 1 year or 1 person 3 years to make a unit of manufactured goods. The unit of manufactures can be thought of as a composite basket of manufactures.

Consider the constant cost labor inputs

$$a_{LS} = 2 \quad \text{and} \quad a_{LM} = 3$$

The way to read a_{LS} is labor per unit of services. Labor inputs are fixed, and since labor is the only input, substitution with other inputs is impossible. These labor inputs describe *constant cost technology*.

Let S be the output of services. The labor employed in the service sector is $2S$. It takes 2 workers to produce a unit of services, and S units are produced. For instance, if output in the service sector is $S = 30$, the service sector must employ $2 \times 30 = 60$ workers.

Suppose the labor force is fully employed. The quantity of manufactures is M. If the total amount of labor L in the entire economy is 120, then

$$L = 120 = 2S + 3M$$

It takes 3 workers to produce a unit of output in manufactures, and $3M$ workers are employed in manufacturing. Employment in services ($2S$) plus employment in manufactures ($3M$) must sum to the entire labor force ($L = 120$). The economy is constrained in the outputs it can produce. With only a certain quantity of labor and constant labor inputs, more output in one sector implies less output in the other.

EXAMPLE 2.1   *Capital Input and Labor Productivity*

Capital raises labor productivity and lower unit labor inputs. As the ratio of capital to labor K/L in the US grew since 1950, labor input per unit of output a_{LQ} fell as reported by the Department of Commerce.

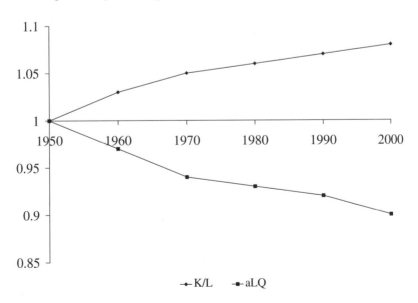

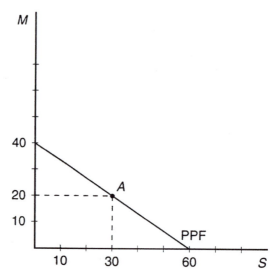

Figure 2.1
A Constant Cost Production Possibility Frontier
With constant input requirements, the opportunity cost of production remains constant as output moves along this straight production possibility frontier (PPF). The labor force is 120 and labor inputs are $a_{LS} = 2$ and $a_{LM} = 3$. The economy can produce at the endpoints $(M,S) = (40,0)$ or $(0,60)$ or at any point in between. At point A, production and consumption is $(M,S) = (20,30)$.

Constant Cost Production Possibility Frontier

With this simple production structure, the production possibility frontier (PPF) is easily derived. The PPF shows the various combinations of outputs that the economy can produce given its resources and technology.

In Figure 2.1, manufactured output is measured on the vertical axis and service output is measured on the horizontal axis. If the entire labor force worked in manufacturing, service output S would be zero and $120/3 = 40$ units of M could be produced. At the other extreme if no M were produced, $120/2 = 60$ units of S could be produced. The two endpoints of the PPF are $(M,S) = (40, 0)$ and $(M,S) = (0, 60)$.

Since labor inputs per unit of output do not vary, the PPF is the straight line. Each additional unit of S costs the same amount of sacrificed M down along the PPF. This is the sense in which costs are constant. The opportunity cost of one additional unit of one product in terms of the other is constant.

The domestic relative price of services in autarky is the absolute value of the slope of the PPF, $|-40/60| = 2/3$. This price is the same all along the PPF. The same amount of M must be given up to acquire an additional unit of S. To produce an extra unit of S requires 2 units of labor. Since the economy has full employment, these 2 workers must come from manufacturing. Output of manufactures will drop by less than 1 unit because 3 workers are required to produce 1 unit of M. When the 2 workers leave manufacturing, output drops by 2/3 of a unit. The equation of the PPF is

$$120 = 2S + 3M \quad \text{or} \quad M = 40 - 2/3S$$

The opportunity cost of one additional unit of output is a constant amount of the other output throughout the PPF. Home consumers in autarky must choose a point along the constant cost PPF in Figure 2.1. Consumers choose among available goods and services according to the satisfaction each provides, given limited incomes and the relative price of the goods.

Suppose consumers spend an equal share of their income on both goods. Each unit of S is valued at $2/3M$. An equal share of income is spent on each good when 2/3 as much M is consumed as S. Substituting into the equation for the PPF,

$$L = 120 = 2S + 3(2/3S) = 4S$$

and $S = 30$. Consumption of M must be 20, illustrated by point A in Figure 2.1. Since consumers spend half their income on each good, half the labor force works in each sector.

EXAMPLE 2.2   *How to Increase Labor Productivity*

Labor saving investment and improved technology increase labor productivity. A startling example is long distance telephone calls per operator per day, rising from 64 in 1970 to 1300 in 1994. The 10 firms in the US that cut the most jobs in the 1990s experienced a jump of 25% in labor productivity.

EXAMPLE 2.3 *Increased Labor Productivity in Japanese Manufacturing*

Investment in physical and human capital increase labor productivity. One real success story is Japanese manufacturing over recent decades. Following an amazing 77% reduction in labor input from 1955 to 1965, improving productivity has continued to the present.

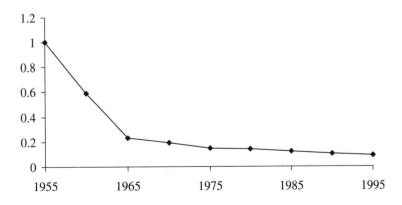

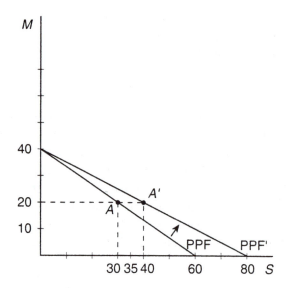

Figure 2.2
Improved Technology in Service Production
If labor productivity improves in service production, the production possibility frontier
(PPF) expands. If a_{LS} falls to 1.5, the maximum point of the PPF along the S axis shifts
out to $120/1.5 = 80$. The economy is able to produce higher combinations of both goods.
For instance, production could jump from point A where $(M,S) = (20,30)$ to point A' where
$(M,S) = (20,40)$.

Improved Technology and Economic Growth

Improved technology is illustrated by a decreasing unit labor input. Improved
technology in services means a lower unit input and an expansion of the
production frontier along the S axis. When a_{LS} drops from 2 to 1.5, the PPF
expands to PPF' in Figure 2.2,

$$L = 120 = 1.5S + 3M$$

Total potential output in services is $120/1.5 = 80$ and more of both goods can
be produced with the improved technology in one sector. The domestic relative
price of services falls to $|-40/80| = \frac{1}{2}$. Increased supply of S relative to M has
led to a lower relative price of S, similar to an increase in the supply of services.

*Improved technology in one sector expands the PPF in that direction, lowers
the relative price of that good, and raises production potential.*

Labor growth is pictured by a parallel outward shift of the PPF. In Figure 2.3,
the labor force expands from 120 to 144. Input requirements are $a_{LS} = 2$ and
$a_{LM} = 3$. The equation for PPF' is

$$L = 144 = 2S + 3M$$

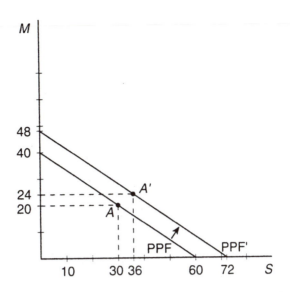

Figure 2.3
Labor Growth
If the labor force grows from $L = 120$ to 144, the economy will expand to a higher production possibility frontier (PPF). With labor input requirements constant, the shift in the PPF is parallel. The economy's ability to produce both goods rises. For instance, the economy's output could rise from point A where $(M,S) = (20,30)$ to point A′ where $(M,S) = (24,36)$.

A total of $144/2 = 72$ units of S or $144/3 = 48$ units of M could be produced with the expanded labor force. The relative price of S in terms of M remains 2/3. With growth, the economy can produce more of both goods. If consumers continue to spend half their income on each good, consumption shifts to $(M,S) = (24,36)$.

Labor growth is an outward parallel shift of the PPF.

EXAMPLE 2.4   *Changing Productivity*

Falling unit labor inputs a_{LQ} indicate industries with investment and innovation. Matthew Shapiro (1987) reports changes in labor inputs in US industries between 1974 and 1985. When unit labor inputs decline, the PPF expands in the direction of those outputs although outputs depend on relative prices.

	$\%\Delta a_{LQ}$		$\%\Delta a_{LQ}$
Communications	−2.3%	Utilities	−1.2%
Agriculture	−1.4%	Construction	1.1%
Manufacturing	−1.4%	Mining	4.3%

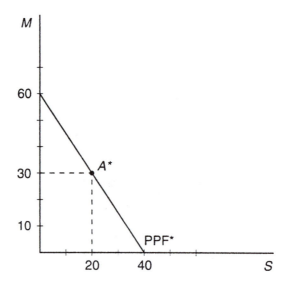

Figure 2.4
The Foreign PPF*
Labor input are $a_{LS}^* = 6$ and $a_{LM}^* = 4$ in this example with a labor force of 240. The end-points of complete specialization are $240/6 = 40$ in services and $240/4 = 60$ in manufactures. The foreign economy can produce anywhere along its production possibility frontier (PPF), for instance at point A* where $(M^*,S) = (30,20)$.

International Differences in Production

Consider a foreign country with its own particular unit labor inputs and relative price. The foreign unit labor input in service production is $a_{LS}^* = 6$ and in manufactures $a_{LM}^* = 4$. The foreign labor force is $L^* = 240$. Asterisks denote the foreign country. The foreign production frontier PPF* is drawn in Figure 2.4. Its endpoints are $60M^*$ and $40S^*$. The equation of the PPF* is

$$L^* = 240 = 6S^* + 4M^*$$

The foreign relative price of services is $M/S = |-60/40| = 1.5$.

Foreign unit labor input requirements are higher for both products: $a_{LS}^* > a_{LS}$ and $a_{LM}^* > a_{LM}$. The home country has an absolute advantage in both manufactures and services but it will pay to specialize just as it will pay the foreign country. Comparative advantage, not absolute advantage, creates the potential to gain from trade.

The relative autarky price of services is higher in the foreign country because the foreign relative labor input requirement is higher in services. The opportunity cost of service production is higher in the foreign country because more manufactures must be given up to produce an extra unit of services. The opportunity cost of service production is lower in the home country.

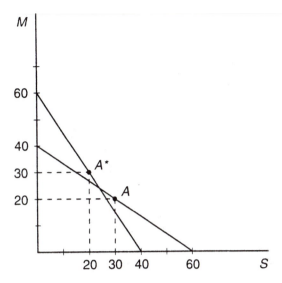

Figure 2.5
Production and Consumption without Trade
Production and consumption in autarky occur at point A in the home country and point A* in the foreign country. Services are relatively cheap without trade in the home country while manufactures are relatively cheap in the foreign country.

If foreign consumers also spend half their income on each good, the foreign labor force will split equally between sectors. With 120 workers in each sector, foreign consumption of services will be $120/6 = 20$, while consumption of manufactures will be $120/4 = 30$.

Consumers in each country are constrained along their PPF when there is no trade. Each economy, on its own, will value a good according to its opportunity cost of production. When production of one good increases, production of other goods must decline. The lost output represents the value of increased production. If consumers were identical in the two countries, they would consume differently because of the different opportunity costs of production.

Figure 2.5 summarizes autarky production and consumption. The home produces $20M$ and $30S$, consuming at point A. The foreign country produces $30M^*$ and $20S^*$, consuming at point A*. Consumers in both countries spend half of their income on each good. Autarky relative prices of services are 2/3 at home and 3/2 abroad. Services are relatively cheap in the home country, and manufactures are relatively cheap in the foreign country. Neither country can consume the bundle of goods consumed by the other country.

With constant cost, potential output is determined by total input supply and the unit input in each productive activity. In autarky, consumers choose the optimal output combination along their PPF.

EXAMPLE 2.5   *High Tech Comparative Advantage*

Opportunity costs determine comparative advantage. The opportunity cost of high tech goods in terms of other manufactured goods is the relative price of high tech goods H in terms of manufactured goods M, M/H. Mordechai Kreinin (1985) compares these opportunity costs for the US, Japan, and Germany. The US has a slight comparative advantage relative to Japan and both have an advantage over Germany.

	US	Japan	Germany
M/H	0.90	0.95	1.08

EXAMPLE 2.6   *International Labor Costs*

Labor costs vary across countries. Estimates of production labor costs across a number of countries and areas reported by the US Bureau of Labor Statistics. In a constant cost model with many products, countries with low labor costs would specialize according to comparative advantage and low wages would determine exports. In trade models with capital and other inputs, countries with low labor costs will specialize in products that use relatively high labor inputs.

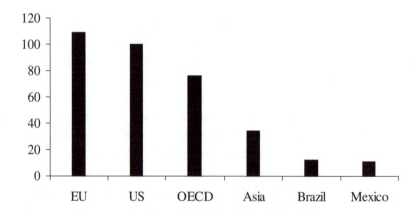

Problems for Section A

A1. Draw the PPF for a country with unit labor inputs $a_{LS} = 4$ and $a_{LM} = 5$ with labor force $L = 220$. Find the relative price of S in terms of M.

A2. In the previous problem, suppose technology changes in manufacturing to $a_{LM} = 4.4$. Draw the revised PPF. Explain whether this is improved technology.

A3. Suppose the economy in Problem A.1 grows until the labor force $L = 264$. Draw the new PPF.

EXAMPLE 2.7   *GDP Breakdown*

GDP in the US was $11.7 trillion in 2004. The US economy is specializing increasingly in services. The share of manufacturing in GDP fell from 19% in 1987.

GDP shares		
Agriculture, forestry, fishing, mining		2%
Utilities, construction		7%
Manufacturing		13%
Services		78%
Largest sectors:		
Finance, insurance, real estate	21%	
Wholesale & retail trade	13%	
Government	12%	
Professional services	11%	

B. SPECIALIZATION AND GAINS FROM TRADE

Differing relative prices are the stimulus to specialize, leading to efficient global production. Consumers in trading economies have the potential to consume more of every product than available without trade.

Relative Prices and Specialization

In the example from the previous section, the home relative price of services is low. Services are relatively cheap in the home country because less of other goods must be given up to produce more service output. In the foreign country, manufactured goods have a lower opportunity cost.

Comparative advantage occurs when relatively less of other goods must be sacrificed to produce a unit of the specialized good. These concepts are equivalent:

- Lower opportunity costs
- Relative efficiency
- Comparative advantage

Nations should specialize in producing the products in which they have a comparative advantage since global potential to produce increases with specialization.

Relative prices or opportunity costs indicate the efficient pattern of specialization. Countries tend to specialize in products with lower relative prices.

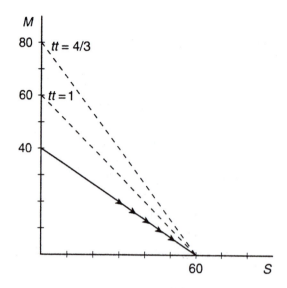

Figure 2.6
Complete Specialization for the Home Country
The high international price of services pushes the home country into complete specialization. All inputs are used in service production and the domestic manufacturing industry
collapses. The economy trades up along its terms of trade (tt) line. Every unit of exported
services brings in 1 unit of manufactures along $tt = 1$. Exporting all 60 units of produced
services would bring in 60 units of imported manufactures. If $tt = 4/3$, exporting all 60
units of services would bring in 80 units of imported manufactures.

The home country sacrifices output of manufactures to produce more services.
Resources are rearranged as the service industry grows with new and expanding
firms. Labor moves to the service sector where its activity is more highly valued
and the manufacturing industry declines.

Figure 2.6 shows the home country in a position of *complete specialization*
in services. The economy has moved down along its PPF to produce only services.
It will enjoy gains from specialization and trade because services can be traded
internationally at a price above the domestic price of 2/3. The higher relative
price of services on the international market is the stimulus for specialization.

The international relative price of services is given by the terms of trade line
$tt = 1$ in Figure 2.6. For the home country, the relative price of services must be
above 2/3. The foreign country of Figure 2.4 will offer less than 3/2 of a unit
of M for each unit of S it receives. For the foreign country, tt must be less than
$M/S = 3/2$.

The *limits to the terms of trade* are minimally acceptable relative prices for
the trading partners:

$$3/2 > tt > 2/3.$$

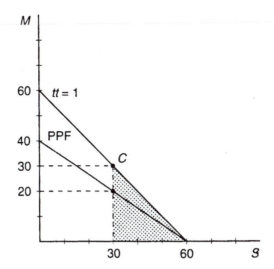

Figure 2.7
Consumption with Specialization and the Trade Triangle
Consumers choose the point along the terms of trade (*tt*) line that they most prefer. In this example, they choose $(M,S) = (30,30)$ at point C. The 30 units of exported services exchange for 30 units of imported manufactures on the international market. The trade triangle illlustrates both the volume and terms of trade.

In the late 1700s, John Stuart Mill contributed to Ricardo's model by showing how the terms of trade could be determined. Mill assumed consumers in both countries spend an equal share of their income on each good. The relative price will be the same in both countries with trade, and trade is balanced.

The terms of trade in this example is $30M$ from the foreign country exchanged for $30S$ from the home country, or $tt = 30/30 = 1$. The terms of trade depend upon labor endowments, productivities and demands in the two nations. The terms of trade have to fall within the limits to the terms of trade. Mills' theory led to the idea of consumer utility, the basis of demand.

The terms of trade is pictured in Figure 2.7. Each unit of exported S brings in a unit of M when $tt = 1$. Consumption takes place beyond the home PPF. The home economy exports 30 units of S and imports 30 units of M.

The *trade triangle* in Figure 2.7 has 30 units of exported S along its base and 30 units of imported M up the *tt* line. Consumption takes place at point C. The trade triangle shows imports and exports. The home economy is left consuming $60 - 30 = 30$ units of S. Imports of M are 30 units. Consumers are better off since they consume more M and just as much S as in autarky. In general, consumers can choose goods along the *tt* line beyond their PPF.

EXAMPLE 2.8   *Revealed Comparative Advantage*

The US exports high tech manufactures, business services, and some agricultural products. High tech manufactures and business services use relatively high inputs of skilled labor and the US has an abundance of skilled labor. Import categories are petroleum, low tech manufactures, and cars. Input availability explains a good deal of production and trade. David Richardson and Chi Zhang (1999) point out that between 1980 and 1995, the US revealed a strong comparative advantage in goods differentiated by quality and a weak disadvantage in standardized goods. They find that regional specialization does not depend on proximity, language, or historical ties.

The Real Gains from Trade

Real gains from trade are measured using prices before trade. The real gains from consumption at point C in Figure 2.7 are measured using the domestic autarky price $M/S = 2/3$. This domestic price line is labeled d in Figure 2.8 and drawn through C parallel to the PPF.

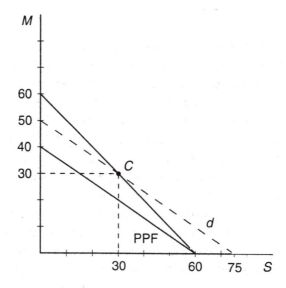

Figure 2.8
The Real Gains from Trade
The consumption bundle at point C is valued at domestic autarky prices to find the real gains from trade. The domestic price line d is parallel to the home PPF and through point C. The value of consumption in terms of either good is found at the endpoint of price line d. Trade creates a real gain of 25%.

The value of consumption at C with trade in terms of good M is

$$30M + (2/3 \times 30S) = 30M + 20M = 50M$$

The 30 units of S consumed are worth 20 units of M at the domestic autarky price. Added to the 30 units of M consumed with trade, the real value of consumption is $50M$. The value of autarky consumption in terms of M is 40, the endpoint of the M axis on the PPF. The real gain from trade is the difference $50 - 40 = 10M$, a $10/40 = 25\%$ increase.

The gains from trade can be calculated in terms of either good. The value of consumption in terms of services after trade is $75S$. Imports of $30M$ are valued at 45 units of S by the autarky price. This is a gain of $75 - 60 = 15S$, in percentage terms $15/60 = 25\%$.

The endpoints of the autarky price line in Figure 2.8 are $75S$ on one end and $50M$ on the other. The value of consumption is found by projecting the consumption point to either axis using the domestic relative price. There is a 25% gain from trade for the home country in this example.

In the foreign nation, there are also real gains from trade. Specialization pushes it into the production of manufactures. There are only two countries in the world and home imports equal foreign exports. Sketch the foreign country in Figure 2.4 with its specialization point P^*, terms of trade line tt, and consumption point C^*. Foreign consumption takes place at $C^* = (M^*, S^*) = (30,30)$ beyond PPF*. In this example the foreign country enjoys 25% gains from trade.

The real gains from trade can be measured in terms of either imports or exports. Every country involved in trade enjoys real gains from trade.

The foreign country in this example has the same percentage gains from trade as the home country. If the terms of trade had been closer to 2/3, the home country would have gained more. If the terms of trade had been closer to 3/2, the foreign country would have gained more.

The more highly valued a country's exports are on the world market, the greater will be its gains from trade. Gains from trade are partly due to the influence of demand. Suppose home consumers value foreign manufactures more than foreign consumers value home services. The terms of trade would move in favor of the foreign country because of international tastes.

If a big country enters into trade with a small one, which can expect to gain more? The typical response is that trade benefits large countries, often pictured as dominating both the level and terms of trade and exploiting available resources in small countries. The terms of trade, however, cannot vary much from a big country's autarky price. The small country adds little to the demand for the big country's exports but the demand for the small country's exports can jump substantially.

A small country gains more from trade if the terms of trade are farther from its domestic prices.

EXAMPLE 2.9   *Ricardo's trade theory*

David Ricardo used the example of constant labor inputs to make the point that comparative advantage is sufficient to bring potential gains from trade even if a country had higher labor requirements for every product. The constant cost model in this chapter builds on the assumption of a single input labor but Andrea Maneschi (1992) points out that Ricardo relied on models with land and capital input as well as labor in *Principles of Political Economy* to develop many of the concepts used in economics today. Tariff disputes between workers, landowners, and manufacturing capitalists were the main topic in political economy during the late 1700s, and nothing much has changed since.

EXAMPLE 2.10   *Iron & Steel Labor Inputs*

The evolution of an industry can be studied through its labor inputs. During the 1970s, Japan switched from a large importer of iron and steel to a large exporter while the US and the UK became net importers. Investment in Japan led to a decrease in unit labor inputs and lower production costs. Mordechai Kreinin (1984) reports these decreases in unit labor inputs occurred between 1964 and 1984. The US and UK lost comparative advantage with the falling labor input in Japan.

	US	UK	France	Germany	Japan
a_{Li}	−16%	−16%	−55%	−56%	−72%

Problems for Section B

B1. Diagram the foreign country in the example from the text. Show production point P^*, the terms of trade line tt, consumption with trade C^*, and the foreign trade triangle. Find the gains from trade in terms of its export S.

B2. Suppose the home country is characterized by $a_{LM} = 4$ and $a_{LS} = 5$ and the foreign country by $a_{LM}^* = 5$ and $a_{LS}^* = 6$. Which country has the comparative advantage in S? Find autarky relative prices of S in both countries and the limits to the terms of trade M/S.

EXAMPLE 2.11 *Wages and Labor Costs Around the Pacific Rim*

Wages and unit labor inputs determine the labor cost of manufacturing. Susan Hickock and James Orr (1989) report a comparison of US manufacturing labor costs with four NICs around the Pacific Rim. Wages in the US are higher but labor inputs lower. There are costs other than labor but the US has a difficult time competing in manufacturing around the Pacific Rim.

	wages	a_{LM}	unit labor cost
Thailand	$0.86	8.3	$7.14
Taiwan	$2.71	3.8	$10.30
South Korea	$2.65	4.3	$10.84
US	$13.90	1	$13.90

C. EXTENSIONS OF CONSTANT COST TRADE THEORY

The constant cost trade model can be applied to issues of international wages and exchange rates. There are two avenues available to improve relative home wages, increased labor productivity and improved terms of trade. For trade to occur, the exchange rate is constrained to limits set by the wages and productivities of trading partners. Constant cost trade theory is also extended to include many products.

International Differences in Labor Productivity and Wages

There is a link between wages across trading partners due to productivity differences and the terms of trade. Trade influences the relative price of outputs which in turn influence payments to productive resources.

In the long run, zero economic profit is expected with free entry and exit of firms in a competitive industry. Accounting profits may be positive but there will be no excess profits. The price of a good in competition moves to the cost of producing it. In other words, price equals average cost: $P = AC$.

The international price of each good is determined in the country where it is produced. In the example of the home country specializing in services, the price of services will be the average cost of producing services in the home nation,

$$P_S = AC_S = wa_{LS} = 2w$$

To produce a unit of services, each unit of labor is paid the home wage w and 2 units of labor are required. The price and the average cost of producing a unit of services equal $2w$.

The dollar price of the manufactured goods produced in the foreign country depends on the foreign wage, the foreign unit labor input, and the exchange rate. Suppose England is the foreign country, and the pound £ is the foreign currency. The price of manufactures is the foreign unit labor input in manufactures a_{LM}^* times the English wage w^*,

$$£/M = w^* a_{LM}^*$$

The English wage w^* is the price of English labor in pounds: $£/L^*$. The dollar price of English manufactured goods is found through the exchange rate $e = \$/£$, the price of pounds in dollars:

$$P_M = e w^* a_{LM}^* = 3 e w^*$$

The expression $3ew^*$ is the dollar price of manufactured goods from England.

The *terms of trade* (*tt*) or the relative price of services in terms of manufactured goods is the ratio of the two dollar prices from the countries of origin:

$$tt = P_S/P_M = M/S = 2w/3ew^*$$

If $w/ew^* <$ less than 1, English wages are higher than US wages. One limit to the terms of trade in this example is that $tt > 2/3$. It follows that $w/ew^* > 1$, which implies that the US wage must be higher than the English wage for the two countries to trade in this example.

The implications are fundamentally important. The wage of home workers relative to foreign workers can be increased through labor productivity and the terms of trade. Labor productivities in the two countries imply $1.5 = 3/2 = a_{LM}^*/a_{LS}$.

Changing productivity affects relative wages. Suppose home labor becomes more productive as a_{LS} falls from 2 to 1.5. Less home labor is required per unit of service output. Then $tt = 1.5w/3ew^*$ and $w/ew^* = 2tt$. The identical outcome occurs if foreign labor becomes less productive, with a_{LM}^* rising from 3 to 4. In both circumstances, home labor becomes more productive relative to foreign labor resulting in a higher home wage. The home wage declines relative to the foreign wage if home labor becomes less productive or foreign labor becomes more productive.

Terms of trade improve for the home country if *tt* rises. Remember *tt* equals *M/S*, the international relative price of home exports. If *tt* rises, services are more valuable and home wages will rise relative to foreign wages. At the same time, foreign workers become relatively worse off. A terms of trade improvement for the foreign country would mean a falling *tt* making foreign workers relatively better off.

The terms of trade depend partly on demand in the two countries. A country that increases its demand for foreign products will see its relative wage falling.

When demand for Japanese manufacturing goods in the US rose during the 1970s and 1980s because of their reputation for quality, the terms of trade worsened for the US and relative Japanese wages rose.

> *Higher productivity and better terms of trade increase home wages relative to foreign wages. Falling productivity and worse terms of trade decrease relative home wages.*

The burden does not fall entirely on labor to increase its own productivity. The quality and quantity of other inputs directly affect labor productivity. With better machines and training, labor will be more productive. Investment spending on physical capital and human capital is required to increase labor productivity. Trying harder may not increase productivity if the right tools and training are not available.

These fundamental lessons emerge:

- payments to inputs are linked across trading partners.
- a factor price is tied to its productivity.
- a change in the demand for foreign products alters the terms of trade and the relative wage

EXAMPLE 2.12 *Wages, Productivity, and Trade*

Steve Golub (1995) tests the theory of comparative advantage with the relationship between relative unit labor costs and bilateral trade flows across pairs of countries. The correlation between exports/exports* and $wa_{Lj}/ew^*a_{Lj}{}^*$ is positive. Countries with low wages also have low labor productivity. As one example, wages and labor productivity in Malaysia were both 15% of the US levels in 1990.

Exchange Rates and International Wages

There is a link between exchange rates and wages across trading economies. For the home economy to export services, the price of services must be lower at home than abroad. The price of services produced by the competitive home industry is $P_S = wa_{LS}$. This home price must be less than the price of services in the foreign country.

With e the exchange rate \$/£ and w^* the foreign currency price of labor £/L^*, the dollar price of foreign labor is ew^*. The dollar price of services produced in the foreign country is $ew^*a_{LS}{}^*$.

If the home country exports services, the dollar price of services produced at home must less than the dollar price of services produced in the foreign country, $wa_{LS} < ew^*/a_{LS}{}^*$. Solving for e,

$$e > wa_{LS}/w^*a_{LS}{}^*$$

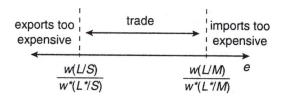

Figure 2.9
Ricardian Limits to the Exchange Rate
If the exchange rate e is too low exports will cost too much abroad. If e is too high imports will cost too much. Only a limited range of e is consistent with trade. Looked at another way, home wages must fall within limits defined by the exchange rate, foreign wages, and international labor inputs.

The price of the £ has this lower limit for the home country to export services. Otherwise, services will be cheaper in England.

For the foreign country to export manufactures, the domestic currency price of manufactured goods produced in the foreign country $ew^*a^*_{LM}$ must be less than the domestic price wa_{LM}. Manufactured goods will be cheaper from the foreign country if

$$wa_{LM}/w^*a_{LM}^* > e$$

The exchange rate has bounds

$$wa_{LM}/w^*a_{LM}^* > e > wa_{LS}/w^*a_{LS}^*.$$

Nothing has been said about the foreign exchange market and how e is determined. There could be an international gold standard, fixed exchange rates, a single clearing house, floating exchange rates, or any other foreign exchange mechanism. However e is determined, it has to fall within these limits if the two countries trade according to comparative advantage. Figure 2.9 illustrates the limits to the exchange rate.

Suppose $w = \$14$ and $w^* = £10$ with $a_{LS} = 2$, $a_{LM} = 3$, $a_{LS}^* = 4$, and $a_{LM}^* = 3$. The exchange rate e would then have to be between $14/10 = 1.4$ and $(14/10)(2/4) = 0.7$ for the two countries to trade. If $e = 2$, both services and manufactured goods would be cheaper in the US. The price of services in the home country would be $P_S = 2w = \$28$ and in the foreign country $P_S^* = 4ew^* = \$80$. The home price of manufactures would be $P_M = 3w = \$42$ and the foreign price $P_M^* = 3ew^* = \$60$. At the other extreme, if $e = 0.5$ both manufactures and services would be cheaper in the foreign country: $P_S = \$28$ and $P_S^* = \$20$ while $P_M = \$42$ and $P_M^* = \$15$.

There are limits to the exchange rate if two countries are to trade. If the exchange rate goes beyond these limits, trade ceases.

For a given exchange rate, the wage can be only so high for the economy to continue exporting. If wages rise too far, the economy loses its cost advantage. In this example, suppose the foreign wage $w^* = £/10$ and the exchange rate $e = 1$. The home wage w must fall between $10 and $20 for trade to take place. Wages outside this range will cause trade to cease.

Home wages are limited by labor productivity in the home country relative to the foreign country. If home labor becomes more productive, the home unit labor inputs a_{LS} and a_{LM} fall. Improvement in home labor productivity will lower the range of e perhaps causing an appreciation.

> *In an open economy, home wages are constrained by foreign wages, the exchange rate, and labor productivity. Governments are constrained in their exchange rate policy.*

EXAMPLE 2.13 *Wages and the Exchange Rate*

A dollar appreciation makes US products more expensive abroad, lowers US exports, and could lower demand for labor and wages. A depreciation could raise wages. Whether the US labor market is exposed to international markets is an empirical issue. Baekin Cha and Daniel Himarios (1995) find evidence that the dollar appreciation during 1983–1985 reduced wage growth but the subsequent depreciation had little effect. Between 1971 and 1988, the exchange rate had effects on wages even for nontraded construction and services industries. In smaller, more open economies labor markets are more exposed to exchange rate changes.

Trade with Many Products

Assuming there are only two products simplifies trade but raises the question of whether similar results hold with many products. The basic lessons with many products can be learned from an example with three. The three major categories of production are services S, manufactures M, and agriculture A.

Compare the unit labor inputs in Table 2.1. Finding the opportunity cost of one good in terms of another is difficult because each country has two sets of opportunity costs. The opportunity cost of one unit of M in the home country is $3/2\ S$ or $3/4\ A$.

Table 2.1 Unit Labor Inputs with Three Products

	a_{LS}	a_{LM}	a_{LA}
Home	2	3	4
Foreign	3	4	2

S = services; M = manufactures; A = agriculture.

This ambiguity is eliminated by comparing countries for each good to see how much labor is required in one country relative to the other. For instance, home services input relative to foreign input is $a_{LS}/a_{LS}^* = 2/3$. It takes 2/3 of a worker at home to produce as much service output as 1 worker abroad. In manufacturing, it takes 3/4 of a home worker to match 1 foreign worker and in agriculture it takes 2 workers.

The home economy has a comparative advantage in services, since home labor is relatively efficient in that activity. In services it takes 3/2 foreign workers to match a home worker. The foreign country has a comparative advantage in agriculture since it takes only 1/2 of a foreign worker to match the output of a home agricultural worker.

In manufacturing, 4/3 foreign workers match 1 worker at home. Manufactures are between services and agriculture, and could be exported by either country or not traded.

Figure 2.10 illustrates the home PPF with the three goods. The home endowment of labor is 120. If all home labor were in agriculture, 120/4 = 30 units of A could be produced. The PPF is the triangle connecting endpoints of complete specialization in each industry.

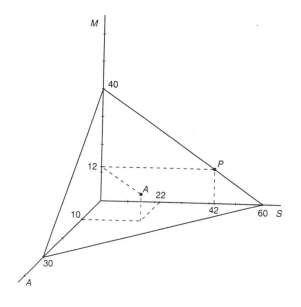

Figure 2.10
A Constant Cost PPF with Three Goods
Labor inputs are in Table 2.1. The labor force in this economy is 120 workers. With three goods, the production possibility frontier (PPF) is a triangle. Autarky production and consumption occur at point A where $(M,S,A) = (12,22,10)$. With complete specialization the economy moves to point P where $(M,S,A) = (12,42,0)$. Agriculture shuts down, manufacturing stays the same, and services expand. Trading services for the agricultural good would move consumption beyond the PPF.

In autarky, domestic consumers would determine production and consumption at point A. Note that 22 units of S and 10 units of A are produced, requiring $2 \times 22 = 44$ workers in services and $4 \times 10 = 40$ workers in agriculture. This leaves $120 - 84 = 36$ workers for manufacturing and $36/3 = 12$ units of M are produced. Point A is $(M,S,A) = (12,22,10)$.

With specialization the home country drops agriculture and moves to point P. Suppose manufactures are not traded and output remains at 12. Service output rises to $84/2 = 42$ with the added 40 workers from agriculture. If the terms of trade are 1 unit of A for each exported unit of S, the economy could trade 15 units of S and consume $(M,S,A) = (12,27,15)$ beyond its PPF. The principles of trade are the same with many goods.

Each country will export goods near the end of the ranking where its industries are relatively more efficient. Consider a hypothetical comparison across 10 types of manufactured goods. Suppose $a_{LM} < a_{LM}{}^*$ for every good. In other words, the home country is more efficient in producing every good. Nevertheless, the 10 goods could be ranked according to $a_{LM}/a_{LM}{}^*$. The foreign country would tend to specialize in goods at the high end of the ranking, and the home country toward the low end.

EXAMPLE 2.14 *US Trade in Services*

These are some major categories of trade in services from the BEA in 1998. Travel is a largest single category. The US spends more with the rest of the world on freight. Royalties and license fees are important in WTO negotiations. Affiliated services are transactions between MNF branch plants. Education of foreign students in US universities generates a surplus. Financial services are a surplus item. The deficit in insurance payments reflects a net outflow of $12 billion due to premiums on foreign insurance offset by a net inflow of $8 billion claims.

	Exports	Imports	Net, $bil
Total private services	$246 bil	$165 bil	$81
Travel	29%	34%	$15
Passenger fares	8%	12%	$0
Freight	4%	12%	−$8
Royalties	15%	7%	$26
Affiliated services	11%	12%	$9
Education	4%	1%	$7
Financial services	6%	2%	$10
Insurance	1%	4%	$4
Telecommunications	2%	5%	$4
Construction, engineering	2%	1%	$3
Other business services	13%	11%	$17

Table 2.2 Unit Labor Inputs with Three Countries

	a_{LS}	a_{LM}
Country 1	2	3
Country 2	3	4
Country 3	4	3

Table 2.3 Unit Labor Inputs, 3 Countries & 3 Goods

	a_{LS}	a_{LM}	a_{LA}
Country 1	2	3	4
Country 2	3	4	2
Country 3	4	2	3

Trade with Many Countries

The constant cost trade model can be applied to many countries. With two goods, the opportunity cost of a unit of one good can be found from each country's labor inputs. Countries with a low opportunity cost will export that product.

To illustrate, suppose there are three countries with labor inputs for M and S in Table 2.2. The relative price of services is $2/3M$ in country 1, $¾M$ in country 2, and $4/3M$ in country 3.

Country 1 has the lowest opportunity cost of services and will export services. Country 3 has the lowest opportunity cost of manufactures and will export M. Country 2 has an intermediate position and the terms of trade will determine trade in country 2. Demand across the three countries will affect the terms of trade. If the terms of trade are above $M/S = 3/4$, country 2 will export services. If tt is less than 3/4, country 2 will export manufactures. The limits to the terms of trade come from the extreme countries,

$$4/3 > tt > 2/3.$$

With many goods and many countries, unit labor input rankings can indicate which goods are exported. Table 2.3 shows a situation with three goods and three countries. The labor input ranking L_A/L_B between countries 1 and 2 in each of the goods is

$$(4/2)_A > (3/4)_M > (2/3)_S$$

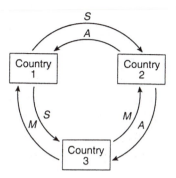

Figure 2.11
Trade with Three Countries and Goods
With the labor inputs in Table 2.3, country 1 has a consistent comparative advantage in
S relative to the other countries. Country 2 has the comparative advantage in A. Country
3 has the comparative advantage in M.

Country 1 will export S to country 2 in exchange for A. Between countries 2
and 3,

$$(4/2)_M > (3/4)_S > (2/3)_A$$

Country 2 will export A to country 3 in exchange for M. Finally, comparing
inputs between countries 1 and 3,

$$(3/2)_M > (4/3)_A > (2/4)_S$$

Country 1 will export S to country 3 in exchange for M.

Country 1 specializes in S, country 2 specializes in A, and country 3 specializes
in M. This pattern of trade is illustrated in Figure 2.11.

Predicting the pattern of trade may not work out as neatly when there are
many countries and many goods. International differences in demand play a role
in determining patterns of trade but there will be products in which each country
has a comparative advantage.

EXAMPLE 2.15 *Labor Productivity and R&D*

Research and development can lower unit labor inputs. Countries that spend
more on R&D enjoy increased labor productivity and higher wages. Figures
from the UN indicate almost all R&D takes place in DCs. Japan's share of
world R&D spending has about doubled from 7% in 1970. The EU share has
remained at about 20% of the world total, while the US share has dropped from
40% to about 30%.

Problems for Section C

C1. Suppose foreign labor inputs are $a_{LM}^* = 5$ and $a_{LA}^* = 3$ and home inputs $a_{LM} = 2$ and $a_{LA} = 3$. Find the international pattern of specialization. Find the relative wage w/ew^* if the terms of trade are 1.

C2. Find the limits to the exchange rate with the unit inputs in the previous problem when $w = \$10$ and $w^* = 1000$ pesos.

C3. If $w = \$16$, $e = \$/\pounds = 1.2$ and $w^* = \pounds10$ find dollar prices of the three goods using the unit inputs in Table 2.1. Predict the pattern of trade.

C4. Diagram the foreign PPF* with the unit labor inputs in Table 2.1 and $L^* = 228$.

EXAMPLE 2.16 *International Wage Differences*

Assembly line production wages vary across countries. Firms considering where to locate production also consider transport costs, local taxes, local work habits, and infrastructure, but wage differences can be overwhelming. The three highest and lowest wage countries in 2000 according to the *World Competitiveness Report* are listed.

Norway	$18.90
Switzerland	$18.10
Germany	$18.03
Hungary	$1.20
India	$0.40
Turkey	$0.40

D. APPLICATIONS OF CONSTANT COST TRADE THEORY

This section reviews tests and applications of the constant cost model. In spite of its simplicity, the constant cost model of trade has proven useful in explaining and predicting trade patterns.

Exports and Imports of the US

The largest categories of US exports are machinery, agricultural products, aircraft, computers, chemicals, and metal products. The largest categories of imports are capital goods, consumer goods, vehicles, oil, iron & steel, and food & beverages.

The largest buyers of US exports and suppliers of US imports are in Table 2.4. NAFTA is the largest trading partner with about 1/3 of export revenue and

Table 2.4 Snapshot of Recent US Trade

	% X		% M	
	1990	**1998**	**1990**	**1998**
NAFTA	28%	34%	25%	30%
EU	26%	22%	20%	19%
NICs	14%	14%	18%	22%
Japan	12%	9%	18%	13%
Americas	7%	9%	7%	5%
ROW	17%	12%	12%	11%
Total, % GDP	7%	8%	9%	11%

Source: US Department of Commerce

Table 2.5 Detailed US Manufacturing Trade

Product	**% X**	**% M**
vehicles	8%	13%
electrical machinery	11%	9%
office equipment	7%	8%
misc manufacturing	5%	5%
telecommunication equip	4%	5%
transport equip	8%	4%
industrial machines	5%	3%
power generation equip	4%	3%
machinery	4%	3%
apparel	0%	4%
nonmetallic mineral mfg	0%	2%
scientific instruments	4%	0%

Source: US Department of Commerce

import expenditure, and the EU accounts for about 1/5 of each. NAFTA is growing in importance as a US trading partner while Japan and the EU are declining. The newly industrialized countries (NICs) supply about 1/5 of imports. A good deal of trade is diversified with the rest of the world (ROW). Both export revenue and import spending are increasing relative to GDP as the US economy becomes more open.

A breakdown of the largest categories of US manufacturing trade is in Table 2.5. Vehicles and electrical machinery are important categories. The top imports are typically consumer goods manufactured on assembly lines by unskilled labor. The top ten categories of manufacturing exports account for

60% of export revenue. For imports, the figure is 57%. There is a lot of diversification in US manufacturing trade.

There is good reason to focus on the example of exported business services. Services include:

Accounting	*Construction*	*Retailing*
Advertising	*Consulting*	*Shipping*
Architecture	*Engineering*	*Tourism*
Banking	*Insurance*	*Transportation*
Computer services	*Lodging*	*Wholesaling*
Communications	*Motion pictures*	

These services represent almost 3/4 of the jobs and 1/3 of US export revenue. These are activities in which US firms are especially efficient and internationally competitive.

In 1900, most workers in the US were in agriculture. The service sector has grown from 30% to 70% and agriculture has shrunk from 40% to 4%. Manufacturing has consistently accounted for about 30% of all jobs.

Trade in services accounts for about one quarter of world trade. The US is the world's leader in service exports. Japan and Germany are net service importers. To explain the evolving pattern of trade, services has to be included since the US is moving into international specialization in service production.

EXAMPLE 2.17 *Top 3 US Trading Partners*

Canada, Mexico, Japan, and now China are the largest trading partners of the US.

	US Exports		
	Canada	Japan	Mexico
1983	19%	11%	5%
2004	23%	7%	13%

	US Imports			
	Canada	Japan	Mexico	China
1983	20%	16%	6%	–
2004	17%	–	11%	13%

Testing Constant Cost Trade Theory

G.D.A. MacDougall (1951) compared exports from the US and the UK in 1937. If labor productivity was higher in a particular industry in one nation, he found

Table 2.6 Labor Inputs in High Tech Products

	1963	**1984**
EU	1.25	1.46
US	1.00	1.06
Japan	1.76	0.92

its share of that export market consistently higher. The essential prediction of constant cost theory is that labor productivity determines comparative advantage and the pattern of trade. More recent studies have confirmed MacDougall's test for many countries and types of products.

Hebert Glesjer, K. Goosens, and Eede Vanden (1982) compare countries in Europe before and after they joined the EU. The EU eliminated trade restrictions. Countries with lower opportunity costs of goods exported those goods to other member countries, the prediction of constant cost theory.

High tech goods are those with relatively high inputs of R&D. High tech manufactures are electronics, chemicals, aircrafts, computers, and specialized machinery. The unit labor inputs a_{LH} where H represents a unit of high tech output in Table 2.6 explain Japan's evolution as an international supplier of high tech products. Unit inputs are rescaled so that $a_{LH} = 1$ in the US in 1963. Note that the EU declined in productivity of high tech goods. The US essentially held its position, while Japan improved productivity. Japan's improvement has been due to its investment in human capital (education) and a high level of investment. In 1963, Japan was the most inefficient producer of high tech products but by 1984 Japanese technology had surpassed the competition. The Japanese PPF expanded along its high tech production axis.

The 1970s was a decade of decline for the US auto industry, as an examination of unit labor inputs largely explains. Imports of Japanese cars rose from less than half a million in 1970 to almost 2.5 million in 1980. Japanese autos went from less than 5% to more than 20% of the US retail market. Labor productivity in Japan increased tremendously, reflected by data from the Japanese Ministry of International Trade and Industry (MITI) and the US Bureau of Labor Statistics (BLS). Rescaling units so that the unit labor input is 1 in the US in 1970, the Japanese unit input was 1.5 the same year. Over the 1970s, the US unit labor input rose to 1.15 while the Japanese fell to 0.75. The Japanese automobile invested heavily, the stock of capital rising 225%.

Since the 1980s, there have been radical changes in the US automobile market. About 30% of all new cars are foreign. In fact, the distinction between domestic and foreign cars is blurred, with a third of the value of a typical "domestic" car accounted for by its foreign parts. Foreign car firms have opened factories in the US. The future promises wider dispersion in the world auto market, with NICs entering international competition.

EXAMPLE 2.18 *Maquiladores*

Maquiladores are MNF branch operations in Mexico that produce goods for export to the US. Labor from Mexico is combined with capital and skilled labor from the US. Before NAFTA, the Mexican government severely restricted investment by US firms except in the maquiladores plants close to the border. Maquiladores hire workers for about $2 per hour, well below US wages. About 1/3 of maquiladores employees are in electric and electronic equipment, 1/5 in transport equipment, and 1/5 in textiles and apparel. US labor unions claim the maquiladores plants steal jobs, but the alternatives are US plants in labor abundant LDCs around the world, or MNF branches from other countries. Competing MNFs from other DCs would also operate branch plants in Mexico. In 1970 there were 20,000 maquiladores employees. There has been steady growth in maquiladores to over 1,000,000 employees and maquiladores have spread over Mexico. NAFTA is resulting in increased foreign investment by US firms as the economies integrate.

Problems for Section D

D1. Considering both imports and exports, which four countries are the largest trading patterns of the US?

D2. High tech manufactures require a large input of skilled labor. Why might the US be able to produce relatively cheap high tech goods?

D3. Investment spending in the US automobile industry lagged far behind its competitors in the 1970s. How would this account for the relatively high cost of producing autos in the US during the 1980s?

EXAMPLE 2.19 *China/US Trade*

Trade between China and the US is increasing dramatically. The figures from the Department of Commerce are in billions of 1997 dollars. Major export categories in 1997 were aircraft 17%, fertilizer 8%, telecommunications equipment 5%, and cotton 5%. Exports are based on high tech production and agricultural comparative advantage. Import categories were toys & sporting goods 16%, apparel 12%, footwear 12%, and other manufactured goods 11%. Imports are generally labor intensive manufactured goods.

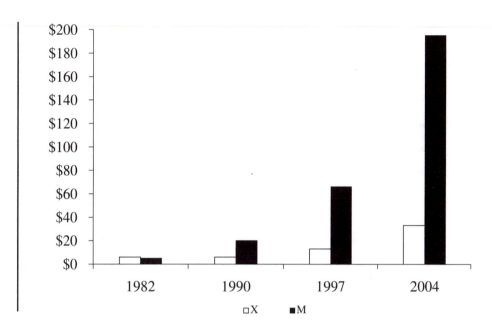

CONCLUSION

The constant cost explanation of international trade strips production and trade to the simplest level. While the theory is sensible, it has shortcomings. Why does one country have lower labor inputs than another? What would cause labor inputs to change? Does including other inputs alter fundamental predictions? Why is there incomplete specialization? Modern theories that include increasing costs of production, various inputs, and different types of industrial structure answer these questions.

Firms combine inputs to minimize cost and maximize profit, varying inputs according to input prices. If labor becomes more expensive, firms substitute toward other inputs. As a radical example of switching inputs, farms in the EU use machinery and very little labor because labor while in India the opposite is true.

Constant cost trade theory does not consider this substitution between inputs, but it remains useful for studying patterns of trade.

EXAMPLE 2.20 *3-Way Trade*

Japan has trade surpluses with NAFTA and the EU. NAFTA has a deficit with the other two, and the EU has a deficit with NAFTA. The following summarizes trade balances in $billion. Japan exports manufactures exclusively. NAFTA is the largest shipper of foodstuffs and has bilateral trade in foodstuffs with the

EU. NAFTA also ships raw materials. Japan and the EU ship more manufactures to NAFTA than to each other.

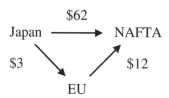

Terms

Absolute advantage
Comparative advantage
Complete specialization
Constant costs
Invisible hand
Labor input ranking

Limits to the exchange rate
Limits to the terms if trade
Mercantilism
Opportunity cost
Relative price

MAIN POINTS

- A constant cost PPF with constant factor inputs has a slope equal to the relative product price.
- Trade with constant costs involves complete specialization according to comparative advantage.
- The gains from trade are illustrated by the increased value of consumption.
- Constant cost trade theory illustrates fundamental international links among wages, productivity, and exchange rates.
- Unit labor inputs indicate comparative advantage and contribute to explaining and predicting trade patterns.

REVIEW PROBLEMS

1. Compare Figures 2.1 and 2.4. Which country has a lower opportunity cost of manufactures? Which country would you expect to export manufactures?

2. Suppose the economy Delta is characterized by $a_{LM} = 4$ and $a_{LS} = 5$. Compare Delta with the home country in Figure 2.1 and predict the pattern of trade. Make a similar prediction for Delta and the foreign economy in Figure 2.4.

3. The workforce of the US totals about 150 million, while the workforce of Japan is 60 million. Find the amounts of high tech goods these economies could produce over the years in Table 2.6 if a quarter of each labor force worked in high tech manufactures.

4. Suppose the H economy is characterized by $a_{LM} = 4$, $a_{LS} = 5$, and $L = 260$. The F economy's production structure is $a_{LM}^* = 6$, $a_{LS}^* = 5$, and

$L^* = 300$. Find the comparative advantage. Suppose each country exports half its production to the other. Find the terms of trade. Diagram both trade triangles.

5. Evaluate the gains from trade for both countries in the previous problem in terms of S. Evaluate the gains from trade for both countries in percentage terms. Explain which country enjoys the largest gains from trade.

6. Find the percentage gains from trade in this same example if the terms of trade are $M/S = 1$ and the same 30 units of S are exported by F. Explain the difference in the gains from trade compared with the previous problem.

7. If the terms of trade are $tt = M/S = 1.4$ between the home economy in Figure 2.1 and the foreign economy in Figure 2.4, find the relative wages w/ew^* implied by free trade. Find the relative wage if instead $tt = 0.7$ and explain the effect of the change in the terms of trade on the relative wage

8. Using the information in the previous problem with each terms of trade, find w if $w^* = 1100 ¥$ and $e = \$/¥ = 0.008$. Compare the limits to the exchange rate under each of the two terms of trade.

9. In the home economy, unit labor inputs are $a_{LM} = 2$ for manufactures and $a_{LA} = 3$ for agriculture. In the foreign economy, unit labor inputs are $a_{LM}^* = 4$ and $a_{LA}^* = 5$. The terms of trade are $tt = A/M = 3/4$. Find the relative wages implied by trade.

10. Find the limits to the exchange rate for the two economies in the previous problem.

11. Find the home wage w if the foreign wage $w^* = 10{,}000$ pesos and $e = 0.001$ in the previous problem. Show what happens to w if
    (a) *tt* worsens for the home country falling to 7/10
    (b) The home labor input a_{LM} subsequently improves to 1.5.

12. Suppose unit inputs for three goods are

	Good 1	Good 2	Good 3
Home	3	5	3
Foreign	2	1	3

Predict the pattern of trade.

13. If the foreign wage is 2250 ¥ and the exchange rate $e = 0.008$ in the previous problem, find the home wage w that makes the price of the middle good the same in both economies. Using this wage, find the prices of the two traded goods produced in each country. Verify the direction of trade.

14. Find the limits to the exchange rate in the previous problem.

15. Consumer goods such as appliances and apparel require relatively low levels of investment and high levels of unskilled labor. Why would the US have little cost advantage in consumer goods?

READINGS

David Ricardo (1817) *The Principles of Political Economy and Taxation*, New York: Everyman's Library, 1969. Chapter 3 "On Foreign Trade" is Ricardo's own presentation.

Andrea Maneschi (1998) *Comparative Advantage in International Trade: A Historical Perspective*, New York: Edward Elgar. An excellent historical review.

Michio Morishima (1989) *Ricardo's Economics: A General Equilibrium Theory of Distribution and Growth*, Cambridge: Cambridge University Press.

Ron Jones & Peter Kenen (1984) *Handbook of International Economics*, Vol. I, Amsterdam: North Holland. Surveys of international trade.

William Allen (1965) *International Trade Theory: Hume to Ohlin*, New York: Random House. A short paperback with readings from the classics.

TRADE: GAINS, PROTECTION AND TERMS

CHAPTER 3

Gains from Trade

Preview

The arguments for free trade are presented in this chapter. Topics are:
- *Production possibility frontier* with increasing costs
- *Utility* and *real income* measures of the gains from trade
- *Less developed countries* and international trade
- *Industrial trade policy*

INTRODUCTION

Firms and industries are constrained in production because of limited labor, capital, and natural resources. Available factors of production play a critical role in determining the pattern of production and trade.

There are different skill groups of labor. Capital goods such as machinery and equipment come in varieties and must be produced. Natural resources are as different as Kansas farmland, Kuwaiti crude oil, Colombian rain forests, and sunny Mediterranean hillsides. Technology to combine imputs into goods and services is continually evolving.

When prices change, resources shift from one industry to another. If the price of copper increases, for instance, mining firms hire more workers, raise wages, and invest in new equipment. The overall limits to what can be produced are described by the production possibilities frontier (PPF).

For output in an industry to increase, resources must come from the rest of the economy, short of resource growth or improved technology. Generally, the opportunity cost of a good increases as its output increases.

Consumers choose between available products according to relative prices, making choices subject to budget constraints. When the relative price of a good increases, consumers choose substitutes. Firms respond to price changes, switching to more profitable activities. When the price of a good rises, profit opportunity increases and firms increase output. In the general equilibrium, relative prices determine output through the interaction of supply and demand.

When a small economy trades with the rest of the world, it accepts international prices for traded products. A small economy cannot influence global supply or demand. Industries inside a small economy rearrange activities toward outputs more highly valued on international markets. A trading small economy has to be ready to specialize according to comparative advantage.

Goods and services that a country can produce cheaply are exported. Another inducement to import is the quality of foreign products. Consumers in an open economy end up with a mix of domestic and foreign products. One measure of whether there are gains from trade is whether consumers can afford more of every product. Another measure uses social utility. This chapter introduces both techniques of measuring the gains from trade.

A move to free trade may bring overall gains, but adjustments in the economy have to be made. Production processes are reorganized according to international prices. Firms expand output in some industries but reduce output in others. New firms may enter an expanding industry while existing ones shut down in a shrinking one. Business is risky business. Workers are forced to retrain or relocate, and will not want to see their industry declining due to international competition. An appeal to overall economic efficiency and long term gains will not change their opinion.

Trade has played a vital role in the development of most economies. Trade is an engine of growth. The US was a prime example of an LDC that relied on trade as a foundation for growth. Cheap agricultural products based on abundant and fertile natural resources were exported during early development. High tariffs were placed on manufactured goods to raise revenue and give the country's "infant industry" a chance to compete. The infant industry tariff is an industrial trade policy and this chapter examines various industrial trade policies.

A.   PRODUCTION POSSIBILITIES AND REAL INCOME

The production possibilities frontier (PPF) summarizes an economy's potential to produce. It illustrates the influence of relative prices on production and lays the foundation for evaluating the gains from trade. This section develops the ideas of

- increasing opportunity costs
- real income and social utility

Activities in an Economy

Resources move to where they are paid the highest. Firms hire extra workers according to the value of the resulting output. The price of the firm's output and the productivity of the input determine its value. The productivity of any input depends on the quantity and quality of other inputs. Wages depend on capital and natural resource inputs.

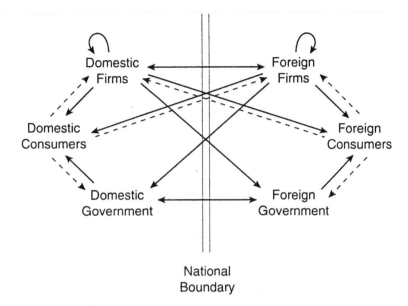

Figure 3.1
The Circular Flow of Economic Activity
National boundaries are incidental to economic activity. Arrows between firms illustrate
trade in intermediate products. Dotted arrows indicate factor markets. International
economics studies the transactions that cross the national boundary.

Consider an economy producing manufactures and services. Prices and outputs
are determined in individual markets. Prices of the factors of production (labor,
capital, natural resources) are determined in factor markets where owners of
productive resources sell to firms that combine the factors into outputs sold to
consumers who have earned income supplying their factors of production. Factor
markets and output markets are linked in the economy.

This activity is summarized by the flow of economy activity in Figure 3.1.
Solid arrows show the flow of goods and services. Dotted arrows represent
factor markets. Payments flow in opposite directions. Some firms sell intermediate
products used to produce other products. The government acts much like a firm,
hiring productive factors and providing services, mainly public goods such as
national defense, parks, police, and public health.

Figure 3.1 is a flow diagram for an open economy. International economics
studies transactions that cross the national boundary. Foreign firms enter the
picture by selling their products to domestic firms, consumers, and government.
Foreign firms also buy intermediate inputs from domestic firms. Factor owners
can supply their labor, rent their capital, or sell their natural resources to foreign
firms or the foreign government.

EXAMPLE 3.1   *Expanding DC Services*

> Investment in the US since the 1950s has tended toward the service sector ac-
> cording to figures from the Department of Commerce. Over half of all investment
> spending during the last half of the 20th century went to services, over 70%
> during the 1970s, and over 90% during the 1980s. About 80% of the stock of
> productive capital in the US is in services and 18% in manufacturing and the
> labor distribution is similar. In 1960, 52% of US workers were in services and
> 41% were in manufacturing. Similar trends toward services have occurred in all
> DCs. The OECD reports that service output has grown from about half to about
> two thirds of DC output.

Production with Increasing Opportunity Costs

In the PPF of Figure 3.2, the economy at point C produces 300 units of manufactured goods *M* and no services *S*. All resources go into manufacturing with
complete specialization. Consider what happens as the economy moves down
along the PPF toward point B due to a higher relative price of *S*. Resources are
bid away from manufacturing by higher payments in the service sector. Firms in
the service sector will want to hire inputs that are more productive in services.

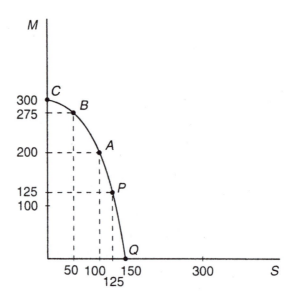

Figure 3.2
A Production Possibilities Frontier with Increasing Costs
Increasing opportunity costs of production result in a PPF bowed or concave to the origin.
The opportunity cost of additional production of (*S*) rises from 25/50 = 0.5 between points
C and B to 125/25 = 5 between points P and Q. The opportunity cost *S* rises with the
production of *S*. The same can be said for production of *M*.

The economy reaches point B when enough resources have been shifted to services so output in that sector climbs to 50. Output of *M* has dropped from 300 to 275. The *opportunity cost* of the first 50 units of *S* is the lost 25 units of *M*. In the transition from points C to B, 1/2 of an *M* is given up for every unit of *S* produced on average.

At any point of the PPF, the slope of the PPF is an estimate of the opportunity cost of *S* in terms of *M*. The tangent at point B estimates how much M production an extra unit of S would cost. The slope of the PPF is called the *marginal rate of transformation* (MRT).

> *The PPF shows the potential of the economy to produce goods when there is full employment and efficient production. The slope of the PPF is the marginal rate of transformation (MRT).*

If the relative price of *S* continues to rise, more resources shift into services. Resources more productive in services continue to go to that sector first. Firms in services must bid resources away from manufacturing. The economy moves down along its PPF toward point A where another 50 units of S are produced and output of *M* has dropped to 200. The opportunity cost of these additional 50 units of *S* is $275 - 200 = 75$ *M*, an average of $75/50 = 1.5$ units of *M* for every unit of *S*. Note that the opportunity cost has increased. The MRT increases moving down along the PPF.

With *increasing opportunity costs,* the PPF is concave to the origin. If the relative price of services continues to rise, production responds by shifting toward point P. The opportunity cost of producing the 25 additional units of *S* to point *P* is $200 - 125 = 75$ *M*, or $75/25 = 3$ *M* per unit of *S*. Moving finally to point Q, the opportunity cost is 5 *M* per unit of *S*.

The PPF is concave all the way from C to Q. Theory and empirical evidence suggest increasing costs. The opportunity cost of *S* increases moving down the concave production frontier due to *diminishing marginal productivity*. With other inputs constant, the *marginal product* or addition to output of an extra worker diminishes as more workers are hired. The same is true for all inputs. Diminishing marginal productivity creates a concave PPF.

> *Increasing costs of production and a concave PPF are due to diminishing marginal productivity.*

In autarky, consumers choose the point along the PPF they want according to their demand. *Producer choice* is represented by the production frontier. *Consumer choice* is the process of choosing the most desired bundle of goods along the production frontier. The interaction of consumer choice and producer choice determines the relative price of services or the amount of *M* that trades for a unit of *S*. Factor markets are at work in the background, determining payments to labor, capital, and natural resources. Incomes of factor owners influence their demands for the final products. All markets in the economy are linked together in the *general equilibrium.*

EXAMPLE 3.2   *Global Growth: Who's been Hot*

Yearly growth rates in output per capita vary across time and regions. The fastest growing region in the world has been the Pacific Rim with its open international commerce and the slowest growing region has been Africa due to its corrupt governments. Latin America and Africa suffered declines during the 1980s. Figures are from the World Bank's *World Development Report.*

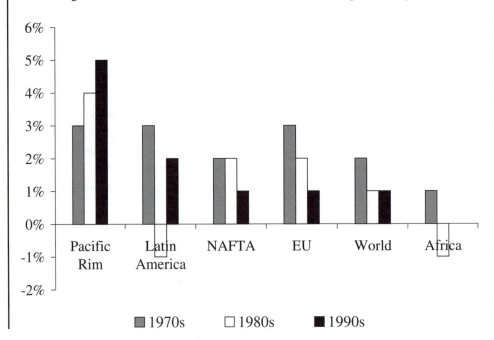

Indifference Curves and Consumer Equilibrium

The choice made by consumers can be pictured with *indifference curves.* Consumers equally value the combinations of *M* and *S* along indifference curve I in Figure 3.3. Every point along I has equal value in consumption. Similarly, consumers equally value any point along indifference curve II. Consumers prefer consuming any point on II to any point on I. More is better and substitution counts. Indifference curve III represents a higher level of utility.

Consumers are constrained to choose a point on the PPF in autarky. Bundles B or P on indifference curve I could be chosen but that would be inferior to point A on indifference curve II. Consumers would like to be on indifference curve III but it lies beyond their PPF. The optimal choice in Figure 3.3 is point A where utility is maximized subject to the PPF.

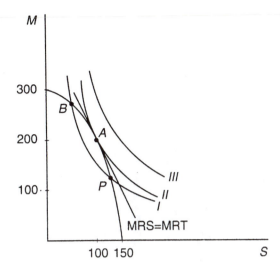

Figure 3.3
Maximizing Welfare and Consumer Choice
Indifference curve I represents a low level of utility, II an intermediate level, and III the highest. Consumers maximize utility subject to the constraint of having to be on their PPF. Point A represents the optimal consumer equilibrium where the slope of the indifference curve (the marginal rate of substitution, MRS) equals the slope of the PPF (the marginal rate of transformation, MRT).

Indifference curve II and the PPF are tangent at point A. The slope of an indifference curve is the *marginal rate of substitution* (MRS). The MRS shows how many units of one good consumers are willing to sacrifice for an extra unit of another. At the consumer optimum, the MRS equals the MRT. Consumers value an extra unit of S exactly the same as its opportunity cost in production at point A.

At point B the MRS is greater in absolute value than the MRT. Consumers value an extra unit of S more than its opportunity cost in production and the relative price of S would be bid up. At point P the MRS is less than the MRT. Consumers value an extra unit of M more than its opportunity cost in production at point P, and the relative price of M would increase.

In market equilibrium, the MRS along an indifference curve equals the MRT along the PPF. Markets push the economy toward this general equilibrium.

EXAMPLE 3.3   *Investment Across Countries*

Countries that invest more are able to produce more in the future. Investment varies across countries as these figures on investment relative to output from the US Department of Commerce indicate. High growth can be anticipated in countries toward the top of the list. The US is toward the bottom of the list but foreign investment is increasing in importance.

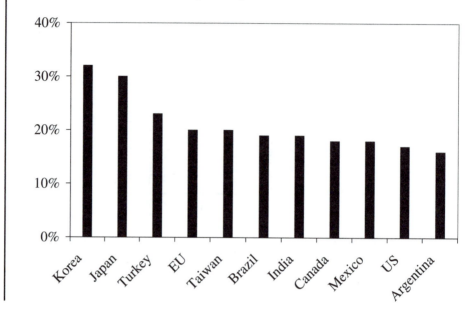

Finding Real Income

In Figure 3.4 the slope of the tangency at the equilibrium is found from the endpoints of the tangent to point A. Slope is rise over run, $-400/200 = -2$. The negative sign indicates that 2 units of M must be given up for the extra unit of S at point A. The endpoints of this *domestic price line* indicate the value of national output expressed in either good.

The value of national income at point A is 400 M. Consumption at point A is 200 M and 100 S. Each unit of S is valued at 2 M, so the 100 S produced and consumed are worth $2 \times 100 = 200$ M. Total output and consumption are thus valued at $200\ M + (2 \times 100\ S) = 400\ M$. Production, consumption, and national income are 200 S.

National income is typically expressed in the home currency. When income is expressed in terms of goods, it is *real income*. Suppose the nominal price of manufactures in Figure 3.4 is $2. Remember that the relative price S at point A is $M/S = 2$. The price of S must then be $2/M \times 2 = $4. National income valued at 400 M is nominally valued at $2/M \times 400 = $800. Alternatively, national income of 200 S is worth $4/S \times 200 = $800.

Comparison of nominal values over time must consider the changing value of currency. Inflation can lead to higher prices and higher nominal income with falling real income. Valuing national income in real terms drives home the point that real income matters.

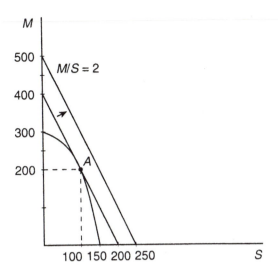

Figure 3.4
Relative Price Lines and the Value of National Income
Production and consumption take place in autarky at point A. The line tangent to the PPF at point A is the relative price line. Its endpoints show the value of national income in terms of that good. National income is 400 *M* or 200 *S*. The parallel outward shift in the price line represents an increase in national income at the relative price *M/S* = 2.

> *Real national income in terms of a good is the projection of the equilibrium relative price line.*

At the same relative price, a price line farther from the origin implies higher real income. The price line at 500 *M* in Figure 3.4 illustrates such an increase in income. Note that relative price is unchanged since *M/S* = 500/250 = 2. National income is 25% higher at 500 *M*, 250 *S*, or $1000. This level of income is unattainable in autarky given the PPF.

A straightforward way to measure the gains from trade will be to see whether trade increases real national income valued at autarky prices. In other words, trade produces gains if consumers end up with a bundle of goods valued higher at autarky prices. Alternatively, gains from trade are illustrated by higher utility increases if consumers can move to a higher indifference curve with trade.

EXAMPLE 3.4 *Expanding PPF and Specialization*

The US production frontier has expanded with production shifting toward services due to international specialization. Patricia Beeson and Michael Bryan (1986) estimate the ratio of services to manufacturing output rose from 2.8 to 3.5 be-tween 1950 and 1985. Output in services grew 252% while manufacturing output rose 178%. The average price of services relative to manufactures fell

26% over the same period as estimated by Lynn Brown (1986). These trends can be expected to continue. The DCs are specializing in the production of business services, and countries with lower production wages are specializing in manufacturing.

Problems for Section A

A1. Diagram a production possibility frontier with points $(M,S) = (100,0)$, $(90,25)$, $(70,50)$, $(40,75)$ and $(0,100)$. Show the increasing opportunity costs.

A2. From the diagram of the previous problem, *estimate* the MRT when consumption is $(M,S) = (90,25)$. What is the value of consumption in terms of S? What is the value of national income in terms of M? If the price of M is $\$/M = 3$ million, find nominal national income.

A3. *Estimate* the change in relative price needed to shift consumption from $(90,25)$ to $(40,75)$ along the PPF in the previous problem.

B.   SPECIALIZATION AND THE GAINS FROM TRADE

An economy trading internationally opens its markets to international prices. Changing prices rearrange production, pushing the economy into specializing. Production of exports expands but imports enter the economy causing cutbacks in domestic industries. This section stresses that specialization and trade lead to overall gains and the potential to consume more of every product. Real income increases and consumers move to higher utility.

Autarky Prices and International Prices

The supply side of an economy is pictured by its production possibility frontier. The upper limits of production with efficiency and full employment are along the PPF. The demand side of an economy is made up of consumers and their preferences for goods and services, summarized by indifference curves. The interaction of supply and demand determines relative prices, optimal production and consumption along the PPF, and national income.

There are two ways for the economy to provide more consumption, higher utility, and higher national income. One way is economic growth through expanding the resource base or improving technology. The other way is international specialization and trade.

Consider an economy with an autarky relative price of services M/S of 2 at point A (for autarky) in Figure 3.5. The economy produces and consumes 200

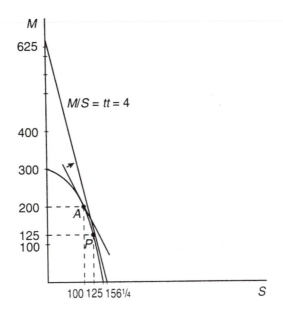

Figure 3.5
International Prices and Specialization
The line $M/S = 4$ is the international price of services. It is higher than the domestic relative price. An open economy will specialize in producing S, moving from A to P. The domestic service industry expands and the domestic manufacturing industry shrinks as the economy specializes.

units of M and 100 units of S. There is an international market for services where each unit of service output is worth $4M$. If the economy opens to free trade, firms producing S have the option of selling at a relative price of 2 or 4. If the price of a unit of M is $2, the price of S is $4 on the home market and $8 on the international market. This higher price is the incentive to export.

In Figure 3.5 sketches the *international price* of $M/S = 4$ along with the PPF. This international price remains the same whether or not the economy trades. The economy is *small* relative to the international market.

Industry inside the economy responds to the higher international price of services through *specialization* in that sector. Resources shift into services, with output rising from 100 units of S at autarky point A to 125 units at specialized point P. Resources leave manufacturing, causing its output to drop from 200 to 125. The economy moves from autarky production point A to production point P, specializing in the good that is worth more on the international market.

EXAMPLE 3.5   *Welcome to Nirvana?*

With both NAFTA and the WTO in the 1990s, protectionists warned of a giant sucking sound that would drain jobs from the US. Instead, the US economy is transforming as it specializes and trades. The Associated Press ran a series of articles called "The Nirvana Economy?" during October 1999. One article "Transforming Middletown USA and the Nation" focuses on Muncie, Indiana. Muncie had been a unionized blue collar working class manufacturing town. Art Emmerling's hands are now cleaner, softer, and free without blisters from working in the General Motors plant. Art is now a chief programmer for Ontario Systems, a company that switched from silverware and jet parts to semiconductor equipment and debt-collection software. "I do more with the mind now," he says. Jobs in the rust belt have switched from manufacturing to services. Foreign investment is playing an important role in this transformation, with joint ventures clouding the distinction between domestic and foreign investment.

Real Gains from Trade

Trade takes place at international prices. In this example, every unit of exported S trades for 4 units of M. With *barter*, one good trades directly for another. In reality, money and the foreign exchange market facilitate trade. Domestic service firms offer their products on international markets. Foreign importers sell their own currency to buy domestic currency in the foreign exchange market. Domestic importers buy foreign currency to pay foreign exporters, then sell the imported products to domestic consumers.

In Figure 3.6 the international price line is labeled *tt* for *terms of trade*. Its slope is -4, representing the 4 units of M imported for every unit of exported S. This economy takes the terms of trade, adjusts production to point P, and trades to the most desired point T along terms of trade line *tt*.

Consumer choice determines point T on the highest indifference curve along the terms of trade line *tt*. Consumption possibilities along *tt* lie beyond the PPF. Point T is a tangency between the *tt* line and an indifference curve. At point T the marginal rate of substitution along indifference curve III equals the terms of trade. In autarky, consumers maximize utility subject to the PPF at point A. With trade, consumers maximize utility subject to the *tt* line. Consumption at point T has higher utility than at point A.

> With free trade, production takes place where the marginal rate of transformation (MRT) along the PPF equals the terms of trade (tt). Consumption takes place where the marginal rate of substitution (MRS) equals the terms of trade tt.

With free trade at point T, 205 units of M and 105 units of S are consumed. Production takes place at point P where $(M,S) = (125,125)$. Consumers would be forced to a lower level of utility (indifference curve I in Figure 3.3) if they had to consume what the economy produces at point P. Exports of services amount

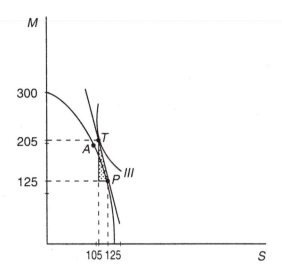

Figure 3.6
Production and Consumption with Free Trade
With international specialization at point P, consumers can consume anywhere along the
terms of trade line. In this example, 20 units of S are exported in exchange for 80 units
of M. At point T, consumption of both goods has increased relative to the autarky at point
A. Consumers move to a higher level of utility at point T.

to $125 - 105 = 20$ units of S. Imports of manufactures are $205 - 125 = 80$ M.
Trade reflects the terms of trade $tt = 80/20 = 4$ M/S.

The shaded triangle in Figure 3.6 with exports as the base and imports as
the height is the *trade triangle*. Point T is northeast of point A. The same would
be true for other economies specializing and trading. The world economy must
be operating more efficiently than without trade. Consumers everywhere can
consume more of every good with free trade.

> *International prices determine the pattern of production and consumption*
> *for an open economy.*

The *real gains from trade* are found by valuing consumption with trade at
domestic autarky prices. The autarky relative price of M is 2 from Figure 3.4.
Each unit of M consumed can be valued at the domestic autarky price of
$1/2$ S. With trade in Figure 3.6, the value of consumption in terms of services is
105 $S + (205$ $M \times 1/2) = 207.5$ S. The 205 M is valued at 102.5 S. Along with
the 105 S consumed, the value of consumption with trade is 207.5 S, beyond
200 S with autarky in Figure 3.4. The gains from trade in this example are
7.5 S. Gains can be also calculated in terms of M.

Consumers choose the point along tt that they prefer. Consumers have the
potential to consumer more of every goods with trade. Trade generates gains

since more of every good can be consumed. Trade allows consumers to enjoy combinations of goods beyond their PPF.

The real gains from trade valued in a numeraire *commodity show the increased value of consumption through specialization and trade.*

International trade helps an economy provide goods and services. From the viewpoint of global efficiency, international boundaries introduce frictions that decrease the capacity to produce goods and services. Governments use trade policy to influence international trade in exchange for the political support of those who benefit.

EXAMPLE 3.6   *From Autarky to Free Trade in Japan*

Before 1858, Japan was an isolated backwards feudal country with no international trade. A fleet of US warships then arrived to pry open the Japanese economy. Over the next 30 years, the level of trade in Japan increased 70 times according to Richard Huber (1971). Japan exported silk, tea, copper, dried fish, and coal, and prices of these exports rose by one third. Japan imported sugar, cotton, and metals, and these prices fell 40%. World prices for these commodities were not affected by Japan's entry into trade, indicating Japan was a small economy at the time. Hubor estimates national income rose over 50% with this move to free trade. Daniel Bernhofer and John Brown (2005) use different techniques and estimate an income gain of about 10%.

Production Adjustment to Free Trade

Domestic manufacturing firms face import competition when the economy opens to free trade. Foreign firms have a cost advantage in producing goods a country imports. A positive role for economic policy is to temporarily assist workers with job training or education as the economy adjusts to foreign competition.

When an economy opens to trade, it will adjust along its PPF toward producing goods with relatively high international prices.

In the example, domestic output of manufactures falls and output of services rises. Viewed as a whole, the economy exports its internationally high priced services in exchange for cheap manufactures. Importing firms buy cheap manufactures from abroad to sell in the domestic market, forcing the domestic manufacturing industry to adopt the lower price. Domestic firms switch some of their activity from production to importing.

Some domestic manufacturing firms will go out of business with adjustment to free trade in Figure 3.5. Some manufacturing workers have to retrain and relocate. Stockholders and investors in the domestic manufacturing industry lose. Only the more efficient domestic manufacturing firms survive. Adjustment

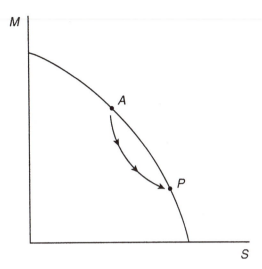

Figure 3.7
Adjustment Frictions
Production may be forced to take the path indicated by arrows below the production possibilities frontier in its adjustment to international prices and production point P. These short run adjustment costs must be paid, pushing the economy temporarily below its long run potential. National income falls during the adjustment.

costs can be large, but they are outweighed by the efficiency gains from free trade.

The friction of adjustment pushes the economy temporarily below its PPF as pictured in Figure 3.7. In the adjustment process, the economy moves along the path with arrows. Resources in manufacturing may not readily transform into inputs for the service sector. These resources may be labor with specialized skills or manufacturing capital not suitable for other production. Some resources may be located away from the growing commercial centers where service production takes place. The costs of retraining, retooling, and relocating must be paid with scarce resources. As adjustments are made, the economy moves to production point P.

The gains from free trade make transition costs worth paying. As firms in an economy open to competition, they adjust to changing world market conditions.

The shape and curvature of the PPF determines how much outputs and factor prices adjust to price changes. Jon Ford and Henry Thompson (1997) examine the curvature of the PPF. Under expected conditions, the PPF is relatively flat. Price changes have large effects on output in the long run. Complete specialization and industrial shutdown are likely outcomes of changing international prices. Input prices also undergo large adjustments due to price changes, although outputs adjust even more in percentage terms. If the PPF were extremely bowed, price changes would have only small effects on output and factor prices.

EXAMPLE 3.7 *Free Trade Fallacy?*

The NAFTA debate brought the issue of free trade into public focus and the headlines. There were newspaper and TV specials on the pro and cons of free trade. Ravi Batra (1992) and Batra and Daniel Slotje (1993) present evidence that the increasing trade since the 1970s caused a decline in US wages and called free trade a fallacy, a claim seldom heard from economists. Higher oil prices, however, had been a big part of the increase in import spending. Declining wages were due in part to both increased import competition and improving technology in labor intensive industries. Sugata Marjit (1994), Farhad Rassekh (1994), and Channing Arndt and Thomas Hertel (1997) disagree that free trade was a fallacy. Free trade may cause real wages to fall in labor scarce countries but investment and training can offset losses. Some groups face losses and adjustments with free trade, but for the nation in the long run protectionism is the fallacy.

Problems for Section B

B1. Evaluate the gains from trade in terms of manufactured goods comparing Figures 3.4 and 3.6.

B2. Starting with Figure 3.4 suppose the terms of trade tt are $0.9\,M$ for every unit of S. How will the economy specialize? Illustrate with a diagram.

B3. At $tt = M/S = 0.9$ suppose production moves to point B in Figure 3.2. Diagram the trade triangle if 72 units of M are exported. Find consumption with trade.

B4. If the domestic autarky price in Figure 3.2 at point $A = 2$, find the real gains from trade in terms of S.

EXAMPLE 3.8 *Compact Pickup Tariffs*

Compact pickup trucks were first imported from Japan to the US during the late 1960s. Tariffs increased from 4% to 25% in 1980 in response to the new compact pickups. The trucks proved durable and imports increased 40% by 1984 in spite of the tariff. Robert Feenstra (1988) estimates the consumer gains from an imported truck at about 20% of its price at the time had it been produced in the US. The tariff reduced consumer gains by 2/3, lowered the quality of US trucks, raised prices for US consumers, and reduced the quantity of trucks in the market. The gains from trade in this example would have been large.

C. GROWTH AND TRADE

Much of the world's population lives in poverty and economic growth is an important branch of economics. International trade and finance are indispensable for growth. Economies that try to develop while closed to international trade are like gardens with no sunlight.

Export Promotion versus Import Substitution

Economies grow by increasing or improving their productive capital and skilled labor. Economies can also improve technology, the techniques used to combine inputs into output.

Human capital (labor skill) is acquired through education and training. Capital equipment and machinery are accumulated through investment spending by firms. There is little capital in the typical less developed country (LDC) and the return on investment can be high. Economic growth is a gradual process with no shortcuts to acquiring the human and physical capital to increase productivity.

Growth is pictured by an expanding PPF. The economy grows to produce more of every good and may also establish new industries.

International trade plays a role in growth. As an economy specializes and exports, it attracts foreign investment. Multinational firms (MNFs) stimulate export industries. As the economy opens, workers intensify training to compete effectively in international markets. The PPF expands faster when the economy concentrates on its export industry. Export led growth occurs when growth is biased toward its export sector. Government policy aimed at pushing the economy toward international specialization is *export promotion*.

Governments of many LDCs have tried *import substitution*, replacing imports with domestically produced goods. The basic motivation behind import substitution is the belief that the economy should provide for itself. "The rich developed nations have an automobile (steel, electronic, or any other) industry, so we must have one to be successful."

In practice, import substitution is protectionism. High tariffs are imposed to protect domestic industry. A domestic import competing industry cannot compete with the rest of the world unless it has an underlying comparative advantage. Protected industries in an LDC operate inefficiently but survive with subsidies and price floors. The economy fails to develop as it would if attention were focused on specialization. Gains from trade are sacrificed.

The former communist countries of Eastern Europe tried for decades to develop with import substitution, which accounts for their dismal economic performance. When these economies began to liberalize with the fall of communism, international trade and investment played important roles and incomes began to rise.

The US imposed high infant industry tariffs after the Great Tariff Debate of 1888. Democratic President Grover Cleveland strongly opposed tariffs, in line with the wishes of the agricultural sector which favored free trade with Europe. Republican Benjamin Harrison favored high tariffs to protect US manufacturing in the North. The Civil War had been caused in part by high tariffs favoring the industrial North. Cleveland won the popular vote, but Harrison won the electoral vote. The high McKinley tariffs of the 1890s followed. The US industrialized heavily in the decades that followed, and the tariffs often get some credit. Douglas Irwin (1998) makes the point that effective protection on iron inputs impeded US industrialization, and that steel and iron prices fell during this period. The high tariffs were a drain on the economy.

Figure 3.8 illustrates losses due to import substitution. Suppose the economy is operating with free trade at production point P, specializing and exporting agricultural goods A. Import substitution policy induces the economy to move up its PPF toward the autarky point and to produce at point IS. The economy then trades at the international terms of trade along line tt' parallel to tt.

Note that tt' lies below the terms of trade line tt from point P. Consumption with free trade is labeled T and consumption with import substitution is labeled

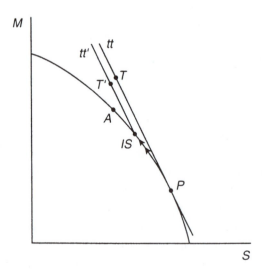

Figure 3.8
Import Substitution
Import substitution encourages the economy to shift resources away from production point P in free trade. Output shifts toward the imported good to point IS. Trade then occurs up along the terms of trade line tt', which lies below tt. Consumption point T' will lie below T, real income falls, and consumers are forced to a lower indifference curve.

T'. Consumers are forced to a lower level of utility with import substitution and real income falls from point T to T'.

Import substitution policies are proven failures, but there remains sentiment that LDCs should not be exploited by developed countries (DCs). When a large MNF builds a plant and produces goods for export, cries of labor exploitation are heard. Firms inside the LDCs that would benefit by avoiding international import competition promote this sentiment. Labor in the LDC is generally happy with the jobs, a step above others available.

National pride may be hurt if some domestic industry cannot compete. Never mind that a huge competitive international market already exists. Each country has its own particular situation and a general prescription for growth is difficult to formulate. Opening to international trade and investment, however, universally increases income.

The development strategy of import substitution has proved unsuccessful, creating more problems than it solves. LDCs should avoid import substitution policy, and open to international trade and investment.

An economy's direction of development is determined by fundamentals such as the availability of capital and natural resources, the training of labor, and the level of technology. Nations with mineral deposits have the potential to develop industries that use the minerals as inputs. Nations with fertile land and climate are suited to develop food industry.

Europe will never produce bananas or coffee. Costa Rica will never produce wheat. These goods could be produced but only at great expense. Hothouses could be built for bananas or coffee, and forests could be cleared to grow wheat. Such projects have been carried out at taxpayer expense, but the goods are too expensive to compete with imports.

Manufactured goods can be produced virtually anywhere, but capital goods, management, labor, entrepreneurship, and *infrastructure* are involved in production. Infrastructure refers to roads, transport, telecommunications, police, public health, airports, and property rights.

EXAMPLE 3.9   *LDC Exports and Growth*

Countries that specialize and trade grow faster. Zhenhui Xu (1996) presents evidence that increases in exports stimulated output in 17 of 32 LDCs between 1960 and 1990. Wenshwo Fang, Wenrong Liu, and Henry Thompson (2000) examine causal links between exports, imports, and output for Taiwan between 1971 and 1995 and find that imports stimulated output and exports weakly stimulated output. Taiwan imported capital goods during this period and exports stimulated output indirectly by stimulating the import of capital goods.

EXAMPLE 3.10 *Trade & the Terms of Trade*

These data from the World Bank summarize broad trends in production and trade. World output has grown at a steady rate of about 3% over the past decades. NICs have grown the fastest, and LDCs growth is higher than average. World trade volume grew 5% during the 1980s and 6% during the 1990s. The terms of trade have risen slightly for DCs but fallen for LDCs. Many LDCs rely on the export of primary products and those prices have declined but there are prospects for rising prices due to depletion of nonrenewable resources, increasing scarcity, and rising demand.

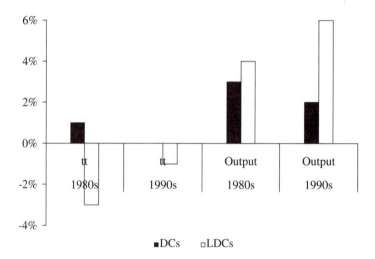

Export led Growth

Figure 3.9 shows economic growth biased toward manufactures. The production frontier expands outward and expansion favors manufacturing. The terms of trade *tt* determine production for an open economy as growth occurs.

In Figure 3.9 the economy starts at point P, producing according to the international price and trading to point T. As the economy grows, its potential to produce manufactures grows more rapidly than its potential to produce agricultural goods A. This bias in growth can be due to international investment, improved labor skills, or the adoption of new technology in manufacturing.

With growth, the economy produces at point P′ and trades at the same terms of trade. The two terms of trade lines are parallel. The economy trades off from point P′ to point T′. Consumers enjoy a higher level of utility and higher real income.

Growth leads to gains because more of both goods can be consumed. With export led growth, production frontiers expand faster. When an LDC trades freely, there is increased incentive and opportunity for the export sector to

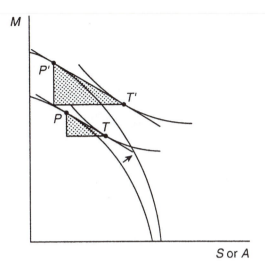

Figure 3.9
Export led Growth
Concentrating on the production of manufactures may lead to enhanced potential to produce manufactures in the long run, illustrated by a PPF that expands more toward the specialized export good.

expand. If the domestic manufacturing industry were protected, the PPF would expand more slowly and there would be less bias toward manufactures. Import substitution impedes expansion of the PPF.

The *developmental gains from trade* refer to the enhanced growth in the production frontier that occurs with specialization. Gains from specialization and trade occur as the economy adjusts production along its PPF. Developmental gains from trade refer to an expansion of the PPF induced by free international trade and investment.

The US provides a classic example of export led growth. Agricultural exports to Europe dominated US export revenue during the 1800s. Frontier farmland increased the frontier, increasing labor productivity. Agriculture in Europe declined with the import competition. Incoming investment and migration contributed to US growth.

Growth biased toward the export industry has the potential to lower the price of the exported good when the economy is a major supplier on international markets. Examples are Chile and copper, Bolivia and tin, Saudi Arabia and oil, South Africa and diamonds, Colombia and coffee. When such a major supplier grows, the international supply of its export rises lowering the international price of the export. If the terms of trade fall enough, the exporter may end up worse off after growth and trade, an outcome called *immiserizing growth.*

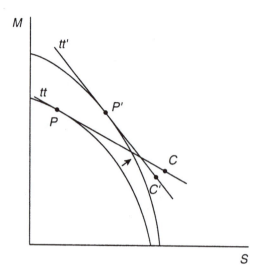

Figure 3.10
Immiserizing Growth
Export led growth can lead to a fall in the terms of trade if the economy is a major supplier on the world market and world demand is inelastic. The fall in the terms of trade from *tt* to *tt'* forces the economy to an inferior bundle of goods at a C'. Immiserizing growth rarely occurs.

Figure 3.10 pictures immiserizing growth. Before growth the terms of trade *tt* led to production at point P and consumption at point C. With growth and increasing exports, the terms of trade fall to *tt'* as supply increases on the international market. This decline in the terms of trade occurs if international demand is inelastic. The terms of trade fall to *tt'* with production ending up at P' and consumption at C', below original consumption at C.

Nations do not generally affect their terms of trade through expanding exports. While there is theoretical potential for immiserizing growth, it has not been realized in practice. Immiserizing growth should not be used as an excuse for protection and import substitution.

Foreign Investment and Growth

The potential to specialize and export is an incentive for investing in exports. LDCs typically depend on DCs for initial investment to begin expansion. For instance, rapid development in the US began with foreign investment in railroads during the early 1800s. Multinational firms provide both physical and human capital in equipment, skilled labor, and management. Successful multinational firms adapt to local customs and laws. Setting up a branch operation can be risky but the returns can be high.

Despite some reluctance to "sell out" to foreign interests, the gains from growth and trade are great. Mexico, Greece, and many other countries have historically limited foreign ownership, curtailing multinational investment. Such restrictive policy restricts long term production potential. Growth and increased production lead to expanded export industries and higher income.

Countries that save and invest more grow faster, as numerous empirical studies have shown. Policies of trade and foreign investment encourage capital accumulation. Robert Lucas (1993) examines the importance of human capital and learning on the job. Workers in fast growing economies quickly learn how to produce more sophisticated products. Economic policy needs only allow free trade and investment. Balanced government budgets encourage saving and investment.

EXAMPLE 3.11 *Comparing LDCs, NICs, & DCs*

LDCs have the lowest income per capita and the highest labor growth, but population growth has been declining for the past 20 years. The DCs specialize more in service production, the LDCs in manufacturing. Investment is risky but returns relatively high in the LDCs, suggesting they have the opportunity to progress. Extreme differences in economic development are indicated by the numbers of tractors per 1000 agricultural workers, personal computers per 1000 people, and percentages of roads paved. The DCs use energy resources intensively as indicated by the consumption of electricity. These figures are from the *World Development Report* of the World Bank.

	LDCs	NICs	DCs
GNP/capita	$2,000	$6,000	$23,000
Labor force growth	2%	2%	1%
% service output	39%	57%	65%
Investment risk index	80	64	19
Investment growth	10%	2%	2%
Income per capita growth	7%	2%	2%
Tractors/1000 ag workers	3	46	877
% roads paved	19%	51%	92%
PCs per 1000 people	4	32	269
Electricity mWh/capita	0.4	1.9	8.1

Less Developed Countries and Newly Industrializing Countries

Less developed countries (LDCs) are typically agricultural with subsistence farming. Newly industrializing countries (NICs) rely on manufactured exports.

A large share of worldwide assembly line production takes place in the NICs. Such jobs require little training. Machinery and techniques are readily available. Global efficiency is improved with expanded manufacturing in the NICs.

Developed countries (DCs) have relatively high wages for handlers and assemblers and cannot compete with the low manufacturing wages in the NICs.

LDCs would like to become NICs. NICs turn to policies of free trade while LDCs are often stuck on policies of import substitution. The infrastructure in NICs is generally better than in LDCs because infrastructure is difficult to build with poor prospects for trade and growth.

The DCs protect their traditional manufacturing sectors. The LDCs and NICs view this protection as a direct hindrance to development. Protection is unfortunate for global economic efficiency. Tariffs on DC imports of manufactures can keep an LDC from selling in the large DC markets. Quotas restrict exports from LDCs and NICs.

Protection of basic industries such as textiles, apparel, and footwear is high in the DCs. Protection is high for precisely the products that would be exported by LDCs and NICs. Nontariff barriers (quotas and other restrictions) of the DCs also inhibit trade. Perhaps 1/5 of manufactured imports from LDCs are subject to nontariff protection. Most LDCs do not take the rich nations seriously when they preach the virtues of free trade.

Imagine yourself the manager of a manufacturing firm in an LDC. Wages and costs are low, but you are unable to sell your goods in the DCs because quotas restrict your exports. Government representatives from the DCs who talk about the benefits of free trade sound hypocritical.

EXAMPLE 3.12 *NIC Manufacturing Exports*

Newly industrialized countries such as Brazil, Korea, Mexico, and Singapore produce manufactures for export. Brazil switched from an exporter of agricultural products during the 1970s. Korea was an agricultural economy up to the 1960s but now earns almost all export revenue from manufactures. Mexico slowly emerged as a supplier of manufactures, now earning about half its export revenue from manufactures. NICs have cheap labor relative to DCs and the infrastructure for manufacturing, and attract international investment to finance capital machinery and equipment.

Problems for Section C

C1. Brazil grows trees and exports lumber. Illustrate export led growth in plywood production.

C2. With growth biased toward manufactures as in Figure 3.9, what happens to the opportunity cost of a unit of manufactures when the ratio of outputs is constant? (Hint: The ratio of outputs is constant along ray from the origin.) How does this changing opportunity cost reflect biased growth?

C3. Growth can be unbiased across sectors. Illustrate unbiased growth with a PPF. What happens to the level of trade in a small open economy that export manufactures when there is unbiased growth?

EXAMPLE 3.13 *Capital and Growth*

Capital machinery and equipment are important inputs essential for growth. Countries with abundant productive capital grow faster, as Bradford DeLong and Larry Summers (1990) show in a study of 61 countries. Japan invested 12% of its income in new capital between 1965 and 1980, leading to yearly output growth of 5%. Argentina, at the other end, invested only 2% of its income and grew at a 1% annual rate. Protection of domestic machinery and equipment industries slows economic growth by raising the relative price of capital inputs.

D. INDUSTRIAL TRADE POLICY

Industrial trade policy is the effort of the government to manage trade. Governments try to help selected industries with favorable policies. Production of some exports is encouraged with subsidies, monopoly franchises, free trade zones, and free enterprise zones.

Export Promotion

Most governments try to devise ways to promote exports of particular products, aiming to help selected industries expand in international markets. At the same time, industries that compete with imports are sheltered with protection. This *industrial trade policy* is carried out under pressure from the industries wanting favors. Political support and financial contributions help keep politicians in office.

The desire to increase export revenue or decrease a trade deficit is often an excuse for trade policy. Promoting the export industry may seem more desirable than a currency devaluation, which would increase prices of imported intermediate inputs and consumer goods and might discourage foreign investment.

A *subsidy* is any device that lowers the cost or increases the revenue of a firm. The simplest type of export subsidy is a direct payment per unit of the good exported. Other subsidies come in the form of reduced taxes, wage subsidies, or waivers on tariffs of imported intermediate products. Labor is subsidized in export industries through direct payments. Government sponsored research and development (R&D) can lower cost in the export industry. The US Department of Agriculture and the land grant universities have historically subsidized US agriculture.

Cost reducing subsidies enable exporting firms to sell at a lower price on the international market. Foreign competing industries view subsidies as unfair. For example, US airline companies claim that European Airbus is subsidized.

Export subsidies are aimed at making exports cheaper on international markets and increasing profit for the exporting firms.

With export subsidies, tax revenue is spent to make goods cheaper for foreign consumers. Put this way, export promotion sounds ridiculous. Export subsidies tax domestic consumers and subsidize foreign consumers.

Nevertheless, there is sentiment to develop a comprehensive industrial trade policy. This may be due to trade deficits or to the perception that foreign governments subsidize their export industries. If foreign taxpayers are willing to subsidize home consumption through government subsidies, it may not be smart to retaliate.

Governments of the DCs subsidize export industries in various ways. *Foreign aid*, giving money to poor countries, often results in the export of domestically produced goods. The countries receiving the foreign aid turn around and buy domestic exports. The US offers *military aid* tied to the purchase of US weapons, amounting to subsidies for the weapon firms. Revenue for foreign and military aid comes from US taxpayers and subsidies the defense industry.

The Export-Import (Ex-Im) Bank of the US Department of Commerce makes loans at low interest rates to exporting firms, particularly in the aerospace industry. Government sponsored R&D in government labs or state supported universities leads to product development, often targeted at export industries. All of these tax supported subsidies make products better and cheaper for foreign consumers.

The industrial countries have extensive industrial trade policies. The political pressures leading to industrial trade policies will always be present.

EXAMPLE 3.14 *DC Subsidies*

Governments support chosen industries with import protection but also with subsidies, direct payments, subsidized loans, and directed R&D. The OECD estimates the level of subsidies as a percentage of total output across DCs. The US has a relatively low subsidy level. All of these countries have increased their subsidy levels since the 1950s except France, which has always had high levels. Taxpayers pay for subsidies and income is redistributed toward favored industries. Some US industries claim their international competition is unfairly subsidized. As some compensation, foreign taxpayers pay their portion of subsidized US imports.

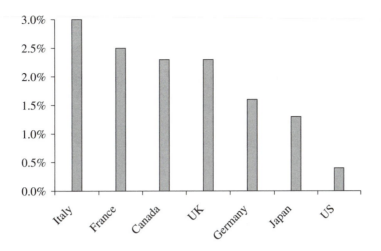

Cost of Export Subsidies

Consider an export subsidy that lowers the cost of production for domestic exporting firms. In Figure 3.11 the domestic supply of exports increases from S to S' with the subsidy. If the international price of the exported good is $10, the export industry will increase output from 100 to 120 units with the subsidy. Domestic quantity demanded remains at 50. Excess supply increases from 50 to 70. Export revenue increases from $10 \times 50 = 500 to $10 \times 70 = 700.

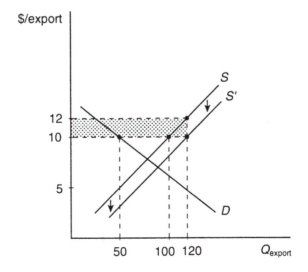

Figure 3.11
Tax Burden of a Subsidy
A subsidy increases domestic supply from S to S'. At an international price of $10, production increases from 100 to 120 and exports increase from 50 to 70. The subsidy costs domestic taxpayers $2 \times 120 = 240, the shaded rectangle.

Firms along the supply curve benefit from the subsidy. The subsidy encourages inefficient production. Moreover, the subsidy does not come from thin air. Taxes are levied to pay the subsidy. A subsidy of $2 per unit, the vertical distance between S and S', costs taxpayers $2 for every unit produced. The tax burden of the subsidy in Figure 3.11 is $2 \times 120 = $240, the shaded rectangle.

Both the costs and benefits of a subsidy have to be considered. There is a tax burden for any export subsidy.

A subsidy can lead to long run gains if it successfully biases growth toward an export industry with rising prices on international markets. This outcome requires that government officials make wise business decisions, which is very ulikely. Subsidies generally have not been used successfully to target growth industries. Economic growth is a complicated process that governments cannot direct.

Even if national income increases with a subsidy, income is redistributed. Firms, stockholders, and workers in the export industry benefit at the expense of taxpayers.

EXAMPLE 3.15 *Wartime Trade Distortions*

During World War II, economic policy funnelled resources into wartime production but fouled markets. *Business Week* (23 October 1943) reports that price ceilings on corn caused shortages of animal feed. Imports of Canadian wheat substituted for the lost corn but these imports displaced shipping on the Great Lakes leading to shortages of iron ore. Also, the wheat had been used to produce alcohol and synthetic rubber. To replace the lost wheat, alcohol producers substituted molasses imported from the Caribbean on freighters that had been carrying petroleum products from the Gulf Coast, leading to petroleum shortages. Meanwhile, hog farmers substituted skim milk for feed, leading to a shortage of adhesives since casein made from skim milk is used to produce adhesives. Casein had to be imported from Argentina. Many prices had ceilings leading to persistent shortages. Arbitrary trade policy has widespread unintended consequences.

Free Trade Zones and Free Enterprise Zones

Another tool of industrial trade policy is the *free trade zone* (FTZ) exempt from tariffs on imported intermediate inputs and capital goods, and free from taxes on foreign investment. Countries around the Pacific Rim use FTZs to encourage foreign multinational firms and export production. FTZs increase international trade and investment by skirting protectionist laws that apply to the rest of the country.

In the US, FTZs are close to ports and international airports. Goods are brought there for storage, inspection, reshipping, and manufacturing. Costly and cumbersome customs procedures are avoided inside the FTZ. The FTZ Board in the executive branch approves and oversees FTZs, a subtle degree of power to skirt the protectionist policies.

Consumers can shop inside a *free enterprise zone* (FEZ) a designated area where protectionism is relaxed. Goods and services are traded freely without tariffs, quotas, or administrative hassle inside an FEZ. Hong Kong and Singapore are classic examples of the economic development that can occur when international trade and finance are unhindered.

For efficiency, economists favor both FTZs and FEZs. If an entire country were an FEZ, there would be free trade.

EXAMPLE 3.16 *FTZs*

An FTZ is an area inside a country exempt from tariffs, quotas, and restrictions on international investment. FTZs first became popular around the Pacific Rim. US manufacturers began using FTZs during the 1970s based on a law dating to the Smoot-Hawley Act. Jafar Alavi and Henry Thompson (1988) report that about 3% of US production occurs inside FTZs. Some industries in the US have *inverted tariff structures* that protect production of intermediate goods: automobile, office equipment, electronics, and printing industries. Production in an FTZ avoids an inverted tariff since intermediate goods are imported without duty, assembled, and shipped into the country at the lower tariff rate for finished goods. The first automobile firm to become an FTZ in the US was Honda and all auto plants are now FTZs. About 80% of the goods shipped from FTZs in the US are sent into the country. In some countries, FTZ production has to be exported. The net effect of FTZs is to move the country closer to enjoying the benefits of free trade.

EXAMPLE 3.17 *Gains from Rice & Fertilizer Trade in Vietnam*

Vietnam has a large agricultural sector with generally poor households. Vietnam liberalized international trade in rice and fertilizer between 1993 and 1998 during a period of market reforms from socialism when the national poverty rate fell by half. Ganesh Seshan (2005) finds that the free trade in rice and fertilizer had no measurable effect on national welfare but does account for about half the reduction in poverty among farm households.

"New" Trade Theory

The debate continues over whether there should be industrial trade policy including export subsidies, protection, and other measures to manage the content and direction of trade. Proponents label this "new" trade theory based on models of imperfect competition. The idea is that intelligent policy makers aided by economists with strategic models could outguess markets.

In truth, the ideas of the "new" trade theory are as old as political economy. The debate over protectionism gave rise to economics as we know it. When it comes to export promotion, taxpayers would be unlikely to lend support if they realized they were subsidizing select industries and foreign consumers. Industries receiving support, of course, will continue to lobby for subsidies.

Any proposed policy should have to pass the economic test of weighing costs versus benefits. Economic theory and evidence from history favor free trade over subsidies or other industrial trade policies. Governments have demonstrated little ability to design and implement successful industrial trade policy. It is unlikely that any theory will improve this record.

EXAMPLE 3.18 *Deadly Import Substitution*

> Two instances of import substitution in pharmaceuticals trade led to deadly consequences (Howard Scripps News Service, May 1993). US drug companies had developed a test for the HIV virus and a method to decontaminate blood for transfusions by 1985. French health officials would not import the product and waited for the domestic Pasteur Institute to develop its own products. As a result, 1200 hemophiliacs received tainted blood and over 250 died. Another twisted tale comes from Japan where government officials would not import a highly reliable vaccine for measles, mumps, and rubella from a US drug company. Japan's Ministry of Health and Welfare directed three Japanese companies to develop a vaccine. Numerous cases of meningitis, encephalitis, paralysis, brain damage, and some deaths resulted. The Ministry first warned of side effects, then made the vaccine voluntary, later allowed Japanese firms to market their own vaccines, and finally banned the import substitute.

Problems for Section D

D1. In what ways is a currency devaluation similar to an export subsidy? In what ways are they different?

D2. As a consumer, would you prefer to live inside an FTZ or an FEZ? As a firm, where would you want to locate?

D3. Predict the effects of a subsidy on an industry competing with imported goods in a small open economy.

D4. If two trading economies both subsidize their export industry, analyze the outcome.

EXAMPLE 3.19 *Productivity and Exports*

Exporting firms perform better than non-exporters in terms of productivity and other measures of success. Good firms may become exporters, or export competition may make firms better. Andrew Bernard and Bradford Jensen (1998) uncover evidence that in fact good firms become exporters. Growth and success are higher for firms that become exporters. Productivity and wage growth are not higher for exporting firms, suggesting exporting does not make a firm more competitive.

EXAMPLE 3.20 *Gains from Used Car Trade*

A natural experiment on the gains from trade occurred in 1993 when Cyprus began to allow the import of Japanese used cars more than two years old as examined by Safronis Clerides (2005). Japan has an excess supply of three-year old cars due to a costly warranty renewal system and steering wheels are also on the right-hand side in Cyprus, generating a natural market. Worldwide, over one million used cars are exported yearly in a lively market with much more price and quality variation and a relative lack of buyer information compared to new cars. Consumers in Cyprus substituted toward the higher quality used car imports, used cars gained a larger share of the total car market, and the total quantities of cars and used cars in the market increased. Consumer surplus gains are a few hundred dollars per consumer.

CONCLUSION

Overall gains are enjoyed with free international trade. Nevertheless, every nation hinders trade with tariffs, quotas, foreign exchange controls, subsidies, and a host of other protectionist tools. Protectionism is the oldest topic in economics and one of the most relevant today. "New" trade theory advocates active trade policy, but successful industrial trade policy has yet to emerge. Tools in the coming chapters lay the foundation for analyzing the causes and effects of trade policy. The goal is to understand the redistribution of income caused by international trade, protectionism, and industrial trade policy.

Terms

Developmental gains from trade

Diminishing marginal returns

Diversification

Domestic relative prices

Increasing opportunity cost

Industrial trade policy

LDCs, DCs, NICs

Marginal productivity

Export promotion	Marginal rate of substitution
FTZs and FEZs	Marginal rate of transformation
Gains from trade	Nominal prices
Human capital	Subsidies
Immiserizing growth	Terms of trade
Import substitution	Trade triangle

MAIN POINTS

- The production possibilities frontier illustrates limited resources and increasing opportunity costs of production. Relative prices determine outputs of goods and services.
- Specialization and trade allow a country to consume a more highly valued bundle of output, the fundamental source of the gains from trade.
- Economic development is illustrated by an expanding PPF. There is solid evidence that export led growth creates higher income.
- Industrial trade policy refers to a comprehensive plan of export promotion and import substitution, but it has never been successful.

REVIEW PROBLEMS

1. If income rises to 220 S in Figure 3.4 with the same relative price of S, find the value of income in terms of M.

2. From Example 3.1 of the changing US production frontier and the shift from manufactures to services, sketch the PPFs and outputs in 1950 and 1986. Estimate the underlying rise in the relative price of services. Show the decline in the ratio M/S of outputs and the growth in the economy.

3. Sketch a PPF with constant costs of production. Use a maximum manufacturing output of 200 as the basis. What is the relative price of M along the PPF? Does the law of diminishing marginal returns hold?

4. Sketch a PPF with increasing costs of production, using outputs of 200, 150, 100, 50, and 0 units of M. Find the opportunity costs of the increased production of M at each step of 50 units. What determines where production takes place?

5. Suppose the domestic autarky relative price $M/S = 1$ and autarky consumption takes place at $(M,S) = (100,100)$. Production with free trade takes place at $(M,S) = (50,160)$ with 50 units exported and 60 units imported. Find the consumption bundle (M,S). Sketch the trade triangle. What are the terms of trade?

6. In the previous problem, find the gains from trade in terms of M and the percentage gains from trade.

7. Illustrate consumer choice and the welfare gains in the previous problem with indifference curves.

8. Comparing unbiased growth with biased growth, which leads to higher gains from trade? Which leads to higher national income?

9. Distinguish between the gains from trade and developmental gains from trade.

10. There is a large FTZ in McAllen, Texas on the Mexican border. Along the border, workers pass freely in both directions. If you were organizing

a firm, what would you consider in deciding whether to operate in the FTZ or across the border in Mexico?

11. Suppose the entire state of California declares itself an FEZ. What would be the effects in California? What would be the effects on the entire US?

12. The most heavily subsidized industry in the DCs is agriculture. There are price supports, government research, direct subsidies, and so on. What would happen to the pattern of trade and income distribution if agricultural subsidies were eliminated?

READINGS

Robert Barro and Xavier Sala-i-Martin (1999) *Economic Growth*, Cambridge, The MIT Press. Excellent textbook.

Robert Solow (2000) *Growth Theory: An Exposition*, Oxford, Oxford University Press. A concise presentation.

Douglas Irwin (1996) *Against the Tide: An Intellectual History of Free Trade*, Princeton: Princeton University Press. The free trade argument through history.

Peter Morici (1995) Export our way to prosperity, *Foreign Policy*, Winter. How the US has gained from trade.

George Crane & Alba Amawi (1991) *The Theoretical Evolution of International Political Economy*, Oxford: Oxford University Press. Readings in political economy.

Paul Krugman (1991) Myths and Realities of US Competitiveness, *Science*, November. Popular misconceptions of competitiveness and trade.

Robert Lawrence (1983) *Can America Compete?* Washington: Brookings Institution. Changing structure of US industry.

Trade Policies for a Better Future (1985) Geneva: GATT. A general argument for the gains from trade.

Anne Krueger (1984) *Trade and Employment in Developing Nations: Synthesis and Conclusions*, Chicago: University of Chicago Press. Summary of trade and development.

Gerald Meier (1989) *Leading Issues in Economic Development*, Oxford: Oxford University Press. Readings on economic development.

David Landes (1999) *The Wealth and Poverty of Nations*, New York: Norton. The big picture of history and economics.

CHAPTER 4

Protection

Preview

The causes and effects of protectionsim are central issues in international economics. This chapter covers:

- *Tariffs* on imports
- *Quotas* and other *nontariff barriers* to trade
- *Distortions* due to protection
- *Political economy* of protection

INTRODUCTION

Government protection of domestic industry from foreign competition began the debate on free trade that led to the discipline of economics. Industrialists have been resourceful when it comes to finding arguments for protecting their industry. International economists have consistently advocated open international competition and free trade.

Protectionism alters the pattern of production and trade, and redistributes income. Protection of an industry creates gains for some but losses for others, and the losses outweigh the gains. Those who enjoy the gains pay the government for protection.

Both theory and evidence suggest that income rises and is more evenly distributed with free trade. Comparative advantage is the foundation of trade and one of the universal principles of science. Nations, firms, or individuals that ignore their comparative advantage are less efficient and poorer. Protectionism restricts the beneficial effects of comparative advantage and free trade.

Economists have yet to persuade governments to give up the protection racket. Tariffs, quotas, and other nontariff barriers are common government policy. The reason for protectionism is simple. Those who benefit, the owners and workers in the protected industry, are organized and willing to lobby politicians. Disorganized consumers and taxpayers do not realize the extent of their losses. The amount of the loss for each individual consumer is not large enough to lobby against the harmful policy. The benefits of protectionism are concentrated but costs are thinly spread, and protectionism prevails.

The partial equilibrium picture of protectionism is developed with market supply and demand. If the country levying a tariff is small relative to the world market, the price of the imported good remains at the world level. The partial equilibrium approach concentrates on the protected market isolated from the economy and is widely used in applications.

The production possibilities frontier (PPF) develops adjustment to protectionism across the economy. The following chapters examine adjustment in international prices and production between economies. Patterns of income redistribution resulting from protectionism with various structures of production are examined.

International trade theory examines the effects of trade restrictions. National income is lower than it would be without protectionism. Resources are wasted on relatively inefficient activities. Lobbyists crowd the halls of government. Taxpayers subsidize the favored industries.

Trade policy affects everyone in measurable ways and we should study its causes and effects. Everyone is involved in international markets and protection.

A. TARIFFS: TAXES ON IMPORTS

A tariff is a tax on a product imported across a national border. As with any tax, the consumer pays a higher price. Tariffs have the double attraction of being inconspicuous and easy to collect. Tariffs have historically been a popular way for governments to raise revenue, and many governments have raised most of their revenue with tariffs. The US government earned almost all of its early revenue with tariffs, more than half of its revenue until 1870, and more than 25% until the 1920s. At present, business and personal income taxes account for almost all government revenue in the developed countries but LDCs rely on tariffs as a major source of government revenue.

The average tariff rate in the US is about 4%, falling from about 10% in the 1960s and 15% in the 1950s. This reduction is due in part to the international negotiations organized under the General Agreement on Tariffs and Trade (GATT) and the World Trade Organization (WTO). In principle, countries are committed to lowering their protection through GATT. The WTO oversees the agreement and acts as a court in disputes.

GATT sprung from a desire to restore the international economy following World War II. There have been eight rounds of negotiations, each successful in some measure in convincing governments to lower protectionism. Average tariffs worldwide have fallen from 40% to below 4%. There are, however, high tariffs on some products in every country, and nontariff barriers have become more popular. Trade is a long way from free, but progress has been made. GATT affords governments a visible mechanism to negotiate and a mechanism to avoid protectionist pressure. In the US for instance, Congress sets tariffs but the President administers the GATT treaty.

The Escape Clause, Section 201 of the Trade Act of 1974, allows Congress to enact temporary protection in the "national interest" for an industry that can prove to the International Trade Commission (ITC) that it has been damaged by imports. Some industries obtain special protection despite the general agreement to lower protection. While the current average US tariff rate of 4% sounds low, tariffs on some goods are much higher. Costs associated with the distortion from protection in some industries are high.

EXAMPLE 4.1   *A History of US Tariffs*

High tariffs in the 1800s on manufactures reduced income in the agricultural South leading to the Civil War. Slavery did not lead to the war, and was quickly becoming uneconomical with mechanization in agriculture. Tariffs provided over a quarter of government revenue until income taxes were made constitutional in the 1920s. The high tariffs of the Smoot-Hawley Act of 1930 stopped international trade and led to the Great Depression as developed by Alfred Eckels (1998). In 1934, the Democrats passed the Reciprocal Trade Agreement Act that allowed the president to negotiate tariff reductions. The RTAA laid the foundation for progress toward free trade, solidifying the political focus of exporters and importers of intermediate products who favor free trade. GATT, the WTO, and NAFTA are legal in the US due to the RTAA. Tariffs now are at a historical low. The average tariff has steadily declined since World War II but quotas and other nontariff barriers have replaced tariffs to some extent and protectionism always threatens. NAFTA will prove an important step in the slow unsteady march toward free trade.

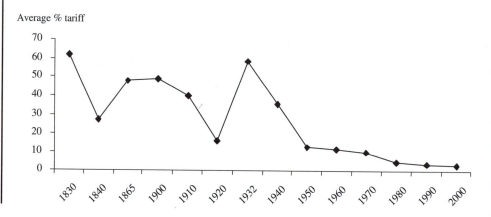

Average % tariff

Table 4.1 Estimated Price Effects of Tariffs

	Free Trade	**Tariffs**
Autos	$7500	$10,000
Box of candy	$2	$5
Bluejeans	$15	$18

Source: "Protection at Any Price?" *Regulation*, 1983.

The Cost of a Tariff

Some idea of the everyday effect of tariffs on prices are in Table 4.1 from Murray Weidenbaum and Michael Munger (1983). The higher price is a windfall to the domestic industry that competes with imports. Tariffs support domestic production that is inefficient relative to foreign production. The government receives revenue by taxing consumers, who pay higher prices for imports.

Tariffs can be levied on finished products like cars and stereos, or they can be hidden in imported intermediate goods like fabric or electric motors. These components and intermediate products are imported and included in goods "Made in the USA" even if only buttons or labels are attached.

The effective rate of protection includes protection on intermediate inputs as well as quotas and other nontariff barriers. Quotas are quantitative restrictions on the import of goods. Nontariff barriers are other devices such as voluntary export restraints or health and safety regulations that limit imports.

Effective protection is the net percentage of domestic value added shielded by tariffs. *Domestic value added* refers to the share of the price of a final product accounted for by domestic inputs. Let V be domestic value added. Protection is valued relative to V. If P^* is the international price of the finished good and T its tariff rate, the tariff raises price inside the country by TP^*. Relative to V, the tariff gives protection of TP^*/V.

Domestic producers may use foreign intermediate inputs in their production. Let p^* be the international price of the intermediate input and t its tariff rate. The tariff t raises the cost of the intermediate input by tp^*. The effective rate of protection (ERP) is then

$$\text{ERP} = (TP^* - tp^*)/V$$

A high enough tariff on intermediate inputs can result in a negative ERP for a domestic producer.

As an example, suppose the international price of a shirt is $20 and the tariff on shirts is 10%. A domestic shirt maker imports materials worth $12 to make a $20 shirt, adding domestic value of $8. The $2 tariff effectively protects domestic

Table 4.2 Effective Rates of Protection

Source: *The Structure and Evolution of Recent US Trade Policy*, University of Chicago Press, 1984.

value added by $2/$8 = 25%$. A 5% tariff on imported textiles taxes the shirt maker by $12 \times 0.05 = $.60$, reducing the ERP to $($2.00 − $.60)/$8 = 17.5%$. A higher tariff on imported textiles reduces the ERP. A tariff rate of 20% on the imported textiles raises their cost by $2.60 = 0.2 \times 12. The ERP becomes negative: $($2.00 − $2.60)/$8 = −7.5%$. The domestic producer operates at a net disadvantage because of the tariffs.

Estimates of the ERP in Table 4.2 from Alan Deardorff and Robert Stern (1984) compare the US, Japan, and Europe. ERPs are generally higher than nominal tariff rates. As the manufacturing process proceeds, the protection of intermediate inputs in each stage is included in the final level of protection. For this reason, ERPs are much higher than the average US tariff rate of 4%. These rates have fallen some under WTO and NAFTA, but it is safe to say the overall tax rate paid by US consumers for all protection is over 5%.

On a more detailed level, a study by A.J. Yeats (1974) finds variation in ERPs. In the US, mill feed products (11%) cottonseed oil (466%), soybean oil (253%), cigarettes (113%), and soft drinks (−10%) are examples. In Europe, sea food (53%), milk (60%), vegetable oil (138%), cigarettes (147%), and soft drinks (−30%) stand out. In Japan, milk (249%), processed food (59%), cocoa (81%), woven fabrics (65%), cottonseed oil (200%), soy bean oil (286%), cigarettes (406%), and animal fats (−2%) are examples of the ERP.

There are different methods to estimate the costs of protection and economists work on improving data, models, and estimation techniques. Howard Wall (1999) uses a more general technique called the gravity model that considers each country's production, tariffs, and distance from each other. Wall estimates 1996 US imports were 26% lower than they would have been without protection, and the country suffered a 1.5% welfare reduction due to protection.

> *Protectionism costs consumers. With protection, consumers have to pay higher prices. All forms of protection tax consumers.*

EXAMPLE 4.2 *Tariff Duties*

> The percentage of duty free goods has slowly increased as tariff rates have decreased in the US. Tariff duties per capita are one measure of the tariff level. The % Free variable reports the percentage of imports without duty. In constant dollars, there has been little decline in duties per capita as estimated by the US Census. Protectionism is alive and well.
>
> | | % Free | Duties/Capita |
> | --- | --- | --- |
> | 1980 | 45% | $79 |
> | 1996 | 51% | $77 |

Market Analysis of a Tariff

The effects of a tariff on the domestic market are in Figure 4.1. The international price of the manufactured good M is $p^* = \$5$. The country can import as much as it likes at $5. The economy is a *price taker* in this international market. At $5, the difference between quantity demanded (300) and quantity supplied (100) is imported. If the economy is open to free trade, 200 units are imported and the domestic price is $5.

With a tariff, the domestic price increases. Suppose a 20% tariff is levied. With $t = 0.2$, the domestic price of M rises to $\$5 \times 1.2 = \$6$. Consumers respond by switching to substitutes and reducing the quantity of M demanded from 300 to 270 up the demand curve. Domestic producers respond to the higher price with an increase in the quantity supplied from 100 to 120 out the supply curve. Imports drop to the difference between the quantity demanded and quantity supplied domestically: $270 - 120 = 150$. The tariff reduces the level of imports by 25%, from 200 to 150.

Tariff revenue for the government is $150, the tariff per unit ($1 = 0.2p^*$) times the level of imports 150. Tariff revenue in Figure 4.1 is rectangle A.

Consumers pay a higher price and consume less with the tariff. *Consumer surplus* gauges the consumer loss. When the price is $5, the quantity demanded is 300. Consumers back along the demand curve would pay more than $5. The first units of M, for instance, could be sold at just under $15. As the price falls

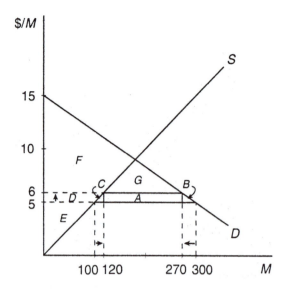

Figure 4.1
The Market Effects of a Tariff
A 20% tariff raises the domestic price to $6 from the world price of $5. The level of imports drops to 150, and tariff revenue of $150 in area A is created for the government. Domestic firms enjoy the increased producer surplus represented by area D ($110). Con-sumer surplus falls with the tariff by area A + B + C + D = $285. The deadweight loss of the tariff is the area of the triangles B + C = $15 + $10 = $25.

from $15, more consumers buy the good. At the world price of $5, all consumers up along the demand curve acquire the good for less than they would be willing to pay. The triangle A + B + C + D + F + G is a measure of the gains to consumers from buying at the market price of $5. This triangle is the consumer surplus, below the demand curve and above the price. In this example, the consumer surplus equals 1/2 [($15 − $5) × 300] = $1500.

Consumers lose the consumer surplus area A + B + C + D with the tariff. When the price rises from $5 to $6 with the tariff, consumer surplus reduces by the area between $5 and $6 over to the demand curve. This lost consumer surplus is a measure of the loss forced on consumers by the tariff. Some consumers are squeezed out of the market, while those remaining pay a higher price. With the tariff, consumer surplus falls to area F + G, which equals ½[($15 − $6) × 270] = $1215. The loss in consumer surplus with the tariff is $1500 − $1215 = $285.

The area above the supply curve and below the price measures gains to firms, the *producer surplus*. Producers gain area D since they end up selling more goods at a higher price. Firms already in the market enjoy the higher price with the tariff. Other firms may enter the industry, attracted by the higher price. Firms up along the supply curve sell at a price above what they would be willing to accept. When the price is $5, producer surplus is area E, equal to

Table 4.3 Income Redistribution from the Tariff in Figure 4.1

Consumer Loss	Producer Gain	Government Revenue	Deadweight Loss
A + B + C + D	D	A	B + C
$285	$110	$15	$15 + $10 = $25

½($5 × 100) = $250. When the price rises to $6 with the tariff, producer surplus increases to E + D, which equals ½($6 × 120) = $360. Area D, the gain in producer surplus, equals $360 − $250 = $110.

This leaves triangles B and C as the *deadweight loss* from the tariff, consumer losses not offset by government tariff revenue or producer surplus. Rectangle A ($150) of the consumer loss ($285) goes to the government as tariff revenue, and area D ($110) goes to domestic industry. The government spends its revenue and firms pay inputs, so the income represented by area A plus D ($260) is redistributed in the economy. Triangles B and C, however represent losses that are not offset. These losses amount to B = $15 plus C = $10, a total deadweight of $25. The redistribution of income as a result of the tariff in Figure 4.1 are summarized in Table 4.3.

Tariffs are taxes that redistribute income and cause net deadweight losses due to inefficiency.

Domestic consumers of the manufactured good are hurt by tariffs. Domestic firms that compete with imports are helped. Workers for these manufacturing firms gain, as do owners of the capital in the industry. These groups, however, must also pay the higher price due to the tariff. Gene Grossman and Jim Levinshon (1989) find evidence that tariffs increase the value of the stocks of firms in protected industries. Shareholders have an interest in keeping their industry protected. There is also some empirical evidence that protection elevates the wages of labor in protected industries.

It is easy to spot the winners from a tariff. Since the gains can be sizeable, the winners find it worthwhile to spend money lobbying for protection. Government officials are happy to accept the money. Tariff revenue on consumer and food products alone was $106 million in 2002. Political support and contributions explain the bias toward protectionism.

EXAMPLE 4.3   *Costs of Protection*

Protection that helps an industry in one country hurts other industries in the country and the same industry in other countries. Some jobs are saved but prices paid by consumers increase. The following partial list of protected US industries from Gary Hufbauer, Diane Berliner, and Kimberly Elliott (1986) rank industries by yearly cost per job saved. The list includes the date of the law, the primary region of the world hurt by the protection, the price increase in the US, and the cost per job saved. The country would be better off paying these workers not to work and allowing free trade. Peanut farmers, for instance, could be paid up to $999 per acre per year not to grow peanuts with free trade and the country would be better off.

Industry	Date	Region	Price	Cost/Job
Steel	1969	Argentina, Brazil	30%	$750,000
Shipping	1789	Global	60%	$270,000
Orange juice	1930	Brazil	44%	$240,000
Dairy	1953	Global	80%	$220,000
Glassware	1922	Europe	19%	$200,000
Meat	1965	Australia, Canada	14%	$160,000
Ceramic tiles	1930	Brazil, Italy	21%	$135,000
Autos	1981	Japan	11%	$105,000
Books	1891	Asia	40%	$100,000
Sugar	1934	Global	30%	$60,000
Textiles	1957	31 countries	30%	$42,000
Peanuts	1953	Global	28%	$1000/acre

Protection Versus Free Trade

Economists estimate deadweight losses from tariffs using this market model. Murray Weidenbaum and Tracy Munger (1983) estimate yearly losses resulting from higher prices paid by consumers of at least $255 per capita. Tariffs are taxes not generally recognized by consumers.

Inefficient organization of production resulting from tariffs creates losses. Firms that cannot effectively compete are encouraged to continue operation. Valuable productive inputs (labor, capital, natural resources) are spent making products available at cheaper prices on international markets. The economy in turn produces less of the products that the rest of the world values more highly, losing income. Instead of concentrating on profitable export production, the economy produces substitutes for products it should be importing. Gains from free trade are based on the improved pattern of production.

Losses are incurred through the lobbying efforts of industry and labor groups. Protected industries employ lobbyists, spending money to bend the ears of politicians. Lobby groups advertise to win popular support.

Economic efficiency calls for elimination of protection. Economists have been making this argument since the beginning of economics as a discipline. The political process of lowering protection is difficult, and the danger of protectionism constant. In the final analysis, it is better to face international competition. Protectionism is a quick fix that undermines economic efficiency.

Tariffs are inefficient but remain part of the political economy because the concentrated winners pay politicians. Protection is for sale.

Developed countries have witnessed declines in some "basic" manufacturing industries including iron and steel, footwear, nonferrous metal, textiles, and apparel. These industries have been forced to face increasing competition from LDCs and NICs where wages are lower. Alarmists claim de-industrialization. Proponents of sagging industries, their managers, stockholders, and workers, clamor for protection. Since the 1950s manufacturing employment has dropped from over 1/3 of the US workforce to less than 1/5, while employment in services has risen from 1/2 to 3/4. This trend reflects underlying comparative advantage and increased international specialization. Rather than using a patchwork of protection for relatively inefficient industries, trade policy might contribute to retrain and relocate workers.

In the DCs, there has been a slight decline in manufacturing with specialization in service production. Imports of manufactures have grown, but so have exports. The mix of manufactured goods produced has shifted toward those more intensive in skilled labor. Unskilled wages have fallen, an incentive for education and job training.

The EU is a free trade area with few internal restrictions. The US, Canada, and Mexico have created the North American Free Trade Area (NAFTA). There is some discussion of a free trade agreement between the US and Japan. There are regional free trade areas in South America, Africa, and Southeast Asia. Negotiations are underway around the world for more free trade areas.

Local government representatives are subject to the constant pressures of protectionism. President Reagan said he was a believer in free trade but the record shows his administration turned the US back toward protectionism. The first President Bush advocated NAFTA, which President Clinton signed. The second President Bush imposed large steel tariffs while advocating free trade. There is increasing free trade in the world but local protectionists are disguised as free traders. The oldest issue in economics promises to persist.

EXAMPLE 4.4 *NAFTA Tariffs & Wages*

NAFTA provides for elimination of protection between Canada, Mexico, and the US. The process began in 1994 and is scheduled to complete by 2008. An assessment of NAFTA was published in *Business Frontier* of the FRB of Dallas in 1999. By 1998, Mexican tariffs on US products had dropped from 10% to 2% and US tariffs on Mexican products from 4% to 0.5%. Trade between Mexico and the US is much larger than between Mexico and Canada. The automobile industry is internationally integrated. Mexican exports are generally labor intensive but some trade is based on natural resources. Trade between the US and Canada is the largest component of NAFTA. Income per capita in $000 and manufacturing wages in the three countries are listed below:

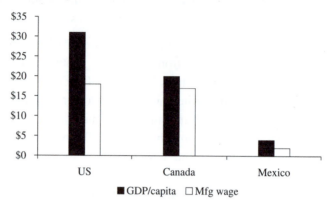

Problems for Section A

A1. Suppose a 40% tariff is levied on imported manufactured goods in Figure 4.1. Find the level of imports, tariff revenue, changes in producer surplus and consumer surplus, and the deadweight loss.

A2. Why is steel protected in the US while toys and games are not?

EXAMPLE 4.5   *Transport Costs, Really*

Transportation costs contribute to determining which products are traded where. Donald Rousslang and Theodore To (1993) find that total transport costs are larger than tariffs for US imports. For imported consumer products, effective tariffs are 6%, international freight 3%, subsequent domestic freight 3%, and wholesale costs 9% of the final product price. High international transport costs keep some products from being traded at all. Both tariffs and transports costs have fallen steadily since the 1950s.

B.   QUOTAS AND OTHER NONTARIFF BARRIERS

A *quota* is a quantitative restriction on the level of imports. Imports cannot exceed a quota even if the goods are free. Quotas force adjustment onto price, generally providing more protection than tariffs. If domestic supply or demand for the import change, quotas maintain an upper limit on imports and force adjustment onto price. In a market with growing demand, price rises more with a quota than with a tariff. Other nontariff barriers are similar to quotas.

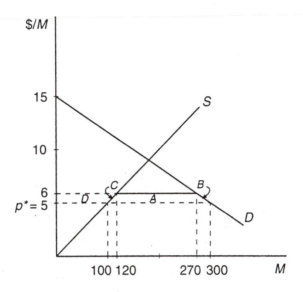

Figure 4.2
Quota on Imports of M
A quota of 150 pushes the domestic price up 20% from the world level of $5. This quota
is similar to a 20% tariff except that no tariff revenue is generated for the government.
The deadweight loss of this quota is the area A + B + C = $175, compared to area B + C =
$25 for a tariff.

Market Analysis of a Quota

In Figure 4.2 there is a quota of 150 units. The international price is $p^* = \$5$. In
the absence of a quota, 200 units of M would be imported. A quota of 150
pushes the domestic price to where quantity demanded minus quantity supplied
is 150. Domestic price rises above the international price, leading to inefficient
production at home and costing domestic consumers.

Notice the similarity between the quota in Figure 4.2 and the tariff in
Figure 4.1. The two figures show equivalent effects. Quotas, however, create no
tariff revenue, are more restrictive, and force all adjustment onto price.

Suppose the import market in Figure 4.2 adopts a quota. Consumer surplus
falls by area A + B + C + D, and D transfers to producer surplus. A + B + C is
the deadweight loss from the quota. If this market switched to an equivalent
tariff, consumers and firms would be indifferent but the government gains the
tariff revenue in rectangle A.

Foreign exporting firms are able to sell at the higher price of $6 with the
quota. Before the quota, foreign export revenue was $5 × 200 = $1000. With the
quota, foreign export revenue falls to $6 × 150 = $900. Rectangle A is a transfer
from domestic consumers to foreign exporting firms.

Area A equals $150 and triangles B and C have a combined area of $25. The deadweight loss from the quota is $175. With a tariff, revenue of $150 in A would go to the government and the $25 in areas B and C would be deadweight loss. Quotas are more costly than tariffs because the deadweight loss is greater. This quota costs the economy $150 compared to the tariff. The tariff costs the economy $25 compared with free trade.

Governments may raise revenue through auctioning quotas to domestic firms buying at the low international price and selling at the artificially high domestic price. The foreign exporter or domestic importer enjoys higher profit. Domestic importing firms can buy at the international price of $5 and sell at the artificially high price of $6. Domestic firms also produce 120 units of *M*, gaining D in producer surplus. Importing firms make a profit of $150 in A. If importers were forced to bid for the right to import, the government could appropriate area A. Firms would be forced to pay this price in a competitive bid for the right to import.

EXAMPLE 4.6   *Costly Quotas*

The cost of a quota can be estimated using Figure 4.1. David Tarr and Morris Morkre (1987) estimate deadweight losses due to various US quotas. All quotas together are equivalent to a 19% tariff but the potential tariff revenue is transferred to foreign firms. Japanese car firms enjoy an annual transfer of $860 million. The average cost to benefit ratio of all quotas is 35 to 1, hardly a bargain.

Product	Annual DWL	Cost to Benefit
Japanese cars	$1.0 billion	24 to 1
Steel	$1.2 billion	115 to 1
Textiles from Hong Kong	$0.4 billion	19 to 1

Market Adjustment with a Quota

Another fundamental difference between tariffs and quotas is that with a quota adjustment is forced entirely onto price. Suppose the domestic demand increases as in Figure 4.3.

With a tariff, the domestic price remains at $6, the world price of $5 plus the $1 per unit tariff. Since price is unchanged, domestic suppliers continue to produce 120. Quantity demanded rises to 320 and the level of imports jumps to 200.

With a quota of 150, the increased demand forces price to rise to $7. Imports remain at 150 but domestic production is spurred to 140. Consumers are worse off with the quota, consuming 30 fewer units at the higher price of $7. With the quota, consumption is 290 but with the tariff it would be 320.

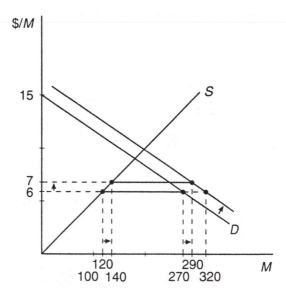

Figure 4.3
Market Adjustment with a Quota
With a quota of 150 in place, an increase in the demand for imports forces all adjustment onto price. Domestic production increases from 120 to 140 but only 150 units of M can be imported. The domestic price is pushed up from $6 to $7.

Protected industries prefer quotas over tariffs when the international price of a good is falling, domestic demand is rising, or domestic supply is falling. In these circumstances the domestic industry can maintain its output with a quota.

Industries would favor tariffs over quotas when the international price is expected to rise, domestic demand is expected to fall, or domestic supply is expected to rise. In these circumstances a quota might become ineffective but a tariff would continue to offer protection.

For any quota there is an equivalent tariff that creates the same production, consumption, imports, and domestic price. Quotas do not produce tariff revenue and force all adjustment onto domestic price.

Quotas can also lower the quality of domestic output. George Sweeney, Randy Beard, and Henry Thompson (1997) show that a quota is likely to lower quality of domestic production when there are high quality imports. Domestic firms relax when they realize imports will fall, and compete less with quality. The quality of foreign products, however, rises.

EXAMPLE 4.7   *The Customary Hassle*

The American Association of Exporters and Importers was founded in 1921 to lobby for free trade and offer technical assistance. The AAEI publishes *US*

Customs House Guide, a formidable tour through US trade policy. Its quota alert system informs traders about changes in quota laws. The following examples illustrate the hassle.

Dolls representing only human beings and parts theoreof:

Dolls, whether or not dressed	
Stuffed	12%
Other	12%
Parts and accessories	8%

Dolls should evidently be imported in at least two parts, dressed or not, stuffed or not, then assembled. Dolls not representing human beings are another story. Tennis rackets should be imported without strings and handles.

Lawn tennis rackets and parts thereof:

Rackets, strung	5%
Rackets, unstrung	4%
Parts and accessories	3%

Tariff laws are a blight on the economy.

Other Nontariff Barriers

There are other *nontariff barriers* (NTBs) besides quotas. The industrialized nations are committed to lowering tariffs under GATT and the WTO. Regional free trade agreements require lower tariffs. More subtle forms of protection afforded by NTBs have become popular because they are more difficult to estimate. Governments are constantly under pressure for protection and are quick to devise methods to skirt free trade agreements.

A popular form of NTB is the voluntary export restraint (VER). Japanese automobile exporters "voluntarily" limit their quantity of exports to the US under threat of tougher protectionism against Japanese imports. The US auto industry puts pressure on the US government, which puts pressure on the Japanese government, which puts pressure on Japanese automakers. VERs are anything but voluntary.

A VER has the same basic effects as a quota inside the nation but it discriminates between trading partners, a violation of GATT principles. European auto producers benefited due to the Japanese VER because they were not subject to quantity restrictions, and sold in the US market at higher prices.

VERs create a cartel for exporters. The Japanese government is coerced to work with various Japanese automakers to restrict competition among themselves in the US market. The VER gives monopoly power to the Japanese auto industry. Monopolies maximize profit by restricting output and raising price. A VER gives monopoly power to the foreign industry. With the restraint on competition, profit for the Japanese auto industry might rise.

Theory and empirical evidence also lead to the expectation of *quality upgrading* with a VER or quota. If Japanese automakers agree to export a limited number of cars per year, it will sell high quality cars if the profit per car is higher. Cars imported from Japan now have all the luxury extras, unlike the simpler models of 25 years ago.

Japan has recently entered into voluntary import expansion (VIE) programs on US goods. Computer chip, coal, beef, and construction industries in the US have benefited from VIE. Such programs discriminate against other countries. Japan buys fewer computer chips from Taiwan, less coal and beef from Australia, and less construction from South Korea. VIEs, like VERs, distort the pattern of trade.

Legal trade restrictions artificially favor domestic firms. Lawyers, doctors, and other professionals are restricted from practicing across borders. The telecommunications and electric utility industries are government franchises protected from foreign competition in most nations.

Health laws are selectively and unfairly applied to foreign goods. Fruits from South America were banned when a test showed evidence of banned insecticides. No other imported fruits samples were positive in tests, and foreign exporters suspected contaminated fruits were purposely placed in the samples. Other examples are banned British exports of beef during the "mad cow" scare, and banned imports of "genetically engineered" crops.

Licensing restricts competition. While there are benefits of standards and licensing, these benefits should be weighed against the costs of restricted competition. Monitoring is necessary to ensure fair application of product standards. International law handles claims of unfair trade practice, and is a growing legal field.

Other more subtle forms of NTBs or discrimination against foreign products can play important protectionist roles. US firms complain that the transportation industry in Japan does not deliver their goods. When shipments sit at the dock, trade becomes unprofitable. Such subtle discrimination against foreign products can curtail imports. The "Buy American" campaign sponsored by US producers tries to prejudice consumers against foreign goods, presumably even when they are better or cheaper. Such campaigns promote inefficient allocation of scarce resources and ask consumers to waste income.

Quotas and other nontariff barriers (NTBs) are more harmful than tariffs. NTBs create distortions that lower real income. Quotas and NTBs protect a status quo of inefficient production.

Jong-Wha Lee and Phillip Swagel (1994) examine the causes of NTBs using data on trade flows, production, and trade barriers for 41 countries in 1988. They find governments tend to protect large, weak, declining industries facing import competition. Governments use a combination of tariffs, NTBs, and exchange rate controls.

EXAMPLE 4.8   *Quota Spillovers*

Japan's voluntary export restraint (VER) on car exports to the US raises the price of cars and benefits exporters in other countries. Car firms in Europe enjoy higher export prices with the Japanese VER. Elias Dinopoulos and Mordechai Kreinin (1988) estimate that the average price of a European car sold in the US was 53% higher in 1984 due to the Japanese VER. The yearly loss per US household was $27 to Japan and $38 to Europe. Each of the 22,000 jobs saved cost $181,000, well above the yearly salary of autoworkers. The country should eliminate the VER and pay the workers not to make cars. Bee Yan Aw and Mark Roberts (1986) examine US shoe imports from 1977 to 1981 and find the quota agreement with Korea and Taiwan resulted in a 12% increase in the price of shoes, and other exporters enjoyed the higher price. Korea and Taiwan shifted to exporting higher quality shoes with more profit per pair. Quotas generally raise the quality of foreign products and downgrade domestic products.

EXAMPLE 4.9   *How to Lobby*

The US steel industry has a long history of special protection from the government. In 1998, it began a sophisticated program to acquire import protection and four years later President Bush invoked Section 201 tariffs on steel imports. The steel industry succeeded with coordinated lobby spending for Congress, government regulators, and the executive branch of government as analyzed by Douglas Brook (2005). Interactions between these different levels and branches of government were critical to success of the lobbying effort. It costs to have friends in high places, but they are profitable.

Problems for Section B

B1. Calculate the deadweight loss and transfer loss resulting from the quota after the demand increase in Figure 4.3. Compare the outcome with a quota to free trade at the world price of $5.

B2. Compare the market adjustment with a quota versus a tariff when domestic supply decreases because of the higher wage in a new labor contract.

B3. Compare adjustment with a quota versus a tariff when the international price falls.

EXAMPLE **4.10** *Winners and Losers with Protection*

The effects of protection vary across industries and regions. Linda Hunter (1990) finds the largest industrial winners in the US are textiles, autos, steel, chemicals, mining, plastics, and utilities. The largest losers are furniture, fixtures, and construction. Regions winning with protection are the Southeast and East with losses spread across the Midwest and West.

C. PROTECTION AND PRODUCTION

Estimates of losses from protection do not include efficiency losses in the pattern of production. An underlying issue is how much extra income the economy could produce if it specialized in producing what it does most efficiently. The relevant tool is the production possibility frontier.

Tariffs and the Production Possibilities Frontier

Along the PPF in Figure 4.4 there is full employment of all resources and complete efficiency in production. The slope of the PPF is the marginal rate of transformation (MRT) telling how many units of manufactures M must be given up to produce an additional unit of services S. If the relative price of services rises, the economy moves down along its PPF toward more S production less M production. A higher relative price of services creates higher profits, attracting new firms and increasing the output of existing firms. The falling relative price of manufactures creates losses in that industry and causes firms to cut back production or go out of business.

Without international trade, consumers pick the point they most prefer along the PPF. Autarky production and consumption is point A in Figure 4.4. Consumers maximize utility subject to the PPF. In autarky at point A, 400 units of each good are produced and consumed, and there is no international trade.

Suppose the relative price of services on the international market is higher than the autarky price. If the economy opens to trade, specialization moves the economy along the PPF from A to P. Resources shift into the production of S and out of the production of M. At point P the MRT equals the terms of trade and the terms of trade line is tangent to PPF. In this example, $tt = M/S = 2$.

From P the economy trades at the world's relative price of services, with 2 units of imported M per unit of exported S. Consumers maximize utility subject to

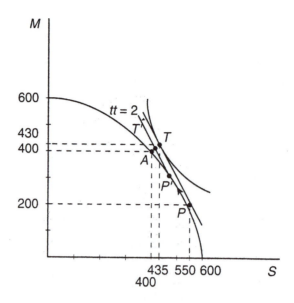

Figure 4.4
Specialization and Trade
A high price of services on the international market induces the economy to specialize from
A to P. Consumers pick point T that maximizes welfare along the terms of trade line $tt = 2$.
The economy exports 115 units of S in exchange for 230 units of M. A tariff pushes the
economy back to P′. Consumers are forced to consume along a lower tt line. Consumption
falls from T to T′.

the consumption possibilities terms of trade line. Consumer equilibrium in free
trade at T where tt is tangent to the indifference curve. The slope of the
indifference curve is the marginal rate of substitution MRS. With free trade,
$tt = $ MRT at P and $tt = $ MRS at T.

More of both goods are consumed at T compared to autarky A. Consumers
are better off in that real income and the level of utility are higher. The community indifference curve tangent to T lies above the autarky level of utility at
A. This country has a low relative price of services in autarky and a comparative
advantage in services.

A tariff on imports of M distorts the efficient pattern of specialization. The
relative price of services inside the country falls. Production moves back from P
to P′ in Figure 4.4. The economy specializes less in S, which is unfortunate
because S has a relatively high value on the international market. This *production
distortion* of the tariff wastes resources in the protected production of M that
has relatively little value on the world markets.

The *efficiency loss* of this production distortion is more difficult to estimate
than the deadweight losses of Figure 4.1. It takes time for the country to change
its pattern of production. There are adjustment costs of moving and retraining.
Investment in the expanding industry takes time.

When the economy arrives at point P′, it trades up along the terms of trade line. Note that 2 units of *M* are still imported for each unit of exported *S* but the economy has reduced its consumption possibilities. The new *tt*′ line from point P′ lies below the free trade *tt* line from point P. Note also that MRT < *tt* at point P′. Consumption falls to T′. The community indifference curve tangent to *tt*′ at T′ lies below the one tangent at T. The tariff reduces utility. Domestic consumers are hurt because their potential to consume both goods is reduced. Real income falls measured in terms of either good at the autarky price.

> *From a global perspective, inefficient production occurs with tariffs that keep an economy from specializing according to its comparative advantage. Tariffs reduce consumption possibilities and lead to less utility and lower real income.*

EXAMPLE 4.11 *Farm Commodity Protection*

Commodity programs reduce supply with "allotments" that limit planting. Price supports are common for agricultural products. Agricultural lobbying during the 1920s and 1930s led to subsidies for milk, sugar, cotton, tobacco, wheat, rice, corn, grain, sorghum, barley, peanuts, and wool. Bruce Gardner (1987) finds that imported goods are more likely to be in such a commodity program. Farmers simply want protection from imports. A price support has much the same effect as a tariff: raising price, stimulating domestic production, restricting consumption, lowering imports, and taxing consumers.

Tariffs and the Terms of Trade

A tariff can improve the terms of trade for a country that consumes a large share of the world market. In the world market, demand for a good falls when a large country imposes a tariff. This decline in demand causes the international price to fall, and the relative price of imports falls. With better terms of trade, the country imposing the tariff might benefit. In Figure 4.4, the terms of trade may improve enough so the new consumption possibilities line *tt*′ swings out beyond T.

Conditions for such an *optimal tariff* are hard to find. The optimal tariff argument is not a generally accepted reason justification for tariffs. Even if conditions for an optimal tariff are found, imposing one can lead to a *tariff war*. Other nations will retaliate with tariffs of their own, and the conditions that led to the optimal tariff are washed away.

The most famous tariff war occurred during the 1930s when countries raised tariffs to prohibitive levels. The Smoot-Hawley Tariff Act created the high US tariffs. More than 1000 economists formally protested, inducing one senator who obviously had never lectured on international economics to claim that professors in ivory towers do not make an honest living by sweating. International trade came to a virtual halt, explaining in large part the duration of the Great Depression. The Federal Reserve Bank simultaneously carried out a sharp reduction of the money supply. Although the stock market crash receives much of the credit for the Great Depression, falling stock prices were only a symptom of the irrational economic policies of excessive tariffs and the drastic money supply reduction.

Although tariffs have the potential to improve the terms of trade, for political reasons this use of tariffs should be avoided. Protectionism inhibits an economy's potential to provide goods and services. Free trade offers a country the potential to arrange production more efficiently and provide consumers with the potential to consume more of every product.

EXAMPLE 4.12 *Smuggling*

Smuggling is illegal trade aimed at avoiding protection or prohibition and may be over 10% of all international trade. A smuggler considers benefits as well as costs including the probability of being caught and penalized. Smuggling increases international specialization and trade but uses more resources than free trade because the goods are more costly to distribute.

Problems for Section C

C1. Explain the relation between the relative price of S in autarky and with trade if the open economy of Figure 4.4 moves northwest from point A up the PPF. Illustrate the effects of a tariff.

C2. What will happen regarding international trade if the relative price of S in the world exactly equals the autarky price in Figure 4.4? What would be the effect of a tariff?

EXAMPLE 4.13 *Tariffs as Tax Surcharge*

People with lower income pay a higher percentage of their income as tariff taxes, making tariffs a regressive tax. Basic items such as food, clothing, autos, and shoes cost more because of tariffs. Lower income groups unfairly spend a larger share of their income on these items. Susan Hickock (1985) estimates the tax burden of tariffs as a percentage of income taxes and the lowest income group pays the highest percentage additional tax. As income rises, the tax surcharge falls.

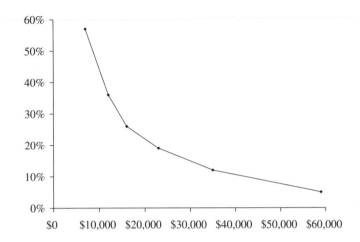

D.   POLITICAL ECONOMY OF PROTECTION

Economic arguments against protectionism are the inefficiency, lost income, and misallocation of resources. Losses deepen over time as the economy ignores its relatively efficient industries. Free trade promotes a more equal international income distribution. Each country can pursue its own redistribution of higher income. Economists have been making these points for 200 years, and business people have pursued the gains from trade since before the dawn of history. Why then does protectionism persist?

EXAMPLE 4.14 *GATT, GATS, WTO*

The GATT concentrated on lowering protection on manufactured goods starting after World War II, and tariffs have dropped around the world. The General Agreement of Trade in Services (GATS) began in 1994. The goal of GATS is to liberalize trade in business services. Many countries maintain protection of inefficient government monopolies in telecommunications, utilities, postal service, banking & finance, and other business service industries. Other governments protect domestic industry by keeping out foreign firms. The WTO began in 1993 as the active branch of GATT and GATS, and administers the negotiations that ultimately can lead to multilateral lowering of protection. The WTO also hears and decides damages from complaints about protectionist trade practices.

Rent Seeking for Protection

Protected industries and workers are willing to spend resources to buy protection. Political representatives are elected from relatively small districts that often have a single large firm or industry that are willing to lobby a sympathetic representative. Political campaign contributions are closely tied to representative voting behavior. Voters in the district want a representative looking out for their interests.

Industries hire lobbyists to put pressure on representatives for protection. This *rent seeking* activity is inefficient because these resources could be used to produce goods and services. Representatives trade votes, *logrolling* to gain enough support for legislation they favor. Laws lump many individual tariffs and quotas together, reflecting vote trading among representatives with narrow interests. A representative who does not protect local industry will find it hard to appeal to global economic efficiency and might not be elected. People may be global free traders but they are local protectionists.

Industries spend resources lobbying to buy protection. Consumers suffer but are disorganized and unable to influence the political process of protectionism.

The choice of tariff levels is a political process. Industries lobby for protection, spending resources for higher tariffs. The marginal benefit of spending on lobbying determines the amount spent by industry, as shown in Figure 4.5. Every dollar spent on lobbying creates some benefit for the industry. Benefits of extra spending

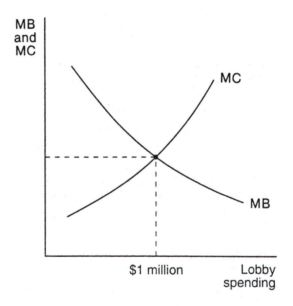

Figure 4.5
Optimal Lobby Spending
The marginal benefits MB to the industry of lobbying come from the protection afforded by higher tariff rates. Marginal benefits from additional spending diminishes and MB slopes down. Given the marginal costs MC of lobby spending, an industry picks the optimal amount of lobbying where MC = MB.

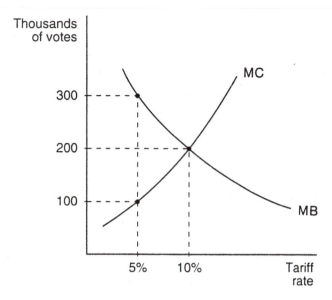

Figure 4.6
Optimizing Votes with a Tariff
A tariff gains votes from those who benefit but costs votes of those who suffer. If the tariff rate is 5%, the marginal cost MC of an increase in the tariff is only 100,000 lost votes while the marginal benefit MB is 300,000 gained votes. The political party seeking votes has an incentive to increase the tariff to 10%.

are positive, but marginal benefits are likely to diminish. The optimal amount of lobbying occurs when the marginal cost MC of lobbying equals the marginal benefit MB. In Figure 4.5, the industry will spend $1 million per year lobbying.

Political parties gain the support of some voters by imposing tariffs. Workers in a protected industry will support political candidates who deliver protection for their jobs. Stockholders and local business interests also favor protection.

Figure 4.6 shows the marginal benefits MB of tariffs for a protectionist political party. As the tariff rate increases, MB decreases since higher tariffs gain increasingly fewer votes.

Tariff protection also creates distortions. Importing firms are disrupted, prices increase, and national income falls, losing votes. These losses are summarized in Figure 4.6 by the marginal cost curve MC. As the tariff rate increases, MC increases. The optimal political tariff is the one that maximizes votes gained by the protectionistic party, where MC = MB at a 10% tariff. At a tariff rate of 5%, the MB of an increase in the tariff is greater than the MC and the tariff would increase.

In the political economy model of protection, industries lobby and political parties set tariffs according to costs and benefits.

EXAMPLE 4.15 *An Appeal for Protection*

The following appeal might be heard in the halls of Congress:

> *Our domestic industry is subjected to the competition of a foreign rival with superior production conditions and cheap labor. They flood the domestic market and steal our customers, killing an important branch of industry. We cannot win this unfair contest. Our workers need tariff protection.*

This appeal is an abridged version of a satire by Fredric Bastiat written in the early 1800s. The foreign rival was the sun and Bastiat appealed for a law to shut all "windows, openings, and fissures" to support the domestic candle industry! Congressional representatives have industries in their districts they protect in exchange for political contributions and votes. Tariffs are passed in bundles with representatives agreeing to vote on other tariffs in exchange for votes on their own.

EXAMPLE 4.16 *Chinese Apparel Quotas in the EU*

Apparel manufacturers in China are facing quotas on their surging exports to the EU, and Beijing might impose export taxes to stall the quotas (*Reuters*, 27 April 2005). China's low wages, highly organized labor, and savvy entrepreneurs have taken advantage of the end of the multifiber agreement that limited LDC exports. China's exports will rise 30% in 2005, too much for the EU. Under China's trade agreements, countries can restrict imports that increase more than 7.5%. "Governments should have foreseen this," says Jun Yeh, chairman and president of Oxwil Apparel Shanghai Ltd, predicting clothing manufacturers in China will shift production to Cambodia.

Dumping: Unfair Competition?

Industries in the US can file claims of unfair trade competition with the International Trade Commission (ITC) of the Department of Commerce. Foreign firms thought to be dumping may face a hearing with the ITC. Subsidies by foreign governments to their export industries are considered unfair even though foreign taxpayers are subsidizing domestic consumers.

Dumping is selling temporarily below cost to drive out competition.

The President can award dumping damages and restrictive quotas can be put in place. During the 1990s, there has been a large increase in the volume of claims investigated and the value of awards. These suits with the ITC offer another political avenue for industries wanting to pursue protection. Dumping allegations cannot be proved, the evidence presented is typically weak, and dumping awards can be made largely for political reasons. Awards for dumping claims have typically been based more on the politics of protection rather than economic evidence.

EXAMPLE 4.17 *Dumping & the ITC*

The WTO oversees protection as a response to alleged dumping. GATT commits countries to lower protection but exceptions are allowed when dumping is proven. In 1990 there were 405 antidumping orders in place, almost half in the US. By 1997, the total had more than doubled with 35% in the US, 28% in the LDCs, 16% in the EU, and 11% in Canada. The US International Trade Commission makes decisions on incomplete evidence. Foreign firms avoid exporting even on a rumor of an ITC hearing. This antidumping circus has worse effects than dumping itself, ultimately not a problem.

EXAMPLE 4.18 *Eliminate Dumping*

Is US trade law passed by Congress and implemented by the ITC designed to maximize the benefits of trade or is it protectionism? Joseph Stiglitz (1997) assesses US trade law and finds it protectionist. There is little hope to engineer trade policies to secure gains in imperfectly competitive markets, and such efforts amount in practice to protectionism. Costly rent seeking activity adds to the losses as industries spend on lobbying. Stiglitz suggests redesigning US trade law to eliminate dumping laws and emphasize trade adjustment assistance to retrain labor for an increasingly competitive international economy.

Eliminating Import Restrictions

Protectionism introduces distortions to the pattern of international production. Inefficiency and wasted resources are promoted. Consumers lose because of higher prices and fewer goods. Most consumers have little idea of the degree to which protectionism increases prices and decreases real income.

The benefits of protectionism can be measured by jobs saved. Costs are measured by lost consumption and higher prices. Ratios of costs to benefits have been estimated to range from 4:1 up to 10:1 and higher.

Even if consumers were completely aware of the costs imposed by protection, they would find it difficult to organize and lobby. Industries and labor unions, on the other hand, are organized.

Consumers are local protectionists even if they are global free traders. Hardly anyone would favor opening a protected industry to international competition if friends or family would lose their jobs and are forced to retrain or relocate.

The only sure way to remove inequities associated with protectionism is to phase it out completely. It is constitutionally illegal to tax exports in the US, unlike other countries. The bias against export duties in the US dates from colonial days when the King of England heavily taxed exports from the colonies and kept the revenues. Outlawing protectionism would eliminate the waste and rent seeking.

The protectionism debate is not new, as this 1696 quote from Charles D'Avenant (*An Essay on the East India Trade*) shows:

> "Trade is in its nature free, finds its own channel, and best directs its own course; and all laws to give it rules and directions, and to limit and circumscribe it may serve the particular ends of private men, but are seldom advantages to the public."

The temptation to pursue narrow local interests at odds with the national interest would be removed if protectionism were simply illegal. Pressures from key employers in their districts often override what representatives might recognize as the national interest. Protection only offers temporary remedies for economic problems and leads to dependence and inefficiency.

Developed countries should lead the way toward increased global efficiency by eliminating all import protection.

EXAMPLE 4.19   *Union Pocketbooks*

Labor unions pursue their narrow goals in trade policy. The AFL-CIO circulates a yearly pamphlet *The Pocketbook Issues* aimed at securing protection. Some of its recommendations are

- Negotiate bilateral trade deficit reductions
- Address unfair trade practices
- Enact domestic content laws
- Extend VERS on steel imports
- Impede imports of foreign products
- Policy to process raw products before export
- Pass laws to increase share of cargo on US merchant ships
- Control foreign investment
- Repeal the Foreign Trade Zones Act

Problems for Section D

D1. Why are large firms and industries typically more protected than small ones?

D2. Why might senators favor protectionism less than members of Congress? Presidents less than senators?

D3. Some industries claim they must be protected because their products are essential for national defense. If you were president, which products would you allow this national defense status?

EXAMPLE 4.20 *Buy American Regardless*

The Crafted with Pride in the USA Council promotes domestic products with advertisements. One large retailer conducted an experiment with identical jeans sold side by side, one with "Made in USA" and the other with foreign labels. More of the domestic jeans sold. Surveys have shown that consumers consider the country of origin in making purchases, or at least say they do. It may be effective to appeal to patriotism. In the long run, however, good quality at a low price maintains customers.

EXAMPLE 4.21 *Shrimp Dumping and Soybeans*

Shrimp has become a leading seafood in the US due to low cost farming techniques and global competition, but hold the hot sauce. US shrimpers won a dumping case with the ITC in 2004 and were awarded tariffs of around 100% on imported shrimp in spite of a lack of evidence of predatory pricing or selling below cost by exporting Asian countries. The money to pay for the ITC filing came from disaster relief for shrimpers, your tax dollars at work. Congress also awarded the shrimping industry the tariff revenue in direct violation of WTO rules, sure to encourage more dumping cases. Shrimp prices are projected to rise by 40% in the US, good news for catfish and salmon farmers. The tariffs might sound like a big win for US agriculture, but the US exports a lot of soybeans to Asian countries for shrimp food. Soybean farmers are lobbying to repeal the shrimp tariffs. The only sure winners are the lawyers and economists working for the lobby industry, as well as government officials receiving lobby payoffs from both shrimpers and soybean farmers. This shrimp soybean tale illustrates why dumping, and for that matter all tariffs, should be eliminated from US trade law.

CONCLUSION

Protectionism is the oldest issue in economics and a contemporary issue as well. The free trade debate will rage as long as the potential benefits to protected industries outweigh the costs associated with lobbying. In a large economy, protection may affect international prices. Japan, the EU, and the US are large economies in their imports of oil, automobiles, and other products. The next chapter shows how the terms of trade are determined between large economies, and how a tariff may improve the terms of trade.

Terms

Antiprotection	Fair trade
Deadweight loss	ITC
Dumping	Logrolling
Effective protection	Quotas
Nontariff barrier (NTB)	Rent seeking
Production distortion	Tariffs
Quality upgrading	Voluntary export restraint (VER)
Quota license	

MAIN POINTS

- Tariffs impose deadweight losses benefiting narrow industrial interests at the expense of the entire economy.
- Quotas and other NTBs have become popular in a wave of new protectionism arising in the face of the WTO and lower tariffs.
- Protection shifts production away from industries in which the economy has a comparative advantage, creating efficiency losses.
- Protection arises when the benefits to the protected industry outweigh the cost of lobbying. Consumers would benefit from free trade. Antiprotection is the lobbying for free trade by industries that export or use imported intermediate products.

REVIEW PROBLEMS

1. Problems 1 through 9 are based on the domestic demand for sports shoes give by $D = 100 - P$ and a domestic supply of $S = -10 + P$. Diagram this domestic market. Find imports if the world price is $30.

2. Suppose a 50% tariff is put on sport shoe imports and the international price is $30. Find and diagram the change in imports.

3. Find the tariff revenue and the deadweight loss with the 50% tariff.

4. Find the *prohibitive tariff* that would eliminate all shoe imports.

5. With an international price of $30, suppose a quota of 10 units is imposed. Find the domestic price with the quota.

6. Find the total loss associated with the quota of 10 units compared to free trade.

7. Find the producer surplus of domestic shoe producers with the quota of 10 units and compare it to free trade.

8. Suppose foreign shoe producers voluntarily agree to limit their exports to the domestic market to 30 units. Find the domestic price with this VER. Compare total losses with the situation of a quota of 10 units.

9. With free trade, suppose all shoe imports come from two foreign countries, A and B. Each foreign country supplies half of imports. Under political pressure, country A agrees to a VER of 15 units and country B agrees not to increase

its export level. Find the price, level of imports, and the change in export revenue of both foreign countries with the VERs.

10. Diagram the PPF of a closed economy where the relative price of manufactures is higher on the international market than at home. In which direction will the economy specialize if it moves to free trade? Describe the direction of trade. Illustrate the effects of a tariff on the pattern of production.

11. Consider an economy producing services, manufactures, and agricultural goods. Describe its PPF. What determines which goods are imported or exported? What are the effects of protection?

12. If all congressional representatives were elected at the state level rather than from particular districts, explain whether protectionist legislation would be easier or more difficult.

READINGS

Ron Jones and Anne Krueger, eds. (1990) *The Political Economy of International Trade*, London: Blackwell. Readings on the economics of protection.

Forrest Capie (1994) *Tariffs and Growth*, Manchester: Manchester University. History of tariffs from 1850 to 1940.

Gary Clyde Hufbauer and Howard Rosen (1986) *Trade Policy for Troubled Industries*, Washington: Institute for International Economics. Potential of policy for US industry facing foreign competition.

William R. Cline, ed. (1983) *Trade Policy in the 1980s*, Washington: Institute for International Economics. Applied studies of trade policies.

I.M. Destler (1986) *American Trade Politics: System Under Stress*, Washington: Institute for International Economics. Analysis of the domestic politics of US trade policy.

Dominick Salvatore, ed. (1987) *The New Protectionist Threat to World Welfare*, Amsterdam: North-Holland. Studies on policy issues.

Inside US Trade, Inside Washington Publishers, Washington, DC. Weekly newsletter on government trade policy.

Jagdish Bhagwati, *Protectionism* (1988) Cambridge: MIT Press. A lively look at the oldest issue in political economy.

Stephen P. Magee, William A. Brock, and Leslie Young (1989) *Black Hole Tariffs and Endogenous Policy Theory*, Cambridge: Cambridge University Press. Political theory of protection.

Robert Baldwin, ed. (1988) *Trade Policy Issues and Empirical Analysis*, Washington: NBER. Articles on empirical analysis of trade policy.

Martin Wolf (2005) *Why Globalization Works*, Cambridge: Yale University Press. Excellent survey of arguments for free trade.

CHAPTER 5

Terms of Trade

Preview

A large country can affect international markets and prices. Consider two countries trading with each other, each producing two types of products. The terms of trade, an international relative price, is determined along with the direction and volume of trade. Each country prefers better terms of trade but better terms of trade for one mean worse terms of trade for the other. With better terms of trade, the same amount of exports could be traded for more imports or less in exports could be traded for the same amount of imports. This chapter presents:

- *Offer curves* and the terms of trade
- *Optimal tariffs* and the terms of trade
- *Tariff games*
- *Natural resources* and international trade

INTRODUCTION

Some countries are large exporters in world markets. Examples are South Africa in diamonds, Australia in wool, the US in airplanes, Canada in lumber, Saudi Arabia in oil, Brazil in coffee, Japan in autos, Germany in chemicals, Greece in tourism, and so on. Some countries also have market power buying some imports, like the US in oil, Japan in food, Latin America in machinery and equipment, and so on. Changes in these national markets affect international prices.

When the economy is large relative to the world market, the national market can affect the international price and level of trade. The terms of trade are variable if shifts in production or preferences are large enough to affect international prices. Such a country is a *price searcher* in the international market.

A complete picture of how the terms of trade are determined between two economies involves the excess supply and demand for traded products. For simplicity, suppose two economies trade two products with each other. The production possibilities frontier and preferences of each country will determine the direction, terms, and level of trade. Changing technology, economic growth, or changes in preferences will impact trade. *Offer curves* illustrate this interplay between trading partners.

A large country tariff lowers world demand for the imported product and can lead to a fall in the international price. A tariff can improve the terms of trade for a large country but the gains come with another country's loss.

If one large country imposes a tariff to improve its terms of trade, the other country can retaliate. Each country adjusts its tariffs and a "game" can arise in which the outcome depends on tariff strategies. *Game theory* predicts what will happen when nations grapple with each other in such *tariff games*. Outcomes depend on the payoffs and strategies chosen. Free trade might not occur even though it leads to higher consumption and efficiency.

There are active international markets in resources such as oil, minerals, and timber. Ultimately only a certain amount of nonrenewable resources such as oil can be extracted. Depletion is a critical issue for oil importers and exporters. How fast should Saudi Arabia deplete its stock of oil? Should the US government subsidize research in alternative energy sources? Should the DCs levy tariffs on oil? What is the optimal rate of depletion of gold for South Africa? Offer curves provide background for analyzing international resource markets and illustrate how the terms of trade evolve.

A. OFFER CURVES

Gains from trade are possible when two economies differ in production potential or consumer preference. Patterns of production and consumption lead to offer curves that show how the terms and level of trade are settled.

Trade Triangles and Offer Curves

The economy starts in autarky at point A in Figure 5.1. The PPF and consumer preferences lead the economy to produce and consume 100 units of each product. Consumer utility is maximized on the highest attainable community indifference curve (I) tangent to the PPF. The autarky relative price of S in terms of M is found at point A. The marginal rate of transformation MRT along the PPF equals the marginal rate of substitution MRS on the optimal indifference curve.

If the international relative price of services is higher than the autarky price, production shifts toward more S. At the international relative price of services $M/S = 2$, the economy moves down along its PPF to the point where the terms of trade line is tangent to the PPF. In Figure 5.1, production at point P is $(M,S) = (50,135)$. The economy trades up along the terms of trade line to the highest indifference curve II to T where consumption is $(M,S) = (110,105)$. Exports of 30 S are traded for 60 M. With trade, tt = MRT = MRS. The shaded trade triangle shows exports of $30S$ on its base and imports of $60M$ on its side.

If the terms of trade improve to $tt = 3$, the value of exported services increases on the international market. The economy increases specialization, producing

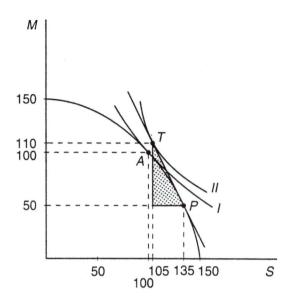

Figure 5.1
International Specialization
When $tt = 2$, the economy specializes in service production and is able to consume more of both goods at T compared with autarky A. The level of trade grows from zero at autarky A to the shaded trade triangle between P and T, with exports of 30 S exchanged for imports of 60 M. Consumers increase their welfare from indifference curve I to II.

more services and less manufactures. Production shifts until the MRT equals 3. Production moves to P$'$ in Figure 5.2 where $(M,S) = (25,145)$. The level of trade increases, pictured by the larger trade triangle. Trade takes place up to the consumer equilibrium at point T$'$ where $(M,S) = (130,110)$. Exports of 35 S are traded for 105 M. More is exported in exchange for increasing imports at the better terms of trade. Consumers are better off on indifference curve III.

The lower relative price of services induces consumers to a higher ratio of manufactures consumption. In the consumer equilibrium at A, 100 units of each good are consumed and the ratio of M to S is 1. At the relative price $M/S = 2$, the consumption ratio is $110/105 = 1.05$. At $M/S = 3$, the ratio is $130/110 = 1.18$. Consumers switch toward a higher ratio of M to S with the higher relative price of imported M.

Figure 5.3 summarizes this response to improving terms of trade. Imports of M and exports of S are plotted on the axes. A ray from the origin represents the terms of trade, the number of imports per unit of export. This is one way of picturing the terms of trade.

When $tt = 2$, 30 S are exported in exchange for 60 M. When the terms of trade improve to $tt = 3$, 35 S are exported in exchange for 105 M. Both trade triangles are in Figure 5.3 and the one with improved terms of trade is larger.

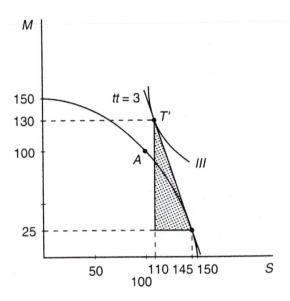

Figure 5.2
Increased International Specialization
If tt rises to 3, the economy specializes more in service production and will consume more of both goods at T′ compared to T in Figure 5.1. The level of trade grows as indicated by the larger trade triangle. Exports of 35 S are traded for imports of 105 M at the improved terms of trade. Welfare increases to indifference curve III tangent to the tt line.

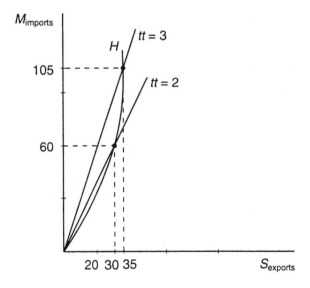

Figure 5.3
Home Offer Curve
An offer curve shows the level of exports and imports for various terms of trade. At the autarky price, there is no trade. At $tt = 2$, 30 units of S are exported in exchange for 60 units of M. At $tt = 3$, 35S are traded for 105M.

Connecting imports and exports as the terms of trade improve leads to the *offer curve* labeled H.

Every point along the offer curve H represents a potential international equilibrium. The country's willingness to export in exchange for imports depends on the relative price. Improving terms of trade creates larger gains from trade and expands the volume of trade up along the offer curve. For any terms of trade, the home country will offer a certain quantity of exports in exchange for imports. The offer curve includes all potential trade triangles.

> *An offer curve shows the exports a country is willing to offer in exchange for imports depending on the terms of trade. Offer curves summarize the behavior of producers and consumers in a trading economy. Improving terms of trade induce the economy to specialize and trade. Con-sumers enjoy increased gains from trade moving out the offer curve.*

Figure 5.4 shows the foreign offer curve. Suppose the autarky relative price of S in the foreign country is 3. If the terms of trade are 3 units of M for every S, the foreign country will not trade. If the terms of trade are 2 units of M for every S, the foreign country will specialize in M and trade for S. At this price the economy exports 60 M in exchange for 30 S. At $tt = 1$, each unit of exported manufactures brings in one unit of services and the foreign country exports 80 M in exchange for 80 S.

EXAMPLE 5.1   *Aggregate tt*

The terms of trade tt are the relative price of exports estimated as a ratio export and import price indices. The tt for the US and all oil importing countries fell during the 1970s due to the OPEC oil embargoes according to estimates of the IMF. US tt generally improved since 1980 and especially during the 1990s. Cheap oil imports were the main reason but oil prices have risen and tt are falling during the 2000s. One reason for improving tt for the US and other DCs is cheaper manufactured imports from NICs and some LDCs.

A higher relative price for M induces more specialization and a higher level of trade for the foreign country. Underlying the foreign offer curve are the foreign PPF and indifference curves. As tt falls from 2 to 1, the relative price of its exports rises and the terms of trade improve. The foreign offer curve bends toward its import axis as does the home offer curve in Figure 5.3.

International Terms of Trade

With two countries, home imports equal foreign exports and vice versa. The international equilibrium determines the direction, volume, and terms of trade. In Figure 5.4 with terms of trade at $M/S = 3$, no trade is offered by the foreign

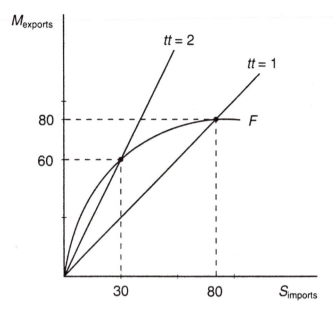

Figure 5.4
The Foreign Offer Curve
As the terms of trade improve for the foreign country, the level of exported M increases.
No trade is offered at the foreign autarky price. If the relative price of M rises from the
autarky levels to 0.5, 60 units of M are exchanged for 30 units of S. At $tt = 1$, the foreign
country offers 80 units of exports.

country because its exports are too cheap. In Figure 5.3 with $M/S = 1$, no trade
is offered by the home country because its exports are too cheap. The terms of
trade must fall between these autarky prices. Autarky prices in each country
determine the *limits to the terms of trade*.

At this *equilibrium terms of trade*, the quantities offered by each country
match. The terms of trade adjust so the quantity each country is willing to
export equals the quantity the other wants to import.

Home and foreign offer curves are combined in Figure 5.5, illustrating how
the terms and level of trade are determined in the *international equilibrium*.
Where the two offer curves intersect, the level of S the home country is willing
to export exactly equals the level of S the foreign country wants to import.
Also, the foreign country wants to export exactly as much M as the home
country is willing to import. Each country would prefer better terms of trade
out along its own offer curve but neither is able to induce its trading partner in
that direction.

*The terms of trade and the level of trade are determined for large countries
where their offer curves intersect.*

To see how the markets work, suppose the international relative price of
services were lower at $M/S = 1.5$ as in Figure 5.6. There is then a *international*

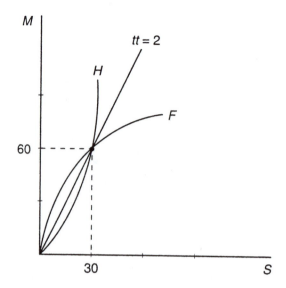

Figure 5.5
The International Equilibrium
Where the home offer curve H meets the foreign offer curve F, the international terms of trade and the level of trade are determined. At any other terms of trade, exports from one country do not match imports into the other country.

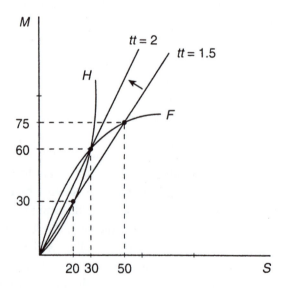

Figure 5.6
International Market Price Adjustment
If the international price were $M/S = 1.5$, there would be a shortage of 30 units of S and a surplus of 45 units of M. These market conditions push the relative price of services up toward the international equilibrium. If tt were above 2, there would be a surplus of S and a shortage of M. The relative price of S would then fall back toward international equilibrium of $M/S = 2$.

shortage of *S*. The level of exports of *S* supplied by the home country is 20 while the foreign demand for imported *S* is 50. This shortage of 30 units of *S* puts upward pressure on the price of services. Competitive buyers in the international market will bid up the price of services and sellers raise the price.

At *M/S* = 1.5, there is also a surplus of *M* in the international market. Desired home imports of 30 are less than the 75 units the foreign country offers. This surplus of 45 units of *M* puts downward pressure on the price of *M*. Foreign producers notice they are producing more *M* than they can sell and lower their price. Buyers purchase more. The relative price *M/S* rises toward the international equilibrium.

The international relative price of services would rise from 1.5 toward the international equilibrium terms of trade at 2. There is stability because the terms and level of trade tend toward equilibrium levels. Any other terms of trade lead the two countries back toward a relative price of 2.

Offer curves illustrate how the terms and volume of trade are found through international competition. In every market, producers and consumers follow their self interest, leading to the international equilibrium. Offer curves can be applied to trade involving groups of nations, between the industrialized North and developing South, for instance, or between the Pacific Rim and North America.

EXAMPLE 5.2   *LDC and DC tt*

World trade continues to grow and countries are becoming increasingly integrated. Trade in the LDCs increased quickly during the 1990s as this data from the IMF shows. The terms of trade have been turning against LDCs over the past 20 years. As nonrenewable resources become scarcer, the *tt* for exporting LDCs will improve. LDCs will also become involved in the production of manufactures.

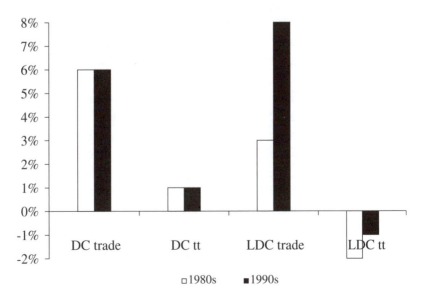

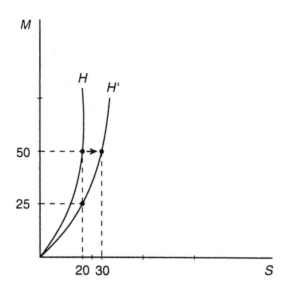

Figure 5.7
An Expanding Home Offer Curve
When domestic technology for manufactures falls, the home offer curve expands away from the import axis. For 50 units of *M*, the home country would be willing to export 30 units of *S* rather than the previous 20. In exchange for 20 units of exported *S*, the home country would accept 25 instead of 50 units of *M*. The economy has become more open to trade.

Adjustments in the Terms of Trade

Offer curves shift with changes in the PPF or consumption preferences. For instance, suppose technology for manufactures declines because of reduced investment. Manufactures would become more expensive to produce domestically and the manufactures importing home country would be more open to trade.

Figure 5.7 pictures an expansion of the home offer curve due to declining technology in manufactured production. The country is more open to international trade because it is less efficient at producing the good it imports. The offer curve expands out from the import axis. For each level of imported *M*, the home country is willing to sacrifice more exported *S*.

In Figure 5.7 before the shift, the home country would have given up only 20 units of *S* for 50 units of imported *M*. After the expansion of its offer curve, it would be willing to export 30 units of *S* for the 50 units of *M*. Looked at the other way, the home country would accept less *M* in exchange for each unit of exported *S* after the shift. For 20 units of exported *S*, it would accept 25 units of *M* instead of the previous 50.

An expansion in the home offer curve results from

- decreased supply of imported products
- increased demand for imports

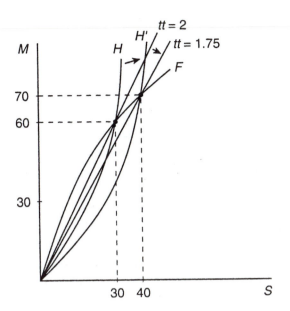

Figure 5.8
An Expanding Offer Curve and the Terms of Trade
A large economy that wants to expand trade will see its terms of trade worsen. As this home offer curve expands from H to H', the terms of trade fall from 2 to 1.75 while the level of trade increases. Expansion of the offer curve could be due to lower tariffs or increased efficiency in the export industry.

- decreased demand for exported products
- increased supply of exports

When demand for M increases, the economy places a higher value on consumption of M and is willing to sacrifice more S to obtain imports of M. A fall in the demand for S would have a similar effect. If technology improves in S production, services become cheaper to produce at home and the home country would be willing to accept less imported M for the same level of S. Manufacturers become more highly valued in the home country with all of these changes.

The expanded home offer curve will change the international equilibrium as in Figure 5.8. At $M/S = 2$, there would be a shortage of manufactures and a surplus of services in the international market after the shift to H'. The relative price of services falls under market pressure. A higher international relative price for manufactures results.

In Figure 5.8, the terms of trade tt decline for the home country and the relative price of services falls to 1.75. An expanding offer curve leads to falling terms of trade. Home exports rise to 40 units of S while imports rise to $1.75 \times 40 = 70$ units of M. Home consumers enjoy more manufactures but they cost more in domestically produced services. The trade triangle in each country expands. A good exercise is to sketch the new trade triangles in diagrams with each of the two PPFs and indifference curves.

An expanding offer curve lowers the terms of trade and raises the level of trade.

If foreign consumers increase their demand for your exports, its relative price increases. Increased demand means higher prices and more revenue. From a national perspective, increased demand for home goods means higher income and utility.

An improved capability to produce exports has the same effect on the home offer curve. Exports can be produced more cheaply and a lower level of imports would be accepted for any level of exports. With investment or improved production technology in the export industry, the economy becomes more open to trade. The volume of trade increases and the terms of trade decline.

Such a fall in the terms of trade may seem a paradox given the popular opinion that a country should become "more competitive" in its export industry. Gains in efficiency in export industries lead to falling terms of trade, similar to the effects of expanding supply on price. There is higher real income and utility with improved technology.

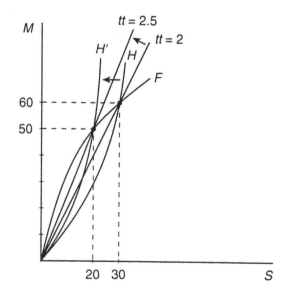

Figure 5.9
A Shrinking Home Offer Curve
A large economy withdrawing from trade will see its terms of trade improving. As the home offer curve contracts from H to H′, its terms of trade rise from 2 to 2.5 and the level of trade decreases. The contraction in the offer curve could be due to increased tariffs, declining efficiency on exports, increased efficiency on imports, or a shift of consumer tastes toward the exported good or away from the import.

A contraction of the offer curve occurs with

- falling demand for imports
- reduction in the supply of exports
- increased demand for exported products
- increased supply of imported products

Figure 5.9 illustrates a shrinking home offer curve. The terms of trade tt improve for the home country to 2.5 but only 20 units of S are exported.

Reduced supply of exports occurs with higher input costs, declining investment, or a fall in technology. The terms of trade improve with the contracting offer curve but the level of trade falls.

Japanese cars were viewed relatively less favorably in the US as the quality of US cars improved during the 1990s. The shrinking offer curve improved the US terms of trade. As another example, suppose new technology makes fuel cells efficient for automobiles, and carmakers begin equipping cars for fuel cells. The EU offer curve for oil imports would then contract as EU demand for oil fell. The international relative price of oil would drop along with the level of oil trade.

EXAMPLE 5.3 tt_{US}

The US terms of trade have been fairly constant over the past few decades with yearly changes in the range of a few percent up or down. The chart below shows the average price of all imported and exported products, weighted by the value of the products in trade. Both have trended upwards slightly but there have been no dramatic changes. The US trades a highly diversified basket of products and price changes tend to cancel each other in the averages. The price of oil can have an effect on import prices but export prices tend to rise with it from year to year. Other smaller economies may specialize in particular products and are much more exposed to price changes. Regions, states, cities, and towns within the US are much more exposed to prices changes for the products they import or export.

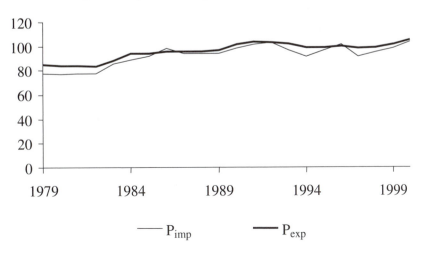

EXAMPLE 5.4   *Predicting Oil Prices*

Oil is a basic commodity on international spot and future markets. Traders buy oil if they believe its price will rise. If the price does rise they make a profit, but if it falls they lose. It is not easy to predict the price of oil or other commodities as illustrated by the following example from *The World in 1999* published by *The Economist*. At the beginning of 1999, the price of oil was $12. By the end of the year, it had doubled. An OPEC agreement restricting output led to the higher price.

> *Oil stockpiles will rise rapidly. The decline in Asian demand for oil has been steeper than expected. On the supply side, the OPEC quota is likely to be ignored. Iraq and Libya will gradually increase output as international restrictions are eased. Russia will try to increase oil production to climb out of its financial crisis. A price collapse to below $10 a barrel cannot be ruled out.*

Problems for Section A

A1. Sketch the production possibility frontier and community indifference curves that lead to the offer curve in Figure 5.4. Illustrate the international equilibrium.

A2. Using offer curves, illustrate two countries that would not trade and explain why no trade occurs.

A3. Explain why the equilibrium in Figure 5.6 is stable starting with a relative price of 2.5.

A4. Diagram the change in Figure 5.5 if foreign demand for services decreases. What happens to the terms and level of trade?

A5. Show what happen to the international equilibrium if home export supply increases and foreign export supply decreases.

EXAMPLE 5.5   *Alfred Marshall Foresees OPEC*

Alfred Marshall, an English economist at the turn of the 20th century, developed many of the principles of microeconomics. He expanded the frontiers of economic theory and wrote on important economic matters of his day. These edited remarks of Marshall (1926) are relevant today.

> *Before another century has passed there may remain only a few areas of rich minerals and raw products. Oil is a good example. With increasing scarcity, sellers will have the upper hand in international markets. Acting together, sellers will have a monopoly and will restrict output and charge monopoly prices. This makes me regard the future of England with grave anxiety.*

A discovery of oil in the North Sea turned England from an oil importer into an oil exporter during the 1980s, allowing Alfred to rest easier in his grave for at least a while.

B.   TARIFFS AND THE TERMS OF TRADE

When a large country imposes a tariff, demand falls on the international market and the terms of trade improve. A large country can achieve net gains with improved terms of trade. This argument has been used in favor of a tariff on oil imports for large developed countries.

Potential Gains from a Tariff

Figure 5.10 illustrates the potential of a large country to increase utility and consume more of both products with a tariff. In autarky, consumption and production occur at point A. With free trade the country specializes in services, producing at P and trading up along the terms of trade line to T. Consumers enjoy the utility on the tangent indifference curve.

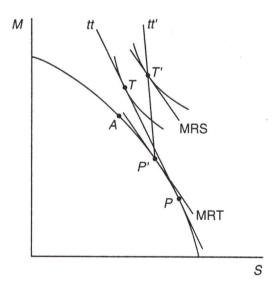

Figure 5.10
Improved Terms of Trade with a Tariff
Autarky production and consumption occur at A. With free trade the economy produces at P and consumes at T with prices at the world level tt. A tariff protects the domestic import competing industry and pushes the economy to P′. The relative price of exports for this large country rise on the world market to tt'. From production at P′, the economy trades up along tt' to consumption T′. At P′ and T′, MRT = MRS ≠ tt'.

A tariff protects domestic manufacturing, pushing the economy away from specialization to point P'. For this large country, the reduction in the international demand for M reduces the price of M on the international market. The terms of trade improve and each unit of exported services trades for more manufactures.

In Figure 5.10 the terms of trade improve to tt'. Each unit of exported S brings more units of imported M. The economy trades up along the new terms of trade line tt', which springs out beyond tt. There is potential to consume more of both goods and consumers pick point T'. Income evaluated at the domestic autarky price increases. As indicated by indifference curves, the level of utility increases.

The terms of trade line tt' is not tangent to the PPF at point P' since the tariff drives a wedge between prices inside and outside the country. The tariff is applied to the imported good when it crosses the border and the relative price of manufactures is higher inside the country than outside.

The terms of trade line tt' is not tangent to indifference curve II. The line MRS is parallel to the line MRT indicating the relative price of manufactures inside the country. In absolute value, MRS = MRT < tt'. Manufactures are artificially expensive inside the country with the tariff.

A large country has the potential to improve its terms of trade with a tariff and might consume more of every good compared to free trade.

If the US, EU, and Japan raised tariffs on oil, their terms of trade would improve. Another example might be Latin American and Chinese tariffs on machinery and equipment.

EXAMPLE 5.6   *Britain, the Large*

Britain was the first country to industrialize. In the early 1800s Britain protected its agriculture with the Corn Laws, tariffs on all grain imports. Economists argued that Britain should move to free trade but recognized that the terms of trade could fall since Britain was a large economy. Douglas Irwin (1988) finds that lowering tariffs in 1841 from an average of 35% to 25% lowered the terms of trade 3.5% leading to a decline of 0.4% in national income. Efficiency gains were outweighed by the falling terms of trade. By the 1880s British tariffs had fallen to 14%, and Europe and the US followed the British example. World specialization and trade increased, and ultimately Britain benefited from its move to free trade.

The Optimal Tariff

When a large country imposes a tariff, its offer curve falls and better terms of trade are one result. Given free reign, the government of a large country can search for the tariff that maximizes utility, the *optimal tariff*. Small countries have no such potential to gain from tariffs because they are unable to affect the terms of trade.

A tariff creates losses because of lost efficiency but can improve the terms of trade. The marginal benefits from improved terms of trade may outweigh the marginal costs of lost efficiency. At higher tariff levels, the marginal costs from decreased specialization would outweigh marginal benefits from improved terms of trade.

From the viewpoint of consumers, imports are an economic good but exports an economic bad. Exports must be produced but are enjoyed by foreigners. Figure 5.11 pictures a set of trade indifference curves for imports and exports. For consumers to remain at the same utility, more exports would have to be offset by more imports. *Trade indifference curves* slope upward. As the level of exports rises along an indifference curve, consumers want increasing levels of imports. For this reason, trade indifference curves bend away from the export axis.

Trade indifference curve I represents the autarky level of utility since it goes through the origin with zero exports and imports. Indifference curves are rated IV > III > II > I. If the foreign offer curve is fixed, the home country can maximize utility subject to the foreign offer curve. Suppose the home offer curve (not

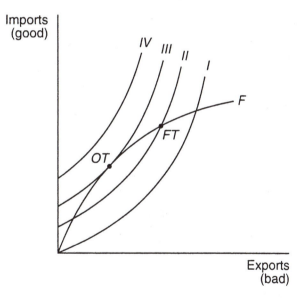

Figure 5.11
Trade Indifference Curves
Imports are an economic good and exports an economic bad. Trade indifference curves I through IV represent consumer preferences. Along any one trade indifference curve, consumers are equally well off. Curve IV is the most preferred, while I is the least preferred. An optimal tariff places the home offer curve (not drawn) through the optimal point OT (optimal tariff) on the foreign offer curve.

drawn) goes through point FT with free trade. Optimizing utility means finding the point along foreign offer curve F tangent to the highest trade indifference curve III. The optimal tariff will shrink the home offer curve to go through the foreign offer curve at point OT. Note that the highest level of utility on indifference curve IV is unattainable. The optimal tariff and trade indifference curve III are preferred to free trade FT and trade indifference curve II, which is preferred to autarky on trade indifference curve I.

The optimal tariff maximizes utility subject to the the foreign offer curve at the optimal terms and level of trade.

Quotas and the Terms of Trade

A quota can have the same effect on a large country's terms of trade as a tariff. A quota lowers the demand for imports on the international market and can improve the terms of trade.

Figure 5.12 shows home and foreign offer curves. Suppose the home country imposes a quota of 50 units of M. The home offer curve becomes horizontal at 50 units of M. This artificially restrained offer curve intersects the foreign offer

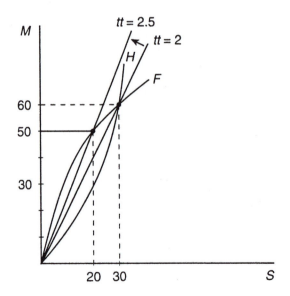

Figure 5.12
A Quota and the Terms of Trade
A quota of 50 imported M will have the same effects on the terms of trade and the volume of trade as an equivalent tariff. The home offer curve is cut off at 50 M. No matter how cheap manufacturers become, no more than 50 units are imported. The modified home offer curve intersects the foreign offer curve where $S = 20$. The home country exports 20 S in exchange for 50 M, with the terms of trade $M/S = 2.5$.

curve at $(M,S) = (50,20)$. This restricted offer curve results in the same equilibrium as the tariff in Figure 5.9.

The terms of trade improve with the quota. There is no tariff revenue and deadweight losses are higher, but the same terms and volume of trade occur in the international equilibrium.

Tariff Wars

If the home country imposes its optimal tariff, the foreign country is bound to notice and can be expected to retaliate with an optimal tariff of its own. This retaliation reduces the foreign offer curve F. Foreign consumption of home exports falls, reducing the international demand and price for home exports. The terms of trade turn against the home country and utility is reduced.

In a *tariff war*, the volume of trade shrinks with each round of tariff retaliation. Imposing an optimal tariff is not a good idea if trading partners might retaliate.

Figure 5.13 shows the steps in a tariff war. The home country fires the opening shot, imposing an optimal tariff based on offer curve F and restricting its offer curve to H'. The international equilibrium moves from A to G, the terms of trade improve for the home country, and it is made better off at the

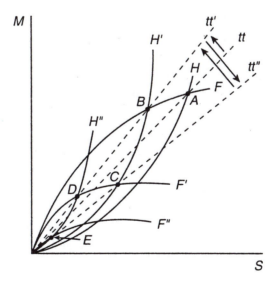

Figure 5.13
A Tariff War
The home country opens the tariff war by imposing a tariff that shifts its offer curve from H to H'. This pushes the terms of trade in its favor from *tt* to *tt'* and reduces the level of trade from A to B. The foreign nation retaliates with a tariff, improving its terms of trade from *tt'* to *tt''* but lowering the level of trade to C. Subsequent of retaliation swings the terms of trade between *tt'* and *tt''* lowering the level of trade to D and E. Nobody wins.

expense of the foreign country. The foreign country notices and imposes an optimal tariff of its own based on home offer curve H′. The foreign offer curve contracts to F′, the international equilibrium moves to C, and the terms of trade shift in favor of the foreign country to *tt″*. The foreign country gains, but the home country loses the second round.

The home country then imposes another optimal tariff based on foreign offer curve F′, restricting its offer curve to H″. The terms of trade shift back in favor of the home country, but the volume of trade falls to D. A subsequent optimal tariff by the foreign country based on H″ turns the terms of trade back in its favor, but reduces the volume of trade to E. This tariff war results in little change in the terms of trade but a diminishing level of trade. Trade ceases if prohibitive tariffs are reached.

Optimal tariffs create gains at the expense of trading partners, reducing the level of trade and inviting retaliation by trading partners.

EXAMPLE 5.7   *Canada/US Tariff Wars*

Canada and the US have historically fired tariffs back and forth, and large US may have more to gain through terms of trade effects. Alok Bohara, Kishore Gawande, and William Kaempfer (1998) examine the pattern of tariff retaliation between Canada and the US from 1868 to 1970. US initiated tariffs persisted and Canada tended to react with its own tariff and stick with it. When Canada initiated a tariff, it backed away and the US did not stick with any reactionary tariff. Internal political forces in the US independent of Canadian tariffs determine US tariffs. The Canadian/US Free Trade Agreement and NAFTA have reduced the habitual tariff feud between neighbors.

Optimal Tariffs in Practice

The WTO dominates the current international political economy. Large industrial nations are unlikely to impose new tariffs, even optimal ones. Participating nations are committed through the GATT treaty to a gradual reduction of tariffs and other protection. Any country stepping out of line is noticed by competing industries around the world. These institutional constraints have led to slowly falling tariffs.

At any rate, the economic calculation and rational policy required to apply optimal tariffs do not exist. Conditions favoring an optimal tariff are unlikely and may not be recognized. The political process of protection is anything but scientific. Industries have the incentive to protect themselves, and what is best for a particular industry is not best for the country. Tariffs benefit the protected industry, which pays politicians for the protection. Protectionist legislation should not be promoted under the guise of an optimal tariff.

There is some sentiment that small countries should be allowed to impose their own tariffs without retaliation from industrial nations. LDCs are exempt from WTO rules and generally are allowed to set their own tariffs. LDCs are typically small in relation to the international markets for their imports and their optimal tariff is zero. Tariffs promote relatively inefficient industries inside the LDCs but persist because they are easily collected taxes.

Every economy should be free to develop its own comparative advantage. In a world with so many goods and services, it makes more sense to search for those with a comparative cost advantage than to artificially encourage those without it. LDCs especially should avoid tariffs.

It is difficult to apply an optimal tariff. The economy must be large relative to the international markets and must not face retaliation. For small countries, the optimal tariff is zero.

EXAMPLE 5.8   *US Energy Imports*

The US has increasing energy consumption and imports. The figures from the Department of Commerce show consumption, production, and imports of all energy products including coal, oil, natural gas, hydroelectric, and nuclear in oil equivalence. The %imp shows the percentage of consumption imported. Japan imports 68% of its energy consumption and Germany 57%. The US uses coal for 40% of its energy production, natural gas for 27%, oil for 18%, and hydro/ nuclear for 14%. Due to international environmental agreements, coal input will decline and natural gas input will rise over the coming decades. Alternative backstop energy sources will ultimately become economical as these fossil fuels are depleted. Nuclear power is the obvious backstop but it has political issues and waste disposal is a problem.

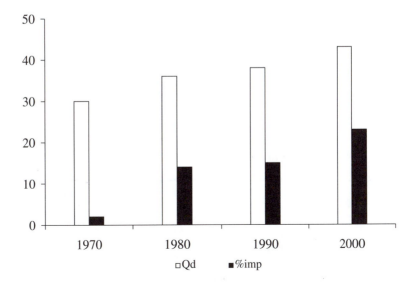

Problems for Section B

B1. Illustrate foreign potential gains from a tariff with a diagram similar to Figure 5.10.

B2. Illustrate how a tariff war could lead to the elimination of trade.

B3. The terms of trade may improve with a tariff but the volume of trade falls. Explain the analogy with monopoly revenue and price. What is the analogy between an optimal tariff and the optimal price for a monopolist?

C.   TARIFF GAMES

Players in games have conflicting goals and have to make choices. The outcome of a game depends on strategies and choices. Popular board games, card games, and sports are strategic games. Skill is as important as luck in strategic games. This section looks at tariffs as a game between countries with an outcome depending on strategies and choices of opposing governments.

Tariffs and the Prisoner's Dilemma

Consider two countries that trade with each other with the potential to levy tariffs. This situation is a *two party game* since there are two players. The two countries can gain with a tariff through improved terms of trade but only at the other's expense.

If one player's gains are offset by the other's losses, the game is a *zero sum game*. Tariffs are a *negative sum game*, since overall losses outweigh gains because of the decline in global efficiency.

Suppose each government decides on January 1st whether to impose a tariff that lasts one year. The two choices are free trade or a 10% tariff. Choices are announced simultaneously and trade takes place.

With free trade, income is $100 billion in both countries as in the payoff matrix of Table 5.1. A tariff increases income by 20% if the other country

Table 5.1 Symmetric Negative Sum Tariff Game
(foreign income, home income)

		Home tariff	
		0%	**10%**
	0%	($100, $100)	($60, $120)
Foreign tariff			
	10%	($120, $60)	($80, $80)

imposes no tariff. A 10% home tariff with no foreign tariff results in home income of $120 billion and foreign income of $60 billion. The home 20% gain is more than offset by foreign 40% loss, a negative sum game.

A symmetric outcome occurs if the foreign country imposes a tariff but the home country does not. In the southwest corner of the payoff matrix of Table 5.1, the foreign country enjoys $120 income while home income falls to $60.

If both nations simultaneously impose tariffs, they each lose 20% relative to free trade. The outcome with multilateral tariffs is an income of $80 for each country, the southeast corner of the payoff matrix. Globally, more income is lost with multilateral tariffs than with only one country imposing a tariff.

If this tariff game is repeated year after year, each country develops a *strategy*, a procedure to follow in deciding whether to impose a tariff. The nations would be better off this year if they both choose free trade. The allure of a quick gain, however, may induce tariffs from politicians eager for donations. If both countries have tariffs it would cost to unilaterally remove the tariff if the other keeps its tariff. If one country promises to remove its tariff, the other might not trust it. This situation is called a *prisoner's dilemma*.

In the classic prisoner's dilemma, police separate two suspected partners in a crime and each is offered a reduced sentence to inform on the other. If they both keep quiet, both go free. If found guilty, each faces a stiff prison term. The police offer a reduced sentence for a confession and tell each suspect separately that their partner has already confessed. While it would be optimal to keep quiet, each prisoner may not trust the other.

Tariffs are the *dominant strategy* in Table 5.1, since income with a tariff is larger regardless of the opponent's choice. A home tariff is the best choice whether the foreign country chooses free trade or a tariff. If the foreign country sets no tariff, the home country enjoys $20 more income with a tariff, $120 opposed to $100. If the foreign country sets a tariff, the home country makes $80 with a tariff and only $60 without one.

Multilateral tariffs are the *Nash equilibrium* in this game. John Nash defined a equilibrium as occurring when each player makes the best choice given a correct guess about the opponent's choice. Equilibrium multilateral tariffs are stable because a penalty is imposed for lifting the tariff. Even though free trade would benefit both countries, they are trapped and do not move to free trade.

The prisoner's dilemma illustrates why international negotiations of the WTO are crucial in moving toward free trade. Each country may be more willing to lower tariffs if it can be assured that the other country will do the same. Without WTO oversight, the other countries cannot be trusted.

The persistence of tariffs may be due to a prisoner's dilemma. Free trade is optimal only if every country eliminates tariffs.

A country can signal a desire to move to free trade by *unilaterally* removing its tariff. This means a temporary loss of income if other countries keep their tariffs but they might follow suit by moving to free trade. As long as each country resists the temptation of the temporary gain of a surprise tariff, free trade persists. Free trade is an unstable equilibrium since there is the temptation to gain at the other's expense.

EXAMPLE 5.9 *The MFA Shirt Off Your Back*

The Multifiber Agreement was an international market sharing plan for textile and apparel trade. The MFA began in 1961 between Japan and the US and grew to encompass a wide range of products and many countries. Its quota schemes were inconsistent with WTO rules against discrimination and bilateral trade agreements. Irene Trela and John Whalley (1995) point out that the quota allocation system awards the right to produce to existing firms and excludes newer more efficient firms. This "lock in" effect makes it difficult for new firms to enter the international market. The end of MFA would result in increased competition, better textiles and apparel, and lower prices. China's entry into the WTO and the international textile and apparel markets has eroded the restrictive MFA. The MFA has officially expired but the DCs are not ready to compete with China and other LDCs and various aspects of the restrictive agreement persist.

Equilibrium Tariffs

Each country has an optimal tariff given the other's choice of a tariff. The process of arriving at equilibrium tariffs can be pictured by the *reaction functions* in Figure 5.14.

The home reaction function H shows the optimal home tariff on the horizontal axis for any given foreign tariff on the vertical axis. With no foreign tariff, the optimal home tariff of 2% improves the home terms of trade and moves the home country to its highest possible trade indifference curve. If the foreign tariff is 12%, the optimal home tariff is 8%. For every foreign tariff rate, there is an optimal home tariff.

The foreign reaction function F shows the optimal foreign tariff for any home tariff. If the home country has no tariff, the optimal foreign tariff is 2%. If the home tariff is 8%, the optimal foreign tariff is 10%. For every home tariff rate, there is an optimal foreign tariff.

The home reaction function has a positive slope because a higher foreign tariff turns the terms of trade against the home country and requires a higher optimal tariff in response. Where the two reaction functions intersect, there is an international tariff equilibrium. Point N in Figure 5.14 is a *tariff equilibrium*.

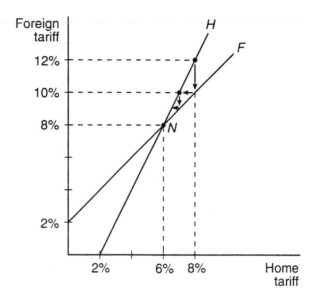

Figure 5.14
Reaction Functions and Equilibrium Tariffs
Each nation reacts to a tariff from the other with its optimal tariff. Starting with a foreign tariff of 12%, the home nation sets its tariff at 8%. The foreign nation then responds to the 8% home tariff with 10% tariff. The adjustment process continues until the Nash equilibrium is reached at point N, with a home tariff of 6% and a foreign tariff of 8%.

Suppose the foreign tariff starts at 12%. The home country reacts with a tariff of 8%. The foreign country responds with a tariff of 10%. The home country reacts with a tariff of 7%, and so on until the tariff equilibrium at point N is reached. The equilibrium home tariff is 6% and the equilibrium foreign tariff 8%.

Reaction functions shift with changing conditions. If the home country becomes more efficient in producing exports, increased excess supply on the world market drives down the price of home exports. The falling terms of trade shifts the home reaction function to the right as in Figure 5.15. The home country compensates for its weaker bargaining position by imposing higher tariffs, regardless of foreign tariffs. The shift from H to H′ drives the home tariff up to 8%, and the foreign equilibrium tariff up to 10%. Increased demand for imports in the home country causes a similar shift in the home offer curve. Decreased supply of exports or decreased demand for imports would shift the home reaction function left and lower tariffs.

An agreement to move to free trade will not be easy to maintain because each country would benefit by imposing a tariff. International negotiations are required to maintain free trade. The WTO offers the forum for continued international negotiation and cooperation on lowering tariffs.

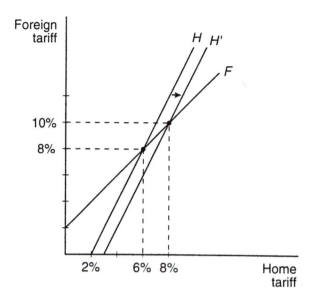

Figure 5.15
Shifting Reaction Functions
If excess supply of exports or excess demand for imports rises in the home country, the home offer curve shifts to H′. To counteract the fall in its terms of trade, the home country imposes a higher tariff. The new Nash equilibrium tariffs are 10% for the foreign country and 8% for the home country.

EXAMPLE 5.10 *Equilibrium Tariffs, US & Canada*

> Canada and the US trade heavily and continually bicker over trade policies. Governments are ready to intervene in exchange for political support. James Markusen and Randall Wigle (1989) use a computer model to evaluate the impact of free trade between the two countries. Equilibrium tariffs in the model are 18% for the US and 6% for Canada. Tariffs are much lower in fact for the US and higher in Canada. The US is the large country and would benefit by raising tariffs to improve its terms of trade. Canada is too small to affect its terms of trade with tariffs and should trade freely. Income in the US would not be affected much by a move to free trade, but Canada would enjoy increased income. Canada avoided the prisoner's dilemma by moving to free trade under NAFTA.

Tariffs Games for Small Countries

A small country cannot improve its terms of trade with a tariff. A tariff creates losses for the small country but does not affect the other country. The situation of a small foreign country is in Table 5.2 where the optimal strategy calls for no foreign tariff and a 10% home tariff. This is a stable equilibrium, since neither

Table 5.2 Tariff Game with a Small Foreign Country
(foreign income, home income)

		Home tariff	
		0%	10%
	0%	($100, $100)	($85, $102)
Foreign tariff			
	10%	($90, $100)	($80, $102)

country can do better given the choice of its opponent. The home country has no incentive to move to free trade but it may on grounds of equity.

The reaction function for this small foreign country is the horizontal axis in Figure 5.14. The optimal tariff for a small country is always zero regardless of the tariff set by the large country.

Small countries cannot play tariff games. With international prices beyond their influence, any tariff creates a deadweight loss.

EXAMPLE 5.11 *Shipping Cartel*

According to data from *Global Trade, Assistance, and Protection* of Purdue University, shipping costs faced by LDCs are higher than the tariffs they face. The two costs together add about 15% to the price of exports from LDCs. International maritime shipping prices are controlled by international cartels. Shipping prices are set at "conferences" with rates published on the internet. Monitoring ensures cartel members do not cheat by offering lower prices. Monopolistic practices would be illegal inside the US but are allowed for shipping between US ports. The WTO encourages competition in shipping but has no legal remedy to enforce it. Competition and efficiency would be encouraged by eliminating the shipping cartel.

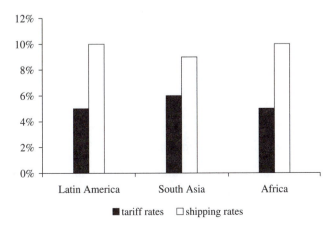

Table 5.3 Mixed Strategy Tariff Game
(foreign income, home income)

		Home tariff	
		0%	10%
Foreign tariff	0%	($100, $100)	($95, $99)
	10%	($101, $97)	($93, $98)

Mixed Strategy Tariff Games

A tariff game may not lead to a tariff equilibrium as in Table 5.3. A tariff would help the home country given a foreign tariff with home income increasing from $97 to $98. If the foreign country has no tariff, a home tariff could lower home income from $100 to $99. When there is a foreign tariff, a home tariff substantially improves the terms of trade for the home country. When there is no foreign tariff, a home tariff has little effect on the terms of trade.

The situation of the foreign country is reversed. A tariff hurts the foreign country if the home country has a tariff, with foreign income falling from $95 to $93. If the home country does not have a tariff, however, a foreign tariff raises foreign income from $100 to $101.

This *mixed strategy game* has no equilibrium. If the foreign country chooses free trade, the home country would benefit by following suit. If the home country picks free trade, the foreign country would benefit with a tariff. If the foreign country then moves to a tariff, the home country would benefit by imposing one of its own. With the imposition of a home tariff, the foreign country benefits by moving back to free trade.

The game in Table 5.3 is called chicken. The countries can be expected to vacillate between free trade and tariffs. It would be optimal for either player to pick a *mixed strategy*, randomly choosing according to the flip of a coin. The countries may realize the overall benefits of consistent free trade and enter into negotiations or agreements to help ensure tariffs are not imposed.

The outcome of a tariff game depends on payoffs and strategies. A tariff equilibrium can be stable or unstable, or there may be no equilibrium. Free trade agreements can help countries move to free trade.

EXAMPLE 5.12 *Global Tariff Elimination*

Eliminating tariffs would alter prices and trade. Some countries and industries would come out ahead while others would lose. Alan Deardorff and Robert Stern (1984) use a computer model and estimate exports for industrial countries would rise 4% with the elimination of tariffs worldwide keeping quotas and NTBs in place. Incomes would increase slightly, less than 1% in the US. The terms of trade and income in the EU would fall as their import prices increase. LDCs would face modest losses. Japan, Australia, and Canada would enjoy small gains. Losing industries in the US would be apparel, footwear, textiles, non-metallic minerals, and rubber. The largest winners in the US would be agriculture, transportation, equipment, chemicals, mining, and electrical equipment.

Problems for Section C

C1. Develop a game with a small home country and show the optimal tariff of a large foreign country.

C2. Explain the adjustment process to the equilibrium at point N in Figure 5.14 starting with a home tariff of 4%.

C3. If the home tariff is dropped from the tariff equilibrium to 5% in Figure 5.14, explain foreign reaction and what ensures.

EXAMPLE 5.13 *Tariffs and the Great Depression*

The stock market crash is associated with the Great Depression but it was only a symptom. The cause was poor government policies, specifically an international tariff war and drastic reductions in money supplies. A steady supply of money is crucial for economic stability and sharp reductions disrupt economic activity. International trade was decimated by the Smoot-Hawley Tariff Act of 1930, raising the average US tariff to 60%. Alfred Eckels (1998) studies the political history of Smoot-Hawley and the business uncertainty it created. Other countries followed suit with prohibitive tariffs to "save jobs." Republican president Hoover favored the act but Democrat Roosevelt followed with a push for more liberal trade. More recently, Republican Reagan advocated free trade but allowed protection to increase. Republican Bush Sr. favored free trade and initiated NAFTA following Mexico's lead. Democrat Clinton signed NAFTA in spite of opposition from Democratic labor unions. Republican Bush Jr. talked free trade but imposed steel tariffs. Both parties say they favor free trade at least if it is "fair" but squirm under the politics of protection. In spite of the melodrama, the average tariff in the US has been declining since 1950 due to GATT and the WTO. Increasing international trade continues to stimulate the US economy.

D. TRADE IN NONRENEWABLE NATURAL RESOURCES

The terms of trade in international markets for nonrenewable natural re-sources like oil and minerals are subject to tariffs and other trade policies. A basic characteristic of nonrenewable resources is their limited available stock. When oil and other depletable resources are used in consumption or investment, they cannot be used in the future. The opportunity cost of using a nonrenewable resource is its use in the future.

Perpetual natural resources including the sun, wind power, geothermal heat, and hydroelectric power have perpetual supply. Trees are a renewable resource, grown and harvested like agricultural crops. The economics of renewable natural resources include planting and harvesting. The economics of perpetual and renewable natural resources are not discussed in this section.

How should OPEC optimally price its oil? How fast should Canada sell its silver on world markets? What determines the price path of such a nonrenewable resource? How will internationally available stocks of minerals such as copper, tin, iron, phosphorus, molybdenum, lead, zinc, sulfur, uranium, aluminum, and gold be depleted? This section looks into the economics of nonrenewable resources.

EXAMPLE 5.14 *The Fuel Bill*

The international price of oil is difficult to predict. OPEC tries to increase the profit of its members by restricting oil supply to keep the price high. New discoveries increase supply and lower price. Demand changes with weather patterns and economic activity. OPEC embargoes caused the price of oil to triple in 1973 and double again in 1980. Oil prices sagged through the 1980s, but then rose with the wars in Kuwait and Iraq. During the 1990s, oil prices slowly fell but immediately jumped 50% in 1999 with an OPEC agreement. Prices declined in the early 2000s but spiked in 2004 with the Iraqi war and increasing demand in China. Oil prices are predicted to climb slowly over the coming decades. James Griffin and David Teece (1982) estimate a long term oil import elasticity of 0.73 for all oil importers making oil imports inelastic. The implication of inelastic demand is that the rising oil prices will cause increased oil import spending, trade deficits for oil importers, and higher export revenue for oil exporters.

Prices of Nonrenewable Resources

Nonrenewable resources loom large in international economics and political relations. OPEC price increases caused economic upheavals during the 1970s and 1980s, including international reorganization of production, redistribution of income, and technological advance.

Owning the right to sell a nonrenewable resource is similar to owning other assets such as stocks representing ownership of private firms, private bonds, government bonds, real estate, precious metals, fine art, and rare coins. An asset produces a yearly return. The *rate of return* is the ratio of this return to the value of the asset:

$$ROR = \text{rate of return} = \text{return/value}$$

If you have money in a bank that pays 3% interest and there is no inflation, the purchasing power of every dollar increases 3% yearly. Your return to $100 would be $3. A *perpetuity* bond that pays $50 per year when the rate of return is 3% has a present value of $50/.03 = $1667. Holding the perpetuity bond is equivalent to having $1250 in the bank. If you own an oil well whose current value is $1 million and the return from the oil sold this year is $30,000, its rate of return is 3%.

For oil, a crucial issue in deciding how much to sell this year is what you expect to happen to its price in the future. You must compare the current price of oil to its *expected price*.

If the price is $20 per barrel and the rate of return on other assets is 5%, an expected price of $21 = $20 × 1.05 next year will leave you indifferent between selling oil this year and waiting to sell next year. Oil in the ground is then worth as much as other assets, all growing at 5%. If you expect the price of oil to fall to $15 per barrel next year, it would be wise to sell more oil now at $20.

The *expected rate of return* on oil depends on its expected price. Other assets whose value would rise by more could be purchased. With the expectation of a falling oil price, oil in the ground is worth less than money in the bank. If you expect the price of oil to rise to $22 per barrel next year, you would want to leave more oil in the ground. Oil in the ground has a higher expected rate of return than other assets.

In deep markets with many buyers and sellers and many decades of oil assets, the price of oil will take the path defined by its perceived opportunity cost. Owners will deplete their oil assets to increase the price of oil at a rate equal to the return on other assets.

As the stock of oil is depleted, its price is expected to rise as depletion falls. The price of a nonrenewable resource will rise in an orderly fashion determined by the real rate of return on assets.

With a 5% rate of return, the real price of oil over a 10-year period starting from $20 will be $24.31 in year 5 and $31.03 in year 10. Each year the price rises by 5% and is found by multiplying the previous year's price by 1.05. The amount of the price increase rises each year. The *optimal depletion rate* involves selling just enough oil to create these prices.

The rate of return determines the expected price path for a nonrenewable resource. The value of the stock of the resource asset will increase at a rate equal to the rate of return on all assets.

If a tariff by oil importers lowers the international price of oil, the depletion rate will increase and more oil will be sold to keep the rate of return on oil assets competitive. Oil producers may restrict supply to raise price, but the risk is a decrease in the value of the asset as technology is spurred to find substitutes. These are very important issues in international trade given the concentration of oil assets in a small number of countries.

EXAMPLE 5.15 *OPEC & Oil Depletion*

> The most famous cartel these days is OPEC. During the 1970s, OPEC was so successful in restricting competitive oil production that prices jumped from $3 to $35 per barrel! This price spike disrupted the oil importing DCs and severely hurt many NICs and LDCs. The oil price increases in the 1970s led to a new generation of efficient cars and the business of energy conservation. OPEC has since diminished in power because of increased production by a fringe of non-OPEC countries but the 1999 OPEC agreement caused an immediate 50% jump in the price of oil. Oil imports are inelastic. OPEC price increases raise OPEC revenue. Over decades, higher oil prices conserve oil in the ground and dampen prices in the future. Ultimately, rising oil prices will make alternative energy sources economical. Proven oil reserves would last another 100 years at the current rate of consumption, but increased scarcity, higher prices, and improved technology will cause oil consumption to fall and reserves will never be depleted.

EXAMPLE 5.16 *Depleting Nonrenewable Resources*

> "Abundant fossil fuels are the source of mechanical motion and chemical change, a chief input in industry, the material source of energy, and part of everything we do. Without them, we are thrown back to the hard work and poverty of earlier times. As we exhaust fossil fuels, it is worthwhile to consider the quantities supposed to remain on earth." This may sound like an energy economist or environmental activist in 2005 but it is an abridged quote from Stanley Jevons in his 1864 book *The Coal Question*. How we deplete fossil fuels (oil, gas, coal) determines their present and future prices, the path of reserves, and how long they last. Technology improves and rising prices discourage consumption so any projections for long time periods are tenuous. Oil is heavily traded and it is easy to predict it will remain the most critical international market during the 21st century.

Energy Substitutes as Backstop Resources

As the price of oil rises, incentives to find substitutes increase. Ultimately the price will become so high that oil will no longer be used as a fuel. Doomsayers base their pessimistic predictions of quickly depleted resources on current prices and consumption, disregarding the conserving character of markets. As a nonrenewable resource becomes more scarce, its price rises and consumption falls. Markets provide the strongest conservation.

Backstop resources are close substitutes that can serve the purpose of a depletable resource. Solar, nuclear, wind, geothermal, natural gas, and coal are backstop resources for oil. Natural gas and coal are also nonrenewable fossil fuels like oil. The stock of coal is much larger relative to oil and gas.

Over time, technology for backstop resources improves. As the price of oil rises, backstop resources become relatively cheaper. OPEC learned from its oil embargoes that an artificially high price of oil leads to improved backstop technology. Huge strides in energy technology were made in the late 1970s and 1980s after the increases in the price of oil.

US energy policy during the oil embargoes encouraged "energy independence" policies of subsidized nuclear investment, increased coal consumption, and increased depletion of US oil reserves. The US has no tariff on oil imports, unlike the EU and most other importing countries. A strategic oil tariff has implications for trade and may invite counter policy from the oil exporters.

EXAMPLE 5.17 *The Historical Steady Oil Price*

The real price of oil in terms of gold or other goods has been fairly constant since the 1880s. Increases in demand have been met with increases in supply, leading to increased quantities but fairly steady prices. Reserves of oil increase with the price of oil and improved exploration, drilling, and extraction techniques. A large jump in the price of oil occurred in the 1970s because of the OPEC embargo. Since 1980, the real price of oil has been declining although there were jumps in 1999 and 2004. The forecast over the coming decades is rising oil prices. Ultimately the endowment of oil is limited and other energy sources will be developed.

Resource Cartels and the Terms of Trade

The oil producers formed OPEC to improve their terms of trade. OPEC aims to restrict oil exports and create a stable higher price for oil.

Figure 5.16 represents an idealized model of the trade between OPEC and the EU, an exporter of manufactured goods. The terms of trade *tt* and volume of trade at point A are based on competitive oil depletion. At point A, oil in the ground is worth as much as other assets. The expected return on oil is the same as the expected return on other assets.

Suppose OPEC imposes a restriction on oil output with a production quota for its members. This restriction cuts off the OPEC offer curve at the *cartel quota*. The offer curve becomes vertical at the cartel quota. The terms of trade improve for OPEC to *tt'*. The relative price of oil increases on the international market. The volume of trade falls to B.

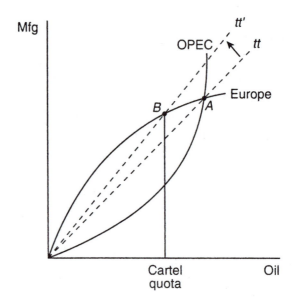

Figure 5.16
Oil Cartel Quotas and Prices
A cartel agreement closes the resource exporter off from international trade at the cartel quota. The terms of trade improve for the oil exporting cartel, but the level of trade falls. Cartel export revenue (price times quantity) may rise or fall. The cartel must maintain restricted output to avoid a surplus (glut) of oil on the international market at the artificially high price of oil (*tt'*).

Revenue from oil imports might rise or fall with the higher price of oil. With a decreased quantity of oil sold, oil revenue might rise or fall. Revenue equals price times quantity, and price rises but quantity falls. There is evidence from the OPEC oil embargoes that oil revenue rose over the first few years with the cartel quotas, but fell back to about what it would have been without the embargo over a decade. There were windfall profits that did not last. The real price of oil in 1988 ended up not much higher than it had been before the oil embargo. OPEC seems to have had little lasting influence.

OPEC and other international cartels have a difficult time agreeing on the quantities each member is allowed to sell under the quotas. To keep the international relative price of oil high, each country must sell only its agreed cartel quota. A surplus of oil would occur in Figure 5.16 at *tt'* if the quota is broken. At the artificially high price *tt'*, OPEC exporters want to sell more than importers want to buy. It is difficult to avoid the temptation of cheating on the cartel.

Cartels in rubber, coffee, tea, bananas, and various minerals have broken down because of the inability of members to maintain their cartel quotas. A cartel member has incentive to sell at the high international price. A windfall can be gained by cheating and selling a large quantity when the price is artificially high.

The war between Iraq and Kuwait stemmed from long standing disagreement over OPEC strategy.

Oil exporters and importers can use economic policy to influence the price of oil. Cartel embargoes, production subsidies, tariffs, subsidized R&D for energy research, auto efficiency standards, pollution emission standards, and other energy resources and policy, all affect the international oil market. Trade policies also affect other international nonrenewable resource markets.

EXAMPLE 5.18 *Slippery Oil Prices*

Short team oil prices are difficult to predict. The price of oil and related products from fuels to plastics to artificial sweeteners depend on OPEC behavior. As an example, at the start of 1999 an oil glut was predicted to cause a collapse in the price of oil to below $10 a barrel. Instead, the price of oil jumped to over $20 a barrel with a successful OPEC agreement. Oil traders following the advice of financial experts would do better with random guesses.

EXAMPLE 5.19 *Global Oil Production*

World oil output has increased almost 50% since 1970. OPEC's share of world output declined over these years, but is now increasing. Saudi Arabia is the largest single producing country, supplying about 15% of world supply. Inside OPEC, the next largest supplying countries are Iran at 6% and Venezuela at 5%. Other OPEC countries are Algeria, Indonesia, Iraq, Kuwait, Libya, Nigeria, and the UAE. Outside OPEC, the US and Russia each supply about 9% of world output. China, Mexico, and Norway supply about 5% each. The US share of world output has declined since the 1970s partly a result of oil tariffs that encouraged domestic depletion. Norway, the UK, China, and Mexico have become major oil producers over the past 30 years. Production upheavals have decreased production in Russia.

Discount Rates and Depletion Rates

Resource depletion rates vary across countries according to time preferences. Poor LDCs are concerned with the immediate future and want income now. This desire for quick income creates a high *discount rate*, a high real rate of return, and faster depletion of resources. Rich DCs discount the future at a lower rate and have a lower discount rate with more conservative resource depletion.

Figure 5.17 illustrates the depletion of a resource in a country with a high discount rate versus one with a low discount rate. The country with a low discount rate knows there will be higher prices for its asset in the future and is willing to wait. The country with a high discount rate is unwilling to wait for

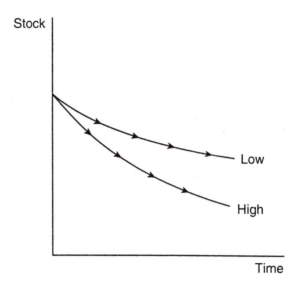

Figure 5.17
Depletable Stocks and Discount Rates
A higher discount rate results in a quicker depletion of the stock of a resource.

the income from selling its resource. Starting with equal stocks, the country with a higher discount rate will deplete its stock of the resource faster. Higher discount rates result in lower prices now but higher prices and increased scarcity later.

> *The discount rate of the owner of a resource determines how quickly the resource will be depleted. Higher discount rates lead to quicker resource depletion.*

Game theory also provides some insight into cartel behavior. A cartel agreement raises price, but members can gain from cheating on the agreement. The incentive to cheat on cartel agreements typically leads to cartel breakdowns. Each cartel member has to choose a strategy and make a decision of whether to cheat on the agreement.

Trade between oil producers and consumers can also be viewed as a game. If oil exporters form a cartel, importers may impose an optimal tariff in retaliation. With the inefficiencies of market restrictions, the gains of OPEC are less in absolute value than the losses of the oil importers. Cartel behavior creates an international misallocation of resources but the cartel goal is to maximize its own wealth. Even that limited goal may not be reached if the quantity of imports of the resource decline enough and cartel export revenue declines. The outcome of the game depends on the strategies and choices of the oil exporters and importers.

EXAMPLE 5.20 *The International Price of Oil*

The international price of oil is destined to rise as the resource is exhausted. When exactly that upward trend will start is a mystery. Supply has increased over the years with improved exploration and refining technology and large areas of the world have not been explored due to political and environmental concerns. Rising prices strongly encourage conservation as shown during the OPEC oil embargoes of the 1970s and 1980s. Demand for oil is increasing with world population and rising incomes in NICs and LDCs, especially China. This chart shows the real price per barrel of crude oil in constant 2003 dollars. The price of oil had been very stable through the 1950s and 1960s with adequate supplies and refining capacity. The price spike in the late 1970s and early 1980s was due to the oil embargoes. Prices then stabilized from 1986 through 2002 before beginning a climb due to rising world demand, market uncertainty over the Middle East and the war in Iraq, and limited refining capacity. The yearly change is difficult to predict but the trend over the coming decades will be upward as the resource is depleted and extraction costs rise.

Problems for Section D

D1. The interest rate is 4%, the present value of an oil well is estimated at $800,000, and the current price of oil is $16 per barrel. How many barrels would be sold this year? How many barrels would be sold at a price of $20?

D2. Find the path of prices over the next 10 years if the present price of oil is $20 and the real rate of return is 6%. Compare this pattern with the example in the text of a 5% real rate of return.

EXAMPLE 5.21 *Major Oil Importers*

Japan, the EU, and US are the major oil importers, relying on imports from OPEC. The % imports variable below is the percentage of consumption that was imported. The % OPEC is the percentage of imports from OPEC. The % PG variable is the percentage of oil from the Persian Gulf. The US gets 14% of its imports from Mexico and 17% from Venezuela, an OPEC member.

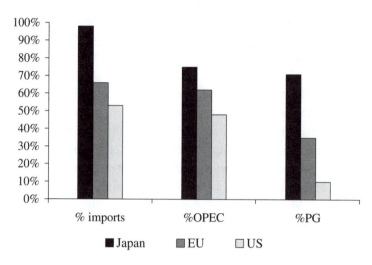

EXAMPLE 5.22 *Resource Curse?*

Countries with an abundance of natural resources do not invest in physical and human capital, relying instead on income from the resource. This "resource curse" slows economic growth and leaves income in the hands of the resource owners. Thorvaldur Gylfason (2004) examines data across countries and finds that resource rich countries tend to have less trade, less foreign investment, more corruption, less income equality, less political liberty, less education, less domestic investment, and weaker financial systems, all important for economic growth. Oil exporting Norway is the exception, providing an example for other resource rich countries, but Norway was a developed country when the oil was discovered. Processing of primary products has a positive effect as shown by Zhenhui Xu (2000) who uncovers evidence that exports of primary products increases industrial exports and national income across 74 countries from 1965 to 1992.

CONCLUSION

The terms of trade contribute to determining national income and utility. Tariffs and other trade policies are not generally successful in improving the terms of trade. Strategic tariff policy assumes the other country is less skillful, a dangerous assumption in any game. Trade policies designed to influence international resource markets result in inefficiencies. The bottom line is that trade policies are unlikely to improve the terms of trade for large countries.

In coming chapters, various structures of production examine the income redistribution among factors of production as the economy adjusts to international changes.

Terms

Backstop resource	Optimal tariff
Cartel	Real rate of return
Discount rate	Repeated games
Dominant strategy	Smoot-Hawley Tariff Act
International equilibrium	Strategic games
Nash equilibrium	Tariff wars
Offer curve	Unilateral tariff removal
Optimal depletion rate	

MAIN POINTS

- The terms of trade are determined between large countries through a process of specialization and bargaining. Supply and demand in each of the trading countries play roles in determining the terms of trade.
- Tariffs can improve the terms of trade for a large country because of decreased demand for imports and lower prices on international markets. Large countries can impose optimal tariffs to maximize utility.
- If one country imposes a tariff, its trading partners follow suit and a tariff war ensues. In tariffs games, the outcome depends on strategies and choices. Free trade is the reasonable policy but tariffs may present an prisoner's delimma.
- International prices of nonrenewable resources like oil and minerals depend on how resource owners discount the future. Resource trade policies generally cause inefficient resource depletion. Resource cartels conserve resources but generally collapse due to the gains from cheating.

REVIEW PROBLEMS

1. When the desire to consume imports increases in a large home country, show what happens to its trade triangle.

2. Show what happens when foreign consumers decrease their demand for home exports using offer curves. Is the home country better or

worse off? Do the home terms of trade improve or worsen?

3. Show what happens to offer curves when the foreign PPF increases because of increased investment in their export industry. How could this growth in the foreign country benefit the home country?

4. Explain what happens when the foreign country supply of its export falls due to higher input prices.

5. Evaluate what might happen if both the home and foreign countries increase demands for imports. Can you tell what happens to the terms or volume of trade?

6. Explain the remark "A tariff on oil imports amounts to a policy of Drain America First."

7. Suppose the terms of trade start at 1 but are improved 10% for both countries by respective tariffs. If each country responds to the other's tariff with a tariff of its own after one year, find what happens to the terms of trade over 5 years. The home tariff is imposed first. Repeat if a foreign tariff is imposed first. Under threat of a trade war, would you wait for the foreign country to impose its tariff?

8. Suppose the foreign country has a policy of imposing a 4% tariff, regardless of what other countries do. Diagram its reaction function. Given the home reaction function in Figure 5.14, describe the adjustment process if the home country enters with a tariff of 3%.

9. Illustrate the shift in the foreign reaction function when foreign demand for the home export falls starting with Figure 5.14. What happens to the equilibrium tariffs?

10. Illustrate a tariff equilibrium at free trade using a payoff table.

11. In Table 5.1, suppose the payoffs to both countries having tariffs is ($80, $110). Predict and explain the outcome.

12. Show what happens in Figure 5.16 if OPEC imposes a tariff on manufactures. How is this outcome different from the cartel quota? Would the EU or the oil importing developing countries be more likely to impose a tariff on oil imports in retaliation?

13. Why is it easier for cartels to form on primary products like oil, copper, minerals, coffee, and tea rather than on manufactures or services?

14. The price of oil is $20 per barrel, and 80,000 barrels are sold. If the interest rate is 2%, find the value of the oil deposit. Explain the difference if the interest rate is 3%.

15. Countries A and B each have oil reserves of 1 billion barrels. Discount rates are 10% for A and 2% for B. How much oil will each country sell?

READINGS

Max Corden (1997) *Trade Policy and Economic Welfare*, Oxford: Clarendon Press. Neoclassical analysis of trade policy.

Bernard Hoekman and Michel Kostecki (1995) *The Political Economy of the World Trading System: From GATT to WTO*, Oxford: Oxford University Press. Analysis of different interests at work in evolution of trade agreements.

Robert Barro (1998) *Determinants of Economic Growth*, Cambridge: The MIT Press. Short book on economic growth.

Daniel Verdier (1994) *Democracy and International Trade: Britain, France, and the United States, 1860–1990*. History of the ideals of trade.

International Financial Statistics, Washington: IMF. Trade data, price data, international financial data.

James Griffin and Henry Steele (1986) *Energy Economics and Policy*, New York: Academic Press. Economies of exhaustible resources.

Ferdinand Banks (2004) *Energy Economics*, New York: Springer-Verlag. Sensible book on energy economics.

Farhad Rassekh (2004) The interplay of international trade, economic growth and income convergence: A brief intellectual history of recent developments, *Journal of International Trade and Economic Development*. Excellent review of the theoretical and empirical literature.

PRODUCTION AND TRADE

CHAPTER 6

Factor Proportions Production and Trade

Preview

Economics is the study of how scarce resources are used to produce and allocate goods and services. This chapter presents explicit models of production and trade emphasizing income distribution across productive factors due to trade and trade policy. This chapter covers:

- *Specific factors* of production and trade
- *Factor proportions* production and trade
- *Four basic proportions* of trade theory
- *Extensions*, *applications*, and *tests* of factor proportions theory

INTRODUCTION

The economics of production is based on firms maximizing profit by minimizing the cost of using inputs to produce output. Firms and industries generate supply, and consumer choice determines demand. Consumers choose goods and services to maximize utility. In markets for productive capital, labor, and natural resources, firms demand inputs for productive processes. People supply these productive factors to derive income. Supply and demand meet in markets for outputs and for factors, which together reach a general equilibrium in the economy. This structure of production and consumption underlies trade between countries.

In partial equilibrium economics supply and demand, things outside the market are assumed to be constant. This assumption is called *ceteris paribus* or "other things equal". *General equilibrium economics* is the study of markets in an interconnected network with all markets allowed to adjust. The deadweight loss of a tariff is calculated in the partial equilibrium market for the imported product. In general equilibrium, the tariff distorts production along the production possibility frontier and consumption possibilities are reduced.

The PPF and offer curves are general equilibrium tools and the present chapter examines what goes on behind these curves. A critical issue is the income redistribution due to tariffs and other trade policies. Payments to some productive factors rise with a tariff, while payments to others fall. This chapter develops the tools to help find out who wins and loses with a tariff or with a move to free trade.

In the specific factors model, each industry uses its own specific capital. Specific machinery and equipment is not used to produce outputs in other industries but all industries share labor input. The specific factors model is a short run model with specific capital not moving between sectors. Adjustment to tariffs, free trade, migration, and foreign investment can be studied in the market for shared labor.

In the factor proportions model, labor and capital both move between sectors in the long run. The concepts of factor abundance and factor intensity lead to the four basic propositions of trade theory. Issues of protection, migration, foreign investment, and income redistribution are analyzed with the factor proportions model.

This chapter extends and applies factor proportions theory. The effect of trade on unemployment is examined. Various inputs and outputs are used in applications of factor proportions theory. An overall picture of the causes and effects of trade is developed with the factor proportions model.

A.   SPECIFIC FACTORS AND TRADE

Specific factors of production are used only in their particular industry or sector. The specific factors model is best understood by concentrating on the markets for productive inputs.

Structure of the Specific Factors Model

Figure 6.1 illustrates the input structure of *specific factors economy*. Labor (*L*) is a productive factor shared by manufacturing (*M*) and services (*S*). Each sector uses its own specific type of capital. K_M is used only to produce *M* and

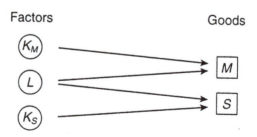

Figure 6.1
Input Structure in a Specific Factors Economy
Each sector in a specific factors economy produces using an input that is sector specific. In this example, manufacturing *M* uses K_M and services *S* K_S. Both sectors share labor (*L*).

K_S to produce S. Services includes telecommunication, banking, construction, consulting, entertainment, and so on.

Factor Demand

Inputs are hired according to the revenue they produce and as the price of an input rises, quantity demanded falls. The demand of all firms using a productive factor summed together is *factor demand*.

Diminishing marginal productivity characterizes production process. Marginal product is the addition to output from an extra unit of input. Diminishing marginal productivity says that the *marginal product* of an input diminishes as the amount of the input increases, holding other inputs constant. Suppose the input of capital is fixed. Extra units of labor produce more output, but the amount of output added per worker declines as more labor is hired.

A firm will hire a worker only if the *marginal revenue product*, the value of the added output, is larger than the cost of the worker. Marginal revenue product is

$$MRP = MR \times MP.$$

MR is the marginal revenue of the output and MP is the marginal product. The MRP slopes downward as in Figure 6.2 because of diminishing marginal productivity. As more L is hired with K input constant, its MP deminishes. Extra units of L add to output, but decreasing increments. MR is the extra revenue the firm gets from selling the added output. MR is constant if the firm is a price taker but decreasing if the firm has some market power.

> The demand for labor is its MRP. Firms hire labor according to the revenue labor produces.

The Market for Shared Labor

Figure 6.2 shows the demand or MRP for labor in manufacturing. Labor input in manufacturing (L_M) is measured on the horizontal axis. If the wage in manufacturing (w_M) is \$20, firms will hire 30 units of L. The output produced by the 30th worker is worth \$20. If $w_M = \$15$, manufacturing firms want to hire 40 workers. If w_M is \$10, manufacturing firms want to hire 50 workers.

The demand for labor in services $D_S = MRP_S$ is in Figure 6.3, and D_S is independent of D_M. The marginal revenue from selling services comes from the demand for services. Labor has marginal productivity in producing services. In Figure 6.3, 50 workers would be hired in the service sector at a wage of \$20, 60 workers at \$15, and 70 when $w_S = \$10$.

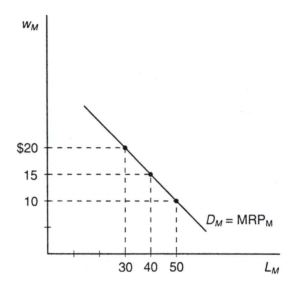

Figure 6.2
Demand for Labor in Manufacturing
The demand for labor is downward sloping because of diminishing marginal productivity. Marginal revenue product (MRP_M) is the marginal revenue of output (MR) times marginal product of labor (MP). Manufacturers would hire 30 workers at a wage of $20, 40 at $15, and 50 at $10.

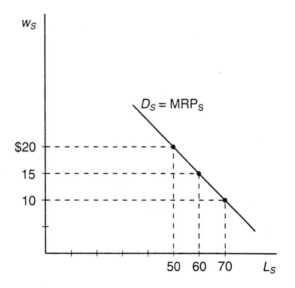

Figure 6.3
Demand for Labor in the Service Sector
The service sector would hire 50 workers at a wage of $20, 60 at $15, and 70 at $10. Labor demand is $MRP_S = MR_S \cdot MP_L$.

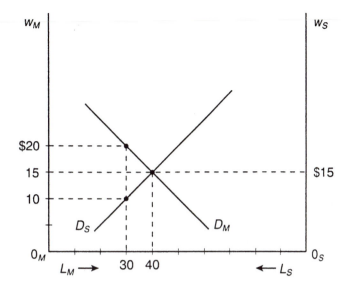

Figure 6.4
The Market for Shared Labor
Labor in manufacturing (L_M) is measured from the origin at O_M. The demand for labor in M (D_M) slopes down to the right. Labor in services (L_S) is measured from O_S and the demand for labor in S (D_S) slopes down to the left. The total endowment of L is 100. In equilibrium, 40 workers are employed in M and 60 in S at a wage of $15.

The economy has a limited amount of labor. Suppose the economy has 100 workers. The length of the axis on the bottom of Figure 6.4 represents the total labor *endowment*.

Figure 6.4 combines the two demands for labor into a single diagram. Labor in manufacturing is measured from the left and demand for labor in manufacturing D_M is also measured from the left. Labor in services L_S is measured from the right. Note that $L_M + L_S = 100$. Demand for labor in services D_S is measured from the right.

Where the two demands intersect, the wage equals $15 and labor is split between the two sectors. In this equilibrium, 40 workers are in manufacturing measured from the left and 60 are in services measured from the right.

Labor can move freely between sectors. If the wage is higher in manufacturing, workers move from services to manufacturing. If only 30 workers are in M, the wage will be $20 in M but only $10 in S. Workers in services would want the higher manufacturing wage and would move to M. The increased labor supply in manufacturing would lower that wage and the falling supply in services would raise that wage. Labor movement continues until the two wages are equal.

When a productive input is shared by different sectors, it moves between them equalizing its price.

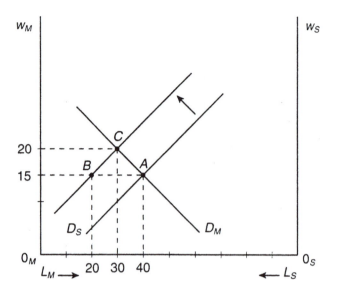

Figure 6.5
Increased Demand for Labor in Services
At the wage of $15, an increase in the demand for labor in services creates excess demand
of 20 units of labor. The wage is bid up to $20 as 10 units of labor move from manufacturing
to services. The equilibrium moves from A to C.

An increase in capital input would increase labor's MP, positively related to
the amount of cooperating input. A higher demand or price of the output would
also raise the demand for labor.

Suppose the price of services rises. This could be due to a rising international
price of services. The higher price of services increases labor demand in the
service sector as in Figure 6.5. A similar shift in demand would occur if the
capital input in services increases.

At the original wage $w = \$15$, there is excess demand for labor across the
economy. The original 40 units are demanded in manufacturing and 80 are
demanded in the expanding service sector. This sums to 120, but only 100
workers are available. There is an excess demand of 20, the distance between A
and B. The payment to labor is bid up to $20. After the adjustment, there will
be 30 workers in M and 70 in S at the equilibrium point C.

The economy adjusts to the higher relative price of services by shifting
resources from manufacturing to services. Movement along the PPF summarizes
this process. Figure 6.5 shows how the market for shared labor adjusts to the
higher price of services, the source of the movement along the PPF.

EXAMPLE 6.1   *Predicting Effects of NAFTA*

There have been numerous studies predicting the effects of NAFTA. Henry
Thompson (1995) applies the specific factors model to predict the immediate

wage and industrial adjustment in the US at the national level will be small. Apparel, furniture, and a few labor intensive industries will decline. Changes in industry specific investment, however, will have substantial long run effects. Predictions of Michael Kouparitsas (1997) below are similar, with the largest benefits predicted for Mexico due to incoming investment. Canada will be less involved with Mexico and projected effects are all under 1%. Predicted effects outside NAFTA are negligible.

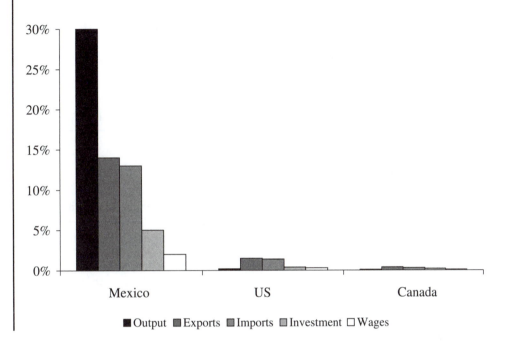

■ Output ■ Exports ■ Imports ■ Investment □ Wages

Markets for Specific Factors

When L moves into service production, the MP of capital in services increases because K_S has more cooperating labor. Higher productivity leads to a higher payment (r_S) to capital in the service sector. As L leaves sector M, the MP of manufacturing capital falls as does its return r_M.

Figure 6.6 shows the market for *sector specific capital* in services, K_S. The vertical supply line is the fixed supply of capital machinery and equipment in the service sector. This capital remains employed, capital owners cannot vary supply, and its return is determined by demand. Capital used in the service sector may be unique or if there might not be enough time to alter the capital. All of the available 100 units of capital are used at a return determined by capital demand.

With the increase in the price of services, the MR of service output increases. Labor moving into the service sector raises the MP of capital in the

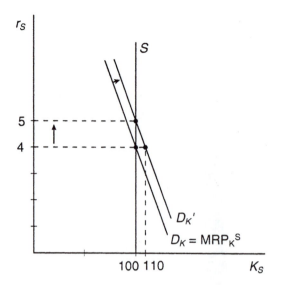

Figure 6.6
The Market for Service Sector Capital
The supply of capital in the service sector is perfectly inelastic at the endowment of 100.
With capital demand at D_K, the capital payment is 4. When demand increases to D'_K, there
is demand for capital and the payment to capital is bid up to $r_s = 5$.

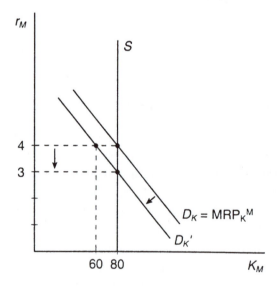

Figure 6.7
The Market for Manufacturing Sector Capital
With the supply of manufacturing capital at 80, demand at the level pictured by D_K creates
an equilibrium capital payment at $r_M = 4$. When demand falls to D'_K, the capital payment
in manufacturing falls to $r_M = 3$.

sector. The demand for capital in services rises on both accounts, as does its payment r_S. In Figure 6.6 the demand for K_S rises from D_K to D_K', creating excess demand of 10 units of capital at $r_S = 4$. Firms want to hire more capital and they bid up for the price of capital. As r_S rises to $5, the excess demand is eliminated.

In the market for manufacturing capital falling marginal productivity of capital leads to lower demand and a lower capital payment r_K. Figure 6.7 illustrates the market for manufacturing capital (K_M). When labor leaves manufacturing for the service sector, the marginal productivity of manufacturing capital falls. The MRP of capital falls, decreasing demand from D_K to D_K'. At the original capital payment $r_M = 4$ there would be excess supply of 20. Firms will hire only along the capital demand curve. Capital owners want their capital gainfully employed, and competitive bidding drives the capital payment down to $r_M = 3$.

When the relative price of output changes, markets for sector specific inputs and the shared input adjust as the economy moves along its PPF.

EXAMPLE 6.2 *Do Tariffs Protect Specific Factors?*

A tariff raises the return to a sector specific input with two inputs in the industry. But with numerous inputs, a tariff could lower the return to the sector specific input as shown by Henry Thompson (1987). A tariff on cars, for instance, could increase demand for labor and energy in domestic car production but lower demand for sector specific capital. It is an empirical question whether tariffs protect specific factors. Gene Grossman and Jim Levinshon (1989) find evidence that protected industries on average have higher than normal stock returns, suggesting tariffs do protect sector specific capital.

Trade and Income Distribution with Specific Factors

Income is redistributed by changes in protection, subsidies, and prices in world markets. Protection raises the price of imports, causing increased production of import competing products and falling output in the rest of the economy along the PPF. With a tariff on manufactures, output of M rises as output of S falls along the PPF. A tariff on M raises the price of M and raises the return to capital specific to M.

Protection helps factors specific to the protected sector. Payments to shared inputs rise with a tariff but payments to factors specific to other sectors fall. This general result illustrates why stockholders, management, and labor unions in an industry all agree that their industry should be protected from foreign competition.

Free trade is the opposite of protectionism. As a nation opens to trade, demands rise for the products in which it has comparative advantage. Suppose the home nation has relatively *abundant* capital in the service sector but relatively *scarce* capital in manufacturing. The country has a higher ratio K_S/K_M than its potential trading partners. Depending on demand, the cost of capital in services r_S would typically be low relative to potential trading partners, while r_M would typically be high. A higher K_S/K_M leads to a lower r_S/r_M unless there are offsetting influences of demand.

For simplicity, assume demands for manufactures and services are identical across countries. Any differences in autarky prices would be due to differences in supply. The home country has relatively cheap service sector capital, and the autarky price of services in the home country should be lower than in its potential trading partners. The home nation has a comparative advantage in services.

With trade, the price of services in the home economy rises due to increased demand. Labor demand in services increases, causing a movement of L to that sector. The wage rises as does the capital payment in services, while the capital payment in manufacturing falls. Free trade raises the price of relatively abundant and cheap service capital. The payment to relatively scarce and expensive manufacturing capital falls with trade.

Free trade arising from cost differences distributes factor income more evenly across countries.

Some disagree, pointing out that income is not very evenly distributed around the world. Trade, however, is not very free. Protectionism and foreign exchange controls inhibit free trade. The argument for free trade is that it will lead to a more even distribution of income.

Free trade might not always distribute income more evenly, however. If both sectors share another input, trade could create wider differences in international factor prices. The expanding service sector could increase demand for skilled labor rather than service capital. Demand for service capital would fall, depressing an already cheap r_S. This is *factor price polarization* with free trade. Still, there is every reason to favor free trade in principle since higher total income can be redistributed to make everyone better off.

Free trade generally creates a more even distribution of income. Examples of steadily rising wages in freely trading economies abound. Japan, Portugal, Argentina, Korea, and Spain are recent examples of the benefits of free trade. Some successful NICs have based their economies on the production of exportables and are opening more to imports. All countries can enjoy the net benefits of increased free trade.

Nations with abundant and cheap unskilled labor will want to produce and export products that use a lot of unskilled labor. DCs should lower their protection on goods produced with a lot of unskilled labor. Examples include apparel, footwear, and consumer goods. Trade would do more to stimulate growth in the

LDCs than any amount of foreign aid but unfortunately the DCs protect themselves from competition with the LDCs.

EXAMPLE 6.3   *Free Trade & Income Redistribution in Japan*

Japan is involved heavily in export production but remains insulated from imports. Increased pressure from foreign exporters in the WTO is leading Japan toward free trade. Three protected industries in Japan that can expect falling prices are iron & steel, agriculture, and business services. Projected impacts on returns to capital and wages in various sectors from 10% decreases in these prices are reported in an application of the specific factor model by Henry Thompson (1994a). These falling prices lower the return to mobile national capital by 5%. Wages in import competing industries fall considerably. Labor in other industries enjoy gains, especially in petroleum & coal (25%) and finance (17%).

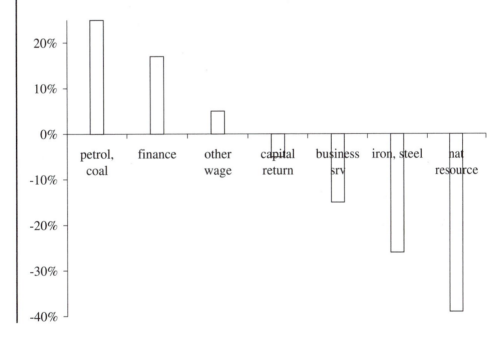

Problems for Section A

A1. Suppose the price of a unit of services is $3 and the fixed input of capital is 10 units. Draw the *MRP* of *L* if the outputs of *S* resulting from increasing *L* input are:

L	0	1	2	3	4	5
S	0	2.5	4.5	6	7	7.5

A2. The marginal product of L in manufacturers is 3.5 when $L = 1$, 3 when $L = 2$, 2.5 when $L = 3$, 2 when $L = 4$, and 1.5 when $L = 5$. The price of M is $1.50. Draw the demand for L in manufacturing.

A3. Combine the two labor demands in the previous problems to determine the equilibrium wage and the employment in each sector when the total labor endowment is 5.

B.   PRODUCTION WITH TWO FACTORS AND TWO GOODS

This section introduces the factor proportions economy with labor (L) and capital (K) both used to produce manufactures (M) and services (S). This model with two factors and two goods is called the Heckscher-Ohlin-Lerner-Samuelson model after the Swedish economists Eli Heckscher and Bertil Ohlin who laid its foundations in the 1930s, and Abba Lerner and Paul Samuelson who developed its structure in the 1950s. This production structure leads to four fundamental propositions of trade theory.

EXAMPLE 6.4   *US Capital and Output Growth*

Output increases with increased inputs of capital and labor. Output and capital stock per worker in the US have both increased since 1940. Before 1970, increases in the capital stock were not dramatic but output responded. Since 1970, there has been a structural change with much higher growth in the capital stock but slower growth in output per worker.

Competitive Pricing

Figure 6.8 pictures a competitive *price taking firm*. A competitive industry has many such firms, each taking the market price $p = \$1$ as given. A competitive firm can sell any amount it wants at this market price. A firm's *marginal revenue MR* is the extra revenue it gains from selling another unit of output. For a competitive firm, $MR = P$. Marginal cost (MC) is the additional cost incurred producing another unit of output. Where MC equals MR, profit is maximized.

If $MR > MC$, profit would be increased by raising output because revenue increases more than cost. If $MR < MC$, profit would be increased by lowering output because cost falls more than revenue. The firm adjusts output until profit is maximized where $MR = MC$.

Entry and *exit* of firms drives price to average cost (AC) in a competitive industry. AC is the total cost per unit of output. If economic profits are positive, firms enter the industry. Supply increases, lowing price and pushing up cost. If there are losses, firms exit the industry, decreasing supply, raising price, and

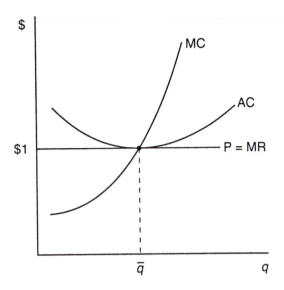

Figure 6.8
A Competitive Firm
This competitive firm takes the market price of $1 and looks for the quantity that maximizes profit. Marginal revenue (*MR*) is price for a competitive firm. Marginal cost (*MC*) is the additional cost of each added unit of output. Where *MR = MC*, profit is maximized at output $q = \bar{q}$. With competitive entry, economic profit is zero and average cost (*AC*) is driven to price.

lowering cost. At the profit maximizing output level of q in Figure 6.8, *AC* is minimized.

Economic profit tends toward zero, implying that all productive resources are paid a normal return and that no surplus or excess profit is left after production. Accounting profit includes only explicit costs, those involving cash payments. Economic profit is a broader concept, including implicit costs and opportunity costs. Accounting profit would be positive when economic profit is zero.

A Look at Substitution

A ditch can be dug with a tractor and a bit of labor or with shovels and a lot of labor. The price of labor relative to capital (tractors and shovels) determines which combination will be the most economical. The firm chooses how to combine L and K to produce its profit maximizing output.

As more of one input is used, less of the other is required. The *isoquant* slopes downward. One input can be *substituted* for the other along the isoquant. For instance, the firm in Figure 6.9 can produce 1 unit of output with 0.1 K and 0.05 L or with 0.06 K and 0.1 L. Any other combination of K and L along the isoquant can be chosen. Firms learn through experience how isoquants are

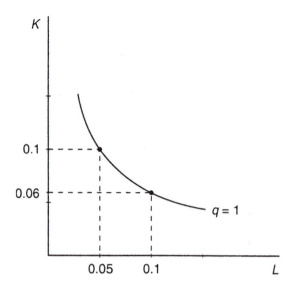

Figure 6.9
An Isoquant of One Unit of Output
With capital and labor substituted along this isoquant, output remains the same. Two possible input combinations are $(K,L) = (.1,.05)$ and $(.06,.1)$. The same one unit of output can be produced with either. Any other point along the isoquant also yields output of 1.

shaped. Economic theory and empirical evidence point to isoquants shaped like the one in Figure 6.9, downward sloping and convex.

The slope of the isoquant is the *marginal rate of technical substitution* (*MRTS*) of capital for labor. As capital input increases, the *MRTS* of capital for labor increases. It takes increasing capital to substitute for labor as capital input increases.

Each level of output has a different isoquant. Isoquants for more output are higher, combining more capital and labor input. Isoquants come from the *production function* $q = q\ (K,L)$ relating inputs to output. Along an isoquant the change in q is zero.

EXAMPLE 6.5 *Convergence of Unit Labor Inputs Requirements*

When increasing trade equalizes factor prices, labor inputs should convergence. David Dollar and Edward Wolff (1988) examine convergence of manufacturing labor inputs across industrial countries between 1963 and 1982. The chart shows unit labor inputs relative to US manufacturing. Relative to the US, Italy used more than twice as much labor per unit of manufactures in 1963 but only 10% more by 1982. There is similar convergence in separate categories of manufacturing output. Other causes of labor convergence are international investment and technology diffusion.

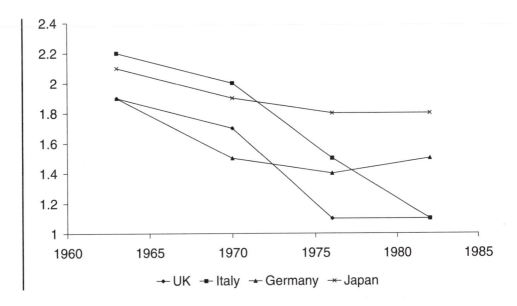

Cost Minimization

The firm is a price taker in its input markets. Suppose the capital rent is $r = \$5$ and labor wage $w = \$10$. The cost of inputs hired to produce one unit of output is the sum of the factor payments. Let a_{Kj} be the capital input and a_{Lj} the labor input for one unit of output. The average cost c of producing one unit is

$$c = ra_{Kj} + wa_{Lj} = \$5a_{Kj} + \$10a_{Lj}$$

Competitive firms have zero profit implying the price of each unit equals average cost. If the market price is $1,

$$P = \$1 = AC = c/q.$$

Figure 6.10 shows combinations of inputs that cost $1. This is the *unit isocost line*. The amount of labor that would cost $1 if no capital were hired is $c/w = \$1/\$10 = 0.1$. The endpoint along the capital axis is $\$1/\$5 = 0.2$, the amount of capital the firm could hire for $1 if $L = 0$. The isocost line connects these endpoints. The slope of the isocost line is its rise over its run: $-(c/r)/(c/w) = -w/r = -2$.

The firm uses a mix of factors. The goal is to minimize the cost of producing the output that maximizes profit. The firm looks for the lowest isocost line that will produce its desired output. The unit isoquant and the $1 isocost are tangent at the cost minimization of Figure 6.11.

The slope of the isocost line is given to the firm by factor prices r and w. The firm chooses the point along its unit value isoquant that just touches the lowest possible isocost line. At this point the isoquant and isocost lines are

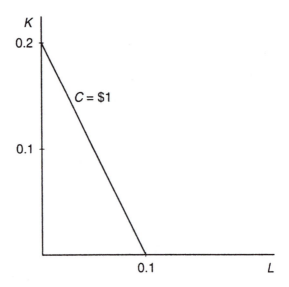

Figure 6.10
The Isocost Line
An isocost line shows combinations of K and L that cost \$1. In this example the wage is \$10 and the capital return \$4. If no K is employed, \$1/\$10 = $0.1L$ can be hired. If no L is employed, \$1/\$5 = 0.2 unit of K can be hired. The unit value isocost line connects these endpoints. The absolute value of its slope $|-.2/.1| = 2$ equals w/r.

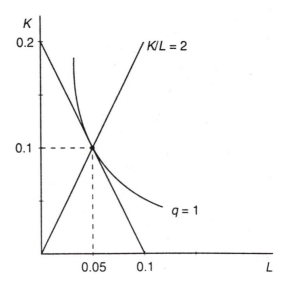

Figure 6.11
Cost Minimization
The firm wants to produce 1 unit of output at minimum cost. Wages are \$10 and the return to capital is \$5. The firm looks for the isocost line with this slope that just touches the unit isoquant. At this cost minimization point, the K/L ratio is 2. Different relative input costs would result in a different input ratio.

tangent and MRTS equals w/r. If the firm produced with any other input combination along the unit value isoquant, the isocost line would cut through the isoquant and cost would not be minimized.

Cost minimization leads to the inputs $L = 0.05$ and $K = 0.1$. Along the *expansion path* cost is minimized. In Figure 6.11, the expansion path shows the optimal ratio of capital to labor, $k = K/L = 2$. Moving out the expansion path, inputs are proportionally increased and output expands to higher isoquants.

If the wage w increases, the slope of the isocost line becomes steeper and the firm substitutes toward more capital. The expansion path shifts upward. If the capital rent r increases, the isocost line becomes flatter, the firm substitutes toward labor, and the expansion path shifts downward.

Firms minimize the cost of production to maximize profit. The factor mix depends on factor prices, and firms substitute away from a factor when its price increases.

The 2 × 2 Production Diagram

Service production isoquants are different from those in manufacturing since the products and processes are different. Capital and labor enter into each production process differently and opportunities for substitution are different.

Capital and labor move freely between the sectors if jobs in the two sectors are essentially the same. Workers are hired in either sector and will want to work where their wage is higher. Labor mobility across sectors equalizes the wage. Similarly, capital mobility in the long run equalizes the return to capital.

Combining the sectors leads to the 2×2 production diagram in Figure 6.12. It is called the *Lerner-Pearce diagram* after economists Abba Lerner and Ivor Pearce. Unit value isoquants are $M = 1$ and $S = 1$ with a unit of each scaled to \$1. The two sectors share the same isocost line since wages and rents are equal across sectors. Cost minimization results in inputs of $(a_{KS}, a_{LS}) = (.1, .05)$ in services and $(a_{KM}, a_{LM}) = (.04, .08)$ in manufacturing.

Expansion paths for the two industries have ratios $k_S = 1/.05 = 2$ in services $k_M = .04/.08 = 1/2$ in manufacturing where k is the capital/labor ratio K/L. Services have a higher k than manufacturing. Manufacturing uses a lot of labor in assembly operations and has a lower k. This production diagram is a compact picture of a productive economy.

EXAMPLE 6.6   *Competitiveness & Growth*

To compete and grow, an economy wants competitive firms, business services, and infrastructure. The *Global Competitiveness Report* surveyed 4,000 business leaders in 1999 and constructed an index of competitiveness based on staff

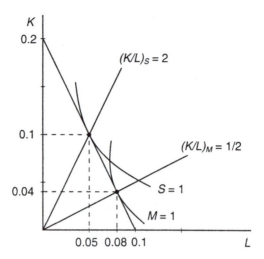

Figure 6.12
The 2 × 2 Production Diagram
When two sectors use the same two inputs, there is a general equilibrium in production. Both industries face the same isocost line. Cost minization leads to different K/L ratios. Manufacturing is labor intensive and services is capital intensive.

training, roads, ports, telecommunications, business information, schools, stock market access, banking, quality of scientists and engineers, and tariff liberalization. The top 3 and bottom 3 countries are listed below along with major US trading partners. More competitive economies tend to have higher incomes, and per capita incomes in $000 are included.

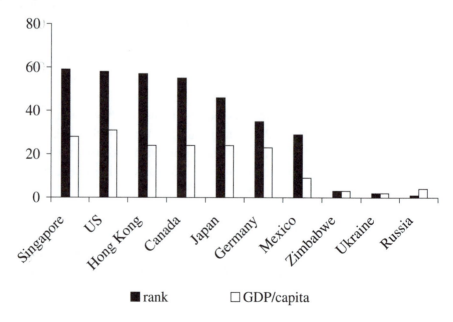

Problems for Section B

B1. Diagram a competitive manufacturing firm's unit value isocost line if $w = \$2$, $r = \$3$, and $c = \$1$. Find the employment of capital if 0.2 units of labor are employed on the isocost line.

B2. Sketch the manufacturing unit value isoquant in the previous problem and show the cost minimization. Draw the expansion path. What is k in manufacturing?

C. FOUR THEOREMS OF PRODUCTION AND TRADE

Trade theory has four fundamental theorems from the 2×2 production diagram that describe the effects of protection, a move to free trade, international migration, and international capital movements on income distribution, the pattern of production, and the pattern of trade.

Figure 6.13 starts with the expansion paths. For each unit of labor L employed in services, there are 2 units of capital. For each unit of L employed in manufacturing, 1/2 unit of K is employed. Manufacturing is labor intensive, and services is capital intensive.

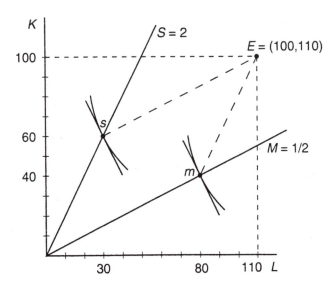

Figure 6.13
Production with Cost Minimization and Full Employment
Cost minimizing firms hire inputs in the ratios $K/L = 1/2$ in manufacturing and $K/L = 2$ in services. The total endowment of K and L in the economy is given at point E: $100K$ and $110L$. Completing the parallelogram from point E determines the inputs in each sector: $40K$ and $80L$ in M and $60K$ and $30L$ in S. Outputs are the isoquants through m and s.

The country has a certain amount of capital and labor, its factor endowment, $(K,L) = (100,110)$ at point E in Figure 6.13. There are unique outputs of M and S consistent with the full employment of labor and capital and with the input ratios that minimize cost in each sector.

Let L_M be the labor and K_M capital employed in manufacturing. Along the manufacturing expansion path, $K_M = 1/2\ L_M$. Along the services expansion path, $K_S = 2\ L_S$. Capital is fully employed in the two sectors, $K_M + K_S = 100$. Substituting, $1/2\ L_M + 2\ L_S = 100$. Labor is fully employed, $L_M + L_S = 110$. Substituting, $1/2\ L_M + 2(110 - L_M) = 100$ which implies $L_M = 80$. Then $L_S = 110 - 80 = 30$. Also, $K_S = 2 \times 30 = 60$ and $K_M = 1/2 \times 80 = 40$.

In manufacturing, the employment of L is 80 while employment of K is 40, giving the cost minimizing input ratio $k_M = 40/80 = 1/2$. In services, $k_S = 60/30 = 2$.

The outputs m and s are unique and represent a production equilibrium. They are located on the isoquants where output is consistent with cost minimization and full employment. Free factor mobility implies that w/r, the slope of the isocost line, is the same in both sectors. The MRTS, the slope of the production isoquants, is also the same in both sectors. These production isoquants are equilibrium outputs for the economy.

Endowments, Production, and Exports

Increased capital would shift endowment point E as in Figure 6.14. The parallelogram becomes taller and thinner. Output of services rises to s' and output of manufactures falls to m'. Both capital and labor leave labor intensive manufacturing. If K increases to 112, $K_S = 76$, $K_M = 36$, $L_S = 38$, and $L_M = 72$. All of the new capital and 4 more units from manufacturing go to the expanding capital intensive sector.

When the endowment of a factor increases and prices are constant, output of the good using it intensively must increase. Output of the other good must fall. This is fundamental theoretical result was first stated by T.M. Rybczynski in the early 1950s:

> **Endowment/output theorem.** *Output of each good is positively related to the endowment of the factor it uses intensively and negatively related to the other factor endowment, holding prices of goods constant.*

In Figure 6.15, the international relative price is the line p and production begins at point P. Output levels m and s correspond to points m and s in Figure 6.14. When capital increases, the PPF shifts out with a bias toward capital intensive services. The new production point P′ is where the new PPF is tangent to the price line p at output levels m' and s'. The *Rybczynski line* R connects these production points and shows how output adjusts to the capital endowment.

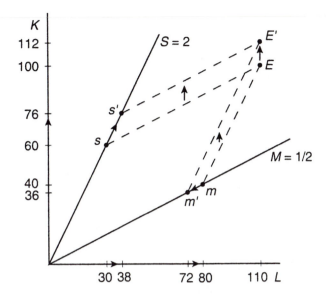

Figure 6.14
Changing Production with Increased Capital
When K/L rises, the economy moves toward capital intensive production. The K endowment rises from 100 to 112, and the service sector gains 16 units of K and 8 units of L input. Output of manufactures falls to m' and output of services rises to s'. All of the new capital goes into the expanding capital intensive sector along with more from the declining labor intensive sector.

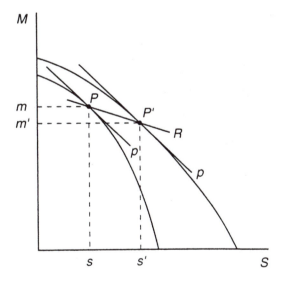

Figure 6.15
Rybczynski Line for Capital
An increase in the capital endowment shifts the PPF out with a bias toward capital intensive services. Production is determined by the paralled international relative price lines p. Production moves from P to P'. The line connecting outputs for different capital endowments is R, the Rybczynski line for capital. There is a Rybczynski line for labor also.

EXAMPLE 6.7   *Labor Content of Exports Relative to Imports*

The US has historically exported agricultural products. Bob Baldwin (1971) estimates that farm labor was 1.4 times more involved in export than in import competing activity in 1962. Estimates of relative export involvement for other types of labor are listed. Professionals are more involved in exports, while operatives and laborers are more involved in import competition. Clerical & sales and operatives are equally involved. Professionals are the most skilled labor group, and skills decline moving down the list of relative export activity. Numerous studies with more recent data verify that the US is a net exporter of products intensive in skilled labor.

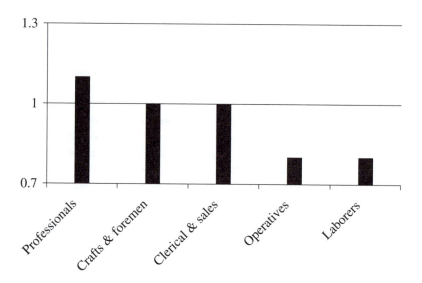

Abundance and Exports

Factor abundance refers to a comparison of factor endowments across countries. Comparing the home and foreign (*) country, the home country is capital abundant if it has a higher capital/labor ratio:

$$k > k^*$$

The foreign country is labor abundant. In Figure 6.14, endowment point E could represent the foreign country and E' the home country. The labor abundant foreign country produces a higher ratio of labor intensive manufactures and the capital abundant home country a higher ratio of capital intensive services.

If consumers in the two countries have similar demands, they will want to consume the same ratio of outputs with free trade and equal prices. The labor abundant foreign country must export labor intensive manufactures and the capital abundant home country must export capital intensive services.

The home country is capital abundant and in autarky it is likely that $r < r^*$. Since the foreign country is labor abundant, $w^* > w$. This difference in factor prices leads to the cheap capital intensive products at home.

The following proposition was developed by Eli Heckscher and Bertil Ohlin in the 1930s and has become part of the fundamental intuition in international economics:

> **Abundance/export theorem.** *Countries export products that use their abundant factors intensively.*

There is a difference between constant cost and factor proportions trade theories. In constant cost theory, different unit labor inputs are the cause of trade. In factor endowment theory, different factor endowments lead to trade. Both theories find support in the data. Each theory makes simplifying assumptions to reach logical conclusions and testable hypotheses.

EXAMPLE 6.8   *Skilled Labor Intensity*

Factor input ratios compare production processes across industries. Ed Leamer (1984) constructs industry rankings with inputs of capital K, labor L, and skilled labor S. Skilled labor includes professional, technical, and scientific workers. This sample of US industries are ranked according to S/L and S/K, with pharmaceuticals standardized to 100. The US has an abundance of skilled labor and a comparative advantage in products with high S/L and S/K ratios. With increased trade, US industries toward the top of the list will prosper in the global economy while those toward the bottom will face more import competition. Instruments and electric machinery have high skilled labor and low capital inputs. Apparel and footwear at the low end have very low capital inputs.

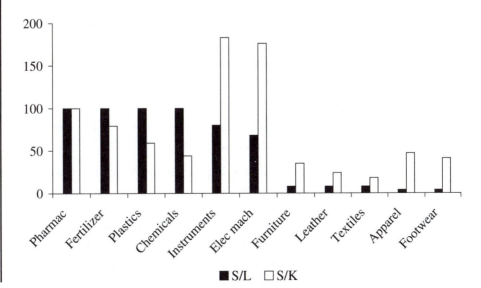

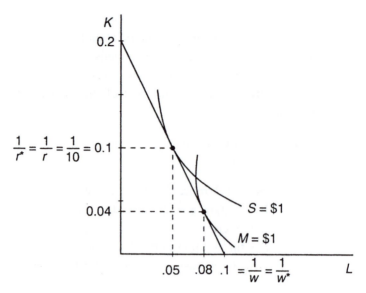

Figure 6.16
Factor Price Equalization
With free trade and identical production functions, the unit value isoquants are the same in each country. The unit value isocost line is $c = 10L + 5K$. Wages are the same in both countries: $w = w^* = \$10$. Capital rents are the same in both countries: $r = r^* = \$5$. The unit input mix in each sector is the same as in Figure 6.12.

Factor Price Equalization

When countries trade freely, output prices are equalized by *arbitrage*. The implication of free trade for factor prices is startling. Isoquants in Figure 6.16 represent \$1 of the two outputs S and M. The quantities of M and S along this *unit value isoquants* are valued at \$1.

When trade equalizes prices and production functions are the same across countries, the unit value isoquants are the same in both countries. Production is carried out by the same cost minimizing inputs in both countries. The unit value isoquants are the same in both countries, implying the same isocost line and factor prices.

> **Factor price equalization theorem.** *Free trade between two factor proportions economies leads to equal factor prices.*

Trading economies can expect factors prices to converge. Countries tend to export products that use their abundant cheap factors, and free trade increases the demand for these inputs. Equal factor prices require that endowment points for the two trading economies lie between expansion paths.

Factor price equalization continues to cause disagreement among economists. Some claim that it proves factor proportions theory useless since observed wages vary so greatly across countries. Others use the potential to equalize factor prices as an argument for free trade. There is empirical evidence that free trade generally brings prices for similar productive factors closer together across countries.

Some labor will want to move between countries seeking a higher wage. This is the primary reason for immigration into the US and the EU. Labor wants to emigrate from labor abundant countries. Immigration increases the host supply of labor and lowers the wage while the wage in the source country rises with decreased supply. Similarly, capital owners want to move capital from the capital abundant countries where r is lower.

> *Free trade has the same effect on factor prices as international factor movements. Free trade substitutes for international factor mobility.*

EXAMPLE 6.9   *Trade & Convergence*

Increased trade can cause both micro convergence of wages and macro convergence of per capita incomes. Farhad Rassekh and Henry Thompson (1998) emphasize the two types of convergence are related but independent. Free trade causes wages in labor intensive countries to increase. David Dollar and Edward Wolff (1993) find wide-spread evidence that micro convergence occurs with trade. Jeffrey Williamson (1996) finds evidence of wage convergence from 1850 to 1910 in developed countries. David Ben-David (1993) shows macro convergence has occured with trade in Europe. Ben-David and Alok Bohara (1997) find macro convergence is stimulated by free trade agreements. Farhad Rassekh (1992) shows there has been macro convergence among the OECD countries. For the LDCs, the prescription is free trade. For the DCs, unskilled labor can expect falling wages with trade, and good advice is to invest in becoming more skilled.

Prices and Factor Prices

Protection drives a wedge between product prices across countries. If trade equalizes prices of factors across countries, protection drives factor prices apart. The following result was proven by Wolfgang Stolper and Paul Samuelson in the early 1950s:

> *Price/payment theorem. A tariff raises the price of the factor used intensively in the protected import competing industry and lowers the price of the factor used intensively in the export industry.*

Consider a tariff that raises the home price of manufactures. The physical amount of the good worth \$1 falls, and the inputs required to make \$1 of the manufactured good falls.

In Figure 6.17 the original unit value isocost line and cost minimization are pictured at points m and s. A tariff pushes the manufacturing unit isoquant toward the origin, forcing a steeper isocost line. The new equilibrium occurs at s' and m' with a higher wage w and lower capital return r. On the labor axis the

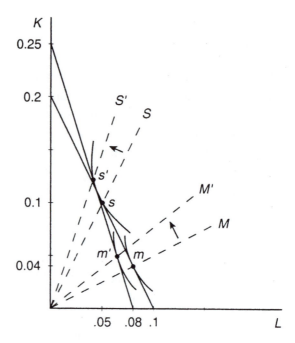

Figure 6.17
The Price/Payment Theorem
An increase in the price of manufactures with a tariff lowers the $1 unit isoquant. With w and r flexible, the isocost line must adjust. The new cost minimization occurs at m' and s'. The wage rises and r falls. The tariff benefits the input used intensively in the protected sector. Both sectors become more capital intensive.

intercept $1/w$ of the isocost line falls, which means w rises. The return to capital falls since $1/r$ rises. With the tariff, the price of relatively expensive labor increases and the price of relatively cheap capital falls. The tariff creates a more uneven distribution of income across countries.

The increase in the relative price of labor causes both industries to switch toward capital. The ratio of capital to labor rises from M to M' in manufacturing and from S to S' in services. Both industries become more capital intensive as outputs change. Protected labor intensive manufacturing increases output while capital intensive services declines. The economy turns away from its comparative advantage and income is redistributed toward the factor with the higher international return.

A tariff increases the output of manufactures and the demand for its intensive input. The wage rises but workers must pay higher prices for manufactures. Are workers better off with the tariff? It turns out that the percentage wage increase is greater than the percentage price increase. With any tariff, one productive factor always enjoys an increase in real income but the other loses. This is the *magnification effect* of Ron Jones.

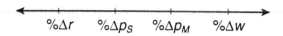

Figure 6.18
The Magnification Effect
Changing prices affect factor payments in a magnified way according to factor intensities. Percentage changes in wages and capital payments flank percentage price changes. The scale can be read in both directions with zero placed anywhere. A tariff causes the real income of one factor to rise while the other falls.

While tariffs create overall losses, the magnification effect implies that some factor owners gain. Factors used intensively in the protected sector gain. With a tariff on manufactures, capital owners are faced with lower income and must pay also higher prices for the goods they consume.

Figure 6.18 illustrates the magnification effect. With a tariff on manufactures, and $\%\Delta p_M > \%\Delta p_S = 0$. Along the scale, $\%\Delta w > \%\Delta p_M$. The wage rises by a larger percentage than the price of manufactures. Since $\%\Delta p_S = 0$, $\%\Delta r < 0$. The return to capital falls.

The magnification effect is based on factor intensity and runs in either direction. A *ceteris paribus* increase in the price of services due to an increase in world demand results in the ranking $\%\Delta r > \%\Delta p_S > \%\Delta p_M = 0 > \%\Delta w$. The return to capital rises by a larger percentage than the price of services. Wages fall. Domestic consumers pay the higher price of services. Capital owners enjoy higher real income, but workers lose.

A tariff on manufactures simultaneous with a smaller percentage rise in the price of services implies $\%\Delta r = 0 < \%\Delta p_S < \%\Delta p_M < \%\Delta w$. Capital owners lose because prices are rising but their return is constant. Workers win because wages rise more than average prices.

There is a *factor intensity link* between factors and goods. Between a good and its intensive factor, the link is positive. Between a good and the other factor, the link is negative. The change in the output of M resulting from a change in L is positive, $\Delta M / \Delta L > 0$ and $\Delta S / \Delta L < 0$. Also, $\Delta w / \Delta p_M > 0$ and $\Delta w / \Delta p_S < 0$. Each good has positive links with the factor it uses intensively.

The four theorems of this section are part of the basic intuition of trade theory. The factor proportions structure plays a central role in trade theory. These four theorems furnish a picture of production as the foundation of trade. New results in trade theory are related to these fundamental theorems.

EXAMPLE 6.10   *FPE as a Scientific Proposition*

Science progresses with theory that makes assumptions to derive testable propositions and the ones that prove themselves empirically become part of accepted science. Farhad Rassekh and Henry Thompson (1993) review the status of factor price equalization (FPE) as a scientific proposition. FPE was pronounced dead at birth in the 1950s by some prominent economists since wages differ so greatly around the world and it has been dismissed offhand by numerous economists over the years. Nevertheless, FPE survives as part of the foundation of international trade theory. FPE can be interpreted as implying that free trade leads toward convergence of wages and other factor prices, and there is widespread empirical support for that proposition. There is increased effort to test the implications of FPE and it remains one of the more powerful scientific theorems in economics.

EXAMPLE 6.11   *Trade & Income Redistribution in Some LDCs*

Trade will raise prices of manufactures but lower prices of business services in LDCs. Production of labor intensive manufactures for export will rise while production of business services fall with import competition. Henry Thompson (1995b) projects the effects of changing prices of manufactures and business services across some LDCs in a factor proportions model. The effects of a 10% increase in the price of manufactures are combined with a 10% decrease in the price of business services. Wages of unskilled labor rise considerably while wages of skilled labor and the capital return decline.

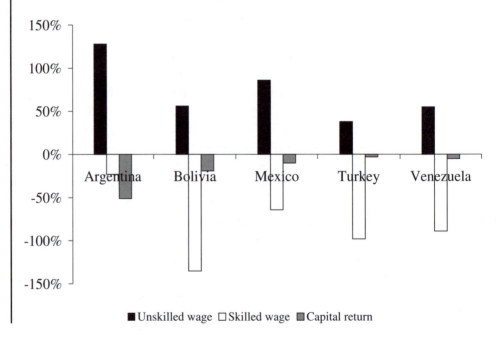

Problems for Section C

C1. Let Figure 6.13 represent the home country. Suppose the foreign country has a factor endowment of $(K,L) = (80,120)$. The two countries have the same production functions and trade freely. Compare the different employments of K and L across sectors in the two countries.

C2. Compare the ratios of foreign outputs in the previous problem with the ratio of home outputs in Figure 6.13. Which country produces a higher ratio of M to S? Which will export M if consumers in both countries have the same preferences?

C3. How would the switch from autarky to free trade affect payments to K and L for each country in the previous problem?

EXAMPLE 6.12 *3 × 3 × 3 Trade*

The $2 \times 2 \times 2$ factor proportions model with 2 factors of production, 2 products, and 2 countries has clear theoretical predictions about the direction of trade and the effects of protection. In a world with various factors, thousands of products, and hundreds of countries, and the theory is not so clear. Henry Thompson (2001) goes a step beyond the two dimensional model to the $3 \times 3 \times 3$ theory of trade. The first practical point is that trade between any two of the countries does not have to be balanced. Each country has to export at least one product, all three can export two products, and there are two intermediate cases. A tariff on an import (or two) has to help at least one factor and might help another but must lower income for at least one. It is impossible to predict which factor price will rise with a tariff given only information on factor intensity since substitution plays a role. A tariff may not protect its industry as anticipated given the range of substitution and other opportunities for adjustment. A tariff on manufactures might raise unskilled wages, increasing demand for capital and skilled labor in the other sectors and draining manufacturing of all inputs. Information about factor substitution is required to predict the effects of a tariff on factor prices and outputs.

D. APPLYING FACTOR PROPORTIONS TRADE THEORY

The factor proportions model is the foundation of trade theory. Conceptually, it captures how an economy adjusts to changes international prices and factor endowments. Like all scientific theories, it must be applied and tested. This section covers some applications, tests, and extensions of factor proportions theory.

EXAMPLE 6.13 *NAFTA and Wages*

International trade between Mexico and the US will raise and redistribute income in both countries. Wages for unskilled workers in the US are expected to decline. Kenneth Reinert and David Roland-Holst (1998) construct a CGE model of NAFTA in which wages of different groups of labor can rise in all three countries. Labor is split into 5 groups in each country: professional, sales, agriculture, crafts, and laborers. With nontraded goods, elastic labor supply, and differentiated exports, there are potential wage increases for all labor groups. Removing tariffs causes wages to increase in all three countries, but by less than 1%. Removing NTBs as well would raise wages 1% in the US, 3% in Canada, and 3% in Mexico.

Tests of Factor Proportions Trade Theory

In an early test of factor proportions trade theory, Wassily Leontief (1953) examined the physical capital and labor content of US exports and imports during 1947 finding labor intensive exports. Since the US was thought to be capital abundant, this was called the *Leontief paradox*. World War II had leveled much of the capital of Europe making this observation more paradoxical. In dollars of capital per person, the K/L ratio was 141 for export production and 182 for imported goods.

Robert Baldwin (1971) found the K/L ratio of US imports and exports in 1962 were virtually identical if agriculture and natural resources were excluded, 116 for exports and 119 for imports. Including agriculture and natural resources, K/L ratios were 143 in exports and 179 in imports. The argument for excluding agriculture and natural resources is that they depend on climate, land, and available natural resources, all geographical in nature. Baldwin also finds that the US exported goods using skilled labor intensively.

Robert Stern and Keith Maskus (1981) used 1972 data and found that the Leontief paradox had disappeared. Keith Maskus (1985) subsequently reported that the paradox is actually a commonplace, the US a net exporter of labor services frequently from year to year.

Ed Leamer (1980) makes the point that the goods actually consumed in the US are much more labor intensive than exports. The K/L ratio in consumption for the Leontief study was 68. Exports were capital intensive ($K/L = 141$) relative to goods consumed. Still, it is odd that imports were more capital intensive.

The Leontief paradox was partly a result of the trade surplus during 1947. Essentially the US exported too much. Francisco Casas and Kwan Choi (1985) calculate what the pattern of trade would have been had it been balanced and find no Leontief paradox.

The US was in fact a net exporter of both labor and capital. William Branson and Nikolaos Monoyios (1977) show that the US exported goods intensive in skilled labor and imported goods intensive in unskilled labor. Capital holds an intermediate position in this factor intensity ranking. Separating skilled labor eliminates the Leontief paradox results in more realistic theory.

Ed Leamer (1984) finds that the factor content of US net exports is largest for scientists, engineers, technicians, and draftsmen. Robert Stern and Keith Maskus

(1981) come to the similar conclusion that US reveals itself as abundant in skilled labor and physical capital.

Comprehensive tests of the factor proportions theory are difficult because data from different countries on inputs, factor abundance, prices, outputs, and trade are not available. Data on service production is rare and the US increasingly exports services that use skilled labor intensively. Industries within manufacturing vary from very capital intensive to very labor intensive. Capital is difficult to conceptualize and measure. Labor, land, and natural resources are very different across countries.

EXAMPLE 6.14 *Industrial Evidence on Prices and Factor Prices*

The link between prices of products and factors depends largely on factor intensity. Farhad Rassekh and Henry Thompson (1997) examine the factor intensity of 9 industries across 12 DCs between 1970 and 1985. A higher price for a labor intensive product increases its share of output, increases labor demand, raises the wage, and raises the capital to labor ratio. A higher price for a capital intensive product should lower the capital to labor ratio and this outcome occurs for 5 of the 9 industries. Predictions of the specific factors model hold for 7 of 9 industries. The ranking compares capital intensity in thousands of dollars of capital per worker across the US, Canada, Germany, and Japan. Canada has the most capital intensive minerals industry by far. Canada and Japan both have capital intensive paper industries. US textile production is the most labor intensive. Germany has low capital intensities in chemicals and basic metals. Canadian manufacturing is the most capital intensive, followed by the US, Germany, and Japan. The average capital input per worker ranges from $40,000 to $60,000 in these four countries.

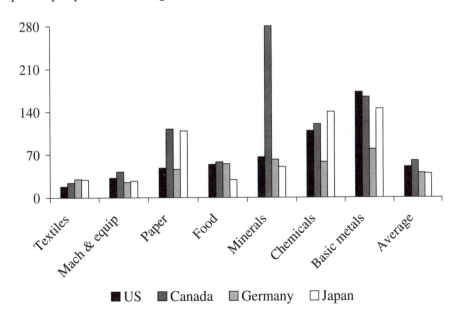

Applications of Factor Proportions Trade Theory

Large economies like the US and the EU trade tens of thousands of goods and services with hundreds of countries. Production processes involve many skill groups of labor, an array of capital inputs, and all sorts of natural resources. The concepts of factor intensity and factor abundance are difficult to interpret when there are many products and many factors of production. One issue in international economics is how to aggregate and classify goods and factors, and then apply the basic trade theorems.

There is increasing importance of trade in business services, a wide variety of activity. Skilled labor is used intensively in the production of business services and the developed countries have an abundance of skilled labor. The evolving pattern of specialization in services and import of manufactures is predicted by factor proportions theory for the DCs.

Computable general equilibrium (CGE) models of production and trade simulate real world economies. CGE models predict the effects of protection, export subsidies, oil price shocks, and so on across many goods and various inputs. CGE models are based on the factor proportion model in this chapter. CGE models have been a major innovation in international economics over the past 20 years.

EXAMPLE 6.15 *Evidence on the Endowment/Export Theorem*

> Ed Leamer (1984) examines the links between endowments and exports in 47 countries producing 10 outputs with 11 inputs: capital, professionals, unskilled labor, skilled labor, coal, minerals, oil, and 4 types of land. Outputs are petroleum, raw materials, forest products, tropical agriculture, animal products, cereals, L intensive manufactures, K intensive manufactures, machinery, and chemicals. Belgium, France, Germany, Italy, Japan, the Netherlands, Sweden, Switzerland, UK, and the US are abundant in capital and skilled labor. They export chemicals (capital and skilled labor intensive) and machinery (skilled labor intensive). Austria, India, Korea, and Spain export capital intensive manufactures. Brazil, Colombia, Cyprus, Egypt, Finland, Greece, Malta, Sri Lanka, Thailand, and Turkey are labor abundant and export labor intensive manufactures. LDCs are capital scarce and export tropical agricultural goods, raw materials, cereals, and animal products. Other countries are diversified in endowments and exports. Trade in agriculture, minerals, and oil is explained by the different types of land and natural resources. Leamer uncovers a dominating underlying influence of factor endowments on exports.

Trade and Unemployment

Unemployment arises for various reasons. It takes time and resources to match firms and workers. Searching for a job is costly. Labor markets require training and experience. Industries expand and contract with business cycles and international competition. Labor contracts create inflexibility. For these reasons, some unemployment is likely to be observed.

The pattern of outputs with unemployment will differ from full employment. Firms hire workers according to their marginal revenue product. If the minimum or contract wage is higher than the market wage, unemployment will be the result. With less labor employed, the economy will be below its PPF.

The *probability wage model* of James Harris and Michael Todaro (1970) provide an alternative explanation of persistent unemployment. Rural wages (w_R) are low but everyone has a job in the rural area. Urban areas offer higher wages (w_U) but the probability P of finding a job is less than 1. Workers in rural areas who consider moving to the urban area discount the high urban wage by P. Suppose $P = 80\% = 0.8$ and $w_U = \$10$. The discounted urban wage is $0.80 \times \$10 = \$8$. If $w_R < \$8$, rural workers will move to the urban area facing the possibility of being unemployed but with a higher expected wage. Other considerations such as moving costs and tastes for urban versus rural life influence the decision, but the probability wage model suggests how urban unemployment may persist. If a tariff on manufacturing in the urban sector would raise w_U, migration from rural areas will increase and the number of unemployed in the city will rise.

There is a normal level of unemployment associated with job searching, business cycles, and unemployment benefits. Better unemployment benefits lower the cost of not having a job and raise the unemployment rate. In the DCs, it is common practice to draw unemployment benefits and work underground. Official statistics of unemployment can be misleading. LDCs often report high rates of unemployment but everyone is constantly working. Underground economies are very active in most countries, producing valuable goods and services.

Minimum wage legislation and labor contracts create unemployment. In a dynamic economy, continuous change calls for flexibility. A reduction in the demand for labor will result in either lower wages or less employment. While neither is desirable, lower wages are less of a burden. Further, such artificial support of unskilled workers lessens their incentive to upgrade labor skills. Flexibility in wages and hours worked would mean more efficient labor markets.

Given the generally low levels of unemployment typical in most DCs, the conclusions of trade theory are not affected much by unemployment. Trade policy should not be used to lower unemployment.

EXAMPLE 6.16 *Free Trade & Income Redistribution in Bolivia*

Free trade in South America will have a large impact on production and factor prices in Bolivia according to Hugo Toledo and Henry Thompson (2001). Natural gas and manufacturing exports are projected to expand while agriculture and services suffer import competition. Brazil and Argentina are major agricultural producers and Bolivian farmers will lose their protection in Mercosur, the South American free trade agreement. The Bolivian service industries are skilled labor intensive, government owned or subsidized, and extremely inefficient. In a model with skilled and unskilled labor mobile across industries, skilled and unskilled labor lose with the move to free trade. Outputs in services and agriculture fall. Capital in services and agriculture suffer heavy losses, while capital owners in natural gas, manufacturing, and mining enjoy large gains. These large adjustments below suggest substantial changes are in store for the small Bolivian economy as it opens to free trade. There is already some political unrest, making the coming transition more critical.

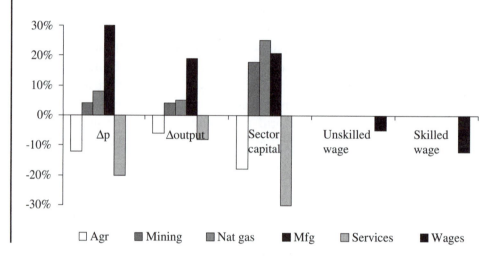

Factor Proportions and Constant Cost

The factor proportions model seems different from the constant cost model but Roy Ruffin (1988) has shown how closely the two are related with the constant cost endowment (CCE) model. The idea behind the CCE model is that trade occurs between different types of labor residing in different countries. Interpersonal trade occurs across borders between people with different skills and training.

The CCE model has characteristics of the constant cost and factor proportions models. Labor inputs determine comparative advantage and endowments of different types of labor determine the trade pattern.

In the CCE model, services (S) and manufactures (M) are produced by unskilled (L) labor or skilled labor (H) where H stands for human capital acquired through education and training. Labor inputs are constant as in the constant cost model.

Suppose L per unit of M (a_{LM}) is 1 and the unit input of skilled labor is $a_{HM} = 2$. In services, the two inputs are $a_{LS} = 2$ and $a_{HS} = 1$. The home country

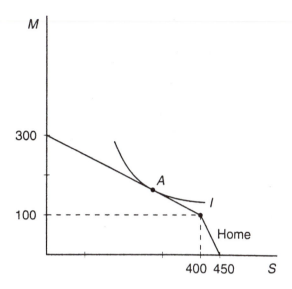

Figure 6.19
Home PPF in the Constant Cost Endowment Model
This home country has 400 units of skilled labor and 100 units of labor. Unit inputs are $L/S = H/M = 2$ and $L/M = H/S = 1$. If all inputs go into M production, $300M$ is produced. On the S axis, $450S$ could be produced. With all skilled labor in services and all labor in manufactures, the pivot point $(M,S) = (100,400)$ is produced. Consumers maximize utility at point A on indifference curve I.

has an abundance of skilled labor with an endowment of $(L,H) = (100,400)$. The endowment of the foreign country is $(L^*,H^*) = (500,50)$.

If all skilled labor at home produces M, $400/2 = 200$ units are produced. Home unskilled labor can produce an additional $100/1 = 100$ units of M. With both skilled and unskilled labor producing M, 300 units could be produced. Alternatively, the H at home could produce $400/1 = 400$ units of S and the L another $100/2 = 50$ units, for a total of 450 units of S. The extremes on the home PPF are $300M$ and $450S$.

Starting at endpoint $M = 300$ in Figure 6.19, skilled labor would begin producing S according to its comparative advantage. If all available skilled labor produces S and only unskilled labor produces M, output would be at the pivot point $(M,S) = (100,400)$.

The home PPF connects this pivot point with the two endpoints with straight segments because of constant costs. Without trade, consumers in the home country would have to pick a point along their PPF. In Figure 6.19, home consumers maximize utility at point A. Some skilled labor is involved in autarky manufacturing production.

The foreign PPF* connects endpoints $M = 525$ and $S = 300$ with pivot point $(M,S) = (500,50)$. Foreign consumers are constrained to consume along their

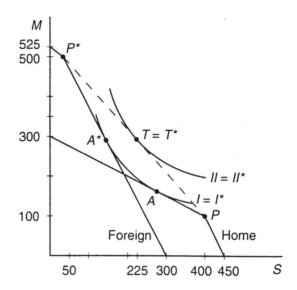

Figure 6.20
Specialization and Trade in the Constant Cost Endowment Model
Each nation will specialize by producing the good that has low inputs of its abundant factor. Abundant skilled labor is all attracted to the home service sector. In the foreign nation abundant unskilled labor is all attracted to manufacturing. In this example the terms of trade $tt = M/S = 200/175 = 8/7$ and each nation consumes $(M,S) = (300,225)$ beyond its PPF at a higher level of utility.

PPF in autarky, maximizing welfare at point A^* in Figure 6.20. Some unskilled labor in involved in autarky service production.

With free trade, production moves to the pivot point for each country. In Figure 6.20, production shifts to P and P^*. The terms of trade are represented by the dotted line connecting the pivot points. Abundant factors specialize in their comparative advantage. All of the skilled labor at home produces S and all of the unskilled labor in the foreign country produces M. The home country exports 175 units of S in exchange for 200 units of M from the foreign country. Both countries consume $300M$ and $225S$ at point $T = T^*$. Tastes are identical across countries and autarky consumption points A and A^* are on the same indifference curve ($I = I^*$). Free trade allows both countries to move to a higher level of utility on indifference curve $II = II^*$ in this example.

International trade produces overall gains, each country consuming beyond its PPF. Real income increases in each country and both increase utility. Income is more evenly distributed as a result of trade. The home country has a relative abundance of skilled labor. Relative wages before trade are likely characterized by $h/w < h^*/w^*$ where h is the wage of skilled labor and w the wage of labor. Labor is relatively cheap in the foreign country and skilled labor is relatively cheap at home. In the home country, trade increases the price of relatively cheap services. With skilled labor pulled into services, the skilled wage rises. In the foreign country, trade increases the price of relatively cheap manufactures and the unskilled wage.

EXAMPLE 6.17 *Trade & Labor Skills*

> Trade leads to overall gains in the economy but redistributes income. With capital input fixed, some types of labor would suffer with a move to free trade and would lobby for protection. William Cline (1997) amasses evidence that unskilled manufacturing wages in the US have fallen and suggests they will continue to fall with increasing trade. Skilled labor enjoys benefits due to increased trade as the US specializes in production intensive in skilled labor. The endowment ratio of skilled to unskilled labor has increased as people respond to market incentives and increase education and training. The effects of trade on income distribution are large enough to lower unskilled wages. The US would benefit by openly facing the challenges of free trade and encouraging education and training for unskilled labor.

EXAMPLE 6.18 *Trade & the Wage Gap*

> Skilled wages have increased relative to unskilled in the US and other DCs exactly as predicted with increased imports of unskilled intensive products. Improved technology may also favor skilled labor, and economists have attempted to determine whether trade or technology has contributed more to the "wage gap" that has grown in size over recent decades between skilled and unskilled labor. Robert Baldwin and Glen Cain (2000) examine the period 1967–1996 and find that the US wage gap declined during the early years due to a net increase in the supply of skilled labor. Since the 1970s, both increased imports of unskilled intensive products and improved technology in skilled intensive industries contribute to explaining the wage gap. Eli Berman, John Bound and Stephen Machin (1998) find evidence of skill biased technical change in both DCs and LDCs during the 1980s but suggest trade also contributes. If technical change is biased toward skilled labor, there would be decreased demand for unskilled labor. Jonathan Haskel and Matthew Slaughter (2002) find evidence that it is sector biased technical change in the skilled intensive industries that best explains the wage gap in DCs during the 1980s and 1990s. Robert Feenstra and Gordon Hanson (1999) model technology as computer investment and trade as intermediate outsourcing, and find that 35% of the wage gap is explained by computers and 15% by outsourcing. More research and different data sets "experiments" are bound to contribute to understanding the wage gap.

Problems for Section D

D1. What is an explanation other than those in the text for the Leontief paradox?

D2. Use a 2×2 production diagram to illustrate the effects of increased unemployment on outputs.

EXAMPLE 6.19 *Labor Movement along the PPF*

The changing prices with free trade move the economy along its production frontier with labor and other factors of production leaving import competing industries and moving to export industries. Romain Wacziarg and Jessica Wallan (2004) examine episodes of trade liberalization from the 1970s to the 1990s across 25 LDCs and NICs looking for evidence of labor movements. Labor market reactions vary across countries. There was no movement between manufacturing, services, and agriculture in the sample but there was movement between industries and firms in manufacturing. The sample countries specialized in different manufacturing industries with free trade. Labor market adjustments to free trade were not as dramatic as the moves following deregulation and privatization of socialized industry.

CONCLUSION

The factor proportions model of production and trade is the foundation of trade theory. It applies when firms are competitive price takers. The specific factors model provides a closely related conceptual framework. These competitive models lead to neoclassical production frontiers and offer curves. The next chapter examines international trade when firms are monopolistic price searchers. Industrial structures in the next chapter are monopoly, monopolistic competition, and oligopoly. Each industrial structure has its own implications for issues in international trade.

Terms

Computable general equilibrium
Cost minimization
Diminishing marginal productivity
Exit and entry
Expansion paths
Factor abundance and scarcity
Factor demand

Isoquant
Leontief paradox
Marginal cost (*MC*)
Marginal product (*MP*)
Marginal revenue (*MR*)
Marginal revenue product (*MRP*)
Price-taking firm

Factor intensity

Factor price equalization

Factor substitution

Probability wage unemployment

Constant cost

Price taking firm

Specific factors

Isocost line

MAIN POINTS

- Tariffs generally protect factors of production specific to an industry but hurt factors specific to other industries. Shared factors may win or lose with protection.
- Firms choose the input mix to minimize their cost of production. With competition, price equals average cost.
- Factor intensity and factor abundance are key concepts leading to the four basic theorems of production and trade. There is a positive intensity link between products and inputs.
- Factor proportions theory does a reasonable job of explaining observed international trade.

REVIEW PROBLEMS

1. In the specific factors economy from the problems in Section A, suppose the price of imported M rises to $2.40 with a tariff. Show what happens in the labor market. Is a shortage of labor created? What happens to the wage?

2. Diagram what happens in the previous problem to markets for sector specific capital inputs. What happens to the outputs?

3. Suppose country A imposes a tariff on imported manufactures and its terms of trade with country B improve. Predict what happens to income distribution in country B using the specific factors model.

4. Sketch the cost minimization that occurs with $w = \$2$, $r = \$3$, $c = \$1$, and 0.2 unit of L input. Find the unit input of capital and sketch the unit value isoquant. Describe what happens in this cost minimization if r falls to $2.

5. Describe what happens to the cost minimization in the previous problem if w rises to $3 when $r = \$3$.

6. Given factor prices $w = \$2$ and $r = \$3$, suppose 0.35 units of labor are used in manufacturing

to produce $1 of output. Sketch the manufacturing cost minimization and the expansion path. Find K/L in manufacturing.

7. Draw the production diagram of the economy with the service sector in problem 4 and the manufacturing sector in problem 6.

8. Two economies have endowments $(K,L) = (100,200)$ and $(K^*,L^*) = (110,190)$. With the technology in problem 7, predict the pattern of trade. Explain which country is labor abundant and labor cheap.

9. If the foreign country described in problem 8 imposes a tariff, what happens to w^* and r^*? Illustrate with a diagram. What happens to the K/L ratios in manufacturing and services?

10. Complete Figure 6.17 showing the changed pattern of production due to the protection of manufactures.

11. Use expansion paths to show an economy that is completely specialized in the production of manufactures.

12. Illustrate factor price equalization using a production diagram when the home country has

twice as much capital and half as much labor as the foreign country.

13. Draw the home PPF in the constant cost endowment model with endowment $(L,H) = (400,500)$ and unit inputs in the text. Draw the foreign PPF* with endowment $(L^*,H^*) = (300,600)$.

14. Find the terms of trade and the final consumption for the two economies in problem 13. Explain the pattern of trade.

15. With the three factors (capital, labor, skilled labor) and the two goods (manufactures, services) define factor intensity.

16. If agricultural output is added to problem 15, define factor intensity and factor abundance.

READINGS

William Baumol, Richard Nelson, and Edward Wolff (1994) *Convergence of Productivity*, Oxford: Oxford University Press. History of convergence across countries.

Brian Berry, Edgar Conkling, and Michael Ray (1997) *The Global Economy in Transition*, New Jersey: Prentice-Hall. Graphical blend of geography, energy analysis, population dynamics, and economics.

David Richardson (1993) *Sizing Up US Export Disincentives*, Washington: Institute for International Economics. Policies leading to lower exports.

John Pool and Stephen Stamos (1994) *Exploring the Global Economy*, Shenandoah University: Durell Institute of Monetary Science. Short excursion into importance of international commerce.

A.G. Kenwood and A.L. Lougheed (1992) *The Growth of the International Economy, 1820–1990*, London: Routledge. A nice economic history.

Alan Deardorff and Robert Stern (1986) *The Michigan Model of World Production and Trade: Theory and Applications*, Cambridge: MIT Press. CGE model of production and trade.

Edward Leamer (1984) *Sources of International Comparative Advantage*, Cambridge: MIT Press, 1984. Quantitative basis of factor abundance and trade.

Ron Findlay (1988) *Factor Proportions, Trade, and Growth*, Cambridge: MIT Press. Clearly written short book.

CHAPTER 7

Industrial Organization and Trade

Preview

Industrial organization refers to the way firms form an industry. The four types of industrial organization are competition, monopoly, monopolistic competition, and oligopoly. These are examples of each industry in international trade. Up to this point in the text, industries have been competitive with many firms producing a homogeneous product. The present chapter examines the influence of different industrial organizations on trade. Topics in this chapter include:

- *Price searching firms* in international markets
- *Intraindustry trade* and product differentiation
- *Oligopolies* and trade
- *Technology, product cycles, increasing returns to scale*

INTRODUCTION

The simplest industry is a monopoly with a single firm. An international monopoly occurs when a single firm is the only supplier for the international market. Compared to a competitive industry, an exporting monopolist produces less output, sells at a higher price, and enjoys positive profit. Importing from a foreign monopoly implies paying a higher price and consuming less. There is monopoly power in international markets for minerals and primary commodities. Members of international producer cartels such as OPEC and the coffee and banana cartels try to join together for monopoly power.

If buyers can be separated into groups with different demands, it pays an international price searcher to discriminate by setting price according to the demand of each group. For a price searching monopoly exporter, buyers can be separated into domestic and foreign and the group with higher or more inelastic demand will pay a higher price.

Some international trade occurs with only a few firms, an oligopoly. In an international oligopoly, a firm in one country competes with a few firms in other countries. Decisions made by one or two foreign auto firms affect US auto firms. An oligopoly can be nearly as competitive as a market with many firms, or the firms may be able to collude and share monopoly profits.

Monopolistic competition, as the name suggests, is an industry with firms having monopoly power to set their own price but ending with zero profit in a competitive equilibrium. There are many firms each selling their own particular brand. Some firms can be foreign and there can be demand in foreign countries for home products, leading to international trade.

Various other industrial organization theories contribute to international trade. If two countries have different production technologies, trade will benefit both. Some countries have a comparative advantage in new products, leading to international product cycle trade. Different income levels across countries can affect demand and trade. Increasing returns to scale are a reason to specialize because unit costs decline as output increases.

All of these industrial organizations and alternative theories contribute to the study of international production and trade.

A.   PRICE SEARCHING FIRMS AND TRADE

A firm that faces its own downward sloping demand can search for the price and quantity to maximize profit. There are unique principles of trade when firms are *price searchers*.

Price Searching Firms

A single firm in an industry is a monopoly. Two general types of monopolies are natural and legal monopolies. *Natural monopolies* occur when average cost declines for the firm all the way to the output that meets market demand.

Average cost declines due to economies of scale for the firm. If average cost continues to diminish at the market output, one large firm is able to operate more efficiently than a number of smaller firms. Small firms would be driven out of business and the monopoly dominates the market. Positive profit persists because a small firm considering entry would be discouraged by its high average cost at a low output level.

Legal monopolies arise from property rights that keep potential competitors from entering. Profits may be high but entry is illegal and there is no natural monopoly. Patents, franchises, licensing, and resource ownership are property rights that lead to legal monopolies.

A newly developed production process can be patented for a number of years. Patent law ensures other firms cannot freely copy a product or process that was costly to develop. Copyright law ensures the property rights of authors, musicians, and movie producers. International patent and copyright agreements have been a focus of the recent WTO negotiations.

Utility companies are granted the sole right to sell their services inside a certain geographical area. Licensing is similar in that it restricts competition. Foreign telecommunication firms and foreign doctors are prohibited from entry. A firm owning a titanium mine in Brazil has the sole legal right to sell the titanium. OPEC and other resource cartels have international monopoly power based on the property rights.

With a single firm in an industry, demand for the firm's output is market demand. A monopolist searches for the price and quantity combination along the demand curve that maximizes profit. Instead of a supply curve, a monopolist chooses a *supply point* on the demand curve. The *profit maximizing* price and quantity are found by comparing the marginal revenue *MR* and marginal cost *MC* of an additional unit of output. If *MR* is greater than *MC*, profit rises if the monopolist produces the additional unit. If *MC* is greater than *MR*, profit rises if the monopolist reduces output.

Suppose all the world's gold is owned by a single mining firm. In Figure 7.1, world demand for gold is *D*. The single gold firm is constrained in setting the price of gold by the demand it faces. There are substitutes for gold: silver in jewelry, titanium in industrial uses, bonds as assets, and so on. If the monopolist in Figure 7.1 sets the price of gold at $1000 per ounce, none will be bought. To sell gold, the monopolist would have to lower price. Since the price on every

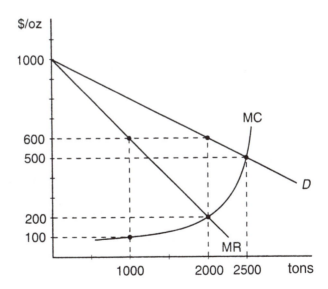

Figure 7.1
A Price Searching Monopoly Exporter
For a monopolist, marginal revenue (*MR*) is below demand *D*. This monopolist produces where *MR* equals marginal cost (*MC*) at 2000 tons. Output is sold according to demand at $600.

ounce sold must be lowered, *MR* will be less than price. The monopoly marginal revenue *MR* lies below demand *D*.

If demand is linear as in Figure 7.1, the *inverse demand function* is $P = a - bQ$ where *a* and *b* are positive numbers. In the demand function quantity demanded is a function of price, and in the inverse demand function price is a function of quantity. Total revenue *TR* is price *P* times quantity *Q*: $TR = aQ - bQ^2$. *MR* is the change in *TR* for a one unit change in *Q*: $MR = a - 2bQ$. Students with calculus background recognize *MR* as the derivative of *TR*. Students who do not know calculus can work through the example of the inverse demand function $P = 1000 - .5Q$ to derive marginal revenue $MR = 1000 - 10Q$. *MR* is twice as steep as linear *D*.

There is another basic constraint on monopoly pricing and output of gold, the cost of mining and refining. At any given time the monopoly has a certain amount of machinery and equipment to use along with the labor it hires. To produce more gold requires more labor, more wear and tear on machinery and equipment, more energy input, and so on.

Marginal cost generally increases with output. The marginal cost curve *MC* in Figure 7.1 is sloping upward. This is a *short run marginal cost* curve that holds capital input constant. *MC* slopes upward due to diminishing marginal productivity. Holding capital input constant, additional workers add to total output but beyond some point these worker increments become smaller. As marginal product falls, marginal cost of output rises. Also, increasing output raises demand for inputs and their prices may rise.

At outputs below 2000 tons, the marginal revenue from selling an extra unit of output is larger than the marginal cost of producing it. Suppose 1000 tons are produced. The MR of an extra ounce of output is $600 in Figure 7.1 but it costs only $100 to produce. The monopolist could raise profit by increasing output, and continues until $MR = MC = \$200$ at the *profit maximizing output* of 2000.

After finding the output that maximizes profit, the monopolist sets the price of gold according to demand. All 2000 tons can be sold at a price of $600, found where the output of 2000 meets demand *D*. The monopolist produces where $MR = MC$ and prices according to demand to clear the market. World gold buyers would pay a price of $600 facing this monopoly exporter.

Price searching firms maximize profit at the output where MR = MC setting price according to demand to clear the market.

EXAMPLE 7.1   *A Snapshot of Exporting Firms*

Manufacturing firms accounted for 69% of US merchandise export revenue in 1997 followed by wholesalers at 13%. Freight forwarders, transportation services, business services, engineering and management services, gas and oil extraction firms, coal mining firms, communication services, and others accounted for another 14%. Large firms with 500 or more employees accounted for 69% of revenue. Intrafirm trade was 42% of total merchandise export revenue. Most firms (62%) trade with only one foreign country. The few firms that trade with 50 or more countries account for about half of all merchandise export revenue. US exporting firms do not generally enjoy price searching market power but there are some examples worldwide.

A Price Taking Firm

At the other extreme, the industry might be made up of many small competitive firms around the world. Each firm would be a competitive *price taker*. A price taking firm in a competitive international gold market is pictured in Figure 7.2. Each price taking firm has no power to vary the international price of $500. The competitive price is found where demand equals supply for the industry. *MR* equals $500 for each firm because every ounce is sold for the same price. For competitive firms, *D* and *MR* are horizontal lines at the market price. Profit is maximized for this competitive firm where $MR = MC$ at a quantity of 25.

Imagine marginal revenue *MR* were equal to demand *D* for the price searcher in Figure 7.1. The monopolist would then maximize profit where $MR = MC$ by setting the price at $500 and selling output Q of 2500, similar to the outcome in

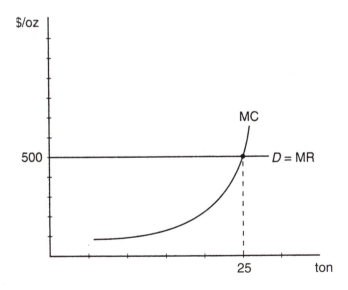

Figure 7.2
A Price Taking Exporting Firm
The international price of gold is $500 in this example and this price taker can sell any quantity it wants at this international price. This firm maximizes profit where $MR = MC$ at 2500 ounces of output.

Figure 7.2. A monopoly prices higher and produces less output than competitive firms with the same costs of production.

EXAMPLE 7.2 *Steel Trigger Prices*

During the 1960s and 1970s, the US steel industry faced increased competition from Japan and Europe after they had rebuilt following World War II and wages were about half those in the US. Ingo Walter (1983) estimates their production costs were about 40% of US costs. The share of imports in steel consumption rose from 5% in 1960 to 18% in 1980. US steel firms pressured the US government, which pressured foreign governments, which pressured foreign steel firms to agree to "voluntary" export restraints to the US. Repeated cases of steel "dumping" resulted in the Carter administration instituting a *trigger price mechanism* in 1978 based on cost data provided by Japanese firms. If the price of steel imports falls below cost plus shipping, imports were stopped. Steel imports dropped, but trigger prices proved impossible to administer since steel traders know more about their product than government administrators. Since the 1980s, competition in the international steel market has increased from NICs such as South Korea, Taiwan, Spain, Mexico, Venezuela, and Brazil, as well as some LDCs. The US steel industry has become internationally competitive mainly by specializing in high tech specialty alloys, but successfully lobbied for steel tariffs in 2002.

Monopoly Profit

If firms in a competitive industry make a profit, other firms enter increasing supply and decreasing price. *Free entry* implies competition and zero profit. Entry is ruled out by law for a legal monopoly or by the cost advantage of a natural monopoly.

Monopoly profit is found by the difference between average cost AC and price P at the optimal output. Suppose OPEC has a legal monopoly on the world's oil deposits. In Figure 7.3, profit is maximized for OPEC where $MR = MC$ at $Q = 100$. Output is sold according to demand at \$15 per barrel.

Consider the lowest cost at AC_1 in Figure 7.3. At the optimal output of 100, $AC_1 = \$12$ and total cost $TC = AC \times Q = \$12 \times 100 = \$1200$. With $P = \$15$ and $Q = 100$, total revenue is $TR = \$15 \times 100 = \$1500$. Price equals average revenue. Profit π is the difference between total revenue and total cost: $\pi = TR - TC = \$1500 - \$1200 = \$300$, the lined area in Figure 7.3. Profit is positive if average revenue is greater than average cost at the optimal output.

At the highest average cost AC_3 in Figure 7.3, $TC = \$18 \times 100 = \$1800$ is greater than $TR = \$1500$. Profit with AC_3 is a loss, $\pi = \$1500 - \$1800 = -\$300$,

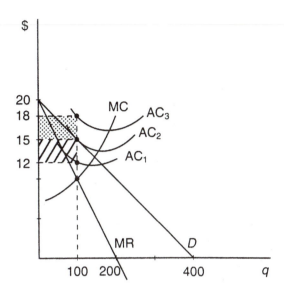

Figure 7.3
Profit for a Monopolistic Firm
Profit is maximized where $MR = MC$ at $q = 100$. Price is set according to demand at $15.
Profit depends on average cost (AC) at the profit maximizing output. With low costs at
AC_1, $AC = \$12$ and profit per unit is $\$15 - \$12 = \$3$. Total profit is $\$3 \times 100 = \$300$. With
high costs at AC_3, $AC = \$18$ with a loss of $3 per unit and total loss of $-\$300$. At AC_2,
economic profit is zero.

the dotted area in Figure 7.3. A monopoly may choose to operate for a time
with a loss if future expected profit is positive.

A monopolist would *shut down* if fixed costs were less than losses. When a
firm shuts down, it lays off labor and ceases operation. Fixed costs including
utilities and rent have to be paid even if the firm shuts down. A monopolist
may *sell out*, selling its capital machinery and equipment if it does not expect
an improvement in market conditions.

With costs AC_2 in Figure 7.3, $P = AC$ and $\pi = 0$. A price searcher has no
guarantee of positive profit. Demand for the product and cost of production
determine profit and whether the firm should shut down. Ultimately, a loss
making monopolist may sell out.

Natural monopolies arise because of a cost advantage associated with large
scale operations and should be allowed to operate without regulation. There is
nothing to fear from a natural monopoly because it has lower cost than smaller
firms. If a natural monopolist tries to extract exorbitant profit, other firms enter
the industry.

A *legal monopoly* can enjoy positive profit as long as the restriction on
competition remains in place. Legal monopolies such as the local utilities are
typically *regulated* by government. Regulators try to induce legal monopolies to

mimick competition. Regulated legal monopolies have a poor efficiency record. Costs are not minimized. Regulators have much less information than the monopolies and can be captured by the monopolist. There is no substitute for competition. Traditional regulated legal monopolies, telecommunications, natural gas, and electricity, are slowly being transformed into more competitive efficient industries.

EXAMPLE 7.3 *Every Year in Trade*

The ITC publishes a yearly summary of US trade agreements, *The Year in Trade*. Recently, the WTO gets top billing. OECD discussions on investment and legal coordination continue. NAFTA continues to evolve according to a schedule of "free" trade by 2008. Negotiations for FTAA (Free Trade Area of the Americas) continue. APEC (Asia-Pacific Economic Cooperation) is involved in preliminary talks over product standards. The US initiated the Transatlantic Economic Partnership designed to coordinate legal issues with the EU. US-Canadian trade is free except for a few agricultural and natural resource markets. Chinese duties on US products dropped and led to a trade agreement between the two countries. Taiwan and the US have problems over pirating of US software, CDs, and videos. There are investigations of trade adjustment assistance for US workers, new antidumping orders, and countervailing duties. The Generalized System of Preferences (GSP) defines which tariff schedules apply to which countries. Textile market sharing quotas attempt to govern textile imports from Asia. Selective economic sanctions are imposed, often in apparent conflict with the WTO. The ITC is the main administrator of trade agreements for the US and a major employer of international economists.

International Monopolies and Trade

If a country imports from an *international monopolist*, a tariff is attractive. Domestic consumers have to pay a higher price for less of the product but the domestic government taxes away some of the profits of the foreign monopoly. Tariff revenue can be transferred to domestic customers or residents.

Domestic demand is D in Figure 7.4. Costs for the foreign monopolist to sell in the home market are MC^* and AC^*. The monopolist would produce where $MR = MC^*$ at $Q = 100$ and $P = \$15$. With AC at $\$12$, profit of the foreign monopolist is $\$300$.

A $2 tariff transfers some of the profit to the home government. The effective demand curve falls by $2 to D' for monopolist, and marginal revenue falls to MR'. Output falls to 90 where MR' equals MC^*. Price in the domestic market rises to $\$15.50$ but the foreign monopolist receives only $\$13.50$. Profit falls for the foreign monopolist with the tariff because average revenue falls and average cost rises.

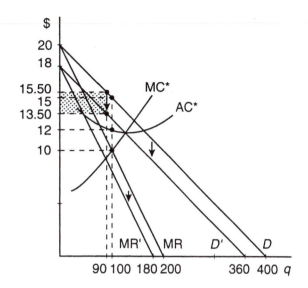

Figure 7.4
Taxing a Foreign Monopolist
A tariff on a foreign monopolist effectively lowers demand from D to D'. Profit maximizing output falls from 100 to 90 and price falls from $15 to $13.50. The $2 per unit tax is collected by the importing country's government. Tariff revenue is $2 \times 90 = $180. Profit falls. Domestic consumers pay a higher price and reduce consumption. The lost consumer surplus is $47.50, less than the tariff revenue.

The home government collects tariff revenue, the shaded area in Figure 7.4 of $2 \times 90 = $180. This tariff revenue can compensate consumers who must pay a higher price for less of the product. The size of the tariff revenue and the lost consumer surplus depend on demand and costs. In Figure 7.4, the transfer to the government is larger than the lost consumer surplus and the tariff is rational.

Reducing the profit of a foreign monopolist might appear to be politically popular. Few consumers would be opposed to the idea of taxing OPEC oil profit but none want to pay higher gas prices.

Dumping or International Price Discrimination?

If a monopolist can distinguish among groups of buyers, it can increase profit by pricing according to the demand of each group. An international monopolist can use *price discrimination* across countries. Consumers in countries with higher or more inelastic demand pay a higher price.

The international monopolist in Figure 7.5 faces domestic and foreign demand, D and D^*. The two groups of buyers have their own marginal revenues, MR and MR^*. For simplicity, MC is assumed constant. Each additional unit of output costs the same to produce, implying AC is constant as well. A price

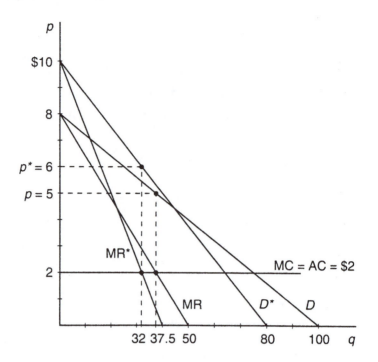

Figure 7.5
Price Discrimination by an Exporting Monopolist
This monopolist can discriminate between home demand curve D and foreign demand curve D^*. MC is constant at $2, and average cost ($AC$) is $2. The monopolist equates MC with MR and MR^*, and 32 units are sold abroad for $6 with 37.5 units sold at home for $5.

discriminating monopolist will produce where marginal cost MC equals MR for each group.

Profit maximization is 37.5 units of output for the home market and 32 for the foreign market. Foreign buyers have higher and more inelastic demand and pay $6, while domestic buyers pay only $5. Profit for the monopolist is higher than if the two demands were treated as a single aggregate demand. Selling in the home market, the monopolist makes a profit of $3 per unit for a total of $3 \times 37.5 = \$112.50$. Foreign profit is $4 \times 32 = \$128$.

Resale of products from home country to the foreign country must be impossible for price discrimination to work. If traders in the low price home country could resell to consumers in the foreign country, the price discrimination of the monopolist would collapse. Resale across markets discourages firms from international price discrimination.

Cries of *dumping* are regularly heard from firms facing foreign competition. *International dumping* is predatory pricing, when a foreign firm sells temporarily below average cost to eliminate domestic competition. The foreign firm plans to enjoy monopoly power and high profit later. In the US, the International Trade

Commission (ITC) hears dumping complaints and can award damages and erect temporary barriers to imports. Other countries pursue similar restrictive measures.

Japanese computer chip firms were found guilty of dumping in 1986 and antidumping duties were imposed. The US steel industry has repeatedly charged European firms with dumping. Without detailed information it is impossible to determine whether a foreign firm is dumping or just using price discrimination. A guilty firm would not open its books to foreign inspection, and data reliability can be questioned. Determinations of dumping by the ITC are based as much on politics as economic evidence.

Trying to police dumping is not worthwhile. Dumping is not a long run problem. If a foreign firm wants to sell goods for less than the goods cost to produce, it is not clear that we should rush to stop them. International price competition across industries is too sophisticated for government officials to uncover. Protection from alleged dumping offers industry another nontariff barrier to trade, and the payoffs are large. Such unholy alliance between industry and government leads to corruption and should be avoided.

EXAMPLE 7.4   *ITC Protection*

> The ITC hears cases and can award protection if foreign industry is competing "unfairly". Antidumping duties are awarded if foreign firms appear to be dumping and countervailing duties are awarded if there appear to be foreign subsidies. Wendy Hansen and Thomas Prusa (1997) examine 744 dumping cases filed between 1980 and 1988. The steel industry has a 37% higher probability of a favorable ruling than other industries. Industries with more Congressional representatives on the House Ways and Means Committee are more likely to receive ITC protection. An extra $200,000 in Political Action Committee (PAC) donations increases the probability of a favorable ruling by 8%, evidently money well spent. If the foreign country has a growing import market share, a duty is 12% more likely. Nonmarket economies are 38% more likely to be hit with a duty. Western Europe is 17% less likely due to the threat of retaliation. Although the law says the decision should be based on economic evidence, politics plays a role. Antidumping awards are a protectionist device that violates the WTO agreement.

Dominant Firm Imports

Some industries have a *dominant firm* that sets price and a number of competitive *fringe firms* that follow. Suppose a dominant foreign exporter with a number of fringe domestic firms characterize the domestic market for video players. Fringe domestic firms supply according to the price set by the dominant foreign firm, a higher price leading to more output by the domestic fringe.

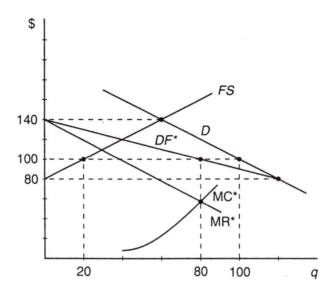

Figure 7.6
A Dominant Fringe Import Market
Domestic demand *D* is composed of the foreign dominant firm demand *DF** and domestic fringe supply *FS* from small firms. The dominant foreign firm produces where *MC* = MR** and prices output at $100. Domestic fringe suppliers produce residual output of 20. A tariff taxes the dominant foreign firm and stimulates domestic fringe firms, but creates overriding losses for domestic consumers.

In Figure 7.6, *D* represents domestic demand that is the sum of demand for the product of the foreign dominant firm *DF** and the residual domestic fringe supply *FS*. If the foreign dominant firm sets price below $80, it captures the entire domestic demand and the domestic competitive fringe supplies nothing. Domestic fringe suppliers cannot produce video players for less than $80.

At the other extreme, the domestic fringe would completely take over the market at $140. While the dominant foreign firm sets price, the domestic competitive fringe responds and with output. For any price between $80 and $140, the domestic fringe shares the market with the foreign dominant firm.

Marginal revenue *MR** for the foreign dominant firm is derived from demand *DF**. The dominant foreign firm maximizes profit by producing where *MR** equals marginal cost *MC**. In Figure 7.6 the dominant firm produces where $MR^* = MC^*$ at $Q = 80$. Price is set at $100 according to *DF**. A price of $100 leaves a residual of 20 units for the domestic fringe on *FS*. With higher costs of production, the dominant foreign firm would be forced to produce less output and at a higher price and give more of the market to the domestic fringe.

A tariff would reduce output of the dominant foreign firm and increase the market share of domestic fringe producers. Domestic consumers, however, would have to pay a higher price for less product. The tariff also produces revenue for the government. The tariff takes away some of the foreign monopoly market power and profit. Nevertheless, deadweight losses occur with the tariff and the loss in consumer surplus is larger than the potential gain.

EXAMPLE 7.5 *Import Quality and Country of Origin*

US imports have become more differentiated since the 1970s with lower quality products coming from lower wage countries as shown by Peter Schott (2001, *NBER Working Paper #W8492*). About 3/4 of all products now come from both high and low wage countries with more expensive varieties from richer countries. As an example, men's shirts imported in 1994 from Japan were 30 times as expensive as those from the Philippines. The implication is that trade data is not detailed enough to test standard factor content theory since the factor content of a product depends on the country of origin with quality variation in each category. In a related study, Schott (2001, *NBER Working Paper W8244*) shows that when products are aggregated according to quality variation rather than product category, the factor content theorem is strongly supported.

Problems for Section A

A1. Explain whether legal monopolies are more likely within a country or internationally. Do the same for natural monopolies.

A2. Why might a foreign monopoly operate temporarily at a loss? Should we be concerned if foreign firms want to export products for less than it costs to produce them?

A3. Illustrate a case of price discrimination in which home consumers pay more. How might home consumers react? Would claims of dumping be heard?

A4. Assume a foreign monopolist has constant marginal cost. Show the effects of a tariff including tariff revenue, lost profit, and the change in consumer surplus.

B. INTRAINDUSTRY TRADE

Imports are classified to apply tariffs and collect data. Television sets, computers, furniture, and plumbing fixtures are examples of the broad tariff categories. Within each category, product differentiation leads to price variation. When a country exports and imports products in the same category, it is called intra-industry trade. The theories of trade up to this point suggest that countries specialize and export some products and import others. This section looks into intraindustry trade, exporting and importing products in the same categories.

Product Differentiation

Markets ideally involve precisely defined products with no variation in quality. Basic commodities like grains and metals are graded and traders know exactly what they are buying and selling. At the other extreme, the market for used cars has no product consistency, even for a given make, model, and year. Most products fall between these extreme examples, with some *production differentiation*.

Within industrial classifications, there is a good deal of leeway for product variety. Economists distinguish between *different products* and *product differentiation*. Within any practical classification of different products, there will be some product differentiation due to quality variation.

For instance, grains are different from fruits although they are both food. Rice is different from barley, although they are both grains. Long grain rice is different from short grain rice although they are both rice. Regardless of how fine the category, some product differentiation will arise in any categories of goods.

The key to designing a workable classification scheme is its purpose. An economist wanting to make predictions about the international rice market next year might aggregate the various types of rice. If the issue is deciding the history of short grain rice or long grain rice, the products should be separated.

Classifying goods is somewhat arbitrary and leaves scope for product differentiation within the categories.

Buyers and sellers in any market, no matter how narrowly defined, are familiar with their product. Firms competing internationally are the experts in their particular markets and they know the products better than anybody else because it is their business. Economists work with categories of products designed by governments interested in applying tariffs and quotas. Categories such as yarn, glass, toys and games, medical products, alcoholic beverages, and telecommunications apparatus leave a lot of room for different products and finer classifications. When goods are disaggregated into a finer classification scheme, product differentiation within each category falls.

EXAMPLE 7.6 *Falling Intraindustry Trade*

The level of trade within an "industry" decreases when industry categories are narrower. As a product narrows (from electronics to computers to laptops) it is less likely to be both imported and exported. An index of intraindustry trade is

$$I = (X - M)/(X + M)$$

If a product is only exported, $I = 1$. If a product is only imported, $I = -1$. If export revenue and import spending for a product are identical, there is perfect intraindustry trade and $I = 0$. As an example, $I = 0.21$ for US harvesting machines in 1985. Part of this category is parts, and for parts $I = 0.47$. There is more intraindustry trade for the broader category. Herbert Grubel and Peter Lloyd (1975) show that intraindustry trade in Australia declines from 43% of total trade in the broadest classification scheme to 6% in the narrowest.

Intraindustry Trade

Intraindustry trade occurs if products in the same category are imported and exported. Cost differences in producing different qualities of a product can lead to intraindustry trade. A consumer buying a shirt, for instance, is interested in shirt *service* including days of dress, warmth, and style. Higher quality means better service in the market for shirt services. Increased quality costs more, implying higher marginal cost.

Figure 7.7 illustrates marginal costs of two qualities of shirts along with the demand D for shirt services. This monopolistic firm distinguishes between the two qualities. Profit is maximized for each quality of shirt by producing where MR equals that MC. The firm will sell 10 units of the high quality shirt for $20, and 20 units of the low quality shirt at $15.

If production of the high quality shirt is capital intensive, a capital abundant country would specialize in it. Labor abundant country would specialize in producing the labor intensive low quality shirt. Consumers in both countries want both types of shirts and *intraindustry trade* occurs.

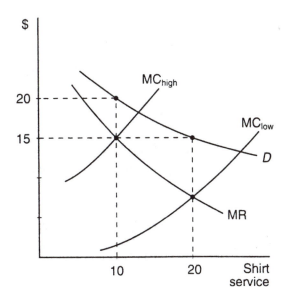

Figure 7.7
Quality Differentiation and Price
When quality varies, consumers demand the services the product provides. A high quality shirt has a higher cost of production than a low quality version. This firm would produce a lower quantity and charge a higher price for the high quality shirt.

Intraindustry trade is the simultaneous export and import of products in the same category. Given the finest classification scheme, about one quarter of all international trade is intraindustry. Increasing the classifications would decrease the level of intraindustry trade.

Another cause of intraindustry trade is transport costs, both international and domestic. Often international shipping is cheaper than crossing land within a country. In large countries, border regions are often closer to other countries for purposes of trade than to domestic regions on the other border. This difference in transport cost gives rise to *border trade*.

As one example, Texas is closer to Central America than to New York. As another, the US exports chemicals from California and imports them from Europe due to the lower cost of shipping at sea compared to across land or through the Panana Canal. Location and transport costs explain a good deal of intraindustry trade.

Intraindustry trade occurs when the same category of good is imported and exported. Intraindustry trade has numerous causes.

Goods with high intraindustry trade are envelopes, transformers, plumbing fixtures, machine tool accessories, synthetic rubber, fans, and sheet metal. Goods within each category have a high degree of price dispersion, reflecting quality variation. Goods more narrowly defined have less price dispersion and less intraindustry trade: women's handbags, soap, radios, TV sets, leather gloves, costume jewelry, refrigerators, and vacuum cleaners.

Manufactured goods are more differentiated than primary products and agricultural goods. As countries develop, they produce a higher ratio of manufactured to agricultural goods. Theory correctly predicts that DCs would have higher levels of intraindustry trade than LDCs.

EXAMPLE 7.7   *Explaining Intraindustry Trade*

Intraindustry trade depends on national and industrial characteristics as well as the level of aggregation. Elizabeth Wickham and Henry Thompson (1989) show that larger and more capital abundant countries have more intraindustry trade. Smaller labor abundant countries produce more homogeneous products, raw materials and basic manufactures. A higher degree of product differentiation revealed by more price variation within a product category implies more intraindustry trade.

Monopolistic Competition and Trade

Firms selling differentiated products have price searching power and face downward sloping demand. Firms making positive economic profit, however, attract other firms to enter the industry. Entry reduces the demand for each firm

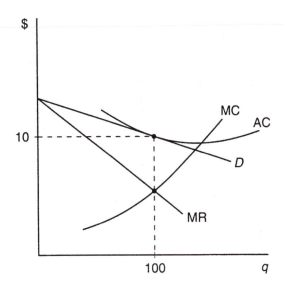

Figure 7.8
A Typical Firm in Monopolistic Competition
This firm faces downward sloping demand and marginal revenue. It maximizes profit
where $MR = MC$ with output $q = 100$ and price = \$10 according to demand. Competition
pushes cost to zero economic profit where price = AC.

and may push up input prices due to competitive bidding. As firms enter, consumers have more substitutes and the demand for each firm falls and becomes
more elastic. With free entry, the result is zero profit. An industry with some
monopoly power but zero profit in the long run is *monopolistic competition.*

Many firms face downward sloping demand for their output because consumers recognize brand name. Such firms are price searchers but market power
is limited and competition can drive profit to zero in the long turn. Monopolistic
competition seems to describe various consumer products.

Figure 7.8 illustrates a monopolistic competition firm with zero profit. The
firm maximizes profit where $MC = MR$ by producing 100 units of output and
price of \$10 equals average cost AC.

When firms are located in different countries and consumers have similar
tastes across countries, intraindustry trade occurs. If domestic firms enjoy positive
profit, entry by foreign firms can lower demand for domestic firms and drive
profit to zero. Increasing intraindustry trade would lower profits in the domestic
industry. A tariff raises demand for domestic firms, increasing profit but attracting
entry of more domestic firms. Profits rise temporarily with a tariff but the
foreign government might retaliate.

When a country is open to free trade, domestic firms are forced to compete
with foreign firms. Suppose the protected domestic automobile industry is making
a positive economic profit and the country moves to free trade. Foreign firms

enter the industry and drive domestic firms toward zero profit with monopolistic competition. Foreign firms make a domestic industry more competitive. The competitive influence of free trade limits market power and encourages efficient production.

EXAMPLE 7.8   *Intraindustry Beer Trade*

The level of international competition, intraindustry trade, and licensing in beer is increasing according to Jeffrey Karrenbrock (1990). International trade in beer is limited by its short shelf life and high transport cost. Foreign firms license production to domestic breweries. Licensed US beer production in Canada, for instance, was 17 times the level of exports to Canada. The countries below are ranked according to the index of intraindustry trade *I*. A value closer to 0 signifies more intraindustry trade. France has the most intraindustry trade but exports only a small share of its output in the *X/Q* variable. Ireland and the Netherlands are the most involved exporters. Consumers in Denmark and Czechoslovakia did not have the option of imported beer due to protection in the late 1980s and import spending *M* relative to consumption *C* was zero.

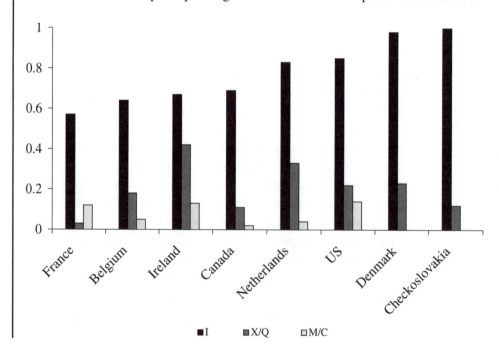

Problems for Section B

B1. The US imports cars with a wide range of quality. Why would a VER on Japanese imports raise the quality of imported cars? What will happen to domestic quality with a VER?

B2. Suppose there are three goods: food, clothing, and household goods. What are the advantages of aggregating clothing and household goods into a new category called manufactured goods? What happens to the level of intraindustry trade with aggregation?

B3. In monopolistic competition with profit below normal, describe what will happen to the number of firms and profit of the typical firm.

EXAMPLE 7.9   *Beer, Wine, Tastes, and Trade*

> Beer is a local product with a short shelf life that is produced and consumed everywhere in the world. Wine is produced where grapes are grown and has been rising in popularity over recent decades with increasing global trade. Joshua Aizenmen and Eileen Brooks (2005, *NBER Working Paper #11228*) examine consumption across 38 countries from 1963 to 2000 and find wine consumption is catching up with beer consumption. Local tastes matters, however. Latin Americans as an example still strongly prefer beer.

C.   OLIGOPOLIES

An industry with only a few firms is an *oligopoly*. In an international oligopoly, the firms are in different countries. An oligopoly can create a range of competition from pure monopoly power to competition. This section examines production and trade in oligopoly markets.

Collusion and Antitrust

Firms in an oligopoly have the incentive to *collude* and act like a monopoly. With only a few firms in an industry, collusion is feasible. Collusion raises price and reduces output, increasing monopoly power. Acting like a monopoly maximizes total profit for all firms together but they face the problem of splitting the profit. *Cartels* must agree on how to restrict output to attain a higher price.

Collusion across international borders is more difficult but is legal and certainly occurs. There are a number of international cartels, mainly in primary industries such as oil, rubber, coffee, tea, and bananas. The various firms try to agree to produce and price their product as though they were a monopoly. *Cartel quotas* limit the production of each firm.

Antitrust laws are designed to limit monopoly power and collusion. Some governments encourage collusive behavior because of increased market "stability". There are no international antitrust laws. As countries become more integrated international laws governing industrial behavior may begin to develop. *International law* is certainly a growing legal field.

EXAMPLE 7.10   *Banana and Aircraft Export Taxes*

There are no export taxes in the US because the American colonists were tired of sending export tax revenue to the King of England and made export taxes unconstitutional. Other countries tax exports. OPEC has a less famous cousin UPEB, the Union de Paises Exportadores de Banano. UPEB is a weak cartel among LDCs in Central America and Africa. Jessica Bailey and James Sood (1987) propose an export tax to maximize banana revenue. The tax would raise price to the calculated monopoly level, helping producers attain a monopoly price. Fewer bananas would be sold but total export revenue would increase. The remaining problems would be to split the profit and maintain a production quota. The US has some market power in the aircraft industry and might tax aircraft exports if it were constitutional, but competition from the EU might make that a moot point.

Kinked Demand

The dilemma of an oligopoly firm is illustrated in Figure 7.9. Suppose the price charged by the firm is $100 and it has the option of raising or lowering price to increase profit.

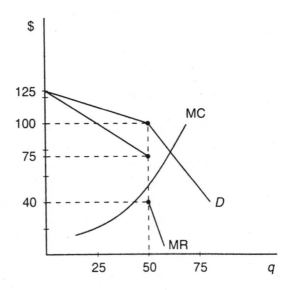

Figure 7.9
The Kinked Demand Curve of an Oligopoly
Suppose the current price is $100 and quantity is 50. If the oligopolist raises price, competing firms will not follow suit and demand is elastic. If the oligopolist lowers price, the competition does also and demand is inelastic. Revenue falls whether the firm lowers or raises price. This kink in *D* creates a break in *MR* and makes it difficult to predict oligopoly behavior.

If the oligopoly firm raises price, consumers buy cheaper substitutes and some of the substitutes could be imports. Other firms in the industry, including foreign firms, enjoy increased demand for their products. In terms of percentages, the decrease in quantity demanded is likely to be larger in absolute value than the increase in price. Revenue of this oligopoly firm falls with the price increase. Demand facing the oligopoly firm is elastic for price moves above $100.

If the oligopoly firm lowers price, other firms have to do the same to keep from losing customers. Foreign exporting firms also lower their price. The percentage increase in the quantity demanded of the firm's output is likely to be less than the absolute value of the percentage drop in price. Revenue of the oligopoly firm falls with the price reduction. Demand is inelastic for price moves below $100.

The demand curve facing this firm is *kinked*. Revenue declines for the oligopoly firm whether price is raised or lowered. Kinked demand implies a broken marginal revenue curve. Changing costs will not necessarily lead to a price change. If other firms lower their price, demand facing this firm will fall but the firm may not change its price.

Each firm in an oligopoly faces a similar dilemma and all firms including foreign ones tend to keep price and output constant. This can occur with an explicit cartel agreement or simply through informal monitoring of prices, outputs, and profits.

In an international market, a domestic oligopoly firm must contend with foreign firms selling locally as it tries to penetrate foreign markets. Foreign firms may try to collude and act like a monopoly and the domestic firm may be tempted to join them. Prices and outputs seem likely to move erratically as firms jockey for profit. In international markets, erratic price movements are more likely because distance, culture, laws, and language separate firms. International collusion is more difficult than domestic collusion but legal and possible.

EXAMPLE 7.11 *Quotas and Domestic Downgrading*

Quotas may cause import quality upgrading as foreign exporters aim to increase revenue per unit sold given the limit on the number of units. Examples include US imports of compact pickup trucks and cheese. A more ominous theoretical result uncovered by Randy Beard and Henry Thompson (2003) is that quotas definitely cause domestic quality downgrading. The domestic producer receives quantity protection from the quota and raises output but reduces quality to the monopoly level. Foreign quality upgrading may occur only relative to domestic quality and is more likely in markets with low quality imports. This theoretical result has not been tested but it presents another potential reason to avoid quotas in markets with quality differentiation.

Table 7.1 An International Duopoly Game
(Home Profit, Foreign Profit)

		Foreign Output	
		Low	High
Home Output	**Low**	($1 mil, $1 mil)	(−$1 mil, $2 mil)
	High	($2 mil, −$1 mil)	($0, $0)

An International Duopoly

A *duopoly* is an oligopoly with only two firms. A duopoly with a home and a foreign firm is an *international duopoly*. Each firm has the option of producing a high or a low output level. Capital machinery might be "chunky" and the firms have to choose low or high output. The profit of each firm depends on its choice and the choice of the other firm. In such a setting, *game theory* can predict how the two firms might behave.

Table 7.1 presents the outcomes with home profit first in parentheses. For instance, if the home firm produces high output and the foreign firm produces low output, profit for the home firm is $2 million and the foreign firm loses $1 million. If both firms produce high output, they both break even with competitive zero economic profit. If the two firms collude and restrict output by producing at low levels, they split monopolistic profit of $2 million.

Collusion and the resulting $1 million profit are preferred to the competitive outcome of zero profit. A dilemma arises in the temptation to cheat on the cartel. If the foreign firm cheats on the cartel by producing high output, it takes $2 million profit and forces the home firm to suffer a loss of $1 million. The home firm can also cheat and cause the foreign firm to suffer a loss.

If this game is repeated, the firms have the incentive to collude and restrict output. An international cartel between the two firms restricts output, resulting a higher international price and profit for the members.

Regardless of the choice made by the foreign firm, the home firm will benefit by producing high output. The game is symmetric and the same is true for the foreign firm. Given a correct guess about the opponent's behavior, each firm will produce high output. If both firms produce high output, however, they make zero profit in a competitive equilibrium. Zero economic profit is the equilibrium in a purely competitive industry. A duopoly may be as competitive as pure competition, depending on the structure of outcomes, the strategy adopted by the players, and their willingness to uphold a cartel agreement.

Both firms will do better by producing high output regardless of the opponent's choice, and the competitive outcome is a *stable equilibrium*. To build an international cartel, the home firm could restrict its own output one year suffering a loss. The foreign firm notices and the home firm established credibility as a cartel member. The foreign firm may then decide to restrict output as well. If the home firm continues to restrict output, an effective cartel has been established. Such a cartel does not require an organization such as OPEC. Consistent cartel behavior is all that is required to establish and maintain cartel profit.

EXAMPLE **7.12** *International Aerospace Oligopoly*

The US remains the world leader in the aerospace industry according to *Aerospace Magazine*. Boeing, Lockheed, and Raytheon are the major US firms. EU Airbus and British Aerospace are also major producers. Boeing and Airbus compete for long term contracts. The two major producers compete to design and sell new and more efficient aircraft. Both design and sell military aircraft and are parts of the "military industrial complex" described by President Dwight Eisenhower in the 1950s.

Sustaining an International Cartel

Payoffs for collusion can be large but cartel arrangements generally break down. International cartels have a hard time holding together during periods of falling demand and prices. Nevertheless, OPEC has enjoyed more success and lasted longer than experts predicted when it formed. The recurring problem for OPEC is keeping its members from selling more than their alloted *cartel quota*. The war in Kuwait caused a split in OPEC as some members produced more to fill the lost production. Whether OPEC can hold together remains to be seen since production by other countries makes collusion more difficult.

In 1997, OPEC accounted for 42% of world oil output. Saudi Arabia had the largest share, 11% of world output. The US produced 10% of world output, the rest of the Americas 16%, Russia and the former USSR 10%, and the North Sea 8%. The US and Canada consumed 28% of world oil, Asia 25%, the EU 20%, and Latin America 9%. OPEC faces competition from other sources. Oil prices generally fell in the 1990s from about $30 per barrel to a low of $10. In 1999, OPEC countries agreed to quotas and prices rebounded to over $25 per barrel. Production costs in some of the OPEC countries is lower than in others, making the quotas difficult to maintain. Prospects are that oil prices will rise with or without OPEC due to increasing scarcity.

International cartels easily break down into competition. Members often have too much to gain by breaking the agreement and selling at the high price. When OPEC speaks of wanting an orderly world oil market, it hopes to avoid increased output by its members and subsequent falling prices. In an oligopoly, price may move around as firms try to outguess their competition. Consumers benefit from the competitive prices of a cartel collapse. A sigh of relief can be heard from the industrial importing countries when negotiations in an OPEC meeting break down.

> *Strategies of firms determine the outcome of an international oligopoly. There are various possible strategies and no general conclusions.*

Oligopolies are made more competitive by the *threat of entry*. Potential entrants closely observe the industry and high profits encourage entry. Existing firms may behave more competitively to discourage entry. Existing firms can discourage potential entrants by making a *credible threat* to lower price. Oligopoly firms may try to keep price near the competitive level to discourage entry. Other sorts of *nonprice competition* such as advertising can also discourage entry. In a *contestable market*, the threat of competition can be as forceful as the real thing.

EXAMPLE 7.13 *Pricing to Market*

When a currency appreciates, prices of its exports for buyers in foreign countries rise. For an exporting monopolist, appreciation causes declines in demand and marginal revenue. The monopolist has the option of lowering price to keep the foreign currency price of its product constant and protect its share of the foreign market. Michael Knetter (1989) finds German exporters price to the US market but US exporters do not price to foreign markets. The dollar depreciation of the late 1980s did not raise the US trade deficit, in part because prices of imports were kept low with foreign pricing to market.

Subsidies for an International Duopoly

Suppose a US firm (Boeing) and an EU firm (Airbus) face the decision of whether to produce and export a new type of passenger jet. Paul Krugman (1987) examines such an international duopoly and questions whether a government subsidy might lead to higher profit.

Table 7.2 presents profits with and without production of the jet, a *one time game*. The decision about whether to produce must be made by the 1st of January. Boeing's profit is first in parentheses. If Boeing correctly guesses that Airbus will produce, Boeing will not produce because zero profit is better than −5. If Boeing correctly guesses that Airbus will not produce, Boeing will be making a profit of 100. If Boeing produces and Airbus does not, Airbus is trapped. Subsequent production by Airbus would create a loss of −5. Once Boeing is established, entry by Airbus is deterred.

The EU government may want to subsidize Airbus to encourage it to begin production before Boeing. The cost of the subsidy may be less than the profit

Table 7.2 A Duopoly Dilemma
(Boeing Profit, Airbus Profit)

		Airbus	
		Produce	**Don't Produce**
Boeing	**Produce**	(−5, 5)	(100, 0)
	Don't Produce	(0, 100)	(0, 0)

enjoyed by Airbus if Boeing is deterred. Such *strategic trade policy* may seem like a good idea.

Governments, however, cannot be expected to recognize or react to such situations. Economists know the theory but typically very little about particular industries, and all industries want a subsidy. Government policy is subject to the whims of politics. Reality is much more complicated than the simple situation in Table 7.2. It is wise to leave important risky business decisions to the experts in the industry, the firms competing with each other in the market. Subsidies based on the theory of strategic trade policy are not recommended.

EXAMPLE 7.14 *Japanese Pricing to Market*

Manufacturers of Japanese transport equipment and electrical machinery price to market according to Richard Marston (1998). These firms adjust yen prices to foreign markets to maintain foreign currency prices. A wedge is driven between the price in Japan and yen export prices. Both planned price changes and changes due to unanticipated exchange rate changes can be seen in the data. Japanese, Canadian, and German exporters to the US are more inclined to price to market than are US exporters according to Michael Knetter (1993). Exporters to the US sell in competitive markets and must keep dollar prices close to the competition while US exporters maintain the dollar prices of their products with less worry about foreign currency prices and competition.

Problems for Section C

C1. Suppose cost rises for the firm in Figure 7.9 so *MC* intersects *MR* at $100 and $q = 25$. Find the price. Explain how other firms in the industry would react to this firm's higher price. Find and explain the change in revenue.

C2. When OPEC income increased dramatically during the 1970s, the OPEC countries did not spend it all. What had to happen?

C3. With an oil import elasticity of −0.6 and a price increase from $20 to $22, find the percentage change in the level of imports. What are the two sources of this decrease? If OPEC raises price to $40, find the reduction in imports. What happens to OPEC revenue with these price increases?

D. OTHER CAUSES OF TRADE

Four supplemental trade theories are *differences in technology*, the *product cycle*, *increasing returns* and *differences in income*.

Technology and Trade

Production depends on *technology*, the processes used to combine various inputs into outputs. Economists look for evidence of differing technologies by estimating *production functions* that describe relationships between inputs and outputs. Firms in different countries may employ the same amounts of capital, labor, and natural resource inputs but get different outputs because of differences in technology.

Figure 7.10 shows unit isoquants of two production functions with different technologies for producing the same good. The same amount of output is produced along isoquant t_1 or t_2.

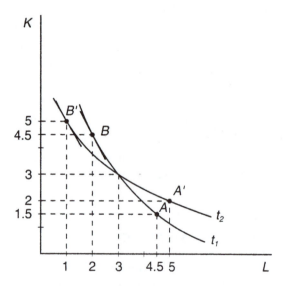

Figure 7.10
Production with Different Technologies
Isoquants t_1 and t_2 represent different ways to produce the same amount of output with different technologies. Less of both inputs may result in the same output, illustrated by A and A'. Cost minimizing inputs will vary, illustrated by B and B'. Different technologies can result in international trade.

When labor input is high, technology t_1 can produce the same output with less of both inputs. At point A, 1.5 units of capital and 4.5 labor result in 1 unit of output with technology t_1. With technology t_2, 2 K and 5 L are required to produce the same unit of output at A′.

If factor prices were the same in two countries, a different mix of inputs would be used according to technology. Points B and B′ illustrate different cost minimizing inputs for the same input prices.

To understand the importance of technology, suppose two countries have identical factor endowments and the same number of consumers with identical preferences. Different technologies would provide an incentive to trade. If the home country has better technology for producing services and the foreign country better technology for producing manufactures, total output in the world rises if the two specialize. Each country can potentially consume more of both goods.

Technology differences across countries can be an incentive for international specialization and trade.

Different input ratios alone give no indication of differing technology. When a firm minimizes cost, it picks the optimal mix of inputs depending on their costs. Firms in different countries using the same technology are likely to use different input quantities when the relative input prices differ. Firms produce with the same production functions, but mix inputs according to local costs making it difficult to determine whether technology varies.

Labor abundant LDCs economize by using labor intensively even with the same production functions as developed countries. Multinational firms are becoming more prevalent, making the same technology available around the world. LDCs send students to the DCs to become familiar with the latest technology. Knowledge quickly becomes a public good and advantages in technology are difficult to maintain. Technology is a public good and technology differences may not explain much international trade.

EXAMPLE 7.15 *Unexposed Manufactures*

The OECD keeps track of various measures of protection and reports the following for 1999 manufacturing industries across countries: average tariffs, NTB share, imports/production, and a measure of exposure. The average tariffs for the US, EU, and Japan are fairly low with the EU the highest at 8%. NTB is the percentage of products subject to nontariff barriers and the three countries are similar. For the second two measures, a larger percentage implies more open manufacturing. Measuring import spending M relative to consumption C, EU manufacturing is again less involved in trade and the US the most involved. Exposure E includes both imports and exports and is constructed to range from 0 with $X = M = 0$ to 100% with $M = C$ and $X = 0$. Japanese manufacturing is the least exposed, consistent with the Japanese *kerietsu* system of trade associations and closed vertical integration. The US has by far the most exposed manufacturing, and is the most involved internationally across all measures.

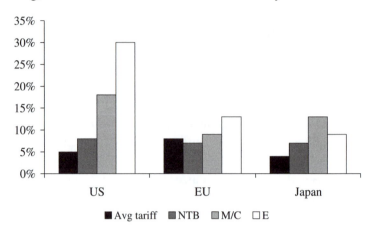

The Product Cycle and Trade

One proxy to measure technology is spending on research and development (R&D). Table 7.3 shows shares of worldwide spending on R&D. Developed countries do almost all of the R&D, some of which is aimed at labor saving

Table 7.3 Shares of World R&D Spending

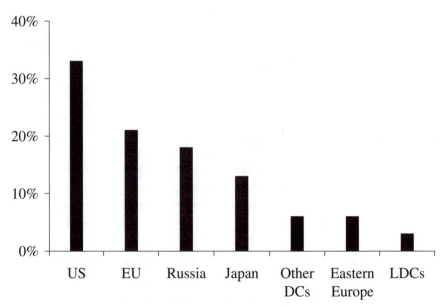

Source: *Trade and Development Report*, United Nations Conference on Trade and Development, 1987, New York: UN.

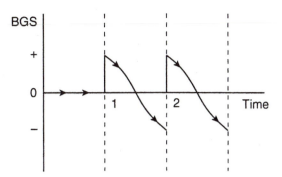

Figure 7.11
The Product Cycle and Trade
The research and development (R&D) country creates innovations at times 1 and 2 resulting in trade surpluses as the new product is exported. Over time, other nations copy the technology and the R&D country loses market power and slips into deficit. Innovations lead to new products that jump the R&D country back to a surplus.

production techniques. In 1985, 27% of US exports were goods using a high intensity of R&D while 9% used low R&D intensity. DCs will continue to develop and exploit comparative advantage in high tech products. Exports with high levels of R&D relates to the product cycle.

The pattern of production and trade that the product cycle predicts is the export of new products from DCs in exchange for low tech products from LDCs. As time passes, new products are picked up by the LDCs and production begins there. Products cycle from new to old and from DCs to LDCs.

New products may require substantial R&D, costly for the firm which must hope for future revenue to recover the cost R&D. Countries with relatively large supplies of scientists and engineers (US, EU, Japan) should have a comparative advantage in developing new products. Goods produced with established techniques require no R&D and LDCs have the comparative advantage in low tech production.

The product cycle is illustrated in Figure 7.11. New products are unveiled at times 1 and 2. The R&D country exports the new products following their development. The R&D country holds a monopoly position in the new product and makes high export revenue. As time passes, LDCs learn to make the new products and begin low cost manufacturing. Soon the DC becomes a net importer of the good and moves to a trade deficit in that product.

Products cycle from new to old and production shifts from innovative to copying countries. Countries putting resources into R&D are net exporters of new products.

Firms that develop new products may plan on eventually being run out of the business but hope to make enough renevue to cover R&D costs for a time.

Data from the United Nations Committee on Trade and Development (UNCTAD) show that exports of manufactures from LDCs to DCs have the largest market shares in low R&D products just as product cycle theory predicts. For low, medium, and high R&D industries, these market shares are 25%, 8%, and 12% respectively. In the low R&D category, the largest market shares are in textiles, clothing, footwear, and leather (38% of all low-tech exports together) and petroleum refineries (40% of low-tech exports). While there may be some innovation in the production of these goods, techniques are well established. In the medium R&D category, the largest market share is nonferrous metal (41%) while in the high R&D category the largest is electronic components (29%). Although classified as a high R&D industry, the production of electronic components is largely standardized and routine. These figures provide some support for the product cycle.

Trade via the product cycle would be more prevalent if DCs did not protect their domestic labor intensive industries. According to 1983 data from GATT, the ratio of manufactured imports from LDCs to total consumption in the US was only 3%. Of the total consumption of manufactures in the US, only 3% was imports from LDCs. Protection may discourage LDCs from adapting routine manufacturing processes. Protection on imports from LDCs should be eliminated.

EXAMPLE 7.16 *R&D and High Tech Exports*

The US has almost half of the R&D scientists in the world according to the National Science Foundation. The US has a comparative advantage in developing new products and leads other countries in the product cycle. Japan and Europe have increased R&D workers since the 1960s. Beyond the US, EU, and Japan, the rest of the world has less than 10% of all R&D scientists. The US has consistent export surpluses in high tech products including aircraft, computers, office equipment, electrical equipment, medical equipment, medicines, plastics, engines, chemicals, and scientific equipment.

Returns to Scale and Trade

Returns to scale refer to how changing inputs affect output in a firm's production. There are *constant returns to scale* (CRS) when a proportional change in all inputs results in a proportional change in output. For instance, output doubles if a firm doubles all of its inputs. With *increasing returns to scale* (IRS) output would more than double. With *decreasing returns to scale* (DRS) output would rise by less than 100%.

Returns to scale can be external or internal to the firm. *External* influences include transportation, communication, utility infrastructure, local suppliers, and

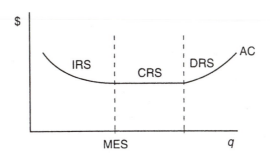

Figure 7.12
Internal Returns to Scale of the Firm
Average cost (*AC*) is decreasing with increasing returns to scale (IRS) up to the minimum efficient scale (*MES*). *AC* is constant in the region of constant returns to scale (CRS). *AC* rises when the firm experiences decreasing returns to scale (DRS).

trained workers. As output expands, the firm becomes more productive if these improve.

Internal returns to scale may occur due to capital equipment. Machines might be used more efficiently as output increases. Proportional increases in inputs then lead to more than proportional increases in output. Nothing outside the firm changes with internal IRS.

Average cost may decrease up to the *minimum efficient scale (MES)*. Declining average costs reflect internal IRS. Figure 7.12 illustrates a typical long run average cost curve with the firm choosing the optimal level of all inputs. The long run AC curve illustrates the lowest cost of producing the range of outputs (*q*). With IRS, *AC* declines. In the region of CRS, *AC* is constant. With DRS, *AC* rises. As the firm expands, DRS might occur due to problems of organization or communication inside the firm. Supervision may become a problem in larger firms, workers may not feel related to the success of a large impersonal organization, and so on. DRS, however, has rarely been uncovered in practice.

With IRS, the firm operates at an output below its minimum efficient scale (*MES*). A firm producing output less than its *MES* could not compete with other firms at their *MES* using the same technology and buying inputs in competitive markets. Firms are typically observed operating in the region of CRS with flat *AC*. IRS would occur at low levels of output. When a firm enters an industry, it could be forced to produce low output and operate in the region of declining AC. Firms considering entry, however, must know their *MES* and would not enter unless they could reach it and effectively compete.

Imagine two countries identical in every way, with IRS. By itself, IRS would provide an incentive to specialize and trade. The two countries could specialize in one good or the other to increase export production. With specialization, world output would be higher and both countries would enjoy higher income.

While IRS and decreasing AC may play a role for some industries at some times, there is little evidence that IRS is fundamental to the overall pattern of trade. Firms tend to operate with CRS.

EXAMPLE 7.17 *IPRs*

Improved intellectual property rights of patent protection would raise the level of trade. Keith Maskus and Mohan Penubarti (1995) find evidence across LDCs that increased patent protection increases the level of trade. Products patented in DCs have to be imported. Foreign firms with patents do not want to sell to countries where their product could be copied and produced locally for consumption or export.

EXAMPLE 7.18 *Returns to Scale & Economic Geography*

The two main causes of trade are the availability of factors of production and increasing returns to scale, and there are differences in opinions about which is more important. Factor proportions models do not perform consistently in tests but there are issues of data, model building, and hypothesis testing. Donald Davis and David Weinstein (1995, 1998) have made important contributions to the empirical testing of trade theory, finding that factor endowments explain almost all trade when models are carefully specified. Most importantly, the cost minimizing factor mix of each country must be used in the tests. The implication that increasing returns less important in the data is not a surprise since there is little evidence of it at the industry level. The geography of production is important for trade, with transport costs and national borders contributing to the explanation of observed patterns of inter-regional and international trade.

Income Effects and Trade

Income affects demand and countries with higher income consume more services and luxury goods. Consumers in low income countries spend income on basics such as food, shelter, and clothing. While comparative advantage determines the pattern of production, income contributes to the pattern of consumption.

The *income elasticity* of a good is the percentage change in quantity demanded divided by the percentage change in income:

$$E_I = \%\Delta Q / \%\Delta Y$$

Goods with positive income elasticities are called *normal goods*. When income rises, the quantity demanded of a normal good rises. Most products are normal.

A positive income elasticity less than one makes the good a *necessity*. A 10% increase in income leads to an increase of less than 10% for necessities like food, transportation, housing, and clothing.

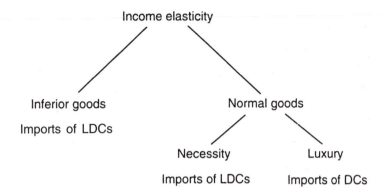

Figure 7.13
Income Elasticity and Trade
Less developed countries (LDCs) have low incomes and tend to import inferior goods and necessities. Developed countries (DCs) have high incomes and tend to import luxury goods.

A good with an income elasticity greater than one is a *luxury good*. If income rises by 10%, consumption of luxury goods like steaks, foreign travel, imported cheese, and restaurant meals rises more than 10%.

Goods with negative income elasticities are *inferior goods*. Higher income leads to less consumption of inferior goods. Examples of inferior goods are public transport, used clothing, economy cars, and red beans.

High income countries tend to import luxury goods while poor countries tend to import necessities and inferior goods.

Figure 7.13 illustrates the associated pattern of trade between DCs and LDCs. If production of inferior goods, necessities, and luxury goods is uniform across countries, LDCs would be net importers of necessities and inferior goods while DCs would be net importers of luxury goods. Imports of high income countries in fact include more luxury goods and LDCs import larger shares of necessities. Income and trade composition are linked.

Linda Hunter and James Markusen (1988) use data from 34 countries to study the effect of income on trade in 10 basic commodities and their estimated income elasticities are in Table 7.4. Four of the goods are necessities with income elasticities below 1: food, furniture, fuel, and education. A 10% increase in income would raise the quantity of food consumed by 5%, furniture 8%, fuel and power 8%, and education 9%. Low income countries should be net importers of these goods. The rest of the goods are luxuries. A 10% increase in income brings about a 19% increase in medical services, not typically viewed as a luxury item. Low income countries simply rely on folk medicine and home treatment. Recreation fits the concept of a luxury good. The influence of income on consumption patterns across countries is significant but there is no empirical

Table 7.4 Estimated Income Elasticities

Source: *Empirical Methods for International Trade*, Robert Feenstra, ed., 1988, Cambridge: MIT Press.

connection between income and trade, suggesting the location of production is critical.

The Bottom Line on Other Trade Theories

The supplemental theories in this section contribute to an overall understanding of international trade and can be applied to various issues. In particular markets, one or the other of these other theories may explain observed trade.

Factor proportions theory remains the fundamental tool for explaining international patterns of production and trade. The relative abundance of different skills of labor, productive capital, and natural resources is the fundamental explanation of international trade.

EXAMPLE 7.19 *Coca Production and the International Drug Market*

The tropical Chapare region in Bolivia specializes in producing coca leaf used to manufacture cocaine as well as some traditional and commercial legal products. Hugo Toledo (2005) analyzes how much it would cost to eliminate illegal coca production using a model of production and trade for the region. Small competitive farmers earn $3000 per acre from selling coca leaves but perhaps only a third as much under government programs to eradicate coca and substitute other commercial crops such as pineapples, bananas, and pepper. Low wage workers in the region are especially vulnerable, facing decreases in income of up to 25% with coca elimination. The social unrest in Bolivia will worsen unless incomes can be maintained at the level of illegal coca production. The cocaine is exported suggesting countries like the US wanting to control the international drug market might directly compensate workers and landowners in Chapare. Lowering the quantity of cocaine traded, however, will require a reduction in demand.

Problems for Section D

D1. Draw the PPFs of a home country with better technology for producing food and a foreign country with better technology for producing clothing. Suppose they are identical otherwise. Show the pattern of specialization and trade.
D2. Would it be wiser for a DC to spend resources protecting its steel industry or developing new steel products?
D3. What do income elasticities predict regarding international trade in inferior goods? Explain what must be assumed about production.

EXAMPLE 7.20 *Regional Competition in Mexico*

Large countries are made up of economic regions that typically adjust differently to free trade. Mexico is an example, opening to free trade in 1985 after decades of misguided import substitution and subsidized nationalized monopolistic industry as described by Gordon Hanson (1998). With free trade, industry became competitive and moved north toward the US border away from congested polluted Mexico City. The attraction was lower transport costs to the US and closer vertical supply chains for intermediate products. Hanson makes the point that northern Mexico is an economic region that includes the southwestern US with little in common with central or southern Mexico, or for that matter with other regions in the US.

CONCLUSION

The industrial organization in this chapter adds some depth to the explanation of international trade. Monopoly power and competition among oligopoly firms characterize some international markets. International economics includes any theory that might help explain trade in particular circumstances. Still, factor proportions trade theory remains the foundation. The next chapter covers the important topics of international labor migration and capital flows.

Terms

Cartel quota	Luxury good
Collusion	Minimum efficient scale (MES)
Contestable market	Monopolistic competition
Credible threat	Necessity
Dominant and fringe firms	Oligopoly
Income elasticity	Price discrimination and dumping
Inferior good	Price taker versus price searcher
International duopoly	Product cycle
International monopoly	Product differentiation
Intraindustry trade	Returns to scale
Kinked demand curve	Technology and trade
Legal versus natural monopoly	Trigger price mechanism

MAIN POINTS

- A price searching monopoly restricts output and raises price relative to a competitive firm. A tariff on imports from a foreign monopolist takes away some of the monopoly profit.
- Product differentiation is a source of monopoly power and can lead to intra-industry trade in monopolistically competitive industries. The level of product differentiation and intradindustry trade increases as goods are aggregated.
- Firms in an international oligopoly have the incentive to collude and form a cartel to collect monopoly profit. Depending on the structure of payoffs and strategic behavior, oligopolies can be as competitive as industries with many firms.
- There are supplemental theories of international trade: different technologies, product cycle, increasing returns to scale, and income differences. Factor proportions theory, however, remains the fundamental explanation of international production and trade.

REVIEW PROBLEMS

1. Complete Figure 7.1 with an average cost curve for a domestic firm showing total profit of $300,000. Illustrate zero profit for a foreign firm. Which firm has higher costs? Could the high cost firm compete?

2. Suppose higher energy costs raise the home firm's cost in Figure 7.1 so that output drops to 1000. What is the price of the domestic firm? Predict the change in its profit. Is demand elastic? If all production is exported, what happens to export revenue?

3. Suppose a monopolist has two plants, one in the US and one in Mexico. The Mexican plant has lower unit costs. Which plant will produce

more? How does the monopolist determine the price of its export to the EU?

4. Find the monopoly profit in the example of price discrimination in Figure 7.5 separating domestic and foreign profit.

5. The following costs were estimated from steel operations in the US and Japan by Peter Marcus in *Comparative Circumstances of Major Steel Mills in the US, European Community, and Japan* (1982). Numbers represent costs per ton of steel for labor, capital machinery, and material inputs:

	Labor	Capital	Inputs
US	$209	$134	$330
Japan	$97	$171	$291

Which country spent more on labor input? What are two possible reasons? If it costs $100 per ton to ship steel to the US, find the cost of Japanese steel in the US if Japanese profit is zero. If Japanese producers make a 2% profit, find the price of Japanese steel in the US. Would US producers want to allow less than 2% profit for the Japanese producers? Where will US producers want the trigger price?

6. Using the cost data in the previous problem, suppose the ratio of wages to capital rent (w/r) is 1 in Japan and 1.4 in the US. Explain whether the country with relatively expensive labor use labor intensive production techniques.

7. Explain which categories of goods are likely to have more intraindustry trade: yarn or medical products; computers or laptop computers? Explain which categories will have less price dispersion.

8. In the international aircraft industry, suppose there is a dominant domestic firm and a competitive foreign fringe. At a price below $3 million, the foreign fringe cannot compete. At prices above $10 million, the fringe will take over the market. Diagram this market with an international price of $7 million. Show the effects on market shares of an increase in domestic costs resulting from a new labor contract.

9. Find the index I of intraindustry trade (Example 7.3) for the following categories of goods.

Figures are in millions of dollars for the US in 1985. Compare and explain the likely cause of the different levels of intraindustry trade:

	Exports	Imports
Footwear	$128	$354
Cotton	$1671	$258
Leather	$287	$425
Leather goods	$121	$374
Toys and games	$271	$2968
Automotive electric equipment	$443	$568

10. Table 7.5 presents a hypothetical duopoly production game between Saudi Arabia and Libya in the international oil market. Figures are economic profit in millions of dollars. The first figure in parentheses is Saudi Arabian profit. Find the equilibrium. Is it stable? Who has the greater incentive to cheat on a cartel agreement? How can the other discourage cartel cheating?

Table 7.5 An International Oil Game (Saudi Arabia, Libya)

		Foreign Output	
		Low	High
Home Output	Low	(30, 10)	(−20, 40)
	High	(40, −30)	(0, 0)

11. Classify the following as internal or external returns to scale:
    (a) Labor in the firm becomes more experienced
    (b) A better public port is built near the factory
    (c) New imported machines result in lower unit costs
    (d) Public schools and education are improved
    (e) International telecommunication is improved

12. Show what happens over time to the PPF as a country specializes in manufactures when there are external IRS. What happens to the level of trade with the external IRS?

READINGS

Gerald Meier (1988) *The International Environment of Business*, Oxford: Oxford University Press. International political and business institutions.

Roger Blair and David Kaserman (1985) *Antitrust Economics*, Chicago: Irwin. Tools of industrial organization and regulation.

P.K.M. Tharakan and Jacob Kol, eds. (1987) *Intra-industry Trade: Theory, Evidence, and Extensions*, New York: Macmillan. Articles on intraindustry trade.

Stefan Linder (1961) *An Essay on Trade and Transformation*, New York: Wiley. Linder's original.

Paul Krugman, ed. (1986) *Strategic Trade Policy and the New International Economics*, Cambridge: MIT Press. Some "new" trade theory.

Ryuzo Sato and Paul Wachtel, eds. (1987) *Trade Friction and Prospects for Japan and the United States*, Cambridge: Cambridge University Press. Collection of articles

Yves Bourdet (1988) *International Integration, Market Structure and Prices*, London: Routledge. Range of issues on international industrial integration and market structures.

INTERNATIONAL INTEGRATION

CHAPTER 8

International Labor and Capital

Preview

International migration and investment are based on the underlying markets for labor and capital. International labor and capital movements increase and redistribute global income. Immigration is the source of population for many countries, and international investment has stimulated most successful economies.

The main points of this chapter are:

- *International migration* arises from wage differences across countries
- *International investment* is the result of differences in the return to capital
- *Income redistribution* occurs due to international migration and investment
- International trade adjusts due to *international factor movements*

INTRODUCTION

When people leave their homes and emigrate to other countries with different languages and customs, they are typically looking for higher wages and a better standard of living. If the wage in one country is higher than the wage in another, workers have an incentive to migrate. The international difference in wages has to be large enough to offset costs of relocation and readjustment.

Capital also moves between countries. International capital movements are increasing and vital for the trade and development of most countries. International capital movement is created by variation in returns across borders. The owner of a machine wants it where it can earn a higher return. As with labor, the incentive to relocate capital is based on differences in returns.

Governments restrict and control international movements of labor and capital. There are various incentives to erect barriers to the free flow of workers and foreign investment. Laws in one country might keep out immigrants while laws in another might restrain capital from going abroad. EU law keeps its neighbors from freely entering the EU labor market where the wage is substantially higher. Restrictions in Latin America hinder US investment seeking the higher return. The primary considerations shaping migration and investment policy is the income redistribution and production adjustments due to the shifting factor supplies.

When unskilled labor immigrates, the unskilled wage falls due to its increased supply. Skilled worker and capital become more productive, however, and enjoy higher payments. When capital leaves the country, the return to the remaining plant and equipment rises because of its decrease in supply, but labor productivity and wages fall.

International factor movements also influence the prices of productive factors that are not moving. With the immigration of doctors, some factors will benefit but others will lose. Doctors inside the country see their wage fall due to the increased competition. Nurses become more productive with the increased cooperating doctors and their wage rises. Capital equipment in the medical industry becomes more productive and its return increases. The price of medical services falls with the lower wage of doctors, the price of medical insurance falls, consumers spend less on medical care, and demands for other products are affected. Outputs and income adjust in this manner to international factor movements.

These effects can be understood by studying interactions between markets for the various products and factors. An overall picture of the economy including input markets is important to understand the causes and effects of international factors movements. This chapter continues the general equilibrium approach to international production and trade.

A. INTERNATIONAL MIGRATION

A comparison of labor markets across countries explains the fundamental cause of migration. In markets for productive labor, capital, and natural resources, these factor prices are determined by market equilibrium. Labor markets determine the wages of electrical engineers, teachers, construction workers, and so on. Capital markets determine the return to investments in oil refining, the iron and steel industry, the computer industry, and so on.

EXAMPLE 8.1   *A Land of Immigrants*

Relative to most countries, the US is populated by recent immigrants. There have been periods of massive immigration into the US. From 1850 until World War I the rate of immigration averaged almost 1% of the population per year. If such an immigration rate were to occur this year, a new city as large as Minneapolis could be filled. In the first part of this century, 1 million people immigrated per year, about the current estimate of immigration. The Census Bureau predicts San Antonio will become the second largest city in the US largely due to immigration.

Marginal Revenue Product and Marginal Factor Cost

A firm gains revenue by selling the output produced by the various factors it hires. A firm's demand for a factor of production is the value of what it produces. The *marginal revenue product* (*MRP*) of a factor is its marginal revenue (*MR*) times the marginal product (*MP*) of the factor:

$$MRP = MR \times MP$$

In equilibrium, *MRP* is the value of the last unit of the input. Suppose price and *MR* of output are constant at the competitive market price of $2. If the *MP* of an extra worker is 5 units of output, $MRP = \$2 \times 5 = \$10$.

A firm would be willing to hire an input if the value of what it produces is greater than the cost of hiring it. The *marginal factor cost* (*MFC*) is what it costs to hire an extra unit of the input. The input's *MRP* must be greater than its *MFC*:

$$MRP > MFC$$

In a competitive labor market the firm can hire any number of workers it wants at the market wage and the market wage is the *MFC*. If the *MFC* of an extra worker is $8/hour and the *MRP* is $10/hour, the firm increases its profit by $2/hour hiring the worker.

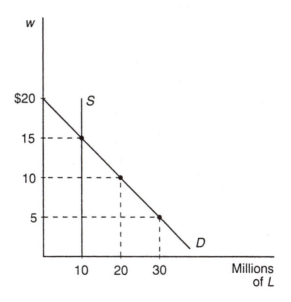

Figure 8.1
The Labor Market
Labor supply *S* is assumed to be inelastic for simplicity. This labor market clears at the market wage (*w*) of $15.

Labor Demand and Labor Supply

Figure 8.1 illustrates the *labor market*. According to the *MRP* of labor, firms will hire from 30 million workers with *MFC* = $5, to no workers if *MFC* = $20. Labor demand slopes downward due to diminishing marginal productivity.

Labor supply is the vertical line at 10 million workers. Perfectly inelastic labor supply means workers accept any wage. Labor supply slopes upward at low wages and may bend backward at higher wages where workers choose to work fewer hours and enjoy more leisure. The perfectly inelastic labor supply in Figure 8.1 simplifies analysis.

The labor market clears where labor demand equals labor supply at a wage of $15. If the wage is over $15, there is a labor surplus and workers would offer to work for a lower wage rather than remain unemployed. The wage is bid down toward the equilibrium $15. At a wage below $15, there is a labor shortage and firms would compete for available workers by bidding up the wage.

Labor markets clear where the market wage equates quantities demanded and supplied.

EXAMPLE 8.2 *International Labor Growth*

Labor growth rates are highest among the LDCs, labor abundant countries evidently trying to maintain their comparative advantage. While free trade would raise wages in the LDCs, there will be continued pressure for migration to the DCs. These figures are average annual rates from the World Bank. Labor growth rates are higher in LDCs than DCs. LDC exporters of manufactures Mfg have lower labor growth. Labor growth rates in DCs are declining.

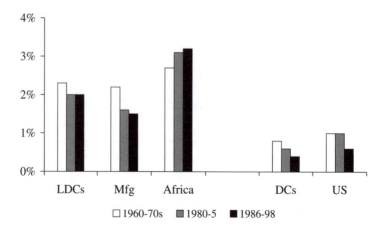

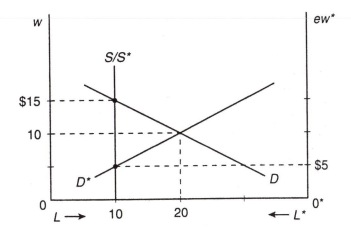

Figure 8.2
The International Labor Market
The home labor market with demand D and wage *w* is measured from origin 0. The foreign labor market with demand D* and wage *ew** is measured from 0*. There are 10 (million) workers in the home country and 30 (million) workers in the foreign country, as indicated by the relative supply line *S/S**. The home wage is $15 and the foreign wage $5.

International Labor Market

Figure 8.2 presents a picture of international wages developed by economist Stanley Jevons over 120 years ago. The vertical axis *w* measures domestic wages and relates to domestic demand D. Foreign demand for labor D* is measured from the vertical axis *ew** on the right side. The foreign wage *w** relates to the domestic wage *w* through the exchange rate *e*. The foreign wage in terms of the domestic currency is *ew**.

The length of the bottom axis represents the total endowment of labor in both countries, a total of 40 million workers. Home labor *L* is measured from the left and foreign labor *L** from the right.

The vertical supply line at *L* = 10 indicates that 10 million workers are in the home country and 30 million are abroad. Demand for labor in the two countries is the same in this example but the home labor supply is low. The home wage is found where home labor demand intersects supply at $15. Foreign labor supply is high and the foreign wage is only $5.

With no migration restrictions, workers are free to come and go between the two countries as they please. Free migration occurs in *common markets* such as the EU. Cultural differences and distance separate the two countries and relocation costs may be important.

With free migration and zero relocation cost, foreign workers would migrate to the home country where the wage is higher. *Emigration* decreases the abundant labor supply in the foreign country and *immigration* increases the scarce home supply. The supply line in Figure 8.2 shifts to the right with migration.

With zero costs, migration would continue until wages are equal internationally at $w = ew^* = \$10$ with 20 million workers in each country. World output increases with the migration because labor is moving to a capital abundant country where its marginal productivity is higher.

With migration the host country enjoys an expanding resource base. In terms of production possibilities and national income, the host country gains and the source country loses. Migrant workers typically repatriate part of their earnings, compensating the source country. Workers who remain in the source country benefit from the higher wage that results from emigration.

The distribution of a resource across countries affects international resource prices. Labor abundance results in a low wage and scarcity a high wage. Migration diminishes international wage differences.

EXAMPLE 8.3   *Recent US Immigration*

Immigration into the US has increased since 1970 and is now about 1 million per year returning to the level of the early 1900s before the disruptions of two World Wars and the Great Depression. Since 1950, immigration has grown steadily and now accounts for almost half of the yearly population increase, suggesting a much different country at the turn of the next century. At present, 53% of the foreign born in the US are from Latin America, 25% from Asia, and 13% from Europe. Income levels and unemployment rates are not much different between immigrants and native born but there are differences in occupations for immigrants from different countries. The chart below shows the steady growth in immigration since 1970 with a spike around 1990. Immigration law limits the number of legal immigrants and is decided in an ongoing political process.

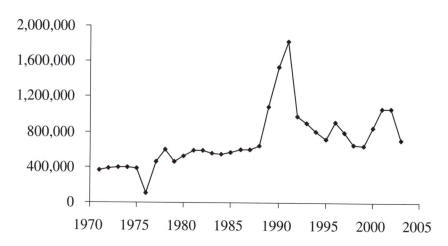

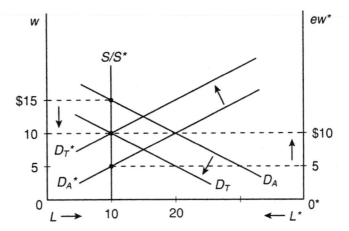

Figure 8.3
Free Trade and International Wages
With free trade, the labor abundant foreign country increases production of the labor intensive good and D_A^* rises to D_T^*. In the home country, production of the labor intensive good falls as does the demand for labor, from D_A to D_T. With free trade, wages are equalized at $w = ew^* = \$10$.

Trade and Migration

Trade between countries also leads to international equalization of wages through factor price equalization. Trade increases demands for cheap products and inputs. Free trade is a *substitute* for migration. Protectionism increases the incentive for migration.

In the international labor market of Figure 8.3, the foreign country is labor abundant and labor cheap in autarky. Autarky demands for labor in the two countries are D_A and D_A^* and supplies of labor are $L = 10$ and $L^* = 30$.

With free trade, the foreign country exports labor intensive products to the home country. The price of labor intensive goods and the demand for labor rises in the foreign country from D_A^* to D_T^*.

The home country lowers production of labor intensive goods as its prices of labor intensive goods fall. Demand for labor in the home country falls from D_A to D_T. The equilibrium with free trade occurs where D_T intersects D_T^* at $w = ew^* = \$10$.

Free trade raises the wage in the labor abundant country and lowers the wage in the labor scarce country by shifting demand while labor migration shifts supplies.

International trade is a substitute for labor migration and both lead toward equal wages across countries.

Substitution of trade for migration is part of the motivation for the EU and NAFTA. Wages will rise in low income countries due to increased production of labor intensive products and the incentive for emigration is lowered.

Free trade may be preferred politically to immigration. The choice faced by the DCs is whether to import manufactured goods from the LDCs or to continue to be inviting for immigration. Illegal immigration remains a problem and an important result of free trade is the decreased incentive for migration.

Migration creates international efficiency as labor moves to where its productivity and wage are higher. Free trade creates similar efficiency gains with specialization. Labor scarce countries like the EU and the US can discourage immigration by trading freely. Migration is a more costly way to reach international efficiency since it is easier to move products than people.

EXAMPLE 8.4   *Early US Immigrants*

Immigration to the American Colonies was open to Europeans and the population of the US in 1790 was close to 4 million including about 700,000 African slaves. About 300,000 slaves had arrived prior to the Revolution, and 100,000 more between then and the Civil War. Some English, Irish, and Germans had immigrated to the Colonies as indentured slaves serving from 4 to 14 years of labor. The slave trade ended in 1808, and African and Asians were generally excluded from immigration. Up to 1850, immigrants were generally English, Scotch-Irish, Dutch, German, and north Europeans. Most were fleeing religious political persecution. Between 1850 and the early 1900s, immigrants tended to be Italians and other central and southern Europeans, and nearly 1 million French Canadians fled Canada during this period. The early history of the US is largely a history of recent immigrants building and defining a new nation.

Legal Immigration

There are many different types of labor: physicians, laborers, engineers, butchers, machinists, accountants, bakers, college professors, fast food workers, migrant farm workers, and so on. More insight comes from examining markets for different types of labor.

High demand and low supply are the two basic influences creating high wages. Hakeem Ollajawan received a high wage for playing basketball after migrating due to his high marginal revenue product based on high demand for tickets and television, and the limited supply of quick coordinated people over seven feet tall. People who make the highest wage are the most productive workers in expanding and high priced industries. People making the lowest wage are the least productive workers in industries with low and falling prices.

Table 8.1 US Census Skilled Labor Groups

L1 = professionals
L2 = craft, repair workers
L3 = transportation workers
L4 = operatives, machine operators
L5 = administrative support, sales personnel
L6 = handlers and laborers
L7 = agricultural, forestry, fishing workers
L8 = janitors, restaurant workers, etc.

Source: Census of Population.

Every worker prefers higher to lower wages, making it important to understand wage differences.

There is data on the various skilled groups of workers listed in Table 8.1. Groups are listed from the highest paid and most skilled to the lowest paid and least skilled. Projections of wages in more detailed occupations are available for college students not wanting to spend the time and resources to train for a particular occupation only to find that wages are low or falling. Lower wages might be due to increased labor supply from immigration, or decreased demand in an industry facing international competition.

Handlers and laborers, agricultural workers, and service workers are the lowest paid labor and the groups most immigrants enter in the DCs. This immigration keeps the wages of these relatively unskilled workers low. Many union members compete directly with the immigrants, and unions have long favored strict enforcement of tight immigration laws. Business people who hire the immigrants benefit directly with their lower wages. Wages of other groups of workers are also affected by immigration and the pattern of production changes.

Wages for the immigrating unskilled workers in the EU and the US are much higher than they would receive in their source nations. The DCs have a relative scarcity of labor and large amounts of cooperating capital, skilled labor, and natural resources. The high levels of cooperating inputs increase labor productivity.

The wage of each group is lowered by its own immigration. When the US Congress cut off the immigration of foreign trained physicians in the 1970s, the main beneficiaries were domestic physicians. The American Medical Association (AMA) lobbied for the cutoff arguing that the quality of foreign doctors is unreliable. Without immigration, the supply of doctors fell and their wages rose. Relaxing the restrictive immigration policy would lead to immigration of foreign doctors and lower medical bills.

The DCs attract different types of skilled workers from around the world. The *brain drain* refers to emigration of skilled workers from LDCs. Resources are spent by LDCs to train engineers, scientists, doctors, and other skilled workers who then emigrate to a DC where they can earn higher wages. Students from LDCs sent to study in the DCs often stay to work. The brain drain hinders growth in source nations. Skilled labor is scarce in the LDCs but there is not enough capital or the right sort of production for skilled workers to be highly paid. Industry in LDCs may not have progressed to the point of demanding electronic engineers and neurosurgeons. In many LDCs, skilled workers are underemployed by inefficient government monopolies.

Well educated people are less likely to emigrate if their incomes are higher. A Swiss business school IMD ranks countries according to the likelihood that skilled workers will stay home. The brain drain is most likely in Russia and South Africa. Sweden with its high tax rate is close behind. Most NICs rank in the middle. The brain drain is least likely from the US, the Netherlands, and Chile.

In the 1970s there was an influx of Vietnamese political refugees to the US. As they entered, wages in their line of work were depressed. An example occurred along the Texas Gulf Coast when Vietnamese shrimpers entered what had been a closely knit local group. The price of shrimp fell as did the wage of shrimpers.

When workers immigrate, payments to capital and natural resources are affected. Groups hurt by immigration want stricter quotas and groups helped favor letting immigration continue. Without a doubt, immigration increases national income and stimulates economic growth. Immigrants into the US have been relatively unskilled and more from Asia and Latin America during the past 30 years.

The income redistribution caused by international labor movement is one key to understanding why some groups favor immigration while others oppose it.

EXAMPLE 8.5   *US Population: Immigrants*

The Immigration and Naturalization Service provides a profile of US immigrants. Before 1940, most immigrants were European. Since the 1960s, many have been political refugees. The first data are millions of immigrants. The second shows how large the immigrants of the period would have become with a conservative 1% growth rate, adding to 254 million, nearly the US population. Almost 40% of the total has immigrated since 1900, the largest group between 1900 and 1920. Present immigration policy will shape the US population at the end of the next century.

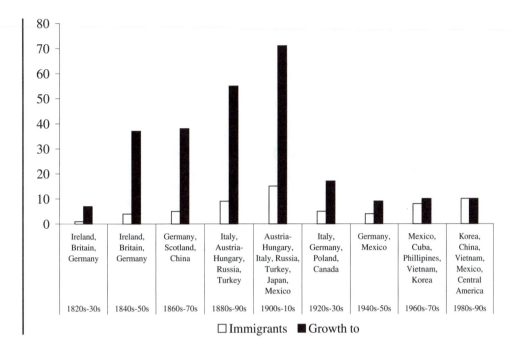

Illegal Immigration

Many workers enter the EU and US from bordering countries as illegal immigrants. The risk of being detained enters into the migration decision but all costs may be outweighed by the international wage difference. Many firms depend on immigrant workers.

Only a limited quota from any country is admitted each year on economic grounds. Some immigrant workers can work legally in the DCs. Temporary workers may enter for limited periods if employers verify their employment.

For illegal migrants, the gains from illegal immigration must outweigh the costs. Part of the cost is the probability of the penalty of being caught. Laws penalize firms that hire illegal immigrants but enforcement is difficult. There is too much to gain through immigration both for the migrants and the firms employing them. Illegal immigration seems likely to persist.

Illegal immigration can be reduced by lowering its marginal benefits or raising its marginal costs. The marginal benefit (*MB*) curve in Figure 8.4 illustrates the difference between wages in the host and source countries. As illegal workers enter, wages fall in the host country and *MB* slopes downward. The marginal cost (*MC*) schedule reflects the cost of relocation and the discounted cost of penalties. The first few illegal immigrants might know the language and live close to the border, and a small inflow might not attract much enforcement. As the number of illegal immigrants rises, so does *MC*.

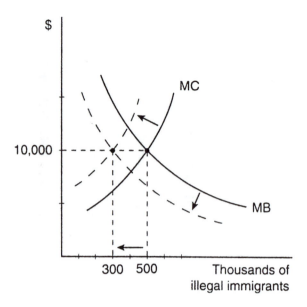

Figure 8.4
Controlling Illegal Immigration
MB represents the marginal benefit from migration for the potential migrant and *MC* is the marginal cost of the move. Illegal immigration can be controlled by lowering *MB* or raising *MC*.

Making it more difficult for firms to hire illegal workers would reduce *MB*. Free trade would reduce *MB* by lowering the international wage difference. Free international investment attracts capital to low wage countries and lower *MB*. Increased patrolling of the border and stiffer penalties raise the *MC* schedule.

The main cause of illegal immigration is the wage difference between the source and host countries. Solutions to illegal immigration must take this difference into account. Free trade and investment reduce the international wage difference.

EXAMPLE 8.6   *Sources of Illegal Immigration*

Almost all immigration to the US from Europe is legal while more than half from Mexico is illegal according to the Census of Population. The largest group of foreign born (FB) residents are from Europe at 5 million. Asia counts for just over half as many FB residents as Europe but now has more immigration. Relatively high percentages of FB immigrants from Mexico, Central America, and the Caribbean are illegal.

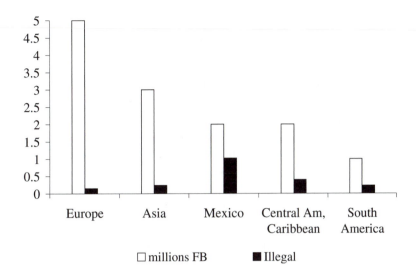

Problems for Section A

A1. Find the wages in each country that would result from migration of 5 million workers to the home country from the foreign country in Figure 8.2.

A2. Suppose the relocation and readjustment cost is $2/hour in Figure 8.2. Find the equilibrium distribution of labor between the two countries when there is no immigration quota. How many workers emigrate from the foreign country?

A3. Name other ways to reduce illegal immigration using Figure 8.4.

EXAMPLE 8.7   *Migrants Worldwide*

The UN reports that out of a world population of 6 billion in 2002, 3% are migrants with 0.2% of world income paid as remittances. In the DCs, 9% of the population is migrants and 0.1% of income is remitted. Immigration to the DCs occurs at a rate of 2 per 1000 of population. In the US, 12% of the population is migrant, 5% of GDP is remitted, and the immigration rate is 5 per 1000. Among the developed countries in the OECD, the US and EU admitted about 1 to 1.5 million immigrants annually between 1990 and 2001. Among the DCs, Australia has the largest stock of immigrants relative to population at 23%. Many small countries have similar and larger stocks of immigrants.

B.   INTERNATIONAL INVESTMENT

Owners of productive capital input seek the highest international return. Capital is more mobile internationally than labor because people do not have to move with their capital. The owner of capital machinery and equipment can be in one country and the capital employed in another. International movement of productive capital is critical for the world economy.

International Capital Markets

Capital machinery and equipment provide the means to produce more and better goods and services. Most LDCs rely heavily on DCs for productive capital and a great deal of FI occurs between DCs. FI accounted the recovery of the US automobile industry in the 1980s. Some FI occurs to avoid persistent protectionism, for instance Japanese and EU firms producing cars in the US to avoid protection.

Tariffs and other forms of protection limit the range of available products. Paul Romer (1994) uses a specific factors model to make the point that protection on capital good imports can eliminate products from production. Losses associated with trade restrictions would be larger than the usual calculated deadweight losses if some products are lost.

The international integration of investment is reflected by *stock markets*. Stocks represent ownership of the capital of firms. When *investment portfolios* contain stocks and bonds from around the world, they are internationally diversified. Anyone with a savings account at a local bank is indirectly involved in international markets.

An important difference between international labor and capital movement is that all capital earnings are *repatriated*. In the host country, incoming capital raises the productivity of labor. The production possibilities frontier and the value of production expand. Earnings on the foreign capital, however, are sent back to the source country. With migration, the owner of the productive resource moves with the resource and the labor income stays mostly in the host country. When capital comes into an economy, wages rise and the capital return falls.

Incoming capital contributes to economic growth. Jong-Wha Lee (1994) finds that imported capital goods are more of a stimulus to economic growth than domestic capital goods, examining data across countries between 1960 and 1985. Countries wanting to grow should not restrict foreign investment.

Figure 8.5 presents the fundamental theory of international capital movements. The principles that explain international capital movements are the same as those that explain migration.

The domestic capital market is plotted from the left and domestic demand for capital slopes downward. The marginal productivity of capital decreases, given a fixed amount of other home resources. Foreign capital demand is plotted from the right and slopes downward as well.

The return to capital is expressed as a percentage rate of return, the expected return on investment netting out expected inflation and capital *depreciation*. Depreciation is wear and tear on the capital equipment. If expected inflation is 3% and expected depreciation 2%, a nominal return of 9% implies a 4% real return.

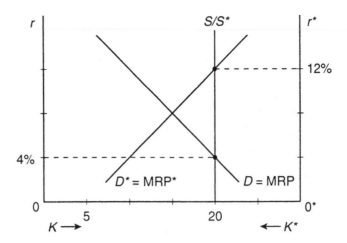

Figure 8.5
The International Capital Market
The domestic capital market with demand D and return r originates from origin 0. The foreign capital market with demand D^* and return r^* is measured from origin 0^*. With 20 units of capital at home and 10 units in the foreign country on relative supply line S/S^*, returns to capital are 4% at home and 12% in the foreign country.

The rate of return is the return divided by the capital stock. The rate of return is typically in the neighborhood of 2% and 4%. A 3% rate of return means $1 invested today will be worth $1.03 after one year. With a 3% rate of return, $100,000 worth of machinery, equipment, and structures produces a net $3000 of output during a year. If this machinery depreciated $2000 over the year, $5000 of output would have to be produced to acquire a 3% real return. This 3% is called the rate of return, the real interest rate, or the rental rate of capital.

In the distribution of capital in Figure 8.5, there are 20 units at home and 10 abroad represented by supply line S. There are 30 units of capital between the two countries. The real return to capital is 4% at home where capital is abundant. The return to capital is 12% in the foreign country where supply is scarce.

The difference in the return to capital will disappear with capital movement between the countries. Policy may limit foreign investment for fear of being "bought out" and controlled by foreign interests. In the DCs, there have been cries to keep foreigners from buying farmland and skyscrapers. LDCs have historically limited foreign investment by requiring majority ownership of domestic investors. Most countries have some restrictive policies and LDCs are unfortunately the most restrictive in their international investment policy.

When capital is transferred to the foreign economy in Figure 8.5, the relative supply line shifts left. The rate of return to capital in the foreign country declines. In the home country the supply of capital falls and the rate of return rises. Capital returns move closer together with international capital movement.

Restrictions on foreign investment in the host country are due to the desire of capital owners to keep their input scarce and return high. Wealth holders can influence government policy makers. If international capital is allowed to enter the economy, capital owners suffer.

In the source country, labor groups want to keep capital from leaving to maintain labor's marginal productivity. Restrictions on the international capital come from both host and source countries.

Given the opportunity, owners of home capital in Figure 8.6 will want to move their capital to the foreign country. With free mobility, an international capital market equilibrium is attained when 5 units of capital move from the home to the foreign country. Each country then has a stock of 15 and the international rate of return to capital is 8%.

International differences in the return to capital arise due to differences in capital demands or supplies. If free to move, capital seeks an international equilibrium with equal returns across countries.

EXAMPLE 8.8   *Sources of FDI in the US*

During the 20th century, the US typically owned more than twice as much capital abroad as foreigners held in the US. During the 1980s this ratio declined. The US now holds net credit positions with Canada and Latin America, and net debit positions with Europe and Japan. Foreign firms invest in the US for various reasons, to locate close to US consumers or producers of intermediate products. With FDI, the foreign parent firm maintains control over its branch operation. Foreign capital increases labor productivity and wages. Net interest payments on the foreign capital are paid in the form of stock dividends and bond payments. The Department of Commerce estimates the largest FDI source countries in $billions.

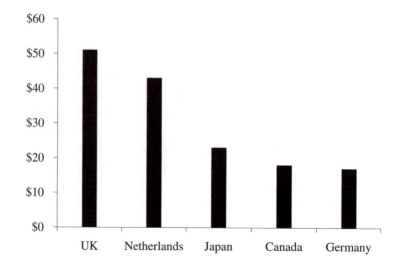

Trade as a Substitute for Capital Movement

Free trade has an equalizing effect on the international capital return, substituting for capital movement as well as migration. The DCs export capital intensive business services and high tech manufactures. Free trade increases the price of these exports and raises the demand and return to capital. In the limiting case, free trade leads to complete factor price equalization and lost motivation for international capital movement.

Free trade lowers the return to capital in countries that import capital intensive goods. The capital return rises in capital abundant countries. Capital abundant countries export capital intensive products and their relative demand for capital rises. Even without capital movement, the international return to capital can be equalized by free trade.

International capital mobility tends to equalize the return to capital across countries. Free trade substitutes for capital mobility by equalizing the return to capital across countries.

EXAMPLE 8.9   *FDI and Trade*

FDI has been growing faster than trade and there are linkages between the two. Linda Goldberg and Michael Klein (1999) investigate whether FDI serves as a complement or substitute for trade in Latin America. FDI from the US causes significant and varied shifts in the composition of output in Latin American manufacturing. Capital intensive production rises. FDI increases production in export industries, complements trade, and stimulates exports in Latin America.

US Foreign Investment

Thousands of US firms have *foreign direct investments* (FDI) and most are totally owned. The largest shares of these foreign assets are distributed across industries as shown in Table 8.2, the remaining highly diversified across numerous industries.

The largest locations of these US assets abroad are in the countries listed in Table 8.2. OPEC and Mexico each have 2% of the total. Mexico is relaxing restrictions on foreign investment. US firms claim Japan is not receptive to foreign direct investment although the Japanese government says it does not discriminate. Each country presents its own legal and policy environment. Some countries are much more open to foreign investment than others.

The largest foreign investments inside the US are from Canada, the Netherlands, UK, Japan, Germany, France, and Switzerland. Many commonly known companies are foreign owned, including Seagrams, Shell Oil, Standard Oil, Mitsui, A&P, American Motors, Mack Trucks, Carnation, Nestle, and Philips

Table 8.2 Distribution of US FDI

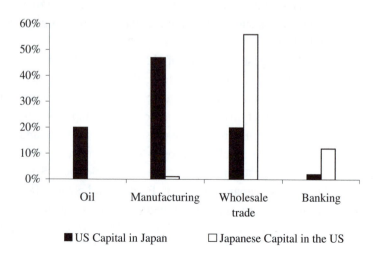

Source: *Survey of Current Business*, Department of Commerce.

Petroleum. About one fifth of all foreign assets in the US are in direct investment, the remaining spread across stocks, bonds, and real estate.

EXAMPLE 8.10 *FDI between the US and Japan*

The pattern of FDI between the US and Japan is the result of investment incentives, underlying trade patterns, and local commercial practices. The US specializes in the oil industry and manufacturing, while Japan focuses on business services. The largest US manufacturing investment is in chemicals. The US has a negative net capital position with Japan according to data from the *Survey of Current Business*.

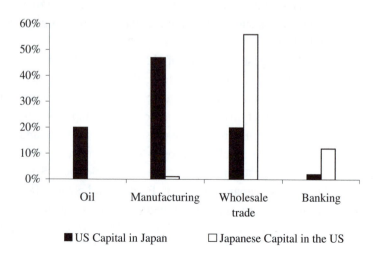

International Loans

Productive capital comes in the form of equipment, machinery, and structures. In application to a particular industry, it makes sense to look at the market for the particular types of capital used in the industry. There is a market for tractor trailers, a market for personal computers, a market for turret lathes, a market for cranes, and so on. The capital market in Figure 8.5 might represent a typical capital good.

International loans are traded in a financial market. In practice, firms borrow to acquire capital input. International loan markets work alongside markets for capital inputs. In the press "capital market" refers to the loan market and it is important to keep the two senses of word "capital" separate. Capital can refer to either productive physical inputs or loans.

There are links between international movements of productive capital and the international loan market. Suppose a US real estate company wants to establish a branch operation in England. It can take funds directly out of its US operations or it can borrow. The borrowing can take place in the US or the UK loan market. The loan market is integrated internationally. International banking is adapting to increased international trade and investment.

When a multinational firm sets up a foreign branch plant, it may attract local or international investment funds. International investment and loans are closely linked.

EXAMPLE 8.11 *FDI from DCs to LDCs*

Foreign direct investment is going from DCs to LDCs and net investment figures from the IMF in 1999 $billion suggest the flow is increasing. Foreign portfolio investment FDI increasingly comes into the DCs. The annual average FDI in the 1980s was about $14 billion and it grew to $58 billion in the 1990s. Firms in the DCs prefer to operate branch plants in the LDCs. Portfolio investment from the DCs rose from a yearly average of $16 billion to $89 billion FI. The increased activity indicates more active international capital markets.

Problems for Section B

B1. Illustrate and explain the effects of trade in Figure 8.5 with an international return to capital of 8% brought about by free trade.

B2. Show and explain what would happen to the international pattern of capital returns in Figure 8.5 with immigration of labor from the foreign to the home country.

EXAMPLE 8.12 *Foreign Capital Stock*

Productive capital seeks locations with higher returns. Tangible assets (machinery, equipment, structures, land, inventories) and intangible assets (patents, trademarks) are valued at historical costs. Firms are typically taxed on their capital assets, not a way to encourage growth. The current market price of an asset is based on the discounted stream of profit from the asset. Book values based on historical costs are typically below market prices. The Federal Reserve Bank of St. Louis reports a comparison of historical and market values of foreign capital. FK is the stock of US owned capital in foreign countries, and FK^* is the stock of foreign owned capital in the US. At historical cost, FK^* has caught up with FK. At market value, FK remains ahead but FK^* is gaining.

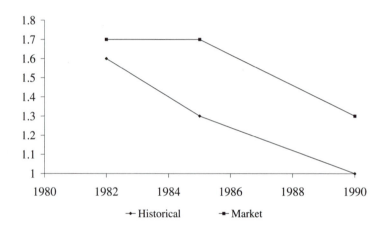

C.   MIGRATION, FOREIGN INVESTMENT, AND INCOME REDISTRIBUTION

When foreign labor or capital enters an economy, there are adjustments in domestic markets. Factor supplies change, outputs adjust, exports and imports change, and factor prices adjust. This section examines the income redistribution caused by international migration and capital flows.

Links between Factor Markets

An increase in the supply of a factor of production reduces its return but national income, the total payment to all productive inputs, rises. The prices of some other factors of production rise due to increased marginal productivity.

If an increased supply of one factor causes the payment of another to rise, the two are called *factor friends*. If payment to another factor falls, those two are *factor enemies*.

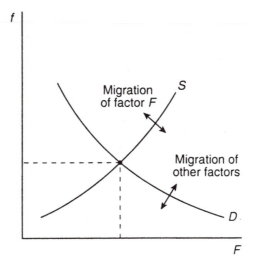

Figure 8.6
Market for a Productive Factor
The domestic market for productive factor F is influenced by international factor movements. When the factor itself migrates, supply shifts. When other factors migrate, its productivity and demand shift. Adjusting outputs also affect the factor demand.

Figure 8.6 presents a picture of the market for factor of production F with payment f. Migration of F changes its supply, and international movements of other factors change the marginal productivity and demand for F.

Suppose F is a friend of immigrating construction labor. The marginal product and demand for F rise when the labor immigrates, and payment f increases. The market for F adjusts in the general equilibrium along with markets for outputs and all productive factors. If F is an enemy of professional labor, demand for F and its payment would fall with immigrating professionals.

International inflow of a factor raises the returns to its factor friends but decreases the returns to its factor enemies.

Labor Skills and Migration

The lowest paid groups of labor are the unskilled: handlers, laborers, agricultural workers, janitors, restaurant workers, and so on. Higher paid groups (professionals, craft workers, transport workers, operators, managers) can be aggregated into skilled labor. The effects of labor migration on income distribution between capital owners and these skill groups of labor depend on the substitution between inputs as the pattern of production adjusts.

Unskilled labor is generally a friend with skilled labor and capital. When unskilled workers immigrate to a DC, demands for skilled workers and capital increase due to higher productivity. Skilled wages and capital returns rise with unskilled labor immigration. Unskilled workers inside the country suffer lower wages due to the increased supply.

Labor unions represent the interests of unskilled labor and have long been opposed to immigration, favoring tighter restrictions and border patrol. Many people in the DCs, however, benefit from immigration of unskilled labor. This benefit explains the reluctance to enforce more active immigration policy. Sanctions on employers of illegal workers may reduce immigration of unskilled workers.

Local effects of unskilled immigration can be startling. Construction wages in Houston, for instance, are kept low by the supply of immigrant workers. Farm workers in California face low wages for the same reason. Lettuce pickers are very much opposed to immigration. Wages of restaurant workers in large cities are kept low by the supply of unskilled immigrants. The Sun Belt in the US bases its recent economic growth on lower wages due in part to increased immigration.

Changes are slow to take effect and may not be noticed right away but the demographics of the US in the 2050s will not be much like the 1950s. California has become the most populous state with Texas second. Various "minority" racial groups will soon make up most of the US population. Both international and interstate migration are playing a role with labor moving into and around the country causing patterns of production and trade to adjust. The high productivity of the US is due largely to its mobile labor force.

Gains from international movements of labor and capital outweigh losses similar to the way free trade improves on autarky. Migration and investment result in higher world output and a more equitable income distribution. Free trade and factor mobility lead toward similar incomes for similar productive factors regardless of their location.

With free trade, a country effectively exports its abundant cheap factors. With free international factor movement, a country in fact exports them. Free trade and free factor movements lead to similar effects on income distribution.

EXAMPLE 8.13 *Immigrant Income and Skills*

Asian immigrants households do better financially than other immigrant groups and have higher income than US natives according to the US Census. Income generally increases with labor skills. Immigrants from Mexico have the highest poverty rate. About 1/3 of immigrant households from Mexico participate in government benefit programs, close to double the rate of the native population. Median income is in $thousands.

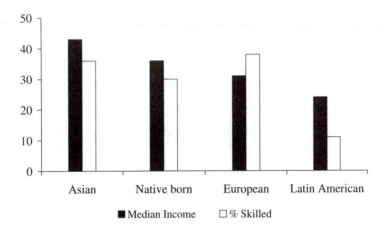

Foreign Investment in the Specific Factors Model

Insight into the effects of foreign investment can be gained with the specific factors model. International capital flows are often aimed at particular industries as when Japanese car firms build plants in the EU or US oil firms build refineries in the Middle East.

Figure 8.7 shows the market for sector specific manufacturing capital. The supply S of capital in manufacturing is 10 and the rate of return to capital 4%.

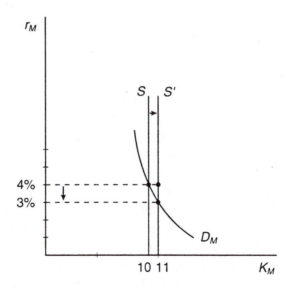

Figure 8.7
Foreign Investment and Manufacturing Capital
This is the market for capital used specifically in manufacturing. When the supply of manufacturing capital (K_M) rises from S to S' with foreign capital, the equilibrium return (r_M) to capital falls from 4% to 3% along demand curve D_M.

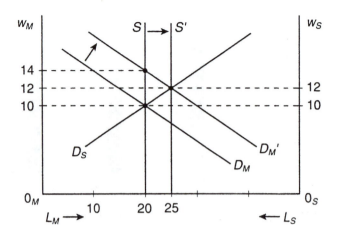

Figure 8.8
Foreign Investment and Labor
When the capital supply rises with foreign capital, the labor productivity rises in manufacturing. Demand for labor in manufacturing rises from D_M to $D_{M'}$. Wages (w_M and w_S) are pushed up from $10 to $12 across the economy as labor moves to manufacturing.

The market for shared labor is in Figure 8.8. The original equilibrium wage is $10 with 20 million workers in manufacturing and 30 million in services along supply line S.

Suppose foreign investment comes into domestic manufacturing and the supply of manufacturing capital rises to S' in Figure 8.7. There is an excess supply of manufacturing capital at the 4% rate of return and capital owners are forced to accept a lower rate of return.

In Figure 8.8, labor demand rises in manufacturing as labor's productivity increases with the foreign capital. With 20 million workers in manufacturing, the wage in manufacturing (w_M) jumps to $14. The wage in services (w_S) remains at $10. Workers notice this difference and move from services to manufacturing causing w_S to rise and w_M to fall. Labor supply shifts to S' as 5 million workers move and the wage settles at $12.

In the market for service sector capital, demand falls as labor leaves the sector. The rate of return to capital in services falls.

Inflows of capital into a sector lower the rate of return to that capital and also lower rates of return to sector specific capital across the economy. Capital owners all oppose incoming foreign investment. The wage is bolstered by foreign investment and workers benefit from foreign investment.

EXAMPLE 8.14 *The Mariel Immigration*

The labor force in Miami increased by a huge 7% in 1980 when 62,000 workers fled Cuba from the port of Mariel. David Card (1989) shows this immigration had little effect on wages in the Miami labor market. Even among unskilled workers competing directly with the immigrants, there was no decline in wages and no increase in unemployment. The reason is that production of goods intensive in unskilled labor, especially textiles and apparel, increased in Miami. Ethan Lewis (2004) finds evidence that the immigration of unskilled Cubans caused slower adoption of computer technology in Miami relative to other cities. The lower unskilled wage in Miami encouraged production intensive in unskilled labor. This episode illustrates the principle that changes in the labor force have very little impact on wages but do affect the pattern of production.

Detailed Models of Income Redistribution

Computer models include markets for the various types of labor and capital inputs as well as markets for many goods and services. A detailed model might tell us what would happen if 10,000 foreign physicians were allowed to immigrate this year. It would predict how much wages of physicians would fall, how much medical costs would fall, how much new hospital construction would result, how much the payment to other health workers would change, how other outputs would be affected, and so on.

Computable general equilibrium (CGE) models are used by various governments to help shape economic policy. CGE models are useful for considering all sorts of adjustments including the income distribution due to international factor movements.

Estimates indicate that migration and capital flows have small long run effects on income distribution. Skilled labor and capital benefit when unskilled labor immigrates to DCs, explaining the lack of persistent opposition to immigration.

Skilled labor and capital are weak enemies in the DCs and capital outflow raises the skilled wage and capital return. Unskilled labor is hurt by capital outflow since it often works with machinery and equipment, especially in capital intensive agriculture and mining.

> *Unskilled labor is a factor friend with skilled labor and capital. Unskilled immigration raises the income of skilled labor and capital owners. The effects, however, are small due to output adjustments.*

EXAMPLE 8.15 *Winners and Losers with Immigration*

Wages for unskilled workers in Mexico remain much lower than in the US, perpetuating the economic incentive to migrate. Clark Reynolds and Robert McClery (1988) calculate the gains and losses from the Mexican immigration rescaled to $100 total gains for the US. US unskilled workers lose but skilled workers and especially capital win. The incoming unskilled labor increases the productivity and demand for the other two inputs. In Mexico, emigrating workers win as do the unskilled workers remaining in Mexico. Skilled workers and capital in Mexico lose because of decreased productivity. The effects in the US are stronger, especially for capital (including land). Total effects would depend on the actual number of immigrants, border enforcement, penalties for hiring illegal workers, and so on. The fact that the US is a net winner explains why there is less than wholehearted enforcement of immigration policy.

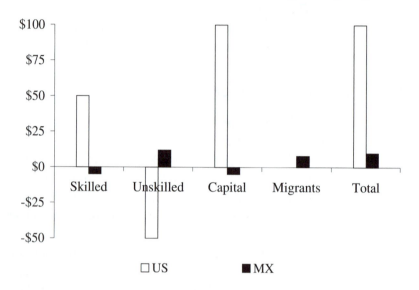

Problems for Section C

C1. Illustrate the effect of unskilled immigration on the markets for unskilled labor, skilled labor, and capital with diagrams similar to Figure 8.6.

C2. Use the estimated factor friendship elasticities in Example 8.7 to predict the effects on unskilled and skilled wages due to a 5% increase in the supply of skilled workers. Suppose the yearly skilled wage starts at $40,000 and the unskilled wage at $20,000.

EXAMPLE 8.16 *FDI and Wages: Skills and Location*

There is no doubt that incoming capital raises labor productivity but the effects might be uneven across labor skill groups and regions. Robert Feenstra and Gordon Hanson (1997) find evidence that FDI into Mexico from 1975 to 1988 raised skilled wages in northern Mexico where there are maquiladora plants. The FDI corresponded with outsourcing by multinationals, shifting production towards products intensive in skilled labor. In regions where FDI was more concentrated, growth in FDI accounted for over half of the increase in the skilled labor income share during the late 1980s. The lesson might not hold in more advanced economies though, as Anna Falzoni, Giovanni Brunno, and Rosario Crino (2004) find an increase in all wages due to FDI in Poland, Hungary, and the Czech Republic during the 1990s.

D. MIGRATION, INTERNATIONAL INVESTMENT, AND TRADE

Production and trade are based on productive factors and international movements of labor and capital change their composition. This section examines how migration and capital movements alter the pattern of production and trade.

Output Adjustments in the Factor Proportions Model

In the factor proportions model, an increase in a factor supply increases output using that factor intensively. Products may be imported, exported, or not traded. If domestic production of an imported product rises due to international factor movement, imports fall. If production of an export rises, so do exports. If output of a nontraded product changes, trade is not directly affected.

Figure 8.9 shows expansion paths for business services and manufactures with skilled labor (S) and unskilled labor (U) inputs. Services use skilled labor

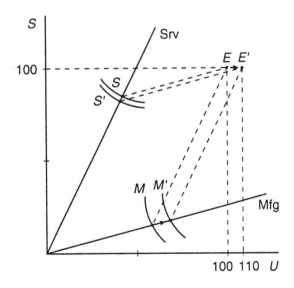

Figure 8.9
Unskilled Labor Immigration and Output Adjustment
Unskilled immigration shifts the endowment point from point E to E'. Production using the immigrating workers intensively rises while other production falls. If services are exported and manufactures imported, exports and imports fall. If manufactures are exported and services imported, exports and imports rise.

and manufacturing uses unskilled labor intensively. Capital input is assumed not to vary or affect the outcome. Point E is the endowment of 100 units of each labor. Outputs occur along expansion paths for services and manufacturers on isoquants S and M.

Unskilled immigration moves endowment point E to E'. There is a 10% increase in the endowment of labor up to 110. Output of manufactures rises to M' and output of services falls to S'.

With unskilled immigration, production shifts toward labor intensive manufactures and both types of labor leave the service sector. All of the immigrating unskilled workers as well as some unskilled workers in services find jobs in manufacturing. Skilled labor also leaves services. Output of manufactures expands up the manufacturing expansion path and output of services declines down its expansion path.

If the immigration alters factor prices, firms adjust their cost minimizing factor mix. Immigration of unskilled labor lowers its own wage while raising the skilled wage. These changes in factor prices are small and the adjustment in the input ratios should be small. Expansion paths are unchanged in Figure 8.9 although they would adjust slightly with immigration.

In a small open economy, prices of traded services and manufactures would not change. If services are exported and manufactures imported, the level of trade must fall. The country becomes less abundant in skilled labor, the input used intensively in exports. Immigration of unskilled labor causes the country to lose some of its comparative advantage if exports are intensive in unskilled labor. Factor mobility substitutes for free trade.

If manufactures are exported, unskilled immigration raises the level of trade. The country becomes more abundant in unskilled labor, the input used intensively in exports. Immigration of unskilled labor causes the country to gain in comparative advantage.

The effect of migration on the pattern of trade depends on the factor intensity of traded products.

EXAMPLE 8.17 *Immigration, Foreign Investment, and Trade*

The effects of immigration and foreign investment on production and trade are relatively large. Kar-Yui Wong (1983) estimates elasticities between US supplies of labor and capital and production of traded goods. Immigration increases exports of nondurable goods and services, which must be labor intensive. Each 1% increase in the labor force increases those exports by 2.2% and durable goods exports by 1.5%. Immigration is about 0.5% per year and the effects accumulate. Imports rise with immigration because of the increased consumption in the economy. Capital increases through FDI have smaller proportional effects on exports and imports.

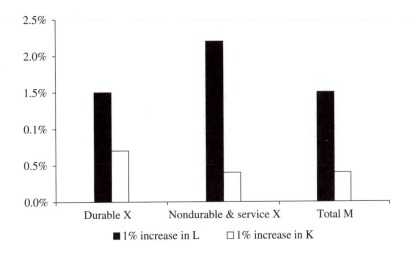

Output Adjustments in the Specific Factors Model

In the specific factors model, a particular type of capital in each sector is combined with shared labor. Figure 8.10 shows the expansion paths for each industry. Supplies of capital in sectors M and S are given by the vertical lines at $K_M = 10$ and $K_S = 10$.

Expansion paths adjust so labor is fully employed in the two sectors combined. With 10 units of capital in sector M, 20 million workers are employed in sector M with a K/L ratio of 1/2. With 50 million workers in the economy, the other 30 million are employed in services at a K/L ratio of 1/3.

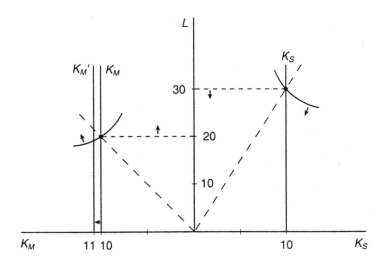

Figure 8.10
Foreign Investment in Manufacturing and Outputs
Foreign investment in manufacturing increases the supply of capital and draws labor from the rest of the economy. Output in manufacturing rises but falls in the rest of the economy.

If foreign investment increases the supply of manufacturing capital from 10 to 11, output of *M* rises. Labor is attracted to sector *M* because of increased productivity and a higher wage. Labor leaves sector *S* and output falls. Output of the sector receiving the investment rises but other outputs fall.

The increased capital raises the wage but lowers the rate of return to capital in manufacturing. In services, the decreased labor input lowers the productivity of capital and its rate of return.

International inflow of a sector specific factor raises the output of that sector but draws resources away from the rest of the economy.

Immigration increases all outputs since the incoming labor is shared by all sectors. Wages fall but the rate of return to capital in every sector rises.

EXAMPLE 8.18 *Recent US FDI*

FDI depends on foreign firms making the private decision to invest in a productive activity inside another country. Net FDI into the US reached $1.4 trillion in 2000, a rather amazing 14% of GDP, but has tapered since. Nevertheless, the $600 billion FDI in 2004 is a substantial amount of investment, over 5% of GDP.

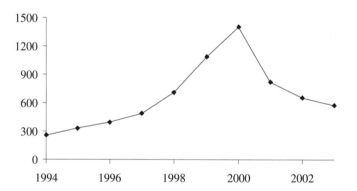

Simulated Output Adjustments to Migration and Investment

The three major industrial aggregates are services (S), manufacturing (M), and agriculture (A). Labor can be split into the eight skill types leads to elasticities of output adjustment with respect to international factor movements. Table 8.3 presents elasticities of outputs with respect to changing supplies of capital and the eight types of labor in the US from Table 8.1.

Changes in input supplies have the largest impact on industries where they are used intensively. Agriculture is very capital intensive, but only 8% of the capital stock is used in agriculture. Capital includes agricultural land. Capital owners receive 58% of all the income in agriculture. A 1% increase in the capital stock resulting from incoming foreign investment would result in a 2.7% increase in agricultural output.

Table 8.3 Output Elasticities of Migration and Investment

	L1	L2	L3	L4	L5	L6	L7	L8	K
				1% Increase in Supply of					
A	1.4	0	0	−0.2	−1.0	0	0.9	−0.2	2.7
M	−0.5	0.7	0.1	1.8	−0.5	0	0	−0.1	−0.4
S	0.5	0	0	−0.3	0.5	0	0	0.1	0.3

Source: "Simulating a multifactor general equilibrium model of production and trade", Henry Thompson, *International Economic Journal*, 1991.

Immigration amounting to 1% of the supply of agricultural workers (L7) would raise agricultural output by 0.9%. The US exports many types of agricultural products but imports others. On net, the US exports agricultural goods. Immigration of agricultural labor increases exports. Farmers confess they would be hard pressed to meet the harvest without immigrant workers. Department of Agriculture programs are aimed at restricting agricultural output and keeping prices high. For the sake of global efficiency, agricultural programs discouraging output in the US should be eliminated.

Operators L4 operators receive 29% of manufacturing income, the largest share, and 54% of all operators are employed in manufacturing. Immigration of L4 workers would cause manufacturing output to rise but outputs in services and agriculture would drop. Manufacturing output is elastic with respect to the supply of operators. Immigration of L4 amounting to a 1% increase in supply would spur manufacturing output by 1.8% but lower outputs in agriculture by 0.2% and services 0.3%. The US currently a deficit in manufactures trade. Immigration of L4 workers would decrease manufactured imports. International factor mobility would substitute for trade.

A majority of professionals, craft, and sales (L1, L3, and L5) are employed in services. Professionals and sales (L1 and L5) receive 27% and 21% of the income in services. The largest output effects on the service sector come from immigration of these two high skilled groups. The US is a net exporter of services and immigration of skilled labor increases comparative advantage, the degree of specialization, and exports.

Output adjustments resulting from international factor movements are tied to factor intensity. International factor movements alter comparative advantage.

EXAMPLE 8.19 *FDI by State*

The FDI stock in the US increased from under $200 billion in 1980 to over four times that billion by 2000 when foreign firms employed 5 million US workers or about 5% of the workforce. This ranking of states shows those with higher than average percentages of workers employed by foreign multinationals.

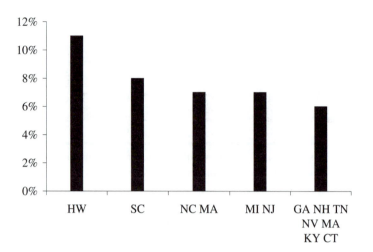

EXAMPLE 8.20 *Why FDI Can Be Important*

These figures from *International Financial Statistics* show net FDI relative to GDP for some big international FDI magnets during 2001. It would take a few years to manage to invest as much out of national income. Still, the largest quantitative international FDI recipient by far was the US at $314 billion (only 3% of US GDP but 38% of world FDI). During 2002, FDI fell worldwide. China took over as the world leading host with $49 billion FDI in 2003.

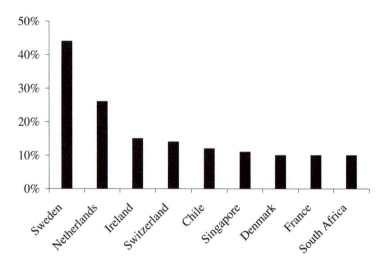

Problems for Section D

D1. Show what happens in Figure 8.10 with emigration of skilled labor. If services are exported, predict what will happen to exports and imports.

D2. Predict what will happen to the pattern of production and trade with outflows of skilled labor from a DC and an LDC.

EXAMPLE 8.21 *Global FDI: Up, Down, Up again?*

Global foreign direct investment increased through the 1990s but tailed off following 2000. FDI below is reported in $billion. The recent decline is due to investor concerns about global recession, increased protectionism, and terrorism. Only about 30% of global FDI goes to the capital poor LDCs. By region in 2003, the largest recipients are the EU at 47%, Asia-Pacific 16%, and North America 15%. China is an emerging FDI recipient that still receives less than half of the leader, the US. This data is from *World Investment Prospects* published by The Economist Intelligence Unit forecasting increased FDI over the coming decade unless there are increases in protectionism and Middle East tensions. The *Prospects* blames poor government policy and property rights for keeping global FDI well below its potential.

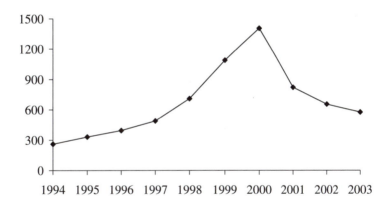

EXAMPLE 8.22 *US Immigrant Remittances to Mexico*

Mexican born immigrants to the US are about a third of foreign born workers in the US and their remittance payments are an important source of income in Mexico. Catalina Amuedo-Dorantes, Cynthia Bansak, and Susan Pozo (2005) review the evidence from a survey of Mexican workers and find the motivations for remittances payments are to support families, meet a goal for savings, or pay of debts. Over the past 50 years remittances have been declining perhaps due to improved living standards in Mexico but Mexicans are also staying longer in the US, opening bank accounts, and becoming permanent residents. Undocumented workers with low education and family members in Mexico remit a larger share of their income. The same principles likely apply to other immigrant workers, for instance Turkish workers in Germany, Albanian workers in Greece, and Pakistani workers in the Arabian Gulf.

CONCLUSION

International labor and capital movements are vital forces in the global economy. The returns to factors and outputs adjust with international factor movements. Countries can integrate their economic activity through steps of free trade, open migration policy, or unrestricted international investment. The next chapter examines the process and politics of international economic integration.

Terms

Brain Drain
Capital depreciation
Emigration and immigration
Factor endowment
Factor friends and enemies

Host and source countries
International capital mobility
International factor markets
Marginal factor cost (*MFC*)
Marginal revenue product (*MRP*)

MAIN POINTS

- Workers respond to international wage differences by migrating toward higher wages. Migration leads to equalize wages across countries. International trade substitutes for migration as it leads toward wage equalization.
- Capital moves between countries seeking a higher return. Free international capital movement leads to the same result as free trade, international factor price equalization.
- When a factor immigrates, national income rises but the price of that factor falls. National income rises, and factor friends gain, but there might be losing factor enemies. International factor movements redistribute income among factors of production.
- International factor movements affect the pattern of production and trade. Migration and capital movement may stimulate trade or substitute for it.

REVIEW PROBLEMS

1. Free trade between the two countries in Figure 8.2 would raise the price of the labor intensive product in the labor cheap foreign country and lower the same price at home. Illustrate this adjustment with wages equalizing at $10.

2. What else could wages of the various labor groups reflect besides the skills and training needed to enter each group?

3. Predict how an inflow of foreign capital into the auto industry will affect wages of the various labor groups.

4. Given the current trends in US immigration, predict the evolving pattern of regional production and trade.

5. If wealth holders in the US traded evenly, at present value, their capital assets with wealth holders in the EU, what would be the net effect?

6. Explain how the industries in Table 8.1 in which the US has substantial foreign investments abroad compare with comparative advantage.

7. Which groups in an economy most favor restricting foreign investment? Which groups most oppose such restrictions?

8. The service industry includes categories such as wholesale trade and banking as in Example 8.6 of investment in the US and Japan. Assume capital is sector specific. What have been the effects on income redistribution and outputs of the observed investment?

9. Emigration of professionals occurs as firms in the DCs expand their foreign branch operations. Predict what will happen to wages of the various types of labor with emigration of professionals.

10. Explain what happens to the income of the various types of labor and capital when the Japanese open a new factory in the US. How are the local effects different from the national effects?

11. What happens to the long run distribution of income when US firms decide to open factories in Mexico rather than in Texas? What would be the difference if the plant was opened on the Texas side of the border but Mexicans were allowed to cross over and work?

12. Explain whether it is more likely that the US would join a *common market* (free trade and free movements of labor and capital) with Germany or Brazil. Consider the income redistribution for each.

13. Given that birth rates in the US are higher among unskilled groups in the West and South, predict what will happen to the pattern of production and trade with the rest of the country.

14. *Free trade zones* are set up partly to attract investment by foreign firms through the elimination of customs procedures. Do they promote or inhibit trade based on comparative advantage?

15. Describe the effects on outputs of the three sectors of the economy when there is a 10% immigration of machine operators L4 using Table 8.3. Predict the effects on imports and exports.

READINGS

Edward Graham and Paul Krugman (1991) *Foreign Direct Investment in the United States*, Washington: Institute for International Economics. Loads of information and detail on FDI

Aad van Mourik (1994) *Wages and European Integration*, Maastricht: BIV Publications. Detailed analysis of integration.

Kaz Miyagiwa (1990) *International Capital Mobility and National Welfare*, New York: Garland. Review of theory.

Barry Chaswick, ed (1982) *The Gateway: US Immigration Issues and Policies*, Washington: American Policy Institute. Studies on immigration.

International Migration Review, New York: Center for Migration Studies. Journal on migration.

"The New Refugee," *US News and World Report*, October 23, 1989. A startling look at migration.

John Shoven and John Whalley (1984) Applied general equilibrium models of taxation and international trade, *Journal of Economic Literature*. Survey of CGE models.

Julian Simon (199) *The Economic Consequences of Immigration*, London: Blackwell. Economic analysis of immigration.

CHAPTER 9

Economic Integration

Preview

International economic integration has accelerated with numerous free trade agreements around the world. From the viewpoint of global economic efficiency, national borders introduce barriers to production and trade that decrease efficiency. Economic integration involves steps to lower the barriers. This chapter covers:

- *Multinational firms* and their role in international economic integration
- *International externalities* that call for coordinated policy
- *International political economy* of free trade agreements
- *Steps of economic integration* to increase productivity

INTRODUCTION

Multinational firms have increasing importance in the world economy. Roughly a quarter of international trade occurs between branches of multinational firms. Direct investment by firms in foreign branch operations is an increasing portion of foreign investment. International franchising and licensing are critical for the world economy.

Thousands of multinational firms (MNFs) have foreign investments. According to the US Department of Commerce, more than 80% of foreign branch firms are majority owned suggesting management of the parent firm is important for typical branch operations. One-fifth of US multinational branches are in the business service industry followed closely by energy companies. Only a quarter of these branches are located in countries where English is the native language. Foreign MNFs employ over 3% of the US workforce.

Multinational branches form when activity inside the firm is more economical than between firms. MNFs "avoid the market" by internalizing market transactions. Often an MNF wants to use its patent, process, or management technique in the foreign country.

Multinationals can be horizontally or vertically integrated. With horizontal integration, the MNF operates similar plants in different countries. Horizontal integration has increased over recent decades. Vertical integration has historically occurred in extractive natural resource industries. A domestic firm can buy raw inputs from foreign suppliers or it can open a branch to produce the inputs itself.

Many countries have restrictions to minimize the influence of MNFs. The motives are control of the economy, mistrust of foreign motives, cultural purity, and national pride. In fact, MNFs bring skilled labor and capital that lower the return to the host skilled labor and capital, explaining their opposition. MNFs increase the demand for local labor and raise wages.

In labor abundant LDCs, multinationals should be most welcomed since they encourage specialization and efficient production. Income increases but is redistributed. Established industry and the wealthy support the government and do not want traditional income distribution upset.

One aspect of production that should induce governments to integrate is pollution, a negative production externality. People close to polluting firm pay part of the cost of production by living in a polluted location. A pollution tax on output forces the firm to consider the costs of its pollution and to restrict output. Alternatively, civil liability would lead to cleaner production.

International pollution externalities are difficult to solve. What incentive does the EU government have to force reduction of pollution and the amount of acid rain falling on Turkey? How can US farmers be convinced to cut back on their use of fertilizers and pesticides that drain into the Colorado River and cause downstream problems in Mexico? There are no international pollution taxes or liability laws, and few accepted precedents for handling international pollution externalities.

Difficult issues lie at the heart of international political economy. As with domestic political economy, insight can be gained by considering the income redistribution resulting from a policy. Every group in every country would like more income distributed its own way.

The world is shrinking due to improved transportation and communication. Economies are becoming more specialized and dependent. International trade and investment lead to gains all around and the various stages of economic integration facilitate international commerce and raise income.

Governments enjoy autonomy and have an incentive to impede economic integration. Governments want to set trade policy to enhance power and protect supportive industries. Governments want to control and tax foreign investment. Governments want to control their money supplies since printing money enables governments to spend more than tax revenue. Economic integration progresses through steps as governments give up these powers.

The gains from economic integration are large and ultimately prevail over narrow local interests. The EU provides an example of the vitality that can be introduced by opening borders to trade, migration, and investment. As the closed economies of eastern Europe open, living standards are steadily rising. The US, Canada, and Mexico have formed NAFTA and free trade throughout North and South America will not be far behind. A Pacific Rim free trade area that would include Japan and the US is under negotiation. There are various forms of international economic integration in the Caribbean, South America, the Middle East, Southeast Asia, and Africa. Even large political differences such as those between the US and China can be overcome by the gains from free trade and economic integration.

A. MULTINATIONAL FIRMS

A *multinational firm* (MNF) has headquarters in one country with branch operations in other countries. This section examines the causes and effects of MNFs in the source and host countries. MNFs account for most of the surge in foreign investment since the late 1980s. By investing abroad, an MNF attempts to remain competitive. There are critics when an MNF "exports jobs" investing abroad but the alternative may be not investing at all or foreign production. *Intrafirm trade* within MNFs now accounts for about half of US trade. The role of policy in influencing MNFs is important part of international political economy.

International Marketing

A firm selling in another country can use four techniques, requiring increasing familiarity with the foreign markets:

- Produce at home and *export*. Foreign importers buy and distribute the export.
- Make a *licensing agreement* with a foreign firm, giving the foreign firm the right to produce. The foreign firm pays the source firm a royalty.
- Form a *joint venture* with a foreign firm to develop and produce for the foreign market.
- Invest in a *branch plant* in the foreign country and become an MNF. Management from the home firm operates the branch plant.

The choice is based on familiarity with the foreign country, legal restrictions on MNFs, transport to costs to the foreign market, contacts among foreign firms, levels of foreign protection, local economies of scale, fixed costs of establishing a branch plant, relative cost of foreign labor, home and foreign skilled labor, the level and elasticity of foreign demand, and other influences. Underlying comparative advantage must make foreign production more profitable for an MNF to invest in a branch plant or the firm would remain an exporter. Foreign carmakers have set up plants in the DCs largely to avoid high protection.

Licensing with a foreign firm is the easiest way for a domestic firm to produce in a foreign country. Licensing lets the firm penetrate the foreign market if there is protection. If the source firm has a special production process, licensing allows *technology transfer*. The branch firm may attach its label to the product and receives a royalty.

Joint ventures are another way to penetrate foreign markets. Agreements are made between firms in different countries to share management, production processes, market information, raw materials, and so on. Joint ventures have become popular with improvements in intranet and internet. By specializing in providing R&D, management, or marketing, firms lower costs and carry out projects that would not be feasible if each operated independently.

If a firm wants to protect a process, it will export or set up a branch plant avoiding licensing and joint ventures. The firm specific input or production process might have a *patent*. International patent recognition is improving under the rules of the WTO. A particular style of management is maintained with exporting or branch plants.

No simple model encompasses all of the decisions facing a potential MNF. The four basic options of a firm wanting to sell its product in foreign markets are export, licensing agreement, joint venture, and branch plant.

EXAMPLE 9.1   *MNFs in Business Services*

Over the past three decades, a large part of MNF growth has occurred in business services. The UN reports that almost half of FDI in the US and just over half of Japanese FDI is in business services. For other DCs, the percentage is about one third. Most investment coming into the US is in business services. IT&T is an example of a US firm becoming involved in services and FDI, a US telephone equipment manufacturer in the 1970s that has grown into a diversified MNF based on telecommunications. About half of IT&T revenue comes from its foreign branch operations. Similarly, IBM developed the original computers but has evolved into a computer service MNF.

International Management and MNFs

The DCs have an abundance of entrepreneurial and management talent and specialize internationally in management. This comparative advantage is revealed by the net export of business services. The US is a leader in the global *business service industry* including telecommunications, computer software, banking, finance, consulting, information services, engineering, construction, and so on. The US has an underestimated trade surplus in business services. Another comparative advantage in the US in higher education, and most PhD students in the US are foreign students who come to the US to learn valued skills in engineering, sciences, and economics.

Like other productive factors, entrepreneurs and managers migrate from countries where they are abundant and cheap to countries where they are scarce and expensive. With internet and intranet communication, managers may not have to move physically.

An increase in MNF activity lowers the return to management inside the host. Domestic managers will oppose the unfettered inflow of foreign MNFs and management. Other factors generally benefit from MNF management as they become more productive.

Firms in an industry have to compete with new MNF branch plants. Local politicians come from districts where existing firms feel threatened by MNFs and there will always be political pressure to keep out foreign competition.

The automobile industry provides an example of the potential foreign MNFs have to increase productivity of the domestic industry. Protection on autos provides an incentive for Japanese and European firms to locate branch plants inside the US. Domestic auto makers have opposed new foreign owned plants, and the entry of foreign MNFs since the 1980s has forced them to become more competitive. There is little difference in domestic value added between domestic cars and "foreign" models produced in the US. The overall quality of cars in the US has increased dramatically over the past 30 years at least partly due to the competition from imports and MNFs.

MNFs increase the level of international management.

EXAMPLE 9.2   *MNF Branches in the US*

There are more Japanese MNF branch operations in the US than from any other country. The UK has about half as many branch operations, and Canada and the EU each have about a third as many. States with the most MNFs are California, Georgia, New Jersey, Illinois, Texas, and Washington.

MNF Horizontal Integration

Horizontal integration occurs in an industry when firms produce the same output at different locations. A horizontally integrated MNF must decide how much to produce in its branch plants. A multiplant MNF is shown in Figure 9.1. The firm wants to produce where marginal revenue *MR* equals marginal cost *MC* to maximize profit, and considers *MC* in its domestic and foreign branch plants separately.

Demand leads to the *MR* curve in Figure 9.1. Both plants make the same product and the foreign branch has lower marginal costs, MC^* in the foreign plant and *MC* in the domestic plant.

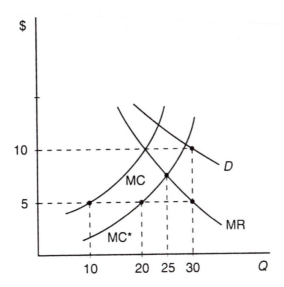

Figure 9.1
Horizontal Integration of an MNF
The MNF produces the same product in two countries and wants to equate *MR* and *MC* across plants setting price according to demand. The foreign plant has lower costs and produces 20 units while the higher cost home plant produces 10 units. At the total output of 30, *MR* = \$5 = *MC* in both plants, and price = \$10.

> *With international horizontal integration, an MNF produces the same product at different locations. Output is higher at lower cost plants.*

Optimal outputs involve equating each plant's *MC* with the firm's *MR* and summing outputs to total demand. Profit is maximized in Figure 9.1 where *MR* = *MC* = \$5 at both plants. Domestic output of 10 plus foreign output of 20 adds to total output of 30. At any price above \$5, the two quantities from the *MC* and *MC** add to more than the quantity on the *MR* curve. Under \$5, the two quantities from the *MC* curves add to less than the quantity on the *MR* curve. The output of 30 units is sold according to demand at a price of \$10. Output will be higher at the lower cost plant.

If there is more than one foreign branch plant, the firm sets outputs where *MR* equals *MC* at each branch plant and total output sums to marginal revenue. There are higher outputs at plants with lower costs.

One question is why the firm in Figure 9.1 would continue to operate the higher cost plant. If the domestic plant has higher average costs, perhaps all production should be shifted to the foreign plant. The firm might operate where *MC** = *MR* at *Q* = 25.

The profit of each location is found with each plant's average cost. Profit may be higher from operating both plants than from operating a single low cost plant for various reasons. Transport costs may be an incentive to keep plants operating. Some buyers may be closer to the home plant. Plants may be located close to a particular natural resource. Costs of shutting down the domestic plant and expanding the foreign plant might lead firms to operate parallel plants. Import protection in the home country can make shipments from the foreign branch plant too expensive. If management is located in the home country, it might continue domestic production to train its managers. If the firm expects costs to rise at home or abroad, it might operate branch plants as a hedge.

EXAMPLE 9.3   *Patterns of FDI*

> FDI in new plant and equipment in the US is concentrated in a few industries and comes mostly from the EU, Japan, and Canada. Ed Ray (1991) summarizes the $211 billion of FDI between 1979 an 1987. FDI on average comes into large firms with market power in large growing industries intensive in skilled labor and capital. FDI increases when the dollar depreciates due to the increased purchasing power of foreign currencies. FDI avoids unionized labor and does not seek protection. Most FDI goes into buying shares of firms rather than establishing independent operations. Manufacturing accounts for 40% of FDI and services the rest. FDI is spread across many industries. The top three manufacturing industries account for only 3% of FDI: motor vehicles (1.8%), car parts (0.7%) and semiconductors (0.5%).

MNF Vertical Integration

Multinational *vertical integration* occurs when an MNF produces an intermediate product in a foreign plant and uses it in the home plant to produce a final product, or vice versa. Natural resources products may be produced in one country and shipped to another for processing as intermediate products.

Figure 9.2 shows a vertically integrated MNF with demand and marginal revenue for the final product television sets on the left. The marginal cost of producing TVs is included. Part of the cost of producing TVs is the electronic components (ECs) produced in the foreign branch on the right side of the diagram. The demand for ECs is their marginal revenue product MRP, the marginal revenue of TVs times the marginal product of the ECs. The foreign marginal cost of producing ECs is included.

The sides of Figure 9.2 work simultaneously. The demand for ECs is derived from the demand for TVs since the MR of the ECs depends on the price of TVs. If the demand for TVs rises, the MRs of both TVs and ECs increase, raising the output of ECs and their price implied price since there is no market transaction. The firm ships the ECs from its foreign branch operation to the TV assembling plant at home.

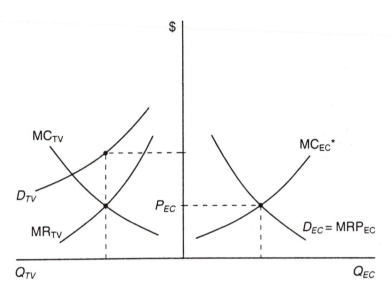

Figure 9.2
Vertical Integration in an MNF
This MNF producing TVs is vertically integrated producing electronic components (ECs) in the foreign country. Demand for ECs is derived from the upstream demand for TVs. An increase in the demand for TVs would raise their price and the MRP and price of ECs.

> *An MNF can avoid the market through vertical integration by producing its own raw materials or components in foreign branch plants.*

The MNF may use a *transfer price* when it buys components from its own foreign branch operations. Understating the price of imported components, the foreign branch firm will appear less profitable and less tariff will be paid on the imported intermediate product. The transfer price of the ECs in Figure 9.2 would be less than its true price. If the transfer price of the components is overstated the foreign branch firm will appear more profitable.

An MNF can manipulate the transfer price to shift profit to the country where taxes are lowest. If taxes are higher in the home country, the transfer price of components can be overstated to make the home assembly operation less profitable. If profit taxes are higher in the foreign country, the transfer price of components can be understated to make the foreign branch operation appear less profitable.

> *Transfer pricing can be an incentive to avoid the market by setting up a foreign branch.*

EXAMPLE 9.4   *Obstacles to International Business*

International commerce is more difficult than domestic because borders introduce various frictions. Transport costs are sizeable for some products. There are different languages and legal systems. A survey by the World Bank of firms in 69 countries led to this ranking of obstacles to international commerce. Taxes top the list, hardly a surprise. Corruption involves having to pay government officials for permits or licenses. In paying local thugs for "protection" is a normal part of business in some countries. Financing may be more difficult internationally. Poor infrastructure results from a lack of efficient government.

Obstacle
1. Taxes
2. Corruption
3. Financing
4. Poor infrastructure
5. Crime & theft

Problems for Section A

A1. Explain why the domestic automobile industry disagrees with the domestic steel and electronics industries on the desirability of foreign MNF car plants. How should domestic consumers feel about the issue?

A2. Speculate on whether a textile factory or an insurance company would be more likely to license a foreign operation. Explain which would be more likely to set up a foreign branch.

EXAMPLE 9.5 *Does FDI Promote Development?*

Whether foreign direct investment (FDI) spurs economic growth or development remains controversial. Theodore Moran, Edward Graham, and Mangus Blomström (2005) find evidence of benefits in countries with high human resources, sophisticated private sectors, competition, and open trade and investment. When FDI coincides with trade, economies expand. Mandatory joint ventures with domestic firms and tax incentives are a hindrance to growth. Sound policy is to focus on the fundamentals by improving local infrastructure, supplying information to investors, and educating or training local workers.

B.   INTERNATIONAL EXTERNALITIES

This section examines externalities in international markets. *Externalities* occur when some of the costs or benefits of a decision made by an economic agent are paid or enjoyed by others. *International externalities* occur across national borders.

Negative Production Externalities

A *negative production externality* occurs when a firm does not pay some of its cost production. Pollution is a negative externality. People near a polluting plant pay part of the implicit production costs by breathing dirty air, diminished health, frequently painting houses, rusting cars, and so on.

One economic solution to pollution is illustrated in Figure 9.3. Demand for the output of the firm is D and marginal revenue MR. *Marginal private cost* (*MPC*) is the explicit costs paid by the firm based on inputs of labor, capital, energy, intermediate inputs, and raw materials. There are also *implicit costs* due to pollution, the $6 distance between *MPC* and *marginal social cost* (MSC). If the firm is insensitive to external pollution costs, it produces where $MR = MPC$ with output of 12 and price $20.

A firm aware of its external pollution costs might produce according to *MSC*. The firm would then produce where $MR = MSC$, restricting output to 10 and raising price to $22.

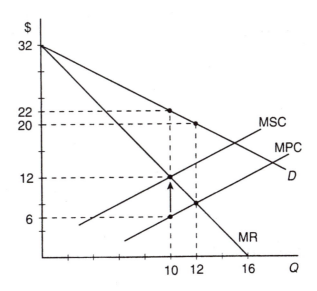

Figure 9.3
A Negative Production Externality
The difference between marginal social costs (*MSC*) and marginal private costs (*MPC*) is the external pollution cost. In this example the external pollution cost is $6 per unit of output. A myopic profit maximizer disregards external cost and produces where *MPC* = *MR* at $Q = 10$ and $P = $20. A pollution tax of $6 per unit of output raises *MPC* to *MSC*, restricts output ot 10, and raises price to $22. There is optimal pollution with a pollution tax.

Firms that want goodwill may choose to operate along the *MSC* schedule. The $6 difference could be spent on R&D to lower the level of pollution. A firm that totally ignores its pollution may make higher temporary profit but bad publicity can lower ultimate profit.

> *Negative externalities are the costs of production that are not explicitly paid by the firm. Firms interested only in short run profit ignore implicit costs and overproduce.*

If the firm in Figure 9.3 is legally responsible or liable for the costs it imposes on others, it will cut output back to the social optimum. With civil liability, property rights govern pollution.

If the firm is not liable, residents could pay the firm to produce the optional amount of pollution by negotiating. The *Coase theorem* says the socially optimal output is reached if there were costless negotiation, but negotiation is typically costly. Those paying the external costs may not be aware of the costs. If the externalities are international, negotiations will be costlier. A positive role emerges for policy to nudge the market toward accounting for social costs.

The government can tax a firm into internalizing its external costs with a tax equal to the difference between *MPC* and *MSC*. In Figure 9.3, the tax would be $6 per unit forcing the firm's *MPC* up to *MSC*. The *pollution tax* forces the firm to explicitly consider the cost of pollution, restricting output to 10 at a price of $22. Tax revenue of $6 \times 10 = $60 could be allocated to those paying the pollution costs. Revenue of the firm with the pollution tax is $160 = $220 − $60.

The US Environmental Protection Agency (EPA) imposes arbitrary limits on pollutants with little apparent regard to costs. Firms in the US face fines when random and uneven sampling turns up pollution outside arbitrary limits. As a policymaker setting scientific standards, the EPA has performed poorly.

> *Civil liability leads to efficient pollution levels. Otherwise, pollution taxes are a solution to pollution. Command and control policy is the least efficient method of pollution control.*

International Externalities

International externalities occur across borders. Pollution externalities are a problem inside a country but are more difficult to solve when the external costs are paid across boundaries. Governments may have different standards and pollution policies, and may want to ignore externalities across their border.

When a US steel plant produces smoke that pollutes Canada, civil liability is not recognized and a pollution tax is impractical. When US farmers use insecticides and fertilizers that drain into the Colorado River and cause problems downstream in Mexico, civil liability and taxes do not work.

There are few international legal precedents that offer remedies for international externalities. There is no international civil liability. Cooperation among governments, industries, and citizens groups across countries is difficult. Awareness of negative externalities and the desire for goodwill and consistent profit are ultimately powerful forces, even internationally.

International externalities pose special problems in that civil liability and pollution taxes do not apply.

Different pollution control standards have been cited as an influence on the decision of where to locate branch plants. LDCs typically have less strict environmental enforcement than DCs, and those relaxed laws may attract industry. The WTO has the goal of consistent international pollution standards.

Pollution can be technologically, but not economically, eliminated. The cost of reducing pollution should be weighed against its benefits. From the perspective of the firm, pollution control adds to the cost of production. Countries with less stringent pollution practices may attract industry but residents will have to pay high pollution costs. For LDCs, the cost of pollution control may outweigh the benefits. In WTO negotiations, LDCs generally want to avoid international pollution standards. As incomes rise, the demand for a clean environment increases.

EXAMPLE 9.6   *International Environmental Agreements*

Various international treaties include environmental issues. The *Antarctic Treaty* specifies Antarctica will be used for peaceful purposes. The *Basel Convention* reduces the movement of industrial wastes across borders. The *Biodiversity Convention* is an agreement to preserve wildlife diversity. The *Convention on International Trade in Endangered Species of World Fauna and Flora* requires permits on trade in some species. The *Climate Change Convention* encourages countries to stabilize greenhouse emissions. The *London Convention* regulates dumping of hazardous waste at sea. The *Montreal Protocol on Substances that Deplete the Ozone Layer* phases out trade in such substances. The *Nuclear Test Ban Treaty* aims to control production of nuclear weapons and waste. The *International Whaling Agreement* has the goal of preserving whale species. The US has signed all but the Basel Convention and the Biodiversity Convention, making the rest the law of the land. Austria, Brazil, Canada, Denmark, Finland, Italy, Netherlands, Norway, Poland, South Africa, Spain, Switzerland, and the UK have signed all agreements. Japan has signed all but the whaling agreement.

Positive International Externalities

Positive externalities are benefits enjoyed by someone other than the decision-maker and *positive international externalities* cross borders. One positive externality is the learning that takes place with a new productive activity. In LDCs, this positive externality can be vital to economic growth. Education is an activity with positive externalities. Students become more productive with exposure to different ideas. LDCs send their brightest students abroad to study. International trade in education has positive externalities. Returning students take back technical training and habits from the DCs that help the LDC develop.

Another example of an international positive externality occurs around ocean oil rigs that supply breeding grounds for fish that can be caught by fishing boats of other countries. Other examples of products with positive externalities are electricity, roads, water and sewer, radio, television, and telecommunication.

Figure 9.4 illustrates a positive externality with *MSC* below *MPC*. Spillover benefits of production make social costs lower than private costs. A firm that does not consider the positive spillover produces where *MPC* = *MR* at an output of 8 and price of $24. Those enjoying the external benefits would compensate the firm to increase output. Otherwise, there may be an incentive for the government to subsidize the firm to increase production, collecting taxes from those enjoying the benefits. The aim of policy is to match *MPC* and *MSC*.

With no compensation from those enjoying the external benefits of a positive externality, a firm produces too little and overprices.

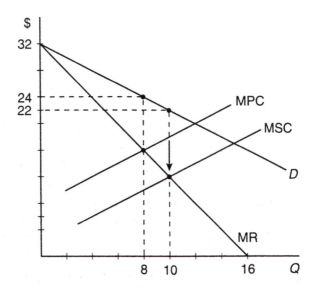

Figure 9.4
A Positive Production Externality
When *MSC* < *MPC* benefits of the production extend beyond the firm. A myopic firm would produce where *MPC* = *MR* at *Q* = 8 and *P* = $24. A subsidy would induce the firm to produce the optimal *Q* = 10 and price = $22.

International Public Goods

Public goods like police, national defense, public health, parks, roads, highways, and safe air travel create positive externalities. Production of public goods suffers the *free rider problem*. Free riders enjoy the product without paying. Markets may fail to provide public goods because some of those enjoying the product do not pay. Nonexclusion is a characteristic of public goods since it is impossible to provide a public good exclusively for part of the population.

Because of the free rider problem, markets underproduce public goods.

Governments produce public goods but across national boundaries production is more difficult. Public goods may be undersupplied close to national boundaries. Parks close to a border might be used heavily by foreign citizens. Governments not wanting to subsidize foreign citizens would reduce the supply of public goods close to the border. Some public goods cross national borders. Police and military, public health, and safe ports and airports benefit citizens of both countries.

International externalities and public goods raise international political issues. There are efforts to integrate electricity systems. International telecommunications faces local protection. Highways that span borders require international coordination. Defense spending in one country affects others. Other countries paid part of the US cost for the Kuwait war.

The solution to an international externality or public good must be political. National boundaries and different sets of laws and customs increase the cost of solutions.

EXAMPLE 9.7   *TRIPs and IPRs*

The WTO oversees Trade Related Aspects of Intellectual Property Rights (TRIPs), an agreement to oversee international disputes on Intellectual Property Rights (IPRs). Each county has its own IPR system. International trade and investment would increase if there were an international IPRs system. The TRIPs agreement sets minimum standards for each country and enforcement standards, and settles disputes.

IPRs are divided into two main categories:

copyright — rights of authors of literary and artistic works for a minimum of 50 years after the death of the author

industrial property — trademarks, inventions protected by patents, for 20 years.

Problems for Section. B

B1. Find the revenue of the firm in Figure 9.3 with and without the pollution tax. Find the tax revenue and revenue of the firm with the tax.

B2. Suppose the EPA sets pollution standards to the extent that the firm in Figure 9.3 could produce 10 units of output. Contrast this outcome with the pollution tax.

B3. Comment on the statement "International pollution is harmful to the environment and should be eliminated".

C. INTERNATIONAL POLITICAL ECONOMY

Political decisions that effect every economy are made inside international organizations such as the UN, IMF, GATT, WTO, and the World Bank. Political agreements and treaties are also made between trading partners and allies. Income redistribution is the connecting thread for studying the outcomes of such diverse political choices.

EXAMPLE 9.8   *Unfair Competition?*

> US trade law is designed to counter subsidized imports with countervailing duties. The sale of imports at prices below "fair value" is met with antidumping duties. If imports cause "material damage" duties can be imposed, apparently regardless of WTO, NAFTA, or other trade agreements. Kenneth Kelly and Morris Morkre (1998) examine the impacts of "unfairly" traded imports on the revenue of competing domestic industries between 1980 and 1988, and the effects are small. Out of a total of 174 cases of unfair trade, 117 resulted in loss of less than 5% of revenue. Potential benefits in terms of protection must nevertheless outweigh the costs of filing cases.

International Income Redistribution

An effective way to view international political economy is the activity of governments trying to influence international income distribution. DCs support the status quo and are politically conservative. LDCs try to use politics to improve their situation, some calling for a radical new international economic order.

Laws and customs inside a country are typically well defined. Ownership of goods and resources is settled through the legal system and damages are awarded if a firm or individual is negligent and damages the property of someone else. Such everyday legal affairs are more difficult to settle internationally due to the inability to collect judgments across borders. The laws, practices, and customs of *international law* are developing as international trade and investment increase. As international commerce grows, so does international law.

International political economy is concerned with the laws and practices between countries that affect international commerce and the distribution of income.

One example of an international political agreement affecting economic activity is the Bretton Woods fixed exchange rate system of the 1950s and 1960s. The stable exchange rates of that period allowed international trade and finance to grow steadily. There was little or no risk from fluctuating exchange rates. The US dollar was undervalued during the Bretton Woods period, meaning US goods were cheap abroad and foreign goods were expensive. The US had chronic trade surpluses during the 1950s.

Another international political institution is the IMF, established to help manage fixed exchange rates. The IMF has become a bank for government central banks, imposing constraints on government deficit spending and money creation.

Another example of an active international political agreement is GATT. Through GATT, member countries agree to negotiate lower protection. It is doubtful that individual governments would have been able to weather the constant protectionism without the overriding international GATT treaty. The WTO is the active extension of GATT. Negotiations are organized by the WTO which hears complaints on trade disputes and hands out settlements. Decisions of the WTO have the status of international law.

Protectionism, foreign exchange controls, limits on international investment, and labor migration laws are tools of international political economy. Every country would like to use policy to distribute income its way.

There are conflicting goals of international political economy, with policies helping one country at the expense of others. Outcomes typically depend on the political actions of all countries.

EXAMPLE 9.9 *Regional versus World Trade*

Regional free trade agreements can potentially divert trade from the rest of the world and decrease global efficiency. With NAFTA, the EU, and other regional trade blocs, there is some chance that international trade would diminish as each bloc becomes isolated. Kym Anderson and Hege Norheim (1993) show that trade is increasing both within and between blocs. Trade is returning to its high levels of the late 1920s before the protectionist era of the Great Depression and World War II. Trade is growing fastest in the Americas and Asia, but expanding in Europe as well. There is no evidence that regional trade blocs impede the growth of trade.

Table 9.1 Policy Preferences

	Voting Groups		
	A	**B**	**C**
Protection	1	3	2
Restrict foreign investment	2	1	3
Restrict immigration	3	2	1

Public Choice and International Policy

Governments may try to act on the principle of majority rule with policy based on approval by a majority of voters. Given a choice of policies on protection, foreign investment, and migration, voters can be expected to choose policies that would distribute the most income their way.

Voters may be inconsistent in their choices, the *paradox of voting*. Suppose there are three potential policies:

- protect industry that competes with imports
- restrict foreign investment
- restrict immigration

Three groups of voters rank their preferences as in Table 9.1. Each group knows exactly how the policies will redistribute income and ranks policies according to their own advantage.

If there is a vote between protection and restricting foreign investment, group B would restrict foreign investment while A and C would choose protection. If there is a vote between restricting foreign investment or immigration, C would choose to restrict immigration but both A and B would choose to restrict foreign investment. Protection is preferred to restricting foreign investment which is preferred to restricting immigration.

But consider what would happen if there were a vote between protection and restricting immigration. Group A would choose protection but B and C would choose to restrict immigration.

The paradox of voting inconsistency in public choice may help explain why politics seems irrational.

Voters seem apathetic but may be politically inactive because of *rational ignorance*. Becoming familiar with issues such as protection takes a good deal of effort. The personal benefits that would come from an informed vote may be outweighed by the costs of becoming informed. With trade policies, benefits are concentrated and localized but costs are dispersed and spread out. The average voter may be rational to remain ignorant on particular issues. Rational ignorance is tied to the free rider problem since the average voter may assume that well informed voters are likely to make the right choice.

Principles of public choice are crucial for understanding political economy. International economic policy is open to the inequities created by special interest groups and *logrolling*. Lawmakers logroll by trading votes on issues of their own particular concern. A representative from Iowa, for instance, may agree to vote for a new highway in California if the California representative votes for new post offices in Iowa. Neither keeps the interests of the entire country nor economic efficiency in mind. WTO negotiators enter into similar deals without regard for international economic efficiency.

The WTO may be a step in the right direction. Through WTO, countries are committed to increase free trade. The IMF is a stabilizing influence, leading to more consistent monetary and fiscal policies around the world. The World Bank promotes development in the LDCs by encouraging public goods such as dams and roads. Free trade and investment remain ideals worth pursuing and protectionism will always be active.

EXAMPLE 9.10 *The Escape Clause*

The US government is committed to reduce protectionism in the WTO but industries can legally apply for "temporary" escape if they suffer import competition. The US International Trade Commission (ITC) has the authority to award escape clause protection. Appeals to the ITC may examine available evidence on costs. Foreign firms found to be dumping face tariffs or quotas. Gary Hufbauer, Diane Berliner, and Kimberly Elliott (1986) summarize historical escapes, and some examples are listed below. The charted value is the estimated producer surplus due to the escape clause protection.

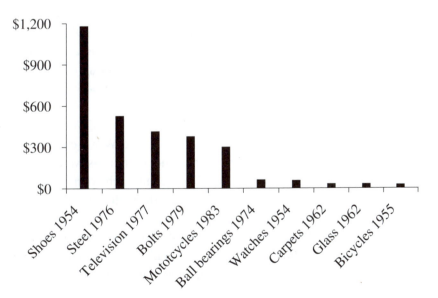

International Political Economy and Growth

In terms of economic growth, the world has two regions: the developed North abundant in capital and skilled labor; and the less developed labor abundant South. For global efficiency the North should specialize in services and high tech manufactures, both intensive in skilled labor, and capital intensive agriculture. The South would specialize in labor intensive manufacturing and agriculture. Much can be gained in both regions with increased specialization and trade.

This international specialization will be painful for the North's traditional protected manufacturing. Imagine how it looks to the LDCs in Africa and South America as they try to specialize and export labor intensive manufactures in the face of protection in the North. The industrial revolution is just beginning to dawn in many parts of the world but the DCs tax the poorest countries with their protection.

The opening of trade in manufactures remains a central issue in international political economy and lower protection of manufactures is central in the WTO negotiations. Adjustment in the North may be less painful with a gradual reduction of protection. If jobs are lost through international competition, workers can receive *trade adjustment assistance* to retrain and relocate. Such positive government policy is much less costly than misguided efforts at protectionism.

The WTO has a fundamental effect on international political economy. Through the WTO, countries are committed to a systematic reduction in trade barriers. The WTO has been successful in lowering tariffs around the world. The industrial countries are committed to the WTO, the first systematic effort to coordinate trade policy internationally. Most countries now belong to the WTO and even though WTO negotiations break down, the process continues.

The IMF is as a bank for national central banks and can loan funds to countries experiencing temporary foreign exchange shortages. The IMF has its own currency, the Special Drawing Right (SDR) accepted by national central banks. The SDR has the potential of becoming an international currency because it is already part of the monetary base of every country. Foreign exchange transactions are costly and global commerce would be much easier with a commonly accepted currency.

The IMF was formed at the end of World War II to create stability in international monetary policy. Prior to World War I, countries used the gold standard. Exchanges rates were stable and currencies were used interchangeably. The 1920s and 1930s were vastly different, each country pursuing its own independent monetary policy. Exchange rates fluctuated greatly and international commerce suffered.

In 1944, representatives of 44 countries met in Bretton Woods, New Hampshire wanting to promote cooperative monetary policy. From 1946 to 1958, the dollar was the stable international currency and the US government traded gold for dollars. The system began to unravel in the 1960s as countries pursued independent monetary policies. Germany revalued, and the UK and France devalued. Money supply growth in the US rose during the Vietnam War with the increased government spending. In 1973, Nixon ended the fixed exchange rate system pulling the dollar off the gold exchange standard.

The IMF has since been a lender of last resort to central banks. During the Mexican financial crisis in 1995, the IMF loaned the Mexican government $18 billion, about 5% of Mexican GDP. The "insurance" provided by the IMF creates a moral hazard problem. If bailouts are readily available, central banks may become careless.

The IMF has also become heavily involved in loans to LDCs, imposing tight monetary policy on the borrowers. One proposal for the IMF is to act as an international bankruptcy court. Nations have bankruptcy laws, proven essential for a successful economy. Bankruptcy insures investors of some repayment in case of business failure. International bankruptcy is difficult and the IMF can establish a forum.

The IMF can provide a stable anchor for floating exchange rates with the SDR. The IMF verifies accounting and financial reporting, and provides financial data that can be used by international lenders.

Free international trade and investment promote economic growth and should remain the goal of international economic policy.

EXAMPLE 9.11 *International IPRs*

International property rights (IPRs) involve protection of private property, one of the principles of English common law and the US legal system. IPRs are patents and copyrights. Keith Maskus (1993) discusses international IPRs in the WTO negotiations. IPRs promote innovation because the owner enjoys monopoly power but IPRs may restrict the spread of technology. DCs have trade surpluses on IPR products. Patents and copyrights are involved with 20% of total US trade. Countries are slowly moving toward reciprocity and an international IPR system. The WTO hears complaints on IPR violations. Some international action has been taken on CD piracy, pharmaceutical patent infringement, and pirated printing of copyrighted books.

EXAMPLE 9.12 *Beef Over Cheese*

Some cattle in the US are fed growth hormones and scientific evidence indicates there are no associated health problems for the cattle or for people from eating the beef. The EU, nevertheless, bans imports of such US beef on the grounds that it is unhealthy. Certainly the competition is unhealthy for EU cattle growers. In 1997, the US appealed to the WTO which ruled that there is no reason to ban the beef but the EU persisted in the ban. The US retaliated with 100% tariffs valued at $117 million, the estimated lost beef sales to the EU, tit for tat. Hardest hit were EU exporters of Roquefort cheese, pork, and mustard, not to mention US consumers of a variety of European food products. The WTO affords a platform for negotiations to eliminate fabricated harmful trade barriers.

Problems for Section C

C1. If all the oil in the world were in one country, would international oil prices over time be any different? What difference would it make if the country tried to maximize profit for the present year or over the next century?

C2. Illustrate the pattern of trade and the gains from trade between the North and South with a production possibilities frontier for each region. Show the effects of Northern protection of its traditional industries. Discuss the income redistribution in both regions that would occur with a move to free trade.

EXAMPLE 9.13 *Libre Mexico*

During the 1990s Mexico made a dramatic switch in trade policy after decades of misguided import substitution and mismanaged socialized industries. Mexico has become more open and competitive. Mexico has made free trade agreements with Chile, NAFTA, Columbia, Venezuela, Bolivia, Costa Rica, and Nicaragua, and negotiations are continuing with the EU. Productivity and income promise to rise substantially in Mexico over the coming decades.

D.   STEPS OF ECONOMIC INTEGRATION

There is a rough idea about what a "nation" is: a central government, borders, territory, language, culture, history, flags, currencies, border patrols, and defense against other nations. Characteristics of nations stressed in international economics involve the government's ability to erect artificial barriers to trade, migration, and investment, as well as the ability to tax and print money.

A political process is leading toward *international economic integration* with countries having common trade, legal, fiscal, and monetary policies. Measured steps can be taken to encourage free trade and investment. Through international economic integration, the political economy of a country changes and economic efficiency improves.

There are four steps of international economic integration:

- *free trade area*
- *customs union*
- *common market*
- *monetary union*

EXAMPLE 9.14 *The Mexican Connection*

The economies of the US and Mexico are more intertwined in NAFTA. Trade between the two countries involves a good deal of shipment back and forth of intermediate products. In the top five categories traded in 2004, the three below appear in both exports and imports in $billion. It is important to remember that there is a huge range of products and qualities of products classified in these official categories. This high level of trade within industry categories suggests manufacturing processes are highly integrated across borders according to labor costs and other costs of production as well as transport costs. The other two top US exports are Chemicals and Machinery at $9 billion apiece. The other two top Mexican exports are Oil & Gas at $14 billion and Apparel & Accessories at $7 billion.

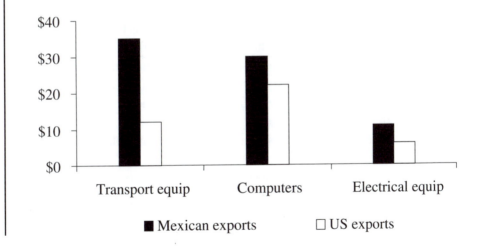

Free Trade Areas

Protectionism is costly but it is difficult to persuade governments to quit protecting industries that offer politicians money and votes. Nevertheless, the countries of the EU, South America, Africa, Southeast Asia, the Arabian Gulf, the Caribbean, and other regions have entered into free trade agreements. The US, Canada, and Mexico are eliminating protection with NAFTA. Countries that agree to eliminate trade barriers enjoy gains, especially in industries that export and use imported intermediate products.

An FTA is the first step toward international economic integration. An FTA removes the temptation of politicians to sell protection. An FTA removes the temptation of industry to rely on politics to maintain profit, forcing it to become more efficient and innovative.

Countries agreeing to free trade can form a free trade area (FTA).

By 2008 in NAFTA, there should be no tariffs between the US, Canada, and Mexico. Countries give up their right to tax imports and protect traditional industries but gain in national income and promote a fair distribution of income. FTAs take trade policy out of the hands of shortsighted politicians.

There is some concern that the world is breaking up into regional *trade blocs* and that trade between these blocs will be reduced. If country A lowers its tariff on country B and not country C, some exports from C could be diverted. Barry Eichengreen and Doug Irwin (1994) examine regional free trade agreements between 1928 and 1938 and find there was very little diverted or lost trade.

NAFTA is a watershed in US trade policy. Protectionism has been the hallmark of US trade policy. The GATT treaty and the WTO have led the US toward free trade since World War II but some industries remain highly protected in the entrenched political system. Canada and the US were fumbling toward an FTA when Mexico approached the US in the early 1990s. By making NAFTA a treaty, the administrative branch of government has taken the power from Congress to levy special interest tariffs. Free trade on all products is the ultimate goal of NAFTA but there are clauses and special deals that will impede progress toward free trade.

NAFTA sets up an environmental agency that will monitor pollution in all three countries. Labor issues will be dealt with separately and could slow elimination of some tariffs. Specific industries may be exempt from NAFTA altogether: peanuts, textiles, frozen orange juice, washing machines, and others. In each case, local industries put pressure on representatives who only agreed to NAFTA with exemptions in side deals. Still, NAFTA represents a large step toward economic freedom and away from special interest legislation.

Another argument used against NAFTA is that it will lower US wages. Factor proportions theory suggests unskilled wages in the US will fall. As free trade with Mexico increases, US workers will have the incentive to increase education and job training as more skilled higher paying jobs open in export industries.

EXAMPLE 9.15 *EU Origins*

The EU has taken over 50 years to progress to its current stage of economic integration. Progress gradually occurs with free trade, investment, and migration. The EU is moving toward common migration policy, transport laws, and tax systems. The following is a short history of progress toward the EU.

1951	France, Germany, Italy, Belgium, the Netherlands, and Luxembourg form the European Coal and Steel Community
1957	These countries sign the Treaty of Rome establishing the European Community (EC)
1968	EC removes internal duties and establishes a customs union
1972	Denmark, Ireland, and the UK join the EC and the "snake" exchange rate links currencies
1985	Spain and Portugal join the EC
1986	Single European Act leads to a common market
1992	Start of common market with free labor and capital mobility
1999	The euro and monetary union

Customs Unions

Beyond an FTA, the next step toward international economic integration is a *customs union* (CU) with common external tariffs and quotas. The step to a CU is much harder because each country has its own particular industries facing international competition from the rest of the world (ROW). Industries might give up their protection from a neighboring country inside an FTA but still want protection from competing industries in the ROW.

A CU is an FTA with common protection for member countries with the rest of the world (ROW).

It is difficult to have an FTA without a CU since goods coming from member countries must be checked to make sure imports from the ROW are not being reshipped. Importers might buy goods from the ROW in the CU country with the lowest protection and ship it to other countries inside the CU. For instance, if Germany has a 25% tariff on shoes and France has a 10% tariff, French importers might buy Brazilian shoes in France and ship them to Germany disguised as French goods. For an FTA to work smoothly with open borders, it must become a CU.

An FTA is easier to form between countries with fewer common industries because there is less call for protection. A CU is easier to form if member countries have the same industries because they can agree on protection from the ROW. The step from an FTA to a CU is difficult.

It is not easy for governments to sacrifice power and accept common trade policy. The process involves compromise between two governments in setting common levels of protection. Given the political difficulties encountered in one country, agreeing to common protection levels across countries is more difficult. The EU countries have struggled through years of political compromise.

Ideally, all protectionism would be eliminated. Imagine you are the dictator of a country where tariffs, quotas, and other nontariff trade barriers are illegal. Your imaginary country trades freely with the world economy, efficiently carrying out activities according to its comparative advantage. Losses would occur if you started to restrict trade. Relatively efficient industries would have to shut down and workers would have to be retrained in jobs that were less productive. Average incomes would fall and the least efficient would enjoy the largest gains. Income would go from those with low income to those with high income. Industries would have to train professional lobbyists and spend rent seeking revenue trying to influence you to protect their industry. Unfortunately, legislators are unlikely to vote to make protectionism illegal because they would be eliminating one of their main income sources.

EXAMPLE 9.16 *Projected Gains from Integration*

Trade within the EU increases specialization across countries. Alasdair Smith and Anthony Venables (1988) project gains for the German and Italian appliance industries, but losses for those industries in the rest of the EU. Industries projected to gain throughout the EU are office machines, fibers, autos, and footwear. Overall income gains are projected between 2% and 5%. Other studies project similar industrial adjustments for regional economic integration.

EXAMPLE 9.17 *EU + EFTA*

The European Free Trade Association (EFTA) is a customs union of Austria, Finland, Iceland, Norway, Sweden, and Switzerland that is moving to join the EU. EFTA is the largest trading partner of the EU followed by the US. The EU is by far the largest trading partner of EFTA. Relative to the EU, the EFTA is small and should gain the most due to improved terms of trade.

Common Markets

The next step in international integration is a *common market* (CM), a CU without restrictions on international movements of labor and capital. The EU is a CM, with workers and firms free to move to any member country.

There is discussion of creating a CM between the US and Canada. Both countries have restrictive immigration policies but it is a large step for the two to open their borders to each other's workers and firms. Common policies for international factor movements with the ROW would also have to be adopted.

With free trade and factor mobility, the economies in a CM are almost completely integrated. Markets operate to create similar living standards throughtout the CM.

EXAMPLE 9.18 *FTAA*

Free trade is the goal of ongoing negotiations in the Western Hemisphere. NAFTA establishes free trade between Canada, Mexico, and the US. The Andean Pact and Mercosur do the same for South America. There are also free trade pacts in Central America and the Caribbean. The next step is to tie them all together in the Free Trade Area of the Americas (FTAA). Countries in FTAA would benefit through free trade and investment. Open migration policy will meet resistance in Canada and the US, and open investment policy will meet resistance in Latin America. A hemispheric monetary union with a common currency would result in economic stability and growth.

EXAMPLE 9.19 *ASEAN Common Market*

In a common market, workers and firms freely move throughout a region. ASEAN free trade is becoming a reality. The Association of South East Asian Nations (ASEAN) includes Japan, China and South Korea and the "tiger economies" of Southeast Asia (Brunei, Cambodia, Laos, Indonesia, Malaysia, Myanmar, the Philippines, Singapore, Thailand and Vietnam). ASEAN is progressing toward becoming a common market.

Monetary and Political Unions

The next step of economic integration is a *monetary union* (MU) with countries sharing a common monetary policy and currency. The step to an MU is the most difficult because governments have a monopoly on printing money, allowing them to spend more than tax revenue.

The EU has become an MU with the euro currency in most of the countries. The prices of most currencies in Europe had been moving with the German mark. Since World War II, Germany has had low money supply growth and inflation. The Italians have a history of much higher money growth and inflation. Each government of Europe has pursued its own independent monetary policy. The euro now circulates in most European countries and each government has lost its ability to spend the money it prints.

Once an MU is formed on top of a CM, little is left of the country from the viewpoint of economics. International economists would be out of a job if all countries of the world formed an MU but everyone else would be better off. National boundaries are inhibiting. Stripping off the inhibitions takes a country through the various steps of economic integration, leading to gains.

A *political union* (PU) is the final stage of integration with commonly accepted legislative and judicial processes. States in the US belong to a PU. Countries in a PU lose most of their political identity.

Economic integration has been proceeding. In South America, Central America, the Caribbean, the Pacific Rim, the Arabian Gulf, Asia, and Africa, numerous agreements are in effect. Countries in Africa have had some success in economic integration. Japan has not integrated with other economies. The move toward free commerce in Eastern Europe will have dramatic effects.

The most powerful influences leading the world toward international economic integration are increased foreign investment and improved communication. Trade continues to grow in size and importance and with direct investment MNFs eliminate borders. Everyone has an interest in increasing productivity and income. Most people in the world live in poverty and many others live by standards well below the DCs. Getting all of the world into the mainstream of efficient economic activity is the main challenge of political economy during the coming century.

EXAMPLE **9.20** *Can You Spare Me an SDR?*

The International Monetary Fund (IMF) is a bank for government central banks, a bank for the banks of the banks. The SDR is an accounting form of money defined in terms of a basket of world currencies. The SDR has the potential to become an international currency. With a stable international currency, central banks would lose their ability to arbitrarily print money to cover budget deficits that could only be financed by the sale of bonds. Foreign exchange markets would be unnecessary. With a stable supply of international currency, there would be steady prices and no inflation. The IMF is poised to become the provider of the international currency although national governments are not prone to give up their practice of printing fiat currency.

Economic Systems and International Integration

The main difference between capitalism and socialism is the ownership of productive factors. Private ownership of productive factors and decentralized decisions characterize *capitalism*. Government ownership and centralized command and control decisions characterize *socialism*. The countries of the world have various mixes of these ideals.

The Soviet Union, China, Cuba, Eastern Europe, and others had planned socialist economies with a system of *material balance planning*. Priorities set by the government for finished products and outputs of intermediate goods were planned and allocated. Many agricultural and consumer products, however, were produced in markets. International trade and finance were controlled by the government to meet arbitrary goals.

The US is a predominantly capitalist economy with market allocation. Markets determine outputs and prices. Production that is efficient and profitable continues, and production that is inefficient and unprofitable ceases. The US has a socialized postal service, some public housing, and partly socialized medical care. Utility companies have been government monopolies since the 1930s. Market forces determine most international trade and finance.

Nations choose economic systems along the spectrum from capitalism to socialism.

Countries in Eastern Europe have been closed to international trade and investment since World War II but are now opening to international markets. Foreign investment and trade between the Western capitalist economies and socialist Eastern Europe is increasing. Russia is beginning to shake off its poor socialist tradition. China has been a closed socialist economy for most of this century but is integrating back into the world economy.

LDCs in South America, Africa, and Asia must choose an economic system. Free market economies rely on free international trade and investment. Planned socialist economies restrict international commerce and stress arbitrary economic targets. Such restrictions are unfortunate from a global perspective because of the potential gains from free international trade and investment. LDCs would benefit from open enterprise and international commerce. DCs should encourage this trend by dropping all protection of imports from the LDCs.

EXAMPLE 9.21 *China and the WTO*

As China integrates into the world economy, real incomes around the world will rise. China negotiated for 13 years before entering the WTO. Protectionist claims against China have been rising due to the increased import competiton in textiles and other labor intensive industries.

Problems for Section D

D1. Eastern European countries were integrated closely with Russia in the Soviet Union. How have they benefited through disintegration of the Soviet Union?

D2. Could two countries agree to free international factor movements with no FTA? How would it work?

D3. Use factor abundance, factor intensity, and the manufacturing wages to constrast the US trade with Mexico versus Canada in Example 9.23.

EXAMPLE 9.22 *Why Not Dump Dumping?*

Antidumping laws of the US are a protectionist relic. No firm will dump by selling its output at a loss for long. The real issue is whether US industry and labor groups will be forced to face international competition. The dumping law may "protect" existing industry but it harms productivity, labor, and other industry by limiting specialization. Chile's government correctly claims that US dumping laws are "a protectionist instrument that has nothing to do with anti-competitive behavior". Jon Jenson, President of the Precision Metalforming Association points out that US industry is at a "comparative disadvantage" because of the higher priced steel inputs due to antidumping restrictions. Dumping provisions of US trade law should be eliminated.

CONCLUSION

Free international trade and investment provide ideals for international political economy. The trend toward international economic integration is improving efficiency and living standards around the world. The final section of the text turns to international money, foreign exchange markets, and macroeconomics.

Terms

Branch plant

Common market (CM)

Customs union (CU)

Economic union (EU)

Externalities

Free rider problem

Free trade area (FTA)

Transfer pricing

Horizontal and vertical integration

Joint venture

Licensing agreement

Marginal social cost

Paradox of voting

Public goods

Rational ignorance

MAIN POINTS

- Multinational firms encourage economic integration and increase international trade and investment.
- Externalities are a rationale for economic policy. International externalities call for policy coordination between countries.
- International political economy examines the causes and effects of political choice across countries. Income redistribution occurs with political choice.
- Nations integrate themselves through various steps to promote free international trade and investment. Each country operates its economic system on the spectrum between capitalism and socialism.

REVIEW PROBLEMS

1. Explain why the US has many MNF branches in construction, business services, and oil.
2. Analyze what happens in a multiplant firm similar to Figure 9.1 if the costs of operation are the same in each plant.
3. How could price discrimination between foreign and domestic markets lead a firm to establish an MNF branch?
4. Analyze what happens to the vertically integrated MNF in Figure 9.2 if costs rise in the foreign country because of a labor contract in the electronic component industry.
5. Smoke from a factor in country A falls across the border onto country B. What are the 3 ways to control this problem?
6. How can a government host to an MNF encourage the positive externalities that come with MNF activity? How will domestic firms react?
7. In some ways the EU acts like a single country and the separate countries in Europe like the states in the US. Where might this sort of international cooperation spread?
8. Illustrate North and South trade with offer curves including protectionism of the North. What happens to the volume and terms of trade when this protectionism is lifted?
9. Speculate on why economic integration has not been successful in Africa. Why has Japan not entered into economic integration?
10. What would be the economic effects of an FTA between the US and Japan? A CU? A CM? An EU? What are the politics of such agreements?
11. Answer the same questions as in #10 for the four stages of international economic integration between the US and the EU.
12. Predict what would happen if the MU between states in the US were eliminated and each state government could print its own currency.
13. What would be the consequences for the US if an FTA was formed for all of North, Central, and South America? A CU? A CM? An EU?

READINGS

Philip Martin (1993) *Trade and Migration: NAFTA and Agriculture*, Washington: Institute for International Economics. Migrant workers and NAFTA.

Gary Hufbauer and Jeffrey Schott (1994) *Western Hemisphere Economic Integration*, Washington: Institute for International Economics. Economic integration in North and South America.

Nora Lustig, Barry Bosworth, and Robert Lawrence, eds. (1992) *Assessing the Impact of North American Free Trade*, Washington: Institute for International Economics. Articles on assessing NAFTA.

Harold Crookell (1990) *Canadian-American Trade and Investment Under the Free Trade Agreement*, New York: Quorum Books. Changes for the two countries.

James Cassing and Steve Husted, eds. (1988) *Capital, Technology, and Labor in the Global Economy*, Washington: The AEI Press. Globalization of production and technology.

Jeffrey Arpan and David Ricks, eds. (1990) *Directory of Foreign Manufacturers in the US*, Atlanta: Georgia State University Business Press. Detailed data on foreign MNFs in the US.

John Carrol, ed. (1988) *International Environmental Diplomacy*, Cambridge: Cambridge University Press, 1988. Articles on the international politics.

Tom Tietenberg (1994) *Environmental and Natural Resource Economics*, New York: Harper-Collins. Very good on production externalities.

James Buchanan and Gordon Tullock (1962) *The Calculus of Consent*, Ann Arbor: University of Michigan Press. The classic in public choice economics.

Jeffry Frieden and David Lake, eds. (1987) *International Political Economy: Perspective on Global Wealth and Power*, New York: St. Martin's Press. Articles on international political economy.

Stephen Easton (1989) Free trade, nationalism, and the common man: The Free Trade Agreement between Canada and the US, *Contemporary Policy Issues*. Free trade from a Canadian viewpoint.

Paul Gregory and Robert Stuart (1985) *Comparative Economic Systems*, Boston: Houghton Mifflin. Perspective on different economic systems.

Melvyn Kraus, ed. (1973) *The Economics of Integration*, London: George Allen and Unwin Ltd. Articles on economic integration.

INTERNATIONAL MONEY AND MACROECONOMICS

CHAPTER 10

Balance of Payments

Preview

This chapter introduces the adjustment mechanisms of the *balance of payments* (*BOP*). Issues include how a country finances a trade deficit and what happens with the foreign currency of a trade surplus. Another issue is the effect of government deficits and surpluses on the BOP. The potential of government policy to influence the *BOP* is examined. Specifically, this chapter examines:

- *Import and export elasticities* and the trade balance
- Components of the *BOP*
- The *government budget* and the BOP
- International roles of *monetary policy* and *fiscal policy*

INTRODUCTION

Excess supply and demand predict how international markets adjust. Adjustments occur continuously in both export and import markets. If the price of an import rises, spending on the import adjusts. As in all markets, quantity demanded falls with the higher price. The higher price increases domestic production, contributing to the decline in imports. Import spending, price times quantity, may fall or rise. If imports fall enough, import spending falls with the higher price.

A higher price for an export will increase export revenue unless the export quantity falls by a larger percentage than price rises. For economies highly dependent on exports, international price changes can be critical. Examples are Colombia and coffee, Saudi Arabia and oil, Costa Rica and bananas, South Africa and gold, and so on. Even for large diversified countries, international prices changes can be important. When the price of imported oil rose with the embargoes of the 1970s, shocks were felt in developed countries.

Given the thousands of international markets and continuous adjustments, no country spends on imports exactly what it earns from exports during a year. The current account of international cash flows in the balance of payments (*BOP*) includes trade in goods and services plus net interest payments. If the current account does not equal zero, there must be international borrowing or lending. A current account deficit is financed through international borrowing or selling assets.

This chapter describes the fundamental mechanisms of such *BOP* adjustment. Current and capital accounts of the *BOP* reflect an international adjustment process.

Government economic policy may influence the *BOP*. Fiscal policy refers to government spending and taxes, and monetary policy refers to control of the money supply. Fiscal and monetary policies are poor tools for influencing the *BOP*.

A. ELASTICITIES AND THE TRADE BALANCE

Changing prices of traded goods affect export revenue and import spending. Imagine you own a warehouse full of athletic shoes and their export demand rises because of a trend toward more exercise. If you also operate a plant producing the shoes, you might plan to increase production, hire and train labor, buy supplies, and perhaps invest in plant and equipment. If athletic shoes are imported, you have to compete with imports.

In the aggregate, changing prices of merchandise imports and exports affect the *balance of trade* (*BOT*), export revenue minus import expenditure. The *balance on goods and services* (*BGS*) includes trade in both merchandise and services:

$$BGS = X - M.$$

Changing Export Prices and the BGS

A country that enjoys a higher price for an export will increase production and export revenue, but domestic consumers pay the higher price. In Figure 10.1 at a world price of $10, exports equal 100 units of business services. Domestically, 200 units are produced but only 100 consumed. Exporters can sell as much as they want at the international price. If it rises to $12, domestic consumers cut consumption to 75 while producers increase production from 200 to 225. Excess supply or exports expand to 150 at the higher international price.

Both producers and consumers respond to the price change but there is no explanation of why the international price rises in Figure 10.1. The price could be increasing because of higher demand in the LDCs for telecommunications, banking, and financial services.

Selling more services at the higher price increases export revenue. The level of exports rises by 50, export revenue rises from $1000 to $1800, and total revenue of domestic firms rises from $2000 to $2700. Total revenue includes export and domestic revenue. Producer surplus increases. Domestic consumers pay a higher price and consume less, and consumer surplus falls. Consumers

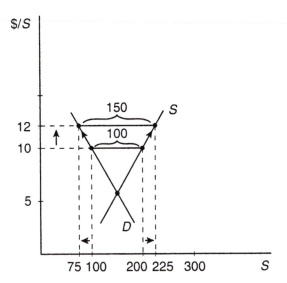

Figure 10.1
Higher Export Prices
When the price of exported services rises from $10 to $12, the domestic quantity demanded falls to 75 and the quantity supplied rises to 225. Exports rise from 100 to 150. Producer surplus rises but consumer surplus falls.

spend $900 on 75 units instead of the previous $1000 on 100 units. The gain in producer surplus outweighs the loss in consumer surplus.

A higher export price can be caused by anything that increases demand among global buyers or decreases supply among global sellers. This principle can be illustrated with an increase in the excess demand for services from the foreign country in Figure 10.2. Eastern Europe, for example, is opening to EU banks and financial firms. In Figure 10.2, foreign excess demand and export revenue increase. Figures 10.1 and 10.2 are consistent. The higher foreign excess demand in Figure 10.2 is the cause of the higher price in Figure 10.1. In Figure 10.2 the price increase is *endogenous*, or explained by the model. In Figure 10.1, the price change is *exogenous*, outside the model.

Higher export prices raise export revenue and the BGS.

EXAMPLE 10.1 *Price Taking Small Open Economies*

Are small economies really price takers in their export markets? Arvind Panagariya, Shekhar Shah, and Deepak Mishra (2001) find that Bangladesh faces an import elasticity of 26 in textiles and apparel products. A 1% increase in the price of these products by Bangladesh reduces the quantity of exports by 26%, not perfect but very elastic indeed. These exporters in Bangladesh have

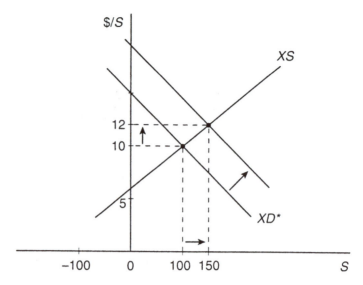

Figure 10.2
Increased Foreign Demand for Home Exports
When foreign excess demand for home exports (XD^*) rises, the international price is pushed up from $10 to $12 and the quantity exported by the home country increases from 100 to 150.

no market power, making the price taking assumption seem reasonable for a wide range of products and countries.

Changing Import Prices and the BGS

Imports are inversely related to their domestic price. If the price of an import rises, its level falls because of a decrease in the quantity demanded and an increase in the domestic quantity supplied. Domestic consumers substitute away from higher priced imports, and domestic firms increase output. Consumers as a group are hurt by the higher price but producers benefit.

An example of increased import prices occurred when the Organization of Petroleum Exporting Countries (OPEC) was able to triple the price of oil in the early 1970s. Domestic consumers had to pay higher prices but the domestic oil extraction industry boomed. As other examples, bad weather in Colombia decreases the supply of coffee and drives up the international coffee price, and depreciation of the dollar raises the dollar price of imported automobiles.

Consider the exogenous increase in the price of imported manufactures from $5 to $7.50 in Figure 10.3. The domestic quantity demanded falls from 300 to 250 as consumers switch to substitutes and their real income falls. Spending by domestic consumers increases from $1500 to $1875. Consumer surplus falls more than producer surplus rises. The quantity supplied domestically rises from

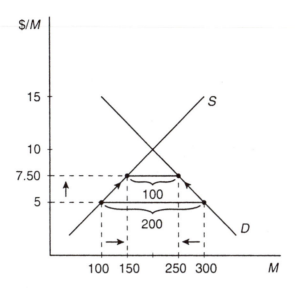

Figure 10.3
Higher Import Prices
An increase in the price of imports from $5 to $7.50 increases the quantity supplied domestically from 100 to 150. The domestic quantity demanded falls from 300 to 250. Imports fall from 200 to 100. Import spending in this example falls. The loss in consumer surplus is greater than the gain in producer surplus.

100 to 150 as the domestic industry responds to the profit opportunity. Revenue of domestic firms rises from $500 to $1125. Producer surplus rises, taking some of the previous consumer surplus. The domestic manufacturing industry benefits from the higher price.

Higher import prices help the domestic import competing industry but hurt domestic consumers.

For the country, the change in import spending with the higher price of imports alters the BGS. Import spending falls from $1000 to $750 in this example, raising the BGS.

Import Elasticities and the BGS

If there is little time or opportunity for adjustment to a higher import price, demand for imports is *inelastic*. A price increase then results in increased import spending because the level of imports does not fall enough to offset the higher price.

If the price of imports and import spending are negatively related as in Figure 10.3, import demand is elastic. If consumers and firms have the time and opportunity to adjust imports, import spending can fall with a higher price.

In the 1970s at the time of the increase in oil prices, consumers were driving large inefficient cars and were not concerned with spending on fuel. There was little opportunity for decreasing oil consumption with the higher prices. Oil imports were *inelastic* and OPEC oil export revenue rose.

In the face of consistently high oil prices, however, cars became smaller and much more fuel efficient. Houses were insulated and heating and cooling technology improved dramatically. Over time, oil consumption fell. On the supply side, domestic drilling was taking place in remote mountains and deeper offshore and government lands were opened to drilling. The quantity of oil supplied domestically increased. England discovered oil in the North Sea, and other nonOPEC production increased. OPEC learned the hard way about import elasticity as their export revenue tapered and imports proved more elastic.

The *import elasticity* summarizes the relationship between import prices and expenditure. It is the percentage change in imports divided by the percentage change in price, in absolute value:

$$\text{Import elasticity} = \varepsilon_{\text{imp}} = |(\%\Delta Q_{\text{imp}})/(\%\Delta P_{\text{imp}})|.$$

The symbol Δ means "change in". Read "$\%\Delta X$" as "the percentage change in X". Quantity Q_{imp} and price P_{imp} are inversely related but the absolute value makes the import elasticity positive and easier to discuss.

To find percentage changes, subtract the original level from the new one and divide by the average. In Figure 10.3, the $\%\Delta Q_{\text{imp}}$ is $(100 - 200)/150 = -.667 = -66.7\%$ and $\%\Delta P_{\text{imp}}$ is $(\$7.50 - \$5)/\$6.25 = 0.4 = 40\%$. The import elasticity in Figure 10.3 is $|-66.7\%/40\%| = 1.67$.

If the import elasticity is greater than one, demand for imports is *elastic*. Price and import spending move in opposite directions if the demand for imports is elastic. If the import elasticity is less than one, the change in the level of imports is not large enough to offset the change in price and imports are *inelastic*. Higher import prices imply more import spending when import demand is inelastic but less import spending when import demand is elastic.

The effect of a price change on import spending depends on the import elasticity. If imports are inelastic, price and import spending are positively related. If imports are elastic, price and import spending are negatively related.

Whether a higher price for imported oil, coffee, bananas, automobiles, television sets, or tires increases or decreases import spending is an empirical issue. Countries reveal their import elasticities in their various import markets.

There are higher import elasticities for goods that

- have more elastic supply
- have more available substitutes

- are larger share of consumer budgets
- are luxuries

If domestic supply is more elastic, price increases cause domestic supply to rise more. If there are more substitutes for a good, consumers can switch away from it when its price rises. If consumers spend a large share of their budget on a good, they will notice an increase in its price and search for substitutes. Purchases of luxury goods such as diamonds are more easily delayed purchase of oil and other basic commodities.

EXAMPLE 10.2 *The Dollar and the BGS*

The balance on goods and services BGS between 1982 and 1998 is indexed to 1 in the final year in the chart below. The trade weighted exchange rate $1/e$ is included to examine the evidence of whether it had an influence on the BGS. During this entire period the dollar appreciated in terms of the countries involved in trade. From 1982 to 1986, export revenue fell with higher priced US products in foreign markets. Exports of machinery, transport equipment, apparel, and primary metals declined. Import spending on oil increased sharply with higher oil prices. From 1986 to 1992, the BGS increased in spite of the dollar appreciation. Finally, from 1992 to 1998 the BGS fell with the dollar appreciation as suggested by theory. Such ups and downs are not unusual, and the connection between the exchange rate and trade balance is difficult to predict.

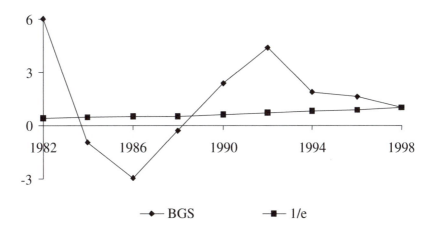

The Terms of Trade and the BGS

Consider a country exporting business services in exchange for manufactured goods at international prices of $5 for M and $10 for S. Each unit of services is traded for 2 units of manufactures. The *terms of trade* (*tt*) or the relative price of exported services is 2.

The increase in the international price of S to \$12 in Figure 10.1 improves tt to \$12/\$5 = 2.4. Each unit of exported S brings in 2.4 units of M, an improvement of 20% in the tt.

Adjustments in tt takes place regularly. The IMF reports that since 1970

- the tt of DCs has fallen
- the tt of oil exporting countries has increased
- LDCs that do not export oil have suffered a decline in tt

The tt is estimated by aggregating traded products and indexing export prices and import prices. Lessons can be learned from aggregation. Changes in the terms of trade can be dramatic and affect the standard of living.

Another illustration drives home the importance of import elasticities. Suppose the home country improves the technology of producing its exports. With the same resources, more output is produced. The home country has become more "competitive" to use a popular phrase.

Improved technology in export production is illustrated in Figure 10.4. With the increase in excess supply it is not clear what happens to export revenue. The country sells more services in the world market and exports rise from 100 to 140. The price of services, however, falls from \$10 to \$8. The change in export revenue depends on foreign import elasticity. In this example, export revenue rises from \$1000 to \$1120. Foreign import demand is elastic because price and export revenue move in opposite directions.

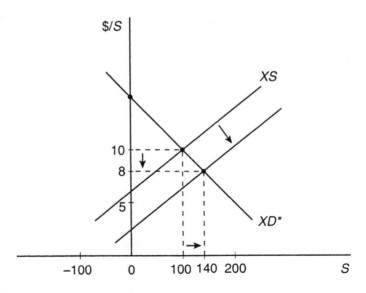

Figure 10.4
Improved Technology in Export Production
Increased excess supply of services drives down the price of exports and increases exports. The direction of change in export revenue depends on the foreign import elasticity.

If foreign import demand is inelastic, becoming more "competitive" lowers export revenue. Improved technology in the production of exports then results in lower export revenue. If the new level of exports were less than 125 in Figure 10.4, export revenue would decline. If the level of exports rose to only 115 with the increased *XS* and the same fall in price, export revenue would drop from $1000 to $920. If foreign import demand is inelastic, increased excess supply at home lowers export revenue. This seems paradoxical because improved technology, increased competitiveness, and a trade surplus are all thought to be beneficial.

In the examples so far, prices in the foreign country are stated in terms of dollars. In reality, the foreign country has its own currency and international trade involves the exchange of currencies. The total transactions in the foreign exchange market determine exchange rates. Changes in the exchange rate affect the price of imports and exports.

EXAMPLE 10.3 *The FX Rate and Agricultural Markets*

> Every market has its own producers and production takes planning and investing. Buyers may be firms in various industries wanting intermediate products around the world. Exchange rates have effects on many markets and the destination can be important. Nathan Childs and Michael Hammig (1987) trace regional exports of corn, wheat, soybeans, and rice from the US between 1968 and 1984. Soybean exports are sensitive to the exchange rate but corn exports are not. Rice and wheat exports to Europe and Asia are sensitive but exports to Latin America are not. The effects of the exchange rate are felt after two to three years in these export markets because of the time required for planning, planting, and harvesting. The market for each product is different. It is difficult to uncover effects in aggregate trade data, but the experts doing the trading are aware of the influence of exchange rates.

Problems for Section A

A1. Start with Figure 10.1 and suppose the exogenous P_{exp} falls from $10 to $8, quantity demanded rises from 100 to 125, and quantity supplied falls from 200 to 175. Diagram this change in the export market and find the new export revenue.

A2. Similar to Figure 10.3, suppose quantity demanded falls from 300 to 270 and quantity supplied rises from 100 to 130 when the P_{imp} rises to $7.50. Find ε_{imp}. What happens to the *BOT* with this increase in P_{imp}?

A3. Construct an example of improved technology in export production and the international price decline based on Figure 10.4 that has unchanged export revenue.

B.   *CURRENT AND CAPITAL ACCOUNTS*

The *BOP* has two main components,

- the current account, *CA*
- the capital account, *KA*

Estimates of the *CA* and the *KA* regularly make the news and provide insight into the economy's international situation. They are also the basis calls for government policy.

Every year taxpayers and firms produce accounting balance sheets that serve as the basis for taxes and financial reports. A balance sheet shows current cash transactions, a credit or positive number when cash comes in and a debit or negative number when cash goes out. At the end of the accounting period the sum of the entries indicates net cash flow.

Borrowing is a credit because cash comes in even though debt increases and future debt payments must be made. Lending is as a debit because cash flows out even though lending sets up future receipts. Wealth holders can accumulate assets other than cash. If an asset is bought with cash, a debit would be entered on the balance sheet. If another asset is sold for cash, cash flows in and a credit is entered. The capital account *KA* reports this borrowing and lending or selling and buying of assets.

EXAMPLE 10.4 *Japan, Inc*

Japan has developed into a leader in world trade and investment as discussed by Naohiro Amaya (1988). Savings rates in Japan are high relative to other DCs. The US is the opposite with a low savings rate and incoming foreign investment. The pattern may change because the *shin-jinrui* (young wealthy) in Japan are spending more and saving less, while baby boomers in the US are saving for retirement. The *keiretsu* business system entails buying supplies from firms in a close knit group, a "buddy system" that competing US firms claim is unfair. Japanese markets were traditionally seen as too small for US firms but that has changed. As an example, Japanese drive on the left side of the road and US automakers tried to sell cars in Japan with steering wheels on the left until only a few years ago. Japan, a traditional society with mistrust of outsiders, has trouble accepting the role of a world leader. The Japanese education system does not encourage innovation. Japanese business managers have trouble dealing with change and international competition. Japan is a world leader facing many internal challenges.

BOP Accounts

Much like firms and individuals, a country keeps its international books on a balance sheet, the balance of payments. The *BOP* is the sum of the *current account* and the *capital account*,

$$BOP = CA + KA$$

Transactions involving current goods and services are in the *CA*. Investment transactions involving international borrowing and lending are in the *KA*.

The components of the current account are the *balance on goods and services* (BGS) and *net investment income* (*NII*)

$$CA = BGS + NII$$

The *BGS* is the *balance of trade* (*BOT*) in goods plus *net trade in services* (*TS*)

$$BGS = BOT + TS$$

TS includes transactions for transportation, travel, accounting, financial services, telecommunications, utilities, entertainment, and so on. This category is sometimes called true, business, or commercial services.

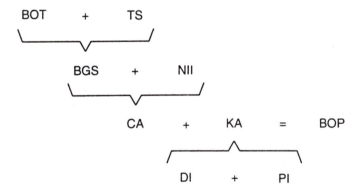

Figure 10.5
Element of the Balance of Payments
The balance of payments (*BOP*) is the sum of two basic elements, the current account (*CA*) and the capital account (*KA*). The CA is the balance on goods and services (*BGS*) plus net investment income (*NII*). The BGS equals the balance of trade (*BOT*) plus trade in services (*TS*). The *KA* is the sum of direct investment (*DI*) and portfolio investment (*PI*).

Table 10.1 Recent *BGS* in the US

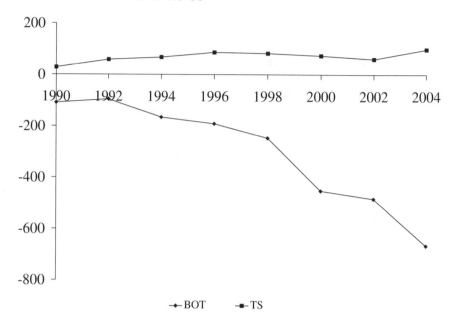

Since 1990, *TS* has been positive and growing in the US. The *BOT* has been negative and falling. A summary of recent *BGS* components for the US is in Table 10.1. Figures are in $billion.

NII includes international incoming payments on assets such as stocks and bonds and international interest payments on loans. When interest payments come in, they are credits and out payments are debits. A positive *NII* indicates the country receives more payments on internationally held assets than it pays out. A negative *NII* indicates the country is an international net borrower.

The *capital account KA* is the sum of *direct investment* (*DI*) and *portfolio investment* (*PI*)

$$KA = DI + PI$$

International investment spending by firms in the form of new plant and equipment is *DI*. International portfolio investment by wealth holders with no control over the foreign firm operation is *PI*. The conceptual difference is that *DI* involves control over branch firm operation.

The distinction between *DI* and *PI* is difficult. Suppose a US oil firm wants to build a refinery in Azerbajan and forms a corporation in Azerbajan. Money is transferred to an Azerbajan bank and construction begins. The oil firm prints stock in the new corporation. Wealth holders buy stock in the new refinery. Stockholders ultimately control the refinery and elect a board of directors and the board appoints a manager. The stock in the refinery is held by international investors. It is difficult to say whether the oil firm controls the branch refinery. The oil firm may own only 10% of the stock but exercise complete control if there are thousands of other stockholders. The oil firm may own 49% of the stock but be excluded from management if a willful stockholder or small group owns the other 51%.

In practice, DI is recorded when 10% or 25% of the stock of a branch firm is held by the investing firm, and investment with less is PI. This cutoff is arbitrary and data are kept up to a 50% cutoff. The distinction between *DI* and *PI* should be eliminated. Roy Ruffin and Farhad Rassekh (1987) conclude that *DI* and *PI* are in fact perfect substitutes. For the US, $1 of *PI* then results in $1 less *DI*. The contribution to management of a branch firm is independent of the ownership of the firm's stock.

EXAMPLE 10.5 *US BOT and GDP*

Consumption *C* has been a fairly stable component of US national income (*Y*). Investment *I* has been stable except for a decline during the Great Depression. Government spending *G* replaced *I* during the 1930s, rose during the 1970s, and has declined slightly since. Both exports and imports have grown. Recent *BOT* deficits are not out of line with history, and similar trade surpluses have occurred.

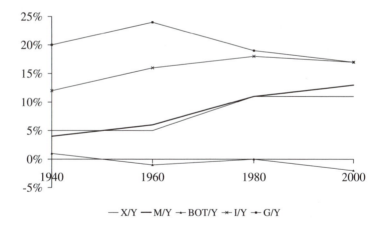

The Recent US BOP

A much publicized trend is the US *BOT* deficit. The last *BOT* surplus occurred in 1975 and it has become steadily more negative since. Domestic import competing industries have used the *BOT* deficit to argue for protection. But while the US has specialized less in manufacturing, it has specialized more in exported services. The *TS* surplus does not always make the news.

Table 10.2 The *CA* in Canada and Mali, *%GDP*

Source: *The Economist*, 16 December 1995.

The *CA* has historically been relatively small compared to *GDP*. In the 1950s and 1960s the *CA* was a surplus of less than 0.5% of GDP and in the 1970s a relative deficit of 0.1% was the average. It is little wonder that the typical US macroeconomics textbook included very little international economics. During the 1980s, there was a fundamental change as the *CA* turned toward deficit. The *CA* deficit peaked at 4% of *GDP* in 1987, with imports 11% of *GDP* and exports 7%.

Current account balances vary widely across countries. In 1993, Singapore had a *CA* surplus of 18% of GDP and Hungary a deficit of 10%. Other relative *CA* balances were Switzerland 6%, Japan 2%, Germany −1%, US −3%, and Mexico −8%. The *CA* balance conceals information. Canada and Mali both had relative *CA* deficits of −5% but the components in Table 10.2 tell a different story. Transfers to Mali came in the form of foreign aid while revenue in Canada came from exports.

The US has traditionally posted *DI* deficits with firms establishing foreign branch operations. A characteristic of *DI* is that management typically goes with the investment. In contrast, European firms historically rely more on *PI* to finance multinational operations. Surpluses in *DI* during recent years have been due to an increase in branch plants of foreign multinationals in the US.

There is no clear trend since the 1970s in *PI*, but the US generally represents a safe haven for investment funds. The volatility and volume of *PI* in recent years reflects increased competition in global financial markets. The New York Stock Exchange now competes with financial centers worldwide and wealth holders have internationally diversified portfolios.

A *CA* surplus in one country must be balanced by *CA* deficits of others. In recent years, Taiwan, Japan, and Germany have been predominant countries with *CA* surpluses. A component of the recent *CA* surpluses in the US has been net official inflow, summarizing investment transactions between central banks. It has been strongly positive, implying foreign central banks have been buying US government bonds.

BOP data are estimated by survey and include large margins of error. The statistical discrepancy is so large some years that it cannot be determined whether the US was a net international lender or borrower. Countries underestimate export revenue. Estimates of US exports to Canada are less than Canadian estimates of imports from the US. If the same margin of error is applied to all trade, the US *BOT* deficit disappears.

> *The BOP accounts provide some indication of the economics international situation but provide no basis for active government policy.*

EXAMPLE 10.6 *FDI and International Capital*

FDI has been slow and steady relative to portfolio investment over the past 30 years according to a study by Robert Lipsey (2000). The only exception is the US where *FDI* has been more erratic. In the 1980s the US switched from the dominant source of *FDI* to the dominant host. In LDCs, the main source of investment has been *FDI*. In 1994, *FDI* was about 1/3 of total international investment. There now is a good deal of *FDI* from Japan to lower wage Asian countries including China.

Problems for Section B

B1. US firms own and operate branch plants in Central America where tens of millions of brassieres are exported to the US annually by US branch plants. These firms supply management, invest, and retain profits. Should these brassieres be counted as imports?

B2. A Japanese carmaker that has been exporting to the US decides to invest $100 million to build a plant in the US to avoid tariffs. Predict subsequent changes in the *BOP* and *NII*.

B3. In 1990, Mexico's *BOP* included $X = 26.7$, $M = 29.8$, $TS = -5.7$, $NII = 3.5$, and $KA = 8.8$ in $billion. Find *BOT*, *CA*, and *BOP*. Find the change in foreign exchange reserves.

EXAMPLE 10.7 *Recent US BGS*

All four components of the US BGS have been growing over recent decades with imports of goods in the BOT growing the fastest as seen in this chart. The figures are in 2004 $billion. The BGS was nearly in balance through the 1970s but import spending on goods began to accelerate with higher oil prices in the 1980s. NAFTA and WTO trade agreements also had an effect during the 1990s as spending on cheap manufactured goods caused import spending to accelerate. Exports of services are also expanding but they are at a lower level. The net effect is a BGS near zero through the 1970s, then a dip in the 1980s due to high oil prices, followed by a recovery to near zero in 1992, then a decline based on rising oil prices and increased spending on imported manufactured goods. Predicting the future trends is not easy but oil prices are destined to continue rising for some decades due to increasing scarcity, rising demand, and an apparent lack of substitutes.

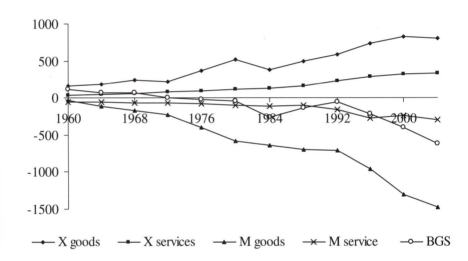

C. INTERNATIONAL DEFICITS AND SURPLUSES

Markets for loans make it possible to borrow and lend, and the country as a whole may be a lender or borrower in the international loan market. The economic implications of financing a current account deficit and examined in this section.

EXAMPLE 10.8 *Easy LDC Debt*

It has been too easy for LDC governments to go into debt. In 2000, LDC debt was $2 trillion according to the IMF and almost half is "official" debt. This total debt is 35 times GDP in the LDCs. This untenable situation is analogous to a person in the US with $50,000 yearly income owing $1,750,000.

Debt service payments of the LDCs are about one fifth of their exports. LDC governments have borrowed excessively from lenders who presume there will be no default on official loans since governments can tax and the World Bank or IMF would rescue defaulting governments. LDC governments run fiscal deficits, increasing their money supplies and causing inflation. The ultimate adjustment to such excessive credit will involve bankruptcy in some form, the only issue whether taxpayers or equity holders pay.

International Debt and Equity

Consumers may spend more or less than their income during a year. College students spend more, borrowing or spending family funds but the investment in human capital increases income potential after graduation making it relatively easy to pay back the debt. Middle aged consumers spend less than their income, saving for retirement.

Firms borrow when they are growing, spending to acquire capital goods and train labor. Firms assume debt by selling bonds and create equity by selling stock. The goal is to raise funds for capital machinery and structures to increase production. A *bond* represents a promise to pay a certain amount of cash at some future date. The rate of return on a bond is fixed. A *stock* entitles the holder to a share of the firm's future profit and its rate of return depends on the firm's profit. Stocks represent ownership of the firm. During years of profitable production, the firm pays off debt and pays dividends on stocks.

What is true for consumers and firms must be true for countries as collections of consumers and firms. Deficits and surpluses in the *CA* are expected and there is no reason a country should have a zero *CA*. If a country spends more on imported goods and services than it receives from exports, it must borrow or spend its wealth.

Borrowing is typical for young and growing consumers, firms, and nations. When there is potential for future income, it is rational to borrow to invest in capital goods or skills to increase productivity. Wealthy consumers, firms, and countries may sell assets to finance deficits. International lending and borrowing facilitate global growth and stability.

EXAMPLE 10.9 *US Expanding KA*

The US invests in the rest of the world and the rest of the world invests in the US. The capital account reports estimates of the change in the net investment position. The recent history of the capital account KA for the US is summarized below. Both outflow and inflow have grown steadily, especially during the 1990s. Figures are in 2004 $billion. US investors prefer FDI in foreign countries and foreign investors prefer portfolio investment in the US. The US net KA has been positive since the 1980s, implying that *NII* will decline in the future. The incoming net investment over 5% of GFP in 2004, raises productivity in the US.

The International Credit Market

If an individual, firm, or country makes more income than it spends, it saves and becomes a lender. A period of lending typically happens at the peak of individual careers, after education and before retirement. Firms with positive profit either invest in new capital or become lenders. Countries with surpluses in their *CA* lend the surplus funds.

The credit market for *loanable funds* is the mechanism for lending and borrowing. When a country has a *CA* surplus, it accumulates assets. A surplus in the *CA* is not inherently good and a deficit is not inherently bad. The same is true for borrowing and lending, or selling and accumulating assets.

It is rational for some people, firms, and countries to be borrowers while others are lenders. Managed debt with a purpose has the potential to increase productivity and income.

People have different habits and desires regarding wealth accumulation. Some are obsessed with accumulating wealth while others seem content with less. Some firms are obsessed with growth while others maintain stable production and size. As collections of consumers and firms, countries vary in their desire for growth and wealth. When it comes to financial planning for individuals, firms, or nations, there are no simple rules to follow. What is wanted for the future is the key to successful financial planning.

EXAMPLE 10.10 *Baby Boom BOT*

Baby boomers were born in the evidently busy years in the US following World War II. The population group born between 1945 and 1955 is now the largest in the US. Michael Bryan and Susan Bryne (1988) examine the influence of baby boomers on US trade and foreign investment. When the boomers entered the workforce in the 1970s, they had low income but high earning potential. Their borrowing led to capital account surpluses and trade deficits for the country. Boomers are now mid career, and saving for retirement. As a result, the US as a whole will save favoring capital account deficits and *BOT* surpluses.

A Borrowing Country

BOT deficits in the US have been in the range of $1000 to $2000 per household since the 1980s, evidence of international borrowing. Much of this borrowing is spent on capital goods that raise productivity and the standard of living. Imports of capital goods are debits in the *BOT* and there is no cause for alarm from importing capital goods. Growing countries can be expected to borrow. Foreign investors must see the US as a good place for funds. Just as consumers and firms borrow to invest, so do countries as a whole.

With a *CA* deficit a country is borrowing or selling assets that create debt as new bonds or equity as new stocks. The sale of existing assets such as stocks, bonds, gold, or real estate also brings in cash to finance a *CA* deficit.

EXAMPLE 10.11   *Government Deficits*

Each government decides on the services it provides and levies taxes to pay for them. Tax revenue *T* and government spending *G* reflect preferences and politics. Data from the World Bank suggests *G* as a percentage of GDP has been on the rise. A negative *T*–*G* indicates a government deficit. Italy has been a country with high deficits and an increasing debt burden, but its deficit has declined in the EU. The US has average government spending. Sweden has nearly balanced its government budget. Governments finance deficits by printing money or selling bonds, promises to pay bond-holders in the future. Bonds represent future tax liabilities. The debt created by most governments is between 1% and 4% of GDP.

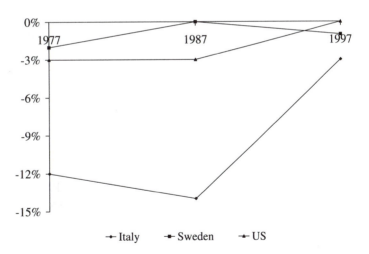

Increasing Foreign Assets

Foreign owned assets in the US have been increasing with the recent *CA* deficits with foreign investors net buyers of US stocks, bonds, and other assets. Investors must expect the US to grow, making the debt sustainable. Rather than causing alarm, the *CA* deficit indicates expected growth.

Special interest groups have fueled fear that foreigners will buy up the country. This issue can be examined by looking at the net position of international stocks of wealth. In 1986, the *Survey of Current Business* estimated the stock of US assets abroad were $1.1 trillion, while foreign assets in the US were $1.3 trillion. This makes the US a net debtor of $260 billion, about $3000 per household but this figure is overstated.

The Department of Commerce values US assets abroad on a historical basis rather than their current value. Suppose a US firm built a foreign branch plant 15 years ago at a cost of $1 million. The current cost of building the same plant might be $5 million because of rising costs and inflation. The current value of the plant might be $4 million, given wear and tear. The asset is valued on the books, however, at its historical cost of $1 million minus depreciation.

Foreigners own about 10% of the gross capital stock in the US. The US has historically bought more into the ROW than vice versa. There is little danger of an impending buyout. Multinational firms continue to expand around the world. International asset diversification has increased dramatically since the 1970s and the increased foreign lending and borrowing is a sign of a healthy economy.

The *KA* per household was a deficit of about $40 per year during the 1970s and a surplus of about $600 during the 1980s (1982 dollars). With these *KA* surpluses, foreign investors were putting more capital assets on net into the US.

Average US investment abroad in the 1970s was $620 per US household, while average foreign investment in the US was $580. US investment abroad continued a steady climb, averaging $800 per household during the 1980s. Foreigners invested more in the US during the 1980s. Foreign investment in the US averaged $1400 per household in the 1980s. As another gauge during the 1980s, payments on foreign assets in the US grew by 200% while receipts on US assets abroad grew by 80%. These figures continued a slow steady climb during the 1990s as the US became more open to international investment.

When a foreign firm builds a plant, the home country as a whole benefits but domestic competing industries suffer. When foreign investment enters, the current owners of capital in the competing industries suffer the most. Owners of the stock of the domestic competing firms are hurt with foreign investment.

A note that sheds light on the transitory nature of political concerns is the chronic US BOT surpluses of the 1950s. There were calls for policy intervention. A wealthy country with trade surpluses created the perception that the US was spending too little. The rebuilding economies of Europe and Japan could not produce more if the US refused to import. Imagine a small town where the richest family was the most frugal. Everyone else would benefit if the rich family went out to eat more often, hired local service labor, and shopped freely in local stores.

International deficits and surpluses are the rule rather than the exception. Deficits are not necessarily bad nor surpluses necessarily good. Avoid any alarmism by special interest groups wanting to use related government policy for their own benefit.

EXAMPLE 10.12 *Pay me Later*

A government budget deficit now implies higher taxes, sooner or later, to pay the debt. If taxpayers realize they will have to pay the debt, they save more now to pay taxes later. Otherwise, a budget deficit would create an excess demand for loans and international borrowing. Robert Barro (1989) develops the *Ricardian equivalence* between a budget deficit and saving for an eventual tax. Government budget deficits do not raise interest rates or foreign investment, evidence favoring Ricardian equivalence. Taxpayers must realize government budget deficits imply higher taxes sooner or later, saving now to pay the tax later.

Problems for Section C

C1. As the average age of a country's population rises from 20 to 40, anticipate what will happen to the *BGS* and the *KA*.

C2. Explain whether Brazil or Austria would be more likely to have a BGS deficit.

C3. Diagram the international excess supply and demand for loans. What is the price of a loan?

EXAMPLE 10.13 *The Ins and Outs of NII*

Receipts on US assets abroad have increased but payments on foreign assets in the US have grown faster. Investors perceive the opportunity for growth and income in foreign investments. As the chart indicates, both in-payments and out-payments have increased and NII has remained fairly constant. The figures are in 2004 $billions. Increasing interest payments in both directions reflect healthy economic activity.

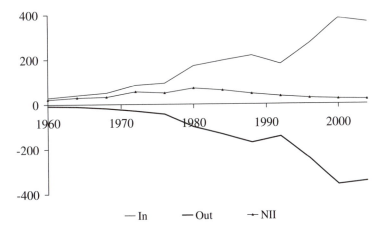

D.   INTERNATIONAL FISCAL AND MONETARY POLICY

Economic policy includes actions of the government to influence the economy. International trade and finance are affected by economic policy. The two general types of economic policy are:

- *fiscal policy* — government spending and taxation
- *monetary policy* — government control of the money supply

There may be calls for fiscal and monetary policy to affect the *CA* or *KA*.

Economists differ in opinions about the role and effectiveness of fiscal and monetary policy. Some favor active policy intervention to deal with unemployment and recession while others favor passive policy and market adjustments with balanced government budgets and zero inflation. This section examines the international role of economic policy.

The Government Budget Constraint

The government produces some goods and services. *Public goods and services* are consumed by the public at large and cannot be consumed exclusively by individuals. Examples of public goods are police, national defense, clean air, health inspectors, sewers, fire departments, highways, roads, oceans and parks. Governments play a positive role by providing public goods that might not be provided by free markets. A free market fails to produce public goods because of *free riders*, people who do not pay but cannot be excluded from consuming the public goods.

Taxes provide revenue which the government uses to produce public goods and services. When the government spends more than its revenue in taxes, it has a *deficit* that creates *national debt* when the government prints bonds that are sold to raise funds to pay its deficit.

A *bond* is a promise to pay the face value to the bondholder at some future date. Government bonds are bought by lenders willing to forego present consumption in favor of the interest premium and higher consumption in the future. Bonds are bought by consumers, firms, the government central bank, foreign investors, or foreign central banks.

If a bond is bought by the central bank, it pays with a new issue of its own, freshly printed currency. In this way a deficit increases the money supply, amounting to *monetary policy*.

With a private sector purchase of bonds, funds are transferred from the private to the public sector. Government spending grows at the expense of consumption and investment since consumers and firms spend on the bonds rather than consumer or investment goods. The demand for loans increases because of the government's desire to borrow, and the *interest rate* or the price of loans is driven up. The price of bonds falls with the increase in supply.

The *government budget constraint* reflects government cash flows. Let B represent the stock of bonds, the national debt. The government must pay an *interest expense* on the national debt rB where r is the interest rate. Total government spending is $G + rB$. Subtract taxes to find the *budget deficit*: $G + rB - T$. A deficit must be financed by selling bonds (ΔB) or raising the money supply (ΔM_S). The government budget constraint is

$$G + rB - T = \Delta B + \Delta M_S$$

Tax revenue comes from numerous sources, mainly income taxes and profit taxes in the DCs. Tariff revenue is small for DCs but important for LDCs. Compared to income taxes, a sales tax would increase saving and investment.

EXAMPLE 10.14 *US Holdings of Foreign Stocks and Bonds*

In 2000 the US held a total of $6 trillion of private assets in foreign countries compared to $8 trillion of foreign owned assets in the US according to Department of Treasury estimates. Of the US assets abroad, 37% were in *DI*, 25% in *PI*, and 11% in bonds. The Western Hemisphere had the largest share of bond holdings, 42%. The EU accounted for 68% of stocks and 38% of bonds.

The Government Budget and the BGS

The *bond market* has implications for an economy open to international finance. A higher interest rate and cheaper bonds attract foreign investment since foreign investors want to buy some of the cheaper bonds. The demand for home currency in the foreign exchange market increases causing appreciation. An appreciating currency implies cheaper imports and more expensive exports, likely to push the *BOT* towards deficit.

> *Government deficit spending can lead to a trade deficit if higher interest rates attract foreign investment causing a currency appreciation.*

Numerous empirical studies have shown, however, that this link is weak. The foreign exchange market is large and quick, and other influences may predominate. The induced effects of the foreign exchange market on the trade balance are small and slow.

One implication is the government budget is a poor tool to combat a trade deficit. Fiscal policy should not be used as a tool to influence the *BOT*. Decisions on government spending and taxes should be based on the costs and benefits of the particular programs or projects but the budget process is political and based on vested interests.

Trade policy including tariffs, quotas, nontariff barriers, and trade subsidies affect trade directly. Trade policy is more efficient than fiscal and monetary policy in dealing with trade issues.

Figure 10.6 presents a summary of the channels of fiscal and monetary policy to their international effects. A foreign purchase of new government bonds can cause an appreciation. Inflation resulting from expansionary monetary policy lowers the value of the home currency relative to other currencies, a depreciation. The direct effect on the *BOT* of increased government spending and lower private spending depends on the composition of imports and domestic goods consumed by the government and the private sector.

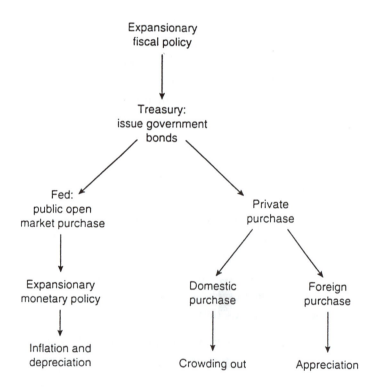

Figure 10.6
International Effects of Economic Policy
Government debt created by expansionary fiscal policy is financed by the sale of bonds. If the central bank makes a public purchase, the expansionary policy amounts to monetary policy. Private purchases can be domestic, crowding out consumption and investment spending. Private purchases can also be foreign and appreciate the currency. Expansionary monetary policy can lead to inflation and depreciation if it is persistent and the growth rate of money exceeds the growth rate of output.

EXAMPLE 10.15   *US T and G*

The *Statistical Abstract* presents US data summaries, breaking federal government revenue and spending into useful categories. Government revenue and spending are summarized in the charts below. Interest on the national debt has risen steadily from about 8% in the early 1960s with more tax revenue being used to pay the holders of US bonds who lent money to the government. Government deficits transfer money now from savers to taxpayers, then later transfer money from taxpayers to bondholders. About 1/10 of the national debt was held by foreigners, which means that about 1.5% of government spending or 0.3% of *GDP* was transferred to foreign holders of US bonds.

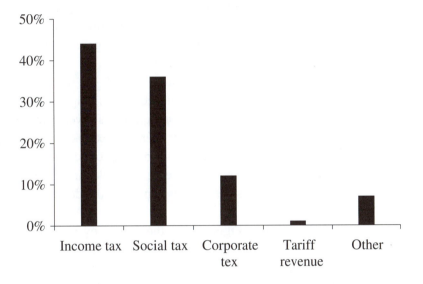

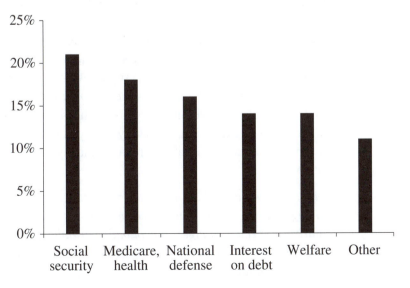

Monetary Policy and the BOP

Monetary policy can affect international trade and finance. Inflation occurs when the supply of money grows faster than the supply of goods and services. Inflation and expected inflation can have real effects on the economy through the credit market and the foreign exchange market. Inflation has little effect as long as it is anticipated correctly. Stable growth in the money supply leads to low and potentially zero inflation.

Mechanical rules have been proposed to control the money supply. Money growth and inflation would be more predictable with monetary rules. Discretion on the part of the central bank, however, may help the economy adjust to external shocks. Zero inflation is an attainable goal and unexpected changes in the money supply hurt consumers and firms. The large monetary contraction leading to the Great Depression and the large monetary expansions of the 1970s had strong effects on the economy.

Business cycles are alternating periods of recessions and booms and may be a natural part of a dynamic economy. Suppose, for instance, a recession starts with firms selling off inventories. As inventories are depleted, firms start building them back. Investment spending expands and an expansion occurs until inventories are full. Firms cut back production to keep inventories from overflowing, and a recession beings with declining output. Ultimately the story repeats. Foreign business cycles can affect the domestic economy through export purchases.

As pictured in Figure 10.7, the frequency of a business cycle is measured from peak to peak. The US has been through six business cycles since 1953. The average business cycle lasted 54 months. The US started an expansion in 1961 that lasted throughout the 1960s and started another expansion in 1982 that lasted throughout the 1980s. The early 1990s were a mild recession and a slight recovery. The economy expanded through the middle and late 1990s.

Central banks manage the money supply to influence the business cycle. The idea is that expanding the money supply would lower the interest rate and encourage investment. The Fed sets the *discount rate*, the rate it lends money to commercial banks. Active monetary policy, however, cannot guide the economy from recession to expansion. Monetary policy is not a tool to tune the economy. It is more important to establish reliable money supply with the goal of zero inflation.

Monetary policy affects inflation, the interest rate, and ultimately the exchange rate. Central banks also actively intervene in the foreign exchange market. Expected changes in economic variables can alter international trade and finance. Monetary policy is a poor tool for influencing international trade and finance.

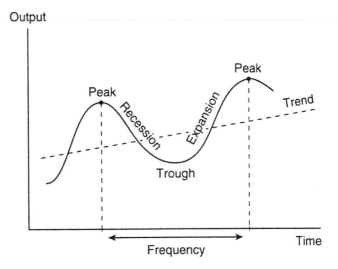

Figure 10.7
The Business Cycle
Output might cycle naturally about an underlying trend. Recessions lead from peaks to troughs, and expansions lead back to peaks. There are various causes of business cycles.

Steady growth of the money supply leads to steady interest rates and a reliable exchange rate. Businesses, traders, and investors are able to make better plans when money growth and prices are stable.

Neither fiscal nor monetary policy should be used to influence international trade and investment. Governments have a range of international policy options: tariffs, quotas, nontariff barriers, voluntary export restraints, export subsidies, free trade areas, free trade zones, managed exchange rates, fixed exchange rates, foreign exchange controls, and foreign investment controls.

One recurring theme is the income redistribution due to any policy. Economics focuses on the costs and benefits of actions. Any policy that alters incentives and behavior will have costs and benefits creating winners and losers. The difficulty is to identify all costs and benefits. Often the secondary or side effects of a policy are as large as the primary effects. It is important to uncover the ultimate winners and losers of any proposed policy.

Problems for Section D

D1. If the government runs a deficit, describe how funds arrive from domestic and foreign sources.

D2. When the government sells bonds to a foreign resident, what are the present and future effects on the *BOP*.

D3. Explain how government surpluses, interest rates, exchange rates, and the *BOT* are related.

CONCLUSION

International markets for goods, services, and assets are active. The world is becoming more integrated economically in trade and finance, and countries more dependent on each another. In some countries the daily change in the exchange rate can affect routine economic decisions. Exchange rates regularly make the news, have an impact on profit in many industries, affect the price of new cars and other goods, and influence the foreign travel. The next chapter studies the foreign exchange market.

Terms

Active versus passive policy	Direct investment (*DI*)
Balance of payments (*BOP*)	Fiscal and monetary policy
Balance of trade (*BOT*)	Government bonds
Balance on goods and services (*BGS*)	Import elasticity
Business cycles	Inflation
Capital account (*KA*)	Net investment income (*NII*)
Current account (*CA*)	Portfolio investment (*PI*)
Debt and equity	Trade in services (*TS*)

MAIN POINTS

- International excess supply and demand are constantly changing, creating adjustments in prices, imports, and exports. Import elasticities determine how price changes affect the *BOT*.
- The *BOP* reports international transactions in the *CA* and investment in the *KA*. A country with a *CA* deficit must have a *KA* surplus, and vice versa.
- *CA* deficits are no cause for alarm since growing countries typically assume debt to acquire capital goods.
- Government deficit spending reduces private spending, raises national debt, and creates inflation. Fiscal and monetary policy are inefficient tools to influence international commerce.

REVIEW PROBLEMS

1. Predict what will happen to foreign excess demand when lower prices are expected for home exports due to improved technology in production abroad. What will happen to international prices, the level of exports, and export revenue?

2. Explain what will happen in the international market for manufactured goods when domestic income rises. What happens to the international price, the level of imports, and import expenditure?

3. Explain what happens to import spending if the increase in import price to $7.50 in Figure 10.3 causes the quantity demanded to fall from 300 to 250 while domestic quantity supplied rises from 100 to 116.67.

4. If the price of M is $5 and the price of S is $12.50, find the relative price of M or the tt for the exporter of M. Do the same if the price of S is $7.50.

5. Find the elasticity and explain what happens to import spending when the quantity of imports rises from 100 to 125 with a fall in price from $10 to $8. Do the same if imports rise instead to 110. Examine the situation if imports rise to 130.

6. With 90 million households in the US, find the 1995 *BOP* account figures per household.

7. Explain current and expected future changes in the *BOP* that occur when an investor in the US buys stock on the Sydney stock exchange.

8. Suppose that a US firm wants to open a manufacturing plant in Costa Rica. It can transfer $1 million of retained earnings to a bank in Costa Rica to build the plant. It might also offer stock worth $400,000 in Costa Rica to raise funds. Describe the current and future BOP entries for the US and Costa Rica under each scenario. Contrast future *NII* for the US and Costa Rica.

9. An saying is that the way to get ahead in business is by using "other people's money". Explain the analogy with the *BOP* accounts.

10. Why do wealth holders like to diversify internationally?

11. Assume you were forced to live without borrowing or lending. How would your life be affected? What is the moral for international economics?

12. During the expansion and recession phases of the business cycle, explain whether *BOT* surpluses or deficits are likely.

13. Does Congress rationally consider the marginal costs and benefits of each newly proposed fiscal program? What law would make such behavior more likely?

14. What effect would reducing import tariffs and imposing export taxes have on the *BOT*?

15. Predict how war in the Persian Gulf affects the CA in the US.

READINGS

Robert Barro (1996) *Macroeconomics,* New York: McGraw-Hill. Analysis of monetary and fiscal policies.

Francisco Rivera-Batiz and Luis Rivera-Batiz (1985) *International Finance and Open Economy Macroeconomics*, New York: Macmillan. Macroeconomics for an open economy.

John Pool and Stephen Stamos (1989) *International Economic Policy: Beyond the Trade and Debt Crisis*, Lexington: Lexington Books, 1989. Facts on government and international debt.

James Rock, ed. (1991) *Debt and Twin Deficits Debate*, Mountain View: Mayfield Publishing. Links between governments deficit and trade deficit.

World Economic Outlook, Washington: IMF. Monetary developments, current and capital account balances, interest rates, exchange rates, and the international oil market.

CHAPTER II

The Foreign Exchange Market

Preview

Anyone involved in international trade, investment, or travel uses the foreign exchange (FX) market, crucial for the functioning of the world economy across countries with different currencies. This chapter covers:
- *FX supply and demand*
- *Floating* and *fixed exchange rates*
- *Stability* and *arbitrage* of FX rates
- *Inflation* and *currency risk* in international commerce

INTRODUCTION

Currencies are bought and sold in the *foreign exchange* (FX) *market*, the largest market in the world. The exchange of goods, services, and assets among consumers, firms, or governments in different countries or *currency areas* requires a currency exchange. The FX market is involved when US tourists fly to Mexico, a Russian importer buys a million tons of French wheat, an investor in Sydney buys shares on the Tokyo stock exchange, a Canadian importer buys a ton of Italian olive oil, or a California electronics firm buys components from Malaysia. There are billions of international transactions daily involving the FX market, each involving the exchange of one medium of exchange for another.

Demand for FX comes from domestic buyers of foreign goods, services, intermediate inputs, capital goods, and assets. Supply of FX comes from foreign buyers of the same range of domestic products and assets. Supply and demand work continuously in the FX market to determine the FX rate, the relative price of traded currencies.

The setting for this currency trading is a global network linking private banks, FX brokers, traders, and central banks. Figure 11.1 summarizes the institutions of the FX market. Currencies are traded at very low costs per transaction.

Although stock markets receive more publicity, trading in FX markets offers more potential profit (and loss). When the demand for a currency rises relative to supply, its price in terms of other currencies rises. Rates of the three major currencies (dollar, mark, yen) are determined in an open market with minimal

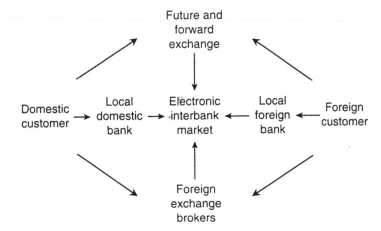

Figure 11.1
Electronic Interbank Foreign Exchange Market
The electronic interbank market is the center for a vast amount of trading. Working through local banks, international traders and investors buy and sell foreign exchange. Brokers bring buyers and sellers together in the central market, buying and selling foreign currencies themselves in search of profit. Future and forward exchange transactions moderate the risk and uncertainty of exchange transactions.

central bank involvement, and these major currencies *float* relative to each other.

Government central banks often buy and sell currencies in the attempt to influence or *manage* exchange rates. Many central banks have a *fixed exchange rate*, arbitrarily setting it to meet some policy goal.

A depreciating or devalved currency means more expensive imports and cheaper exports. A government may devalue its fixed exchange rate to discourage imports and ease a trade deficit. An undervalued currency is a tax on consumers who must pay a higher price for imports. A government might overvalue its fixed exchange rate to encourage foreign investment.

Fixed or managed exchange rates are inherently unstable and cannot be sustained with underlying market disequilibrium. Few governments, however, seem willing to let the FX market work freely. This chapter examines the ways governments try to influence or control the FX market.

A relatively high growth rate in the money supply generally leads to higher inflation and depreciation. Relative money supply differentials explain long term trends in exchange rates. Short term exchange rate changes, however, are difficult to predict.

Uncertainty about the future exchange rates introduces risk into international transactions. The mechanism for avoiding the risk of an unexpected change in the exchange rate is the *forward exchange market* where a contract is signed to buy or sell foreign currency at some future date.

A.   FOREIGN EXCHANGE RATES

The FX market is based on the supply and demand of foreign exchange. Fundamental relationships involving exchange rates include:

- The exchange rate link to import and export prices
- The dynamic response of the BOT to depreciation

The FX Market

When a domestic importer wants to buy foreign products, domestic currency is traded for foreign currency on the *foreign exchange (FX) market*. Consider a US importer buying manufactured goods from a Japanese firm. The importer does business in dollars while the foreign manufacturer does business in yen. The importer can go through a bank to buy the yen and transfer it to the bank of the Japanese exporter. Banks and import agencies specialize in currency transactions and dealing with import restrictions and customs paperwork. If the importer is quoted a price of 625 yen, the role of the FX rate is to translate that price into dollars.

Suppose the exchange rate of the yen is $0.008 in the FX market. As with any commodity, price is expressed in home currency. Apples cost $1/pound, tuition costs $4000/term, and Japanese currency $0.008/yen. One dollar equals $1/.008 = 125$ yen. The price of the manufactured good M in dollars is $\$0.008 \times 625 = \$5$ per M. The decision of whether to import is based partly on the dollar price.

Suppose the price of the dollar rises to yen/$ = 200$. The dollar price of manufactured goods M then falls to $625/200 = \$3.13$. An *appreciating* currency creates cheaper imports and increases the quantity of imports demanded. The importer will want to buy more M at a price of $3.13 than at the $5 price. If imports are *elastic*, import expenditure will rise as will the quantity of foreign currency demanded.

This inverse relationship between $/yen and the quantity of yen demanded is illustrated by the *demand for yen* market in Figure 11.2. The rise in yen/$ from 125 to 200 is equivalent to a fall in $/yen on the vertical axis from 0.008 to 0.005. The quantity of yen demanded rises from 20 to 30 trillion when $/yen falls from 0.008 to 0.005.

On the supply side, Japanese importers buying US exports must sell yen in the FX market. Suppose the price of business services is $10/S$ at home and the exchange rate 125 yen/$. The Japanese price of services is then $125 \times 10 = 1250$ yen. If the yen/$ rate rises to 200, the yen price of the services rises $200 \times 10 = 2000$ yen. At this higher yen price the quantity demanded of imported services is lower.

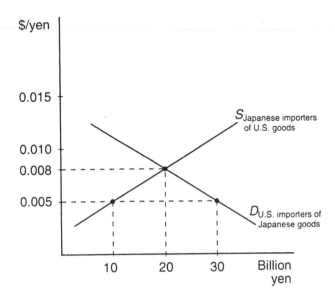

Figure 11.2
The Foreign Exchange Market
The demand (*D*) for FX comes from buyers of foreign goods in the home country. Supply (*S*) comes from buyers of home goods in the foreign country. These "goods" include manufactures, services, and assets.

If foreign imports of services are elastic, spending will fall as will the quantity of foreign currency supplied. The quantity of yen supplied falls from 20 to 10 trillion in Figure 11.2 when $/yen falls from 0.008 to 0.005. The result is the upward sloping supply curve in Figure 11.2.

Where demand and supply of foreign exchange meet, a *market exchange rate* is determined at the market volume of transactions. This equilibrium exchange rate occurs where the quantity of yen supplied equals the quantity demanded. The market clears at the equilibrium exchange rate. The FX market includes trading of assets such as stocks and bonds. In Figure 11.2 the equilibrium exchange rate is $/yen = 0.008 and the equilibrium quantity of FX traded is 20 trillion yen (per hour).

The FX market is based on the demand and supply of foreign currency. The price of foreign currency is the exchange rate, the relative price of the foreign currency in terms of home currency.

EXAMPLE 11.1 *FX Rates*

Exchange rates change continuously and are quoted in newspapers, on the internet, and at banks, airports, and trading houses. In countries highly involved with international trade and investment, exchange rates are on the front page and traders set up exchange windows on busy streets. As the US economy becomes more open, foreign exchange rates grow in importance to the economy. Banks in many small towns in the US now offer foreign exchange service. In countries with quickly depreciating or appreciating currencies, the exchange rate influences everyday business decisions. The column below is the value of the currency in US dollars.

New York FRB, 12 Noon Buying Rates Sat Oct 30 1999	
	In US Dollars
Australian Dollars	0.6376
Brazilian Real	0.5120
British Pounds	1.6425
Canadian Dollars	0.6793
Chinese Renminbi	0.1208
Euro	1.0518
Hong Kong Dollars	0.1287
Indian Rupees	0.0230
Japanese Yen	0.0096
Mexican Pesos	0.1040
Singapore Dollars	0.6013
South Korean Won	0.0008
Swiss Francs	0.6560
Taiwan Dollars	0.0314
Venezuelan Bolivar	0.0016

Depreciation

Depreciation occurs when a currency falls relative to foreign currencies. In the $/yen market, dollar depreciation means $/yen rises. When the currency depreciates, there is a decrease in purchasing power over foreign goods and services, and exports become cheaper abroad. An *appreciating currency* has more power to purchase foreign products but exports become more expensive abroad.

Increased demand for imports of high quality foreign automobiles increases the demand for foreign currency and causes a depreciation. Increased foreign travel leads to higher demand for foreign currency and depreciation. If a home firm develops a new fast personal computer, foreign firms and consumers will buy it, the supply of foreign currency rises, and the currency appreciates. If the government issues new bonds that have a high secure yield, foreign investors will buy them, the demand for home currency rises, and it appreciates. If stocks in Tokyo seem attractive because of growth in the Japanese economy, the demand for yen to buy Japanese stocks increases and the yen appreciates.

The key to the FX market is to understand the markets for the traded products or assets along with the market for the currencies involved.

The FX market is linked to international product and asset markets.

Consider an increase in the price of coffee in Colombia. The higher price of coffee increases the demand for Colombian pesos to buy coffee already under contract. As illustrated in Figure 11.3, the demand for pesos shifts right. The volume in the FX market increases and the peso appreciates. With the increased demand for pesos, the value of the peso rises from $/peso = 0.002 to 0.003 and the dollar depreciates from 500 to 333 pesos.

As the dollar loses value, the US price of imported coffee rises further. Suppose coffee cost 750 pesos/pound or $0.002 \times 750 = \$1.50$ at the original exchange rate. The dollar depreciation increases the price to $0.003 \times 750 = \$2.25$. The FX market strengthens the underlying increase in the dollar price, encouraging substitution away from Colombian coffee.

A depreciation of the dollar from other sources also causes imports to become more expensive. Suppose central banks announce a plan to depreciate the dollar. If traders and investors expect the dollar to fall, the demand for other currencies increases and the dollar depreciates. Few will want to hold dollars if their price

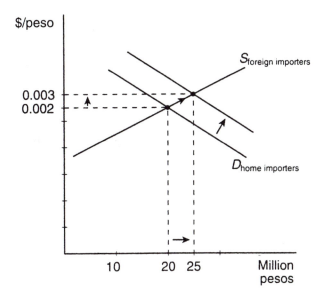

Figure 11.3
Increase in the Demand for Foreign Currency
This increase in demand drives the exchange rate from $0.002/peso to $0.003/peso, and the quantity of pesos traded rises from 20 to 25 million.

is expected to fall. Announced plans to devalue a currency may cause market participants to expect a depreciation. Another cause of a depreciation might be foreign consumers cutting back on imports because of perceived quality problems. When the dollar depreciates, imports become more expensive.

If imports are elastic, currency depreciation makes imports more expensive and import expenditure falls. Simultaneously, exports become cheaper abroad and export revenue rises. Depreciation leads to an increase in the *BGS*.

Imports do not have to be elastic for a depreciation to move the current account toward surplus. It is only necessary that home and foreign imports taken together be elastic. The effects of changing export revenue and import expenditure work together on the *BGS*. If import and export elasticities sum to more than one, depreciation leads to trade surplus. This is called the *Marshall-Lerner condition*, named after economists Alfred Marshall and Abba Lerner.

Empirical evidence indicates the Marshall-Lerner condition holds in the long run, implying depreciation raises the BOT.

EXAMPLE 11.2 *A yen for the ¥*

The Japanese yen has a history of appreciating relative to most currencies including the dollar. This chart shows the overall upward path of the $/¥ since 1976, more than doubling in its dollar value. One major reason is that the growth rate in the supply of yen is kept low with no pressure from the balanced Japanese government budget. As a long term strategy to buy and hold, assets denominated in yen are attractive. For yearly or shorter time periods, however, the currency is difficult to predict.

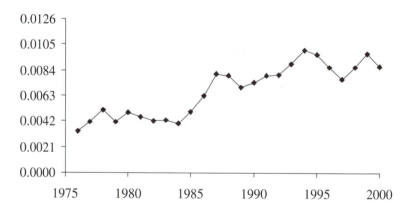

Depreciation and the BGS

The trade balance (*BGS*) is export revenue less import expenditure,

$$BGS = p_X q_X - e p_M^* q_M$$

Exports q_X are aggregated with an average price p_X. Imports q_M are priced in the foreign currency at p_M^* converted to the domestic currency by the exchange rate e. Assume the price indices are constant and $BGS = 0$.

With depreciation, e rises. The higher e raises q_X and lowers q_M due to the effect of e on prices of imports in both countries. If neither q_X nor q_M adjust with the depreciation, the BGS falls.

Suppose q_X does not adjust but q_M falls by 1% with the 1% depreciation. The export elasticity is $\%\Delta q_X / \%\Delta p_X = 0$ and the import elasticity is $\%\Delta q_M / \%\Delta p_M = -1$. Import expenditure and the BGS do not change.

Suppose q_X rises 0.5% and q_M falls 0.5% with the 1% depreciation. The export elasticity is 0.5 and the import elasticity is -0.5. Export revenue then rises by 0.5% and import expenditure rises by $1\% - 0.5\% = 0.5\%$ as well, and the BGS does not change.

Suppose the export elasticity is 1 and the import elasticity is -1. With a 1% depreciation, export revenue rises by 1%, since $\%\Delta q_X = 1$. Import expenditure $(ep_M^* q_M)$ does not change because the 1% rise in e is offset by the 1% decline in q_M and the BGS rises by 1%.

If the export elasticity minus the (negative) import elasticity is greater than 1, depreciation increases the trade balance.

If $BGS < 0$, stronger elasticities are required for a depreciation to have a positive effect. If a country has international market power, a depreciation of its currency would increase demand for exports, raising p_X and p_M^*. International market power strengthens the chance that a depreciation will raise the trade balance.

The effect of a depreciating currency on the trade balance is not easy to predict and varies across countries and for the same country over time. There is evidence of a positive effect in the long run but continued research is required to determine the effects of a depreciation on the BGS. The large exchange rate swings of the 1980s and 1990s provide "experiments" of changing currency values.

The J Curve

A currency depreciation may require some time to have a positive effect on the trade balance, and it can temporarily create a deficit. This relationship is called the J curve because of the shape of the curve describing the trade balance following a depreciation.

Figure 11.4 illustrates the *J curve* with a surprise depreciation of the currency at time d. Contracts for delivery of traded goods and services are already written at time d based on the expectation of a stable exchange rate. The surprise depreciation lowers the price of exports and raises the price of imports

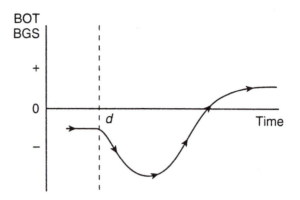

Figure 11.4
The J Curve of a Depreciation
A surprise depreciation at time *d* temporarily worsens the trade balance because contracts are set and products must be delivered at agreed prices. Depreciation causes import prices to rise and export prices to fall. Over time, substitution occurs and the trade balance becomes more positive than before time *d*.

already under contract. During this *contract period*, the deficit in the BGS temporarily worsens. With the quantity of exports fixed and price falling, export revenue must fall. Import expenditure simultaneously rises with the quantity of imports fixed and price rising. Over time, trade adjusts to the new prices, exports rise, and imports fall. The trade balance increases during this *pass-through period*.

> *A currency depreciation that leads to a trade surplus may cause an immediate deficit due to set contracts as pictured by the J curve.*

EXAMPLE 11.3 *The FX Rate and Manufacturing Industries*

The exchange rate affects the price of US manufactured products sold abroad and the price of intermediate products bought by US manufacturers. Between April 1995 and August 1998 the dollar appreciated 30%. US manufactured exports became more expensive abroad but imported intermediate products became cheaper. The large appreciation had an effect on costs and revenues. Linda Goldberg and Keith Crockett (1998) examine exports as well as input purchases of US manufacturing industries and isolate the industries most hurt by the appreciation: instruments, industrial machinery & equipment, electronic & electrical equipment, tobacco products, and chemicals. Profit and investment in these industries declined. Industries that export little but import intermediate products benefited with the appreciation: leather products, petroleum refining, printing & publishing, fabricated metal products, and furniture & fixtures. The FX rate can create winners and losers across industries.

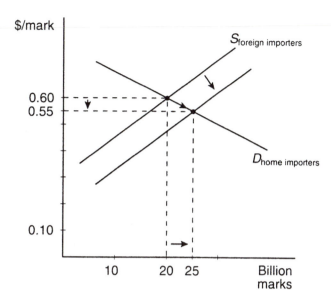

Figure 11.5
Increased Supply of Foreign Currency
This increase in the supply of marks comes from increased demand for US exports. The
mark falls from $0.60/mark to $0.55/mark, and the quantity of trading in the FX market
rises.

Currency Appreciation

On the export side, increased export demand causes foreign buyers to increase
the supply of their currencies on the FX market. As in Figure 11.5, the increased
supply of foreign currency causes appreciation and an increase in the level of
FX trades. This appreciation causes higher foreign currency prices of exports,
strengthening the change in the market price. In Figure 11.5, the dollar rises from
1.667 to 1.818 marks. At a stable price of $12/unit, this appreciation causes a
rise in the foreign price from 20 marks to 21.82 marks.

The accommodating and balancing effect of the FX market is an inherent
and important reason to allow it to operate freely. Induced changes in the
exchange rate work in the same direction as underlying price changes.

EXAMPLE 11.4 *FX and Local Industry*

Between 1975 and 1990 the US dollar exchange rate had some periods with
large swings as this chart suggests. These large swings were the result of erratic
monetary policy, and affected prices of US exports abroad and domestic production. With nationwide aggregate manufacturing data, however, there is little
apparent effect. Henry Thompson and Kamal Upadhyaya (1998) examine two
local industries involved in exporting, chemicals and primary metals in Alabama.

The chemicals industry in Alabama produces petrochemicals and exports about 1/4 of its output, and primary metals exports about 1/5 of its output. Exactly as predicted for exports, chemical output in Alabama declined with the appreciation between 1981 and 1985 then increased with the depreciation from 1985 to 1990. Primary metals production rebounded with the dollar depreciation following 1985. A 10% appreciation lowers output of chemicals by 2.8%, price by 1.4%, and revenue by 4.2%. For primary metals, decreases are 2.1% for output, 2.9% for price, and 5.0% for revenue. These effects illustrate the exposure of local industry to the exchange rate.

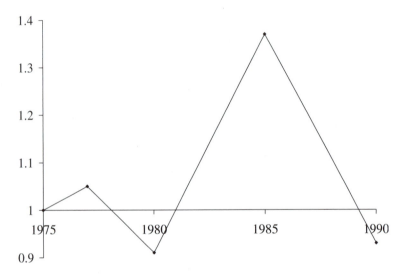

Problems for Section A

A1. Find dollar prices of imported autos costing 880,000 yen when the yen/$ exchange rate rises from 110 to 125.

A2. Illustrate the FX market for the euro with an equilibrium exchange rate of .95 €/$. Suppose the US announces there will be an elimination of all restrictions on European imports after one month. Consumers and firms in the US expect cheaper EU products. Diagram how this announcement affects the current exchange rate. What happens to the current price of EU products in the US?

A3. Suppose a US petrochemical company discovers a cheap way to produce chlorine exported to Germany. Illustrate the effect on the exchange market in its original position at .95 €/$ in the previous problem.

A4. Explain the effect of an appreciation on the balance of trade, similar to the J curve.

B.   *MANAGED EXCHANGE RATES*

Governments resort to various methods to influence international trade and invest-ment. *Managed exchange rates* offer a simple way for governments to influence the price of traded goods, services, and investments. This section examines:

- *Fixed exchange rates*
- Foreign exchange *licensing*
- *Black markets* and FX market controls
- The *pros and cons* of managed exchange rates

Fixed Exchange Rates

Governments may try to keep the price of their currency high for cheap imports or to attract foreign investors. An appreciated currency keeps down the price of intermediate or capital good imports for domestic industry. A stable or appreci-ating currency may attract foreign investment wanting to avoid exchange risk or depreciating currencies. An appreciating currency also makes it easier for a country to pay its debt.

In Figure 11.6 the market exchange rate between dollars and pesos would be \$0.00050/peso, but suppose the Mexican government wants to keep the value of the peso at \$0.00055. The target rate is 1818 pesos/\$ and the market rate 2000 pesos/\$. The fixed exchange rate of \$0.00055/pesos would create an excess supply of 2 billion pesos per day.

At the fixed exchange rate, the excess supply of pesos is equivalent to an excess demand of \$1.1 million. The central bank would have to sell \$1.1 million of its FX reserves every day at taxpayer expense. Supporting a currency's price by depleting FX reserves is expensive when the currency ultimately depreciates because the central bank sells FX assets at a discount, buying high to sell low.

Suppose the Mexican central bank supports the peso as in Figure 11.6 for five days. Mexican FX reserves of \$5.5 million must be sold off in exchange for $1818.18 \times \$5.5$ million = 10 trillion pesos. The Mexican central bank is forced to stop because of declining FX reserves. The exchange rate jumps to the market rate of \$/pesos = 0.00050 and the 10 billion newly bought pesos are worth only \$5 million. An implicit tax of \$500,000 is imposed on taxpayers in Mexico by their central bank.

Overvalued currencies are a popular tax. People do not keep up with the level of FX reserves and believe a highly valued currency is somehow desirable. Many countries repeatedly go through such episodes.

Fixed exchange rates can keep a currency temporarily overvalued at taxpayer expense.

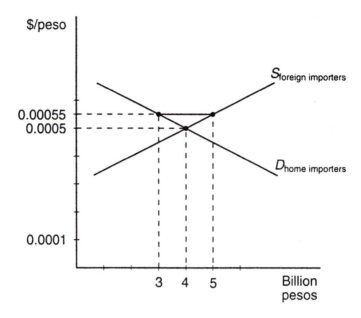

Figure 11.6
A Fixed Exchange Rate
At the official fixed exchange rate of $/peso = 0.00055, the peso is overvalued. There is an excess supply of $5 - 3 = 2$ billion pesos. The central bank keeps the peso above its market rate of $0.0005/peso, requiring exchange transactions at the fixed rate.

EXAMPLE 11.5 *Fixed and Managed FX Rates*

Most governments do not allow the market exchange rate to operate freely, wanting to arbitrarily control their exchange rate and money supply. Ultimately, market forces cannot be denied and a fixed exchange rate must be adjusted so prices of traded products are similar across countries. About 150 currencies are fixed, almost 1/3 of them to a basket of currencies and another 1/3 to a particular currency like the dollar or euro. The others are periodically adjusted. Central banks want their decisions to be difficult to predict because a devaluation takes wealth from domestic citizens and an expected devaluation decreases currency demand. Governments can print and spend money, leading to inflation and ultimate devaluation. Central banks prefer to say their exchange rates are "managed" because it sounds rather businesslike but the term "fixed" in the sense of "rigged" is more appropriate.

FX Licensing

One way to sustain the value of a currency without wasting FX reserves is to limit imports to a level that would occur at an artificially high FX rate by issuing *foreign exchange licenses*.

EXAMPLE 11.6 *Views on the FX System*

Conflicting views of economists attract attention. The *Journal of Economic Perspectives* (Winter 1988) published differing views on exchange rate policy reform. For the past 30 years, there have been large fluctuations in the $/yen and $/mark exchange rates. Ronald McKinnon (Stanford) favors a fixed exchange rate system managed by central banks focusing on stability of the dollar, yen, and mark. Rudiger Dornbusch (MIT) counters that floating rates have worked and there is no "correct" level to fix the currencies. John Williamson (Institute of International Economics) agrees with McKinnon that the disruptions caused by exchange rate swings are large but favors "target zones" rather than fixed rates. All would agree, however, that the market system has gotten the international economy through major disruptions that fixed exchange rate systems would have found difficult.

In Figure 11.7, 15 billion pesos are supplied to importers where the supply of pesos is perfectly inelastic, and importers are unable to buy more foreign currency (or imports). If the pesos demand falls, the government will have to decrease import licenses to keep the value of the peso at the target $0.00055.

Governments can curtail foreign tourism of their citizens and prohibit the purchase of foreign assets. Many countries have such foreign exchange controls.

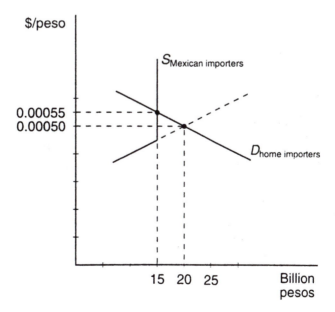

Figure 11.7
Foreign Exchange License
The foreign government can support the peso by licensing imports to 15 billion pesos per period. The peso is kept above its market rate of $0.0005/peso by this import restriction.

People cannot leave the country with more than a fixed amount of cash. Investors are not allowed to buy foreign assets. Such restrictions amount to an implicit tax.

A government can keep its currency overvalued at taxpayer expense by licensing foreign exchange.

EXAMPLE 11.7 *Devaluation and the BOT*

A devaluation is an official decrease in the value of a fixed exchange rate. Governments fixing exchange rates are forced to redefine their currency when inflation rates vary across countries. A devaluation makes imports more expensive at home and exports cheaper abroad. Daniel Himarios (1989) reports on the effects of 60 devaluations of fixed exchange rates prior to 1973. Devaluations raised the *BOT* in 80% of the cases. There were immediate increases in the *BOT* and lagged effects 2 or 3 years after devaluations. Similar results occurred for 15 countries with fixed exchange rates between 1975 and 1984. There were J curves for Salvador, France, Greece, and Zambia. Murli Buluswar, Henry Thompson, and Kamal Upadhyaya (1996) find that devaluations had no effects on the trade balance in India.

FX Black Markets

A *black market* for foreign exchange can arise if the fixed rate is too far from the underlying market rate. The black market exchange rate is the market rate less the risk of penalty for illegal transactions. In the example of an overvalued peso, US tourists, importers, and investors holding dollars would be tempted by black market rates but there can be punishment for black market trading.

An artificially supported peso is expected to eventually *devalue*, and nobody would expect the peso to appreciate. Such expectations ensure the value of the pesos will stay low. Suppose the official exchange rate is 1.818 pesos/$ and a black market operates at 2000 pesos/$. Nobody would expect the official rate to fall toward 1800. US exporters would not discourage black market trading because their goods are cheaper at the unofficial rate.

Merchants dealing with tourists are happy to accept foreign "hard" currency at a rate more favorable to tourists than the official rate. Such trading is illegal, as armed guards inform tourists at some border crossings.

Some governments allow unofficial transactions in what is called a *parallel exchange market*. Official markets work openly alongside the black market and settle for a share of transactions at the official rate.

EXAMPLE 11.8 *FX Policy Disputes*

Peter Kenen (Princeton) argues that governments should intervene to stop harmful effects of international investors. Ronald McKinnon (Stanford) argues for active intervention and management of the dollar value. John Williamson (Institute for International Economics) favors active intervention and thinks joint action by central banks has been successful. Jacob Frankel (IMF) thinks better fiscal and monetary policy should be the focus. Paul Krugman (Stanford) believes that there is no reason for official intervention in exchange markets. Martin Feldstein (Harvard) similarly believes market forces should be allowed to determine the value of the dollar. These experts differ but they all recognize the power of the foreign exchange market. Foreign exchange intervention means little without the fundamental policies of a balanced budget and steady monetary growth. Foreign exchange markets have grown and matured over the past 30 years and now link all economies into a functioning system of trade and investment. No system of fixed exchange rate system could last, and government FX intervention has no lasting influence.

Fixed versus Float

Speculators feed on instability and enjoy exchange rate movements. FX brokers want to "churn" the market to create high turnover and trading fees. A prime historical example is the Mexican peso, typically kept above its market level. In that situation, Mexican central bank support will collapse and a depreciation of the peso will occur. The only question is when. Traders sell the peso short. All speculation is on one side of the market, in favor of a devalued peso.

There is some disagreement over floating exchange rates. Exchange rates have fluctuated greatly since the floating system began. For instance, the US dollar dropped 13% from 1974 to 1979, then rose 63% by 1985, before falling 62% by 1990. Starting at $/yen = 0.05, an imported car costing 2,000,000 yen would cost $20,000 in 1974, $22,600 in 1979, $14,200 in 1985, and $23,000 in 1990. This roller coaster ride then smoothed before the dollar appreciated 29% between 1995 and 1998.

High oil prices during the 1970s and 1980s led to large current account deficits in the importing countries. Governments inflated their way out of debt, leading to large changes in price levels and exchange rates. Governments used expansionary fiscal policy to ease recessions associated with the high oil prices. With the swings in exchange rates, international markets were unsettled due to changing import prices.

There is an argument that a more regulated or governed FX market would be more efficient. The Bretton Woods fixed exchange rate system operated from the end of World War II until the oil price hikes of the 1970s. The US was the dominant economy of the world and the dollar was standard currency. The Bretton Woods system is looked upon by some as reliable and stable. Others yearn for a return to the gold standard of the late 1800s or some other common standard or definition for currencies.

Any fixed exchange rate arrangement would have collapsed under the economic upheavals since the 1970s. The Bretton Woods system succeeded only because the US was the dominant economy at that time. Europe and Japan had been devastated by World War II. Conservative US monetary policy led to stable prices and a reliable international currency standard.

The last three decades of the 20th century were vastly different due to oil price swings, LDC debt, the emergence of Japan as an economic leader, European integration, the success of newly industrializing countries, high levels of international investment, the collapse of communism, and large inflation differentials. The level and intensity of international transactions continue to grow and there is no possibility to form a fixed exchange rate system.

Fundamental forces determining the supply and demand of FX are not affected by central bank management. Further, active exchange rate policy has a tendency to exacerbate the exchange rate volatility it tries to manage.

Individual governments want to maintain their right to print money to increase spending without raising taxes. Each country chooses its inflation rate through a political and economic process. If inflation rates vary across countries, exchange rates must adjust. An alternative to fixed exchange rates would be a single international currency, with the money supply beyond the control of any single government. Such a step has been taken in Europe with the euro but now the European government in Brussels may be tempted by its ability to print money.

The floating exchange rate system works. Governments have propensities to create different inflation rates and floating exchange rates allow continuous adjustment.

EXAMPLE 11.9 *Appreciation and Labor Demand*

Dollar appreciation during 1980–1985 reduced prices, domestic production, and labor demand for 38 import competing manufacturing industries as documented by Ana Revenga (1992). There was a 6% reduction in the labor force and a 1.5% reduction in wages. The reduced labor demand forced the labor market down along its supply curve, revealing a supply elasticity of 0.25. Most of the adjustment was for employment, not wages. Elastic labor supply would imply smaller effects on employment than on wages.

Problems for Section B

B1. Suppose the EU tries to undervalue the euro. Diagram the market for euro and illustrate an artifically low exchange rate. Using FX reserves, how could the central bank sustain this value? Why would it want to?

B2. How could the EU government use exchange controls to keep the euro below its market value?

C. FOREIGN EXCHANGE TRADING

The FX market involves buying and selling foreign currency. Topics in foreign exchange trading include:

*   *Expectations* and exchange rates
*   *Stability* of exchange rates
*   *Triangular arbitrage* across currencies

Expectations and Exchange Rates

If traders expect a currency to appreciate, they demand it in the FX market. This increased demand appreciates the currency. Market expectations make themselves come true.

Much of the hourly and daily movement in exchange rates is due to FX traders looking for short term gains. Investors want to hold assets denominated in currencies expected to maintain or improve their FX rate. This is a motivation for investors with cash in high inflation countries to buy real estate in Houston, Japanese stock in Mitsubishi, or German savings bonds. The dollar, mark, and euro are expected to hold or improve their rate relative to currencies with high inflation.

Expectations influence the *spot exchange market*. This is an explanation of the dollar depreciation that started in 1985 when the major central banks of Germany, France, Britain, Japan, and the US (the Group of Five or G5) announced in September 1985 they would act to depreciate the dollar. Traders and investors paid attention to the agreement and expected the dollar to depreciate. The volume of central bank purchases of other currencies was trivial but expectations of traders and investors moved the market. In an episode between May and July 1989, the dollar appreciated in spite of concentrated selling by central banks illustrating the futility of central bank strategies.

Expectations affect the FX market. Central bank buying and selling is unable to affect the FX rate

FX trading occurs alongside international trading and financial activity in commercial centers. In small countries, the amount of currency traded may not support a competitive exchange market and the central bank may enjoy monopoly profit. Central banks should not interfere with a competitive FX market, and central bank intervention appears unable to affect FX rates.

EXAMPLE 11.10 *Chartists versus Fundamentalists*

A lot of people trade foreign exchange. Chartists look for patterns of FX rate behavior, trends, break points, shoulders, cliffs, spikes, bubbles, and other hints in charts, a bit like reading tea leaves. Fundamentalists examine the underlying theory and variables that should affect exchange rates, including price levels and money supply growth across countries. Fundamentalists have the right idea but theory and practice are far apart. An increase in the relative growth rate of a money supply will lead to depreciation, but when? Jeffrey Frenkel and Kenneth Froot (1990) report that chartists are more prevalent among FX traders. Almost all foreign exchange trading takes place between financial firms, banks, and brokers. Profitable foreign exchange transactions stabilize exchange rates, and unprofitable traders are soon out of business. Because of this stabilization, the FX market should be allowed to operate freely.

Exchange Rate Speculation

A debate continues over exchange rate speculation. Milton Friedman has argued since the 1950s that speculation lowers exchange rate fluctuation.

Figure 11.8 presents a picture of the market for yen at two different times. On the left, the exchange rate at time 0 is determined at e_0. On the right at a later time, the exchange rate is e_1. The supply of yen at time 1 (S_1) is less than the supply of yen at time 0 (S_0). Perhaps Japanese investors at time 1 have shifted to keep more of their assets in Japan because of a change in tax laws or expected stock returns.

Speculators at time 0 who correctly anticipate the coming change in the market and the higher value of the yen at time 1 will want to buy yen at time 0 and sell them at time 1. Buying yen at e_0 and selling them later at e_1 yields a speculative profit.

Profitable speculators dampen variation in the exchange rate over time. Increased D_0 raises e_0 and increased S_1 lowers e_1. Variation in the exchange rate over time is reduced with profitable speculation.

Unprofitable speculators would increase variation of e but they would soon be out of business. Only profitable speculators persist. Speculation is likely to lessen exchange rate fluctuation, transferring currencies from times when they are plentiful to when they are scarce.

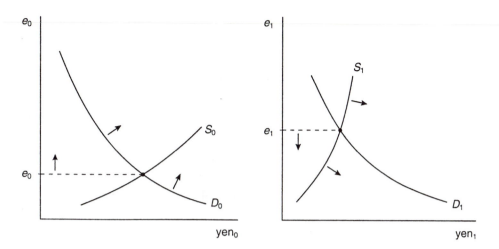

Figure 11.8
Stabilizing Profitable Speculation
The supply and demand for yen at time 0 is pictured on the left and at a later time 1 on the right. The supply yen at time 1 (S_1) is less than supply at line 0 (S_0). Speculators at time 0 who anticipate the higher e at time 1 will buy yen now (increasing D_0 and e_0) and sell yen later (increasing S_1 and lowering e_1). Profitable speculation reduces FX fluctuation.

Detractors of this theory argue that speculators may jump on the bandwagon of a trend in the exchange rate and create speculative bubbles that widen the variation in e. If the yen is appreciating, speculators will buy yen on the expectation that the trend will continue. This speculative buying pushes the yen up faster and further. When the climb stops, speculators rush to sell yen, causing it to crash. Some speculators may make a profit and exacerbate exchange rate swings.

Even if some speculation is definitely linked with higher variability in an exchange rate, any scheme of fixed exchange rates or central bank intervention creates speculation on one side of the market and is likely to worsen matters. Free exchange markets are the best alternative short of a universally accepted international currency controlled by a world central bank targeting zero inflation.

EXAMPLE 11.11 *Currency Game*

Financial funds and money managers put some of their efforts into trading currencies for profit. The *Wall Street Journal* (Craig Karmin, "Currency Game is Plenty Big, Plenty Tough," 6 May 2005) reports that the top ranked professional fund managers lost 1% trading currencies during 2004 after earning only 1% the previous year. Trading currencies is riskier than trading other assets and the return should be higher. Somebody must be earning more than these professionals since the market expanded 25% during the year. New traders include hedge funds and online trading. Daily volume in the global exchange market is about $2 trillion, doubling from 1996 to 2005 and almost matching US GDP during a work week. The market is becoming more complicated, a three ring circus with the US dollar losing its place at center stage. It is more difficult to make profitable speculative predictions about which currency to buy.

EXAMPLE 11.12 *Official Foreign Exchange*

The foreign exchange reserves of the Fed are only a fraction of the volume of daily trading. The Fed periodically enters the foreign exchange market for policy objectives. The Federal Reserve Bank of New York summarizes foreign exchange transactions. An abridged 1998 report states:

> The Fed intervened in the FX markets on one occasion on June 17 selling a total of $833 million dollars for yen. The yen had fallen 4.1% against the dollar during the quarter. The intervention was carried out in coordination with Japan. In the following days, the yen strengthened on heightened expectations that the Japanese government would produce effective domestic policy.

The yen could only have strengthened because traders anticipated a change in Japanese monetary policy. The $833 million purchase of yen could have had no effect itself. The daily volume of foreign exchange is well over 100 times that amount, and daily volume in the US alone is 10 times. The Fed had $14 billion of foreign exchange reserves at the time of the intervention. The entire Fed reserves would be a drop in the daily bucket. Of course, the Fed and the Japanese central bank can print new dollars and yen, and the yen purchase might have been taken as a signal of monetary policy.

Stability of Exchange Markets

Demand for foreign exchange has a negative slope and supply has a positive slope if import demand is elastic as evidence suggests, at least over long time periods. The FX market may, however, be inherently unstable from day to day.

The equilibrium in Figure 11.2 is stable. An exchange rate above the equilibrium $/yen = 0.008 implies excess supply and a falling exchange rate. If $/yen = 0.009, traders see their yen inventories increase and dollar inventories decline, and respond by discounting the yen. If the exchange rate is below the equilibrium at $/yen = 0.007 buyers clamor for yen but too few are offered to meet demand. Yen are scarce and their price is bid up.

An unstable FX market occurs if imports are inelastic causing supply to have a negative slope. Suppose foreign imports are inelastic and supply slopes downward as in Figure 11.9. A lower $/yen rate leads to an increase in the

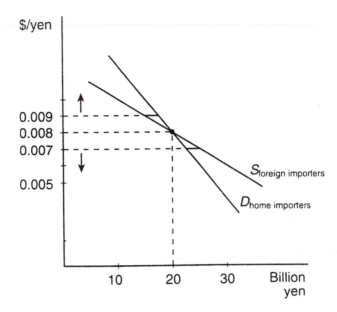

Figure 11.9
An Unstable FX Market
At any price above the equilibrium rate, excess demand occurs and the exchange rate is pushed up. At any price below the equilibrium, there is excess supply and the exchange rate falls. Instead of stabilizing, the exchange rate would rise and fall without bound.

quantity of yen supplied along the supply curve. The supply of yen might slope downward during the contract period.

At an exchange rate of $/yen = 0.009 there is an excess demand and $/yen is bid up. At $/yen = 0.007 there is excess supply of yen and $/yen falls. Figure 11.9 is *unstable equilibrium* and the exchange rate would crash or skyrocket.

Large swings in the dollar occurred during the 1980s. The dollar appreciated 87% from July 1980 to February 1985, then depreciated 42% to December 1988. Such large swings have strong price effects on international transactions.

On an hourly, daily, or weekly basis, there can be substantial exchange rate movement, best understood as participants looking for an equilibrium. Some evidence indicates that immediate changes in supply and demand create explosive situations. With short term movement in the exchange rate, some traders profit while others lose. High risk and return keep the FX market a busy place.

A Public Television program follows three exchange rate dealers, one at a bank in Hong Kong, a private trader in New York, and a third at a bank in London. During one day in June 1986 the three dealers trade a total of $1 billion. Following an emotional morning of trading, the New York dealer makes a profit of $30,000 in one transaction, happily closes shop, and sends his staff home before lunch.

With the large dollar appreciation during the early 1980s, import spending rose and export revenue dwindled. These changes indicate import elasticity and downward sloping long run demand in the FX market. In the early 1980s, the recession in the US can be attributed to low export production and imports of cheap foreign products. As the dollar depreciated after 1985, import prices rose and export revenue climbed. Import expenditure continued to climb primarily due to inelasticity of oil imports. Imports of most goods are elastic with respect to the exchange rate. Export revenue accelerated during the late 1980s and the US experienced trade surpluses early in 1991.

Exchange rates have been volatile but FX markets are stable and should be allowed to operate freely.

EXAMPLE 11.13   *Predicting FX Rates*

Economists are often asked to do the impossible and will gladly do so for a fee. Predicting weekly or monthly exchange rates is impossible. If a lucky economist stumbled on the correct theory for predicting exchange rates, it would remain a secret. The popular press is full of conflicting "wisdom" about what has happened in exchange markets. For instance, *The Economist* magazine reported on 20 May 1989 in "Every Which Way But Down" that rising US output caused the dollar to appreciate because foreigners wanted dollars to buy US products, but then slower US output growth caused the dollar to appreciate because of the perception that there would be no inflation! The thousands of foreign exchange traders have their own reasons for trading and no theory is likely to explain exchange rate movements. Over years and decades, purchasing power parity and relative money supplies explain long term exchange rates. FX trading, however, takes place over shorter time intervals.

EXAMPLE 11.14   *FX Banks in the US*

Banks do not take open positions in foreign currencies but provide broker services for transactions fees. The magazine *FX Week* publishes news on the foreign exchange trade. The 2 October 1999 issue lists the foreign exchange revenue of US banks for the third quarter. Citigroup reports the largest FX revenue at $358 million, followed by Chase Manhattan with $199 million, and Bank of America with $138 million. FX traders make commissions on volume and do not care about the direction of change. Consider the comments of a dealer at one New York bank: "There was some good movement, but it came mainly in the latter part of the quarter. That activity kept FX desks reasonably busy and generated some good profit making opportunities. Volatility was not as high as in 1998 when the Asian and Russian crises were breaking out." There is nothing like a good currency crisis to increase commissions. Traders in the FX markets taking long or short positions are the ones that make profits or losses. Banks have learned the hard way to avoid exchange risk.

Triangular Arbitrage

The millions of banks, brokers, and traders in the FX market instantaneously know market rates through the internet and interbank electronic links. Increasing amounts of foreign exchange trading take place on the internet. Brokers "make" the market, continuously matching buyers and sellers. The FX market is highly competitive. Thousands of brokers and traders operate profitably on volumes minuscule relative to the total market.

Any difference in FX rates results in an opportunity for *triangular arbitrage* that keeps relative prices of currencies in line. Suppose current exchange rates are posted at mark/\$ = 2, yen/mark = 62, and yen/\$ = 125. A trader could take yen, buy marks, and then buy dollars at $62 \times 2 = 124$ yen/\$. This cross rate is lower than the market rate of 125. Dollars are cheaper at the cross rate than at the market rate. Arbitrageurs will buy dollars at the cross rate and sell them at the market rate for a profit of 1 yen per dollar. This arbitrage decreases demand for the dollar and pushes the cross and the market rates together.

Trillions of dollars of currency are involved in continuous triangular arbitrage. Among any three currencies, there are two independent exchange rates. Cross rates between any two currencies determine the value of the other currency through triangular arbitrage. Among any number n of currencies there are $n-1$ independent exchange rates due to triangular arbitrage.

In many places you can witness and take part in the global FX market. Most banks have an FX desk that trades currencies. In large US cities especially near the Canadian and Mexican borders where foreign currency is often used alongside the dollar, FX traders specialize in quick service. Travelers in Europe notice an abundance of FX windows. Airports have FX windows where travelers can buy and sell foreign currencies. There is an increasing volume of currency trading on the internet.

The FX market is a vast competitive market made up of banks and traders profitably trading currencies.

EXAMPLE 11.15 *Growth in the FX Market*

The volume of trade in the FX market grew an average of over 10% annually since the early 1990s according to the Bank for International Settlements (BIS), a Swiss international institution that acts as a bank for central banks. Volume in the FX market now stands at \$2 trillion per day. As a scale, GDP in the US is about a week of trading. The volume of exports of goods and services is a small fraction of the volume of foreign exchange trading. Spot FX transactions are about 1/3 of total transactions. Trading is focused geographically in major centers in each of three 8-hour time zones. London handles the greatest volume of foreign exchange transactions. New York is the major center in the Americas. Tokyo and Singapore are the major centers in Asia. Only a very small fraction of foreign exchange sales and purchases directly involve traders of goods and services. Most FX trades take place between professional traders at banks and financial institutions.

EXAMPLE 11.16 *Corporate Profits and FX*

Corporations pay their labor, energy, rent, and other expenses out of revenue, then distribute profits to shareholders. Corporations acquire equity by printing stocks in exchange for a share of future profits. Stocks represent ownership of the corporation. Corporate profit in the US is between 20% and 30% of GDP, much higher than in Japan and Germany at about 12% and Canada at 5%. Merih Uctum (1998) reports that rising costs of energy and labor in the 1970s lowered corporate profits. In the 1980s, the appreciating dollar meant more import competition and lower US profits. Japanese corporate profits are less exposed to import competition.

Problems for Section C

C1. If the lira/$ exchange rate is 1050, the peso/$ rate is 175, and the lira/peso rate is 5.95, describe a way to make profits through triangular arbitrage. Start with $1000.

C2. Suppose the demand for yen slopes upward due to inelastic demand for Japanese bonds. Diagram an unstable exchange market with upward sloping demand and describe its behavior.

D. EXCHANGE RISK

Over years or decades, exchange rates reflect relative inflation and currency purchasing power and are easy to predict. International transactions cover shorter time periods, however, and involve unpredictable changes in exchange rates. This exchange rate risk is an element of international trade and finance.

EXAMPLE 11.17 *The Early Euro Market*

The euro fell relative to the US dollar in 1999, the year it was introduced. US products in Europe became more expensive than they had been at the start of the year and European products were cheaper in the US. The supply of euros is controlled by the European government in Belgium. Without the ability to create money, national governments in Europe have to more nearly balance their budgets. The exchange rate will depend on growth rates of the two money supplies. Both the US and Europe have the monetary policy goal of low inflation. If that occurs, the value of the $/euro exchange rate would stabilize over the long term. Between 1999 and 2004, however, the euro ranged from 0.85 to 1.31.

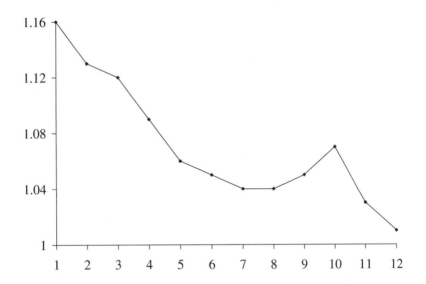

Expected Inflation and Exchange Rates

Inflation occurs when the general price level or the average price of all products rises. If the foreign price level P^* is pesos/good, its inverse is goods/peso, the purchasing power of the peso. If P^* is rising, the purchasing power of the peso is falling. If P^* rises from 100 to 125, the purchasing power of the peso falls from 0.010 to 0.008. Inflating currencies lose relative to the products they purchase.

Currencies have been generally inflating since the 1950s, some much more than others. Periods of currency deflation with the general price level falling have also occurred through history. Changes in the value of a particular currency do not matter as long as the changes are predictable and the exchange rate is free to adjust. Residents in a country readily adjust to any degree of predictable inflation.

If one currency is expected to inflate more rapidly than another, international interest rates will reflect the expected inflation differential. The *real interest rate* is the return on an investment after the eroding influence of inflation. The real interest rate typically does not vary greatly over time or between countries. The *nominal interest rate* is the real interest rate plus an inflation premium.

Suppose the interest rate on a savings account is 6%. If $1000 stays in the account, it will become $1060 at the end of a year. Suppose the expected inflation for the year is 5%. The purchasing power of the $1060 must be discounted to find at the real interest rate, 6% − 5% = 1%. There is an expected 1% increase in the purchasing power of the $1000 since the $1060 next year is expected to purchase $1010 worth of current products.

The Fisher equation, named after economist Irvin Fisher, is expressed

$$i = r + \pi$$

where i is the nominal interest rate, r is the real interest rate, and π is expected inflation.

Suppose expected inflation is 25% for pesos and 5% for the dollar. Expectations are based on the history of inflation in each country as well as information about pending monetary policy. A 28% nominal interest rate in pesos equals a real interest rate of 3% and a nominal interest rate of 8% in dollars. Investing at those nominal interest rates would yield the same purchasing power if actual inflation turns out to be what was expected. The expected increase in purchasing power from investing in either country is 3%. It is never easy to anticipate the path of inflation and choosing among international nominal interest rates is a challenge.

The nominal interest rate discounted by expected inflation is the real interest rate. Choosing between international investments is difficult because inflation is difficult to predict.

Suppose the spot rate is 125 pesos/$ and inflation turns out to be 30% for pesos and 3% for dollars. The peso has lost value relative to the dollar, 27% = 30% − 3% of its value. The exchange rate should be 1.27 × 125 = 158.75 peso/$ at the end of the year.

The trick is that only nominal interest rates are observed. International comparison of real interest rates involves the risk of expected inflation. The difference between nominal interest rates in two countries with competitive exchange and financial markets is the market expectation of the difference between the two inflation rates, the discount of the weaker currency. If nominal interest rates are 28% for pesos and 8% for dollars, the peso would have a 28% − 8% = 20% discount against the dollar and the dollar a 20% premium against the peso.

Holding foreign currency involves exchange risk and investors diversify currency holdings to dissipate risk. Currencies can be ranked according to potential for unexpected depreciation. The following ranking is from the 1993 Australian Export Credit Agency, and there are various rankings. "A" is the safest currency, and "D" the most risky:

A. Austria, Canada, China, Germany, Japan, UK, US
B. Bahamas, Kuwait, Saudi Arabia, Thailand, Turkey
C. Czech Republic, Mexico, Botswana, Chile, Israel, Oman
D. Argentina, Dominican Republic, Honduras, Nicaragua, Russia

Nominal interest rates in currencies with higher expected inflation must be discounted. Nominal interest rates reveal which currencies have discounts.

EXAMPLE 11.18 *The Trade Weighted Exchange Rate*

The US dollar has generally appreciated during the floating exchange rate period, although not relative to other major currencies. The importance of each country in US trade is used to weight the dollar exchange rates. Trade with country i is $T_i = X_i + M_i$ and the sum of trade with all countries is T. The weight of country i is its share of total trade $W_i = T_i/T$. The *trade weighted exchange rate* is $E = W_1 E_1 + \cdots + W_n E_n$ where E is that foreign currency rate. From 1973 when floating exchange rates started until 1981, the dollar remained fairly stable around $E = 30$ (1999 = 100). The dollar then appreciated strongly to 1986. A slight depreciation followed but an appreciation began in 1991. By 1998, the dollar reached 100 and it has depreciated since. For many investors outside the US, holding dollars has been a better investment than holding their domestic bonds. The long term appreciation indicates that the supply of dollars has fallen relative to the average money supplies of US trading partners.

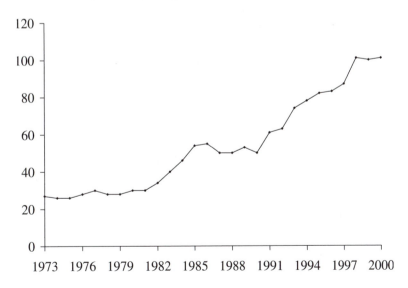

EXAMPLE 11.19 *Peso Crashes*

The Mexican government manages the peso, historically trying to keep it above its market rate. The supply of pesos increases to support government spending.

An excess supply of pesos is created at the fixed exchange rate as in Figure 11.6. To meet the excess demand for dollars, Mexican international reserves fell over 70% in 1994 as the peso depreciated up to the artificial limit. The supply of pesos continued to grow and the peso remained overvalued. Finally the government devalued the peso by 15%, leading to speculation that the peso was ready for a crash. Over the next 3 months the peso lost half relative to the dollar. The price of imports skyrocketed in Mexico and real income fell. Such unfortunate episodes have occurred periodically in Mexico. Fixed exchange rates will not support a currency out of line with underlying relative prices and money supplies. The Mexican government should balance its budget and allow free peso exchange without any effort to manage the exchange market, and has improved its record during the NAFTA years.

Forward and Future Exhange

Currencies with high inflation lose value relative to those with low inflation and FX markets systematically discount inflating currencies. Risk remains, however, in international transactions because of unexpected exchange rate changes. Contracts are written for future delivery, and investors hold assets denominated in foreign currency.

Consider an EU firm assembling personal computers. The firm orders computer chips from a Japanese firm with delivery spread out over the next 6 months and bills to be paid 3 weeks after delivery. The current exchange rate is known but nobody knows what the exchange rate will be when the bills are due. The firm can assume the FX risk and buy the yen on the spot exchange market. International investors face exchange risk when they hold a foreign bond.

To avoid FX risk, firms and investors can *hedge* in the *forward exchange market* where a contract can be signed to buy or sell foreign currency at a date in the future for a price set today. The supply and demand for forward exchange are derived from traders and investors who want to settle the prices of their purchases, sales, or interest earnings in their own currency.

The importing firm can use forward contracts to pin down a euro price for the Japanese computer chips. Suppose the importer knows a bill for 5 million yen will have to be paid in 30 days and the forward exchange rate for 30 days is 0.0069. The importer can sign a contract to buy the yen for 5 million × 0.0069 = 34,500 euros.

The forward market reflects what market participants think the exchange rate will become. Rapidly inflating currencies are systematically discounted by forward rates below spot rates. Currencies with relatively low inflation have a premium in the forward market. If market participants expect the peso to suffer less inflation because of slower money supply growth, the demand for pesos in the forward market rises and the peso discount drops.

Future contracts for standard quantities of foreign exchange and standard time periods have developed for those wanting to trade foreign currencies. Transaction costs of future contracts are very low. Traders and investors can also use the futures market but it has inflexible standard quantities and specified trading dates. The forward and future rates are unbiased predictors of the exchange rate, over and underestimating the exchange rate with equal frequency.

Another sort of agent trades forward and future currency contracts to make a profit. *Speculators* make contracts in foreign exchange when they believe the exchange rate will turn out to be different from the forward rate. Suppose the current spot rate for South Korean won is 760 won/$ and the 3 month future rate is 780 won/$. The won is selling at a discount but the speculator thinks the won will drop to 800 won/$. She will sign a contract to sell won at the forward rate of 780 and plan on buying won later in the spot market. This speculation is leveraged since no current payment is required to make the contract. Such speculation is risky because the spot rate can turn out to be lower than 780 won/$.

Forward and future FX markets offer hedgers a way to avoid exchange rate risk, and speculators a way to assume it.

EXAMPLE 11.20 *Trading FX*

Newspapers, banks, trading houses, and the internet list future exchange rates. Futures contracts are for standard quantities of foreign currency and specified dates. For instance, contracts list for 12.5 million yen on the third Wednesday of September. With futures contracts, numerous buyers and sellers can be involved. Investors and speculators match wits against each other buying or selling future contracts. You can try your hand on internet exchange rate simulations.

EXAMPLE 11.21 *Future Prices*

Foreign exchange is traded in futures markets alongside gold, oil, cotton, beef, and other commodities. The following quotes are for 30 day future contracts from Bloomberg on 8 November 1999. For instance, a trader could contract to buy or sell Japanese yen at yen/$ = 94.94 or $/yen = 0.01053. The spot price of yen that day was yen/$ = 106, indicating investors expected the yen to depreciate. Speculators buy future contracts hoping to outguess the market. Units vary across commodities. The British Pound BP and German D-mark prices are in cents per unit of foreign currency. The change column shows the percentage change from the previous day. Coffee, natural gas, and the S&P futures had busy days.

	Price	Change
Japanese yen FUTURE	94.94	0.14%
British pound FUTURE	162.06	0.05%
C$ FUTURE	68.19	−0.06%
GOLD 100 OZ FUTURE	289.30	−0.58%
S&P 500 FUTURE	1384.60	1.18%
CRUDE OIL FUTURE	23.00	0.61%
COTTON NO. 2 FUTURE	51.11	0.02%
LIVE CATTLE FUTURE	69.10	0.04%

Problems for Section D

D1. Suppose current price levels are $P = \$/good = 100$ in the US and $P^* = €/good = 150$ in the EU. If the same goods are consumed in each country and there is free trade, what is the current exchange rate $\$/€$? Five years later, $P = 120$ and $P^* = 160$. What should the exchange rate be? Which currency has depreciated?

D2. Suppose the nominal interest rate is 12% and inflation is 9%. Find the real interest rate. Starting with $100, find the nominal and real return to saving. If expected inflation rate rises to 15% but the real interest rate is unchanged, find the nominal rate and the nominal and real returns to $100.

EXAMPLE 11.22 *Central Bank Risk*

Central banks may intervene in foreign exchange markets to stabilize currencies if they believe speculation is turning against a currency. Such intervention is thought to reduce volatility temporarily with traders pushing a currency around for no fundamental reason. Richard Baillie and William Osterberg (1997) find evidence of the opposite. Daily foreign exchange interventions by the US, German, and Japanese central banks increase exchange rate variability. Traders view central banks as unpredictable and unreliable. The wisdom in the market is to keep an eye on the central banks and do the opposite, selling what they buy or buying what they sell. Less central bank intervention would lead to less volatile exchange rates.

CONCLUSION

The FX market is a vast lively market and more firms and consumers are becoming familiar with it. As a country integrates more into the world economy, the foreign exchange market becomes more important. The influence of the exchange rate on economic daily life cannot be overlooked. The final chapter turns attention to issues of international finance and the international role of money.

Terms

Black exchange market	Import license
Cross rate	J curve
Currency discount	Market exchange rate
Expected inflation	Marshall-Lerner condition
Fischer equation	Parallel exchange markets
Fixed exchange rate	Real and nominal interest rates
Forward exchange rate	Speculation
FX reserves	Spot exchange rate
FX risk	Triangular arbitrage
Future and forward contracts	

MAIN POINTS

- FX markets are large, active, electronic, efficient, vital to the global economy, and the most important market for many countries.
- The demand for foreign exchange comes from domestic buyers of foreign products and assets. The supply of foreign exchange comes from foreign buyers of domestic products and assets.
- A depreciating currency raises the domestic price of foreign goods and lowers the foreign price of domestic goods, favoring an increase in the trade balance.
- Governments may artificially fix or manage the exchange rate to meet some policy goal. Theory and experience, however, recommend exchange rates float freely.
- High inflation rates are associated with high nominal interest rates and depreciating currencies. Currencies expected to depreciate are discounted by the forward and future exchange rates.

REVIEW PROBLEMS

1. Suppose the domestic demand for the Japanese autos is $Q = 10,000 - P$, where P is the dollar price. Find the quantity of Japanese cars costing 880,000 yen that would be demanded at the exchange rates yen/\$ = 110 and 125. Find and plot the quantity of yen demanded to buy the autos at these exchange rates.

2. Find the yen prices of US rice costing \$4.50 per bushel when the yen/\$ exchange rate is 110 and 125. Demand for rice is $Q = 9,000,000 - 10,000\,P^*$ where P^* is the yen price. Find the quantity of rice demanded in Japan and the quantity of yen supplied at both exchange rates. Plot the supply of yen.

3. Start with $1000 and find a way to make a profit if the lira/peso = 6.05, lira/$ = 1050, and $/peso = 0.00571.

4. Suppose the EU launches a number of communications satellites improving their telecommunications industry relative to the US. Given that the US exports telecommunications services, diagram what happens in the FX market. Predict the subsequent effect on the BGS in the US and the EU.

5. Find the short run percentage change in import expenditure and export revenue with a 5% depreciation when the short run import elasticity is 0.3 and the short run export elasticity is 0.4. Describe what must happen to the trade balance in the short run.

6. If the long run import elasticity is 1.5 and the long run export elasticity is 1.2, find the long run percentage change in the export revenue and import expenditure with a 5% depreciation. Does the trade balance rise or fall in the long run?

7. Illustrate the effect on the foreign exchange market of a limit on cash that can be taken on foreign travel.

8. Explain why a central bank supporting its currency by buying a surplus of its own currency is taxing its citizens. What sort of explicit tax would have the same effect?

9. Which groups of economic agents demand pesos in the forward market? What happens to the quantity of pesos demanded when the forward price of pesos rises? Who supplies pesos forward in the market?

10. The *Foreign Exchange Review* of the First Wachovia Bank reported on its March 12, 1990, issue: "Despite repeated central bank intervention last week, the US dollar rallied to highs of 1.7095 marks, 151.35 yen, and $1.6155/pound". Were the central banks buying or selling dollars? Illustrate with an FX market diagram.

11. Suppose the spot exchange rate for Kuwait dinar is $/dinar = 3.60 and the six-month forward rate is 3.65. Does the dinar have a forward premium or discount?

12. In the example of Korean won speculator, calculate her profit if she signs a contract to sell 10 million won and the spot rate turns out to be exactly what she expected. Find her profit in dollars if the spot rate instead falls to 750 won/$.

13. Start with $1 million and keep an imaginary record buying and selling spot exchange for a week. Check spot rates on the internet. Compete to see who can make the largest profit, assuming zero transaction costs.

READINGS

Mike Melvin, *International Money and Finance* (1989) New York: Harper & Row. Lively text with excellent coverage of the FX market.

Paul Krugman (1989) *Exchange Rate Instability*, Cambridge: The MIT Press. Examines the surprising volatility of exchange rates.

Leland Yeager (1976) *International Monetary Relations*, New York: Harper & Row. A true classic in economics.

Federal Reserve Bank Bulletins. Monthly bulletins with analysis of the FX market, available online.

Internet foreign exchange sites. Various commercial sites with information on the FX market.

CHAPTER 12

International Financial Markets

Preview

Finance refers to borrowing and lending in the credit market. International financial markets involve borrowing and lending across borders. This chapter covers:

- The *international credit market*
- The *exchange rate* and the international credit market
- *Money* and its impact on international prices
- *Relative money supplies* and international financial markets

INTRODUCTION

Money functions as a *medium of exchange* by facilitating trade. People trade labor for food and housing, using money in the form of paychecks, bank deposits, checks, credit cards, and cash. The scarcity of money reflects the scarcity of resources and the necessity of economic choices.

Income for a consumer or firm may be more or less during a year than the desire to spend. To balance income and spending, credit markets develop through the interaction of lenders and borrowers. The interest rate is the return on a loan and the cost of borrowing. Banks make the market by bringing lenders and borrowers together.

A country may also have more or less income than it wants to spend. One country can be a net lender and another a net borrower through international loans. International credit flows through international banks. Each country would have its own loan market in autarky but all countries benefit through the *international credit market*. International interest rates are the result of international lending and borrowing.

Money acts as a *unit of account* for products and assets. Currencies also serve as a unit of account for each other in the FX market. International price comparisons are made through the exchange rate.

Money is also a *store of value*. An inflating currency is a poor store of value that would depreciate in the FX market. Part of currency trading takes place as investors look for currencies that are better stores of value.

International financial flows are reported in the capital account of the balance of payments. Interest payments on international loans are reported as net investment income in the current account because the funds are available for current transactions. Borrowing countries experience cash inflow and capital account surpluses but are committed to future deficits in net investment income. Lenders have cash outflows and capital account deficits but enjoy future surpluses in net investment income. International loans are used to purchase capital or consumer goods and are associated with trade deficits.

While often interpreted as bad news, a current account deficit and international debt is a signal that a country is expected to grow. LDCs can be expected to incur debt to acquire capital goods. As output expands, a growing country can repay its debt.

There is an optimal debt that a country should acquire and debt is harmful if it is not managed well. Borrowing might slow growth if it finances current consumption rather than investment.

Stocks, bonds, certificates of deposit, and "overnight paper" are some of the financial instruments involved in international finance. A firm wanting to raise money for a new building can offer new stocks or bonds. Investors give up cash in hand for more cash later in the form of dividends on stocks or premiums on bonds. When such transactions occur internationally, they affect exchange rates.

Exchange rates also influence the direction and level of international finance. If the home currency depreciates, foreign investors may want to buy more home stocks and bonds because they have become cheaper. A depreciation lowers the relative price of home financial instruments and encourages the country to become a lender.

The international credit market and the FX market are closely related. Arbitrage trading occurs internationally among financial intermediaries including banks, investment houses, and brokers.

The main role that governments should play in international financial markets is to control the money supply. Government central banks have the job of controlling money supplies. A country whose money supply is growing relative to the rest of the world will experience currency depreciation. The foreign exchange market and international credit markets are affected by monetary policies.

International financial markets are active and increasingly important. There are calls for the international integration of monetary policies to stabilize exchange rates. Europe has gone through the process of adopting a common currency, the euro. The debt crisis of the LDCs has fundamentally reshaped international financial relationships. International financial and monetary relations are vital to the everyday life of the world economy.

A. THE INTERNATIONAL CREDIT MARKET

This section examines international credit markets and international financial accounting.

EXAMPLE 12.1 *Credit Markets for the Past 100 Years*

> International credit markets were highly integrated by the 1890s but were disrupted by two World Wars and the Great Depression. International investment relative to output reached an all time low during the 1950s and 1960s. Since the late 1970s, international investment has increased but in real terms remains below the level of 100 years ago. Free markets for foreign exchange and investment would encourage increased international capital flows but many governments do not allow free markets.

Two Senses of "Capital"

Capital has two meanings in economics and finance. In microeconomics, capital is a factor of production, the machinery and structures combined with labor and natural resources. In finance, capital refers to loans. Newspapers or magazines that refer to international capital are speaking of international lending and borrowing.

The two meanings of the word are connected. When a firm borrows from a bank, sells bonds, or sells stocks, it typically invests in productive capital to increase future production. Debt and equity are used to purchase new capital input and the two senses of "capital" go hand in hand.

Economic agents are faced with choosing between current and future spending. Consumers can expand consumption beyond income by borrowing. Governments can increase spending beyond tax revenue by selling bonds. Firms can use profit for investment spending, or they can become lenders in the credit market. If a firm lacks the cash to fund a worthwhile investment project, it can borrow in the credit market.

A firm deciding whether to invest in a project looks at its *rates of return* found by estimating profit created over its lifetime. Suppose a new machine is expected to create revenue of $100,000 per year. Labor to run the machine costs $40,000, maintenance $5000, and material and other expenses $15,000. The net profit would be $40,000 per year. For simplicity, suppose the machine has an indefinitely long lifetime and there is no inflation. The net benefit of the machine is the $40,000 per year it adds to profit. If the machine costs $1 million, its rate of return is $40,000/$1,000,000 = 4%.

To determine whether installing the machine is worthwhile, the opportunity cost of $1 million must be considered. Suppose the interest rate is 3%. With no inflation, this is a real rate of return. If our firm has $1 million cash on hand, it can become a lender and earn $30,000 per year but this is less than the machine would add to profit. The benefit of the machine outweighs the opportunity cost, and the firm should invest in the machine. If the market interest rate were 5%, the firm could earn $50,000 by becoming a lender and should not invest in the machine.

If the firm has no cash on hand, it could borrow to invest in the machine. Suppose the interest rate is 2% and it costs $35,000 per year to pay back the principal and interest on a loan of $1 million. Yearly benefits from the machine of $40,000 outweigh the costs of $35,000 and purchase of the machine should be financed. If the interest rate were higher and it cost $45,000 per year to pay back the loan, the purchase of the machine would not be profitable.

Financial capital is translated directly into productive capital by firms borrowing to invest in new projects, the link between the two senses of capital.

Investment spending varies inversely with the interest rate. The rate of return on potential investment projects is compared to the market interest rate. A higher interest rates means fewer investment projects.

EXAMPLE 12.2 *Emerging Stock Markets*

Financial capital is transformed into productive capital when firms sell stocks and bonds to raise money and spend it on investment projects. Major international stock markets in New York, Tokyo, and London are in the news daily. The World Bank publishes *Emerging Stock Markets Factbook* that summarizes the activity of 27 stock markets in NICs and LDCs. There is a high degree of variation in returns across these emerging stock markets and even more variation across individual firms within each country. Emerging markets have generally high rates of return but also high risks. Yearly rates of return vary from plus to minus a few hundred percent.

The Credit Market

More borrowing will take place at a real interest rate of 2% than 5%. As the cost of borrowing increases, the quantity of loans demanded decreases. At higher real interest rates more people increase saving and decrease current spending. The quantity of loans supplied increases with the return to saving.

Demand and supply for loanable funds (LF) are illustrated in Figure 12.1. The *real interest rate r* represents the price of borrowing and the return to

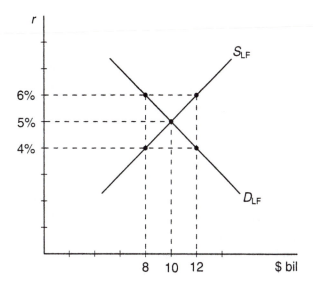

Figure 12.1
The Domestic Credit Market
The real interest rate r represents the expected return on investments after inflation. The demand for loanable funds (LF) is based on the marginal return to various investment projects in order of decreasing expected returns. At higher real interest rates, the quantity of credit demanded falls. The supply of credit comes from those with liquidity who sacrifice current spending, and with a higher real interest rate the quantity of LF supplied rises. Equilibrium occurs at $r = 5\%$ with $10 billion of loans.

lending. The real interest rate equals the nominal interest rate minus expected inflation from the *Fisher equation*,

$$r = i - \pi$$

If $r = 5\%$, saving $100 today results in $105 of purchasing power after a year. If the nominal interest rate i is 8%, expected inflation π is 3%. From the borrower's viewpoint, it costs $5 worth of current goods and services to borrow $100. From the lender's viewpoint, $5 worth of goods and services can be gained by giving up $100.

At a real interest rate of $r = 4\%$, the quantity of loans demanded $12 billion is greater than the quantity supplied $8 billion. Financial intermediaries perceive this excess demand and respond by rationing and increasing the interest rate above 4%.

At an interest rate of 6%, there would be an excess supply of $4 billion and banks would not be able to loan reserves. Idle excess reserves would spur banks to lower the interest rate to encourage potential borrowers. The market equilibrium interest rate is 5% where the quantity of loans supplied equals the quantity demanded.

EXAMPLE 12.3 *Bad International Loans*

> Bad loans, debt problems, and pending bankruptcy are hardly new to the international economy. Scaled to world output, international lending was higher 100 years ago in spite of recent globalization. Barry Eichengreen (1991) surveys the history of bad debt. Latin American countries defaulted on their loans in the 1820s followed by US states during the 1830s and 1840s. Latin American countries defaulted again in the 1880s along with Egypt, Greece, and Turkey. During the Great Depression of the 1930s, every debtor country defaulted. In cases of default, other countries may retaliate with trade restrictions but defaulting countries nevertheless perform better than those continuing the struggle to pay back bad loans. Lenders always turn around and make new loans because of the high potential return. Bankruptcy practice allows bad loans to be written off and business to reorganize but there are no international bankruptcy laws. The WTO has the potential to oversee international bankruptcy proceedings as an international court although sovereinty and commercial interests stand in the way.

International Credit Market

International financial intermediation occurs when banks match lenders and borrowers in different countries. The central issue in the international credit market is comparing real interest rates across countries.

Suppose the real interest rate in the world is 4% and the country in Figure 12.1 can acquire as many loans as it wants at that rate. There will be an inflow of $4 billion, a KA surplus as the country borrows internationally. If the world interest rate is 6%, a national excess supply of $4 billion credit is exported with a KA deficit as the country lends internationally.

> *A small open economy takes the international interest rate. The economy is a borrower if the international interest rate is lower than the domestic autarky interest rate, and a lender if it is higher.*

LDCs with growth potential but a low supply of credit should borrow internationally, running KA surpluses. Rich DCs with low growth potential are likely to be international lenders, with an excess supply of loans and KA deficits. An economy that is small relative to the international capital market is a price taker in the global credit market.

The international interest rate between two large economies is shown in Figure 12.2, analogous to the excess supply and demand of products. Home excess demand (XD) for loans is derived directly from Figure 12.1.

The foreign country has different lenders and borrowers with their own plans and perceptions of the future. The foreign excess supply curve (XS*) is derived from the foreign credit market. Note that the foreign autarky interest

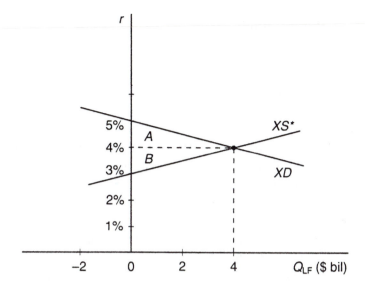

Figure 12.2
The International Credit Market
The excess demand XD for credit from the home country slopes down. Without international finance, the home autarky return to capital is 5%. The excess supply XS* from the foreign country slopes upward and the foreign autarky capital return is 3%. The international equilibrium is $r = 4\%$ with $4 billion of credit from the foreign to the home country.

rate $r^* = 3\%$ is less than the home autarky interest rate $r = 5\%$. Loans are valued more in the home country and the home country will borrow. In the foreign country, loans have less value. At $r = 4\%$, the excess demand for credit at home equals excess supply from the foreign country XD = XS*. The home country borrows $4 billion from the foreign country.

Borrowers are better off at home because loans can be taken at a lower rate. Lenders are better off in the foreign country because they receive higher interest. On the other hand, lenders at home suffer lower returns as they compete with foreign lenders, and borrowers abroad pay more than they would in autarky because they have to compete with home country borrowers.

Net international gains are represented by triangles A and B in Figure 12.2. Net gains for the home country are the area between XD and the international rate of 4%, area A equal to 1/2(.01 × $4 bil) = $20 million.

In the foreign country, lenders gain and borrowers lose. The foreign net gain is the area between foreign XS* and the international interest rate 4%, area B equal to 1/2(.01 × $4 bil) = $20 million. International gains are the sum of the gain in each country, a total of $40 million.

Gains in the international credit market are assessed through the surpluses of lenders and borrowers.

International Investment Accounting

Estimates of international lending and borrowing are reported by governments and the IMF. Financial flows enter the KA of the BOP as foreign investment. Borrowing countries report a surplus as a positive number, and lending countries a deficit with cash flowing out.

NII also enters the BOP. A Japanese investor buying EU stocks expects a yearly return. These dividend payments are a negative entry in the NII of the EU. If someone in China holds a US government bond, the interest payment would enter as a deficit for the US. Payments on international loans enter as deficits in NII.

Suppose home investors have a stock of $2200 billion invested abroad, while foreigners have $1675 billion invested at home. If the international interest rate is 4%, then $0.04 \times \$2200$ billion = $88 billion is received as investment income and $0.04 \times \$1675$ billion = $67 billion is paid out. The NII is then $88 billion − $67 billion = $21 billion. There is a surplus or net cash inflow in NII, approximately what was reported for the US in 1998.

Suppose if the stock of home investment abroad increases from $2200 billion to $2296 billion. This $96 billion investment outflow could be in the form of branch plants built abroad with retained earnings, individual investors buying foreign stocks or bonds, or a domestic bank buying a foreign bank. Suppose during the same year the foreign owned capital stock at home increases by $213 billion from $1675 billion to $1888 billion. The capital account will then report a surplus of $213 billion − $96 billion = $117 billion. There is a net cash inflow in the KA, approximately that reported for the US in 1998. Future increased cash outflows in NII will occur as these international loans are repaid.

Estimates of the KA and NII are done by survey and it is not clear whether the US is a net debtor or creditor some years because the statistical discrepancy outweighs the net KA balance. Financial activity is expanding so quickly that government surveys have a difficult time keeping abreast. Access to financial services on the internet promises to make the job more difficult.

Multinational firms (MNFs) account for an increasing portion of international trade and finance. If a country imports from MNF branches, its management and investment make up part of the value of the imports. If imports from US multinational firms abroad are taken away from import expenditures during the 1980s, reported BOT deficits change to surpluses. The development of international banking tells an analogous story for the KA.

Imagine the branch of a US bank operating in Laredo, Mexico buys $1 million of new stock in a new industrial plant in a free trade zone in Texas which plans to employ 50% Mexican citizens. Further, suppose 49% of the stock of the Mexican bank is owned by a bank in Los Angeles, and 60% of the deposits in the Mexican bank are from Texas. Machinery in the assembly line might be put together by a firm based in Michigan importing components from China. Which way is investment frowing? When the machinery is put into place is this an international flow of productive capital? How should wages earned and spent by the Mexicans in Texas be recorded?

Such international activity presents a quagmire for national income accounting. From a global perspective, accounting dilemmas are immaterial. Imagine the difficulties if every city and town in the US tried to estimate its capital and current accounts! International investment figures may offer some rough notion of the pattern of international investment but they offer no basis for policy action.

International Financial Policy

BOP data provides some indication of the international flows of goods, services, credit, and net interest payments. Loans flow from countries with excess supply where the real interest rate is low to countries with excess demand where the real interest rate is high. International loans finance the expansion of productive capital input. Governments should not control or try to influence international financial flows.

Successful manipulation of international financial markets is beyond the scope of governments but this hardly keeps them from trying. Many governments place direct controls on international investment. LDCs strictly control the outflow of investment. Many governments are reluctant to allow inflows of foreign funds for fear of being controlled by foreign interests. There are calls for capital control policies even in the DCs. Popular magazines in the US run stories of how the Japanese or Saudis are buying farmland, downtown skyscrapers, and golf courses.

A concern typically voiced is the increasing percentage of GDP paid abroad as interest income to foreigners. If a country borrows to finance consumption, it soon loses the ability to repay its debt and loans stop. Financial markets, not politicians, should determine international financial flows.

There will always be political pressure for controls on international investment but controls on free international investment are counterproductive. Through international competition, domestic banks are forced to become more competitive. Financial intermediation, like any other industry, becomes more efficient in the face of competition. Efficiency results in lower costs and better customer services.

A government may protect its financial industry but the country suffers with the inefficiency. Foreign investment and competition in banking and investment are strictly outlawed in many countries. A trip to a bank can then be painful with bank transactions done by hand, people waiting for hours to cash a check, and slow uncaring government workers.

There are sound reasons for free international financial markets. Interntional loan markets allow economic agents to plan, increase productivity, and grow wealthier. International financial competition increases global gains.

EXAMPLE 12.4 *Global Financial Instability*

Recent financial crises in Asia, Mexico, Brazil, and Russia led to abrupt declines in economic growth. International trade and finance virtually halted. Frederic Mishkin (1999) notes that lending of financial intermediaries stopped, interest rates rose, and uncertainties increased during each crisis. Lending booms suddenly stopped. Gerard Caprio and Patrick Honohan (1999) note that political interference in bank regulation was a common theme in every crisis. There are numerous proposals for reform. Jeffrey Sachs (1995) advocates an international bankruptcy court. Paul Krugman (1998) advocates controls on capital outflows but Sebastian Edwards (1999) shows they have been ineffective. Barry Eichengreen (1999) advocates controls on capital inflows. Henry Kaufman (1998) advocates an international financial regulator, perhaps the IMF. Jeffrey Garten (1998) proposes a single world currency and central bank. Kenneth Rogoff (1999) advocates a move toward more equity financing. Stanley Fischer (1999) advocates "transparent" international standards to reduce risk, and notes that the IMF international lender of last resort adds stability to the international financial system. Governments should allow international competition to make banking systems more efficient, should have stable monetary policy, and should target zero inflation.

Problems for Section A

A1. Draw a foreign credit market for loans leading to the foreign excess supply in Figure 12.2.

A2. Find the investment income that will be due on the international loans in Figure 12.2. Which country makes and which country receives the payment?

A3. Find NII given a 5% interest rate at home and a 6% interest rate abroad with a home owned investment stock abroad of $1470 billion and a foreign owned stock at home of $1346 billion. Is there a surplus or deficit on NII?

A4. If there is a 5% increase in the home owned stock abroad in the previous problem while the foreign owned capital stock at home increases 39%, find the capital account. Is it a surplus or deficit? Find the new NII.

EXAMPLE 12.5 *Forgiving LDC Debt*

There have been large loans to LDCs through the international credit market. During the 1970s, OPEC oil embargoes created high oil profits and excess credit supply. These funds filtered through international banks as loans to LDCs. Many were loans to LDC governments with the unfortunate perception that there was no chance of default. Nominal interest rates were high due to high inflation at the time. In the late 1970s and early 1980s, many LDCs suffered in a worldwide recession precipitated by the high oil prices. Paying back the loans became impossible for the LDCs. The funds were wasted and not invested to increase productivity. Many LDCs have essentially defaulted on the loans. There are schemes to reschedule the debt. Rudiger Dornbusch and Franco Modigliani (*Wall Street Journal*, 1989) propose the debt be paid in currency that would have to be spent locally. There is some sentiment toward forgiving debt with taxpayers in the DCs covering the losses so the international banks will not go bankrupt. There was a political movement approaching the year 2000 to raise sentiment among taxpayers in the DCs to absorb the debt. A more efficient option is to let the inefficient banks go bankrupt and their stockholders suffer the bad debt with other more prudent banks taking their place.

B. FOREIGN EXCHANGE AND FINANCE

International financial transactions involve the exchange of currencies through the foreign exchange market. Exchange rates both affect and are affected by international financial transactions. When the exchange rate changes, prices of foreign financial assets change. In the other direction, when international investors buy the stocks and bonds in a currency, it appreciates. This section examines links between the exchange rate and international financial markets.

International Portfolios

There is a large volume of international financial transactions with wealth holders trading financial assets across countries. International transactions are carried out electronically between large international banks and financial intermediaries. Wealth holders want to adjust their portfolios to avoid overexposure in a particular currency. If an international bank exchanges all of its cash for one currency that depreciates overnight, it suffers a loss.

International financial transactions occur due to international trade, exchange rate hedging, international investment spending, and international portfolio diversification of stocks and bonds. Banks and other financial intermediaries perform *arbitrage* across credit and exchange markets, looking for profitable transactions with foreign currencies and international interest rates. There are close links between international financial and FX markets.

The exchange rate affects prices of each country's stocks, bonds, and other financial assets. In the opposite direction, international financial transactions affect exchange rates.

Suppose the nominal interest rate is 20% in a foreign country with peso currency. The price of *perpetuity bond* paying 100,000 pesos per year indefinitely would be 100,000/.20 = 500,000 pesos since a deposit of 500,000 pesos in the bank earns 100,000 pesos interest every year. Suppose the current spot exchange rate is e = $/pesos = 0.002 and both the dollar and peso have the same inflation rate. The dollar price of this perpetuity bond would be 0.002 × 500,000 = $1000. An unexpected peso devaluation to e = 0.0015 would decrease the dollar price of the bond to 0.0015 × 500,000 = $750. Whether the peso bond has suddenly become a bargain depends on the expected future peso depreciation.

EXAMPLE 12.6 *The FX Rate and Foreign Investment*

An appreciating dollar means assets in the US become more expensive for foreign investors. Kenneth Froot and Jeremy Stein (1988) find that a 10% appreciation of the dollar would lower FDI by $5 billion per year, a few percent of FDI. Over half of FDI into the US goes into mergers and acquisitions with no impact on the management or operation of the US firms. Interest rate differentials and expected depreciation affect PI. The exchange rate does not affect PI but expected changes in the exchange rate have an effect, suggesting investors anticipate exchange rate changes and act rationally in anticipation of the changes.

Discounting by Expected Depreciation

A main issue on an international investor's mind is the future value of currencies. For instance, what will the 100,000 peso premium of a perpetuity bond will be worth each year? Suppose investors expect the inflation rate in pesos to remain at its historical average of 20% and the dollar at 4%. The peso, in other words, is expected to lose 16% of its value every year relative to the dollar.

The 100,000 peso yearly earning from the bond is worth $200 at the present exchange rate of e = 0.002. One year from now the 100,000 peso premium is expected to be worth 84% as much, or $168. Two years from now, the 100,000 pesos is expected to be worth 84% of that, $125. The value of the bond to an investor interested in a dollar return must be *discounted* by 16% every year. The present value of the peso bond is only 100,000/(0.20 + 0.16) = 277,778 pesos. At the present exchange rate of $/pesos = 0.002, this peso bond would sell in the United States for $556. If the peso and the dollar had the same inflation rate, the peso bond would sell for $1000.

A *risk discount* may also be associated with the peso bond. Suppose peso bonds have a history of defaulting 12% of the time and dollar bonds default an average of 4% of the time. An additional 8% risk discount would be placed on the value of the peso bond. The present value of the peso bond would be 100,000/0.44 = 227,273 pesos or at the exchange rate $454.

International differences in expected depreciation and risk premiums help investors arrange their international portfolio. While the risk in some countries can be high, potential returns can be high also.

EXAMPLE 12.7 *Country Risk*

Country risk ratings summarize the history and perception of whether private loans will be repaid. Borrowers in countries with higher risk ratings have to pay a higher interest rate. LDCs generally have the highest risk ranking with borrowers paying the highest interest rates. Investors can earn more but face higher default risk. The *Institutional Investor* ranks country risk based on a survey of banks. A few of the top and bottom countries in a recent risk ranking are listed with 100 the riskiest and 0 the safest. Tunisia gets the median of 50 and Jordan the mode of 38.

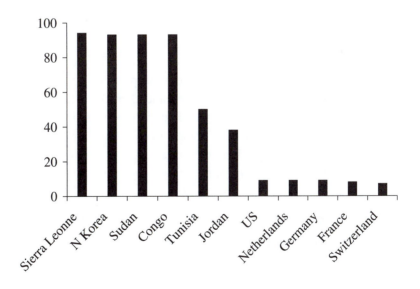

International Investment and the FX Market

The effect that international financial markets have on the FX market is pictured in the market for Korean won in Figure 12.3. Demand for won is based in part

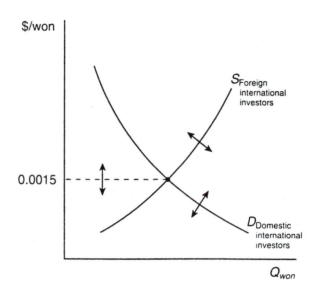

Figure 12.3
International Finance and the FX Market
Demand for won slopes downward partly because a lower $/won exchange rate creates cheaper Korean assets in the US. The quantity of won demanded to buy Korean assets increases. Supply of won slopes upward partly because a higher $/won exchange rate creates cheaper US assets in Korea. Changes in investment opportunities in the United States or Korea shift the supply and demand for foreign exchange, causing exchange rate adjustment.

on domestic investors who are potential buyers of Korean financial assets. As the exchange rate $/won rises, the price of Korean assets in the US rises, the quantity of Korean assets demanded in the US falls, and the quantity of won demanded falls. The demand for won slopes downward.

The supply of won comes from Korean investors, potential buyers of US assets. As $/won rises, the price of US assets in Korea falls, the quantity of US assets demanded in Korea rises, and the quantity of won supplied rises. The supply of won slopes upward.

International investment contributes to supply and demand in the FX market.

Suppose the expected return on Korean investments rises because of an announced policy of increased privatization in Korea. Investors in the US will want to buy more Korean stocks and bonds because Korean firms are expected to prosper under the new economic policy. A higher expected return on Korean stocks and bonds will increase their price because of increased demand. The demand for won also rises, causing the won to appreciate and further raising the price of Korean assets to US investors.

Suppose the expected return on US investments rises because of forecasts of an expansion. Korean investors will want to buy more US assets, increasing the supply of won. This increased supply depreciates the won, raising the price of US assets in Korea.

The FX market works in the same direction as the underlying asset market. Government exchange rate policy is not required to balance international financial markets. In fact, any government policy interfering with the exchange market hinders the complementary adjustment process.

Changes in the exchange rate complement asset market adjustments. Exchange rate and investment policy interfere with the adjustment process.

International investors try to anticipate government intervention in the FX and international financial markets. Erratic behavior in international financial markets has been cited as evidence of the need for more government regulation. The erratic behavior more often than not, however, results from market participants trying to anticipate upcoming government intervention.

An old saying in foreign exchange circles is to watch what the Fed is doing and do the opposite. With central banks intervening, market participants turn their attention away from important market fundamentals. FX traders, hedgers, and speculators should be allowed to operate in a free market.

No scheme of managed or fixed exchange rates and regulated financial markets could have handled the financial upheavals since the 1970s. Innovations in every industry, including banking and financial intermediation, have occurred due to increased competition. International competition is forcing banks and financial intermediaries to become more efficient. Banks favor regulation and enjoy the lack of competition in a regulated industry but those comfortable days are gone. Competition in banking and financial markets has become the rule.

EXAMPLE 12.8 *News and Anticipation*

Foreign exchange traders keep up with the news and economic reports on trade deficits, investment flows, price level changes, national economic trends, and policy discussions. Graig Hakkio and Douglas Pearce (1985) examine empirical links between the exchange rate and economic news. They find only one type of news with immediate and consistent impact, news about money supplies. Exchange rates adjust to money supply news in about 20 minutes. If the US money supply increases unexpectedly, traders expect the dollar to depreciate and begin selling dollars right away. The increased supply of dollars causes the dollar to depreciate and expectation of a falling dollar causes the dollar to fall right away. Prior to money supply announcements, there is decreased exchange rate movement as traders anticipate the news and hold off trading.

Covered Interest Arbitrage

Asset markets are linked internationally with FX markets through the operations of international banks and financial intermediaries. Suppose an investor with $1000 in the US can earn the domestic interest rate of $i = 8\%$. At the end of the year, the investor has $1080. The Malaysian interest rate is $i = 4\%$ and the current spot rate $e = \$/R = 0.26$ where R is the ringgit. The $1000 can be exchanged into $1000/0.26 = R3846$, which will yield $3846.15 \times 1.04 = R4000$ at the end of the year.

The investor can take the position in ringgits and leave it *open* but investors in the US will typically want to turn the ringgits back into dollars at the end of the year. With an open position the investor will wait until the end of the year and sell the 4000 ringgits on the *spot exchange market* at that time. There is some risk of the ringgit depreciating during the year.

This foreign exchange risk can be eliminated by covering the investment in the *forward exchange market*. A *forward contract* to sell 4000 ringgits at the end of the year can be made in the forward exchange market. The forward exchange rate is a market for transactions at a date in the future at a rate set now. Forward contracts can be signed for any time period and any amount.

In the example with $i = 8\%$, $i^* = 4\%$, and $e = 0.26$, this forward rate (f) will invariably be close to $f = \$/R = 0.27$. The reason is that 4000 ringgits will convert back to $1080 at the forward rate, the same return that could be earned in the US. If this were not so, traders could make risk free arbitrage profit. In fact, such *covered interest arbitrage* transactions are made continuously keeping the profit on each transaction small and linking international asset and exchange markets. Simultaneously, triangular arbitrage keeps the cross rates of currencies in line.

> *Covered interest arbitrage is carried out by large international banks and FX traders keeping international interest rates and exchange rates tightly linked.*

Market makers are the financial intermediaries who work at banks, investment firms, and brokerage houses. Market makers are connected electronically by internet, telephone, and computer trading systems. The FX market is very fast and much larger than the more publicized and less competitive stock markets. Stock trading involves only an exchange of existing assets between wealth holders but international trade and investment would collapse without the FX market.

Unexpected exchange rate movements of hundredths of a cent can result in profit or loss of millions of dollars to international investors. Some large international banks have gone out of business due to losses in their FX operations, and many others have found themselves unable to compete in the international market. Banks clamor for protection but continued international competition will ensure more efficient operation.

EXAMPLE 12.9 *FX and Inflation*

> Over decades PPP explains a good deal of the exchange rate. Kenneth Kasa (1995) reports that 60% of the trend during the 1970s and 1980s in the $/mark exchange rate was due to the inflation differential between the two currencies. The dollar on average depreciated 5% versus the mark, and US inflation exceeded German inflation by 2%. For $/yen, only 20% of the exchange rate trend is due to the inflation differential. The dollar depreciated an average of 5% per year versus the yen but inflation in the US exceeded Japan by only 1%. Japanese labor productivity growth has been 2% higher than in the US and has contributed to the appreciating yen.

International Interest and Exchange Rates

The link between interest and exchange rates is summarized by the *covered interest arbitrage* relation,

$$(1 + i) = (1/e)(1 + i^*)f$$

An investor with $1 at home can earn $(1 + i)$ buying a home bond. The alternative is to convert the $1 to foreign currency (divide by e) buy a foreign bond with return $1 + i^*$, and cover the earnings back into dollars (multiply by f). Covered interest arbitrage (CIA) involves making a spot exchange, buying a foreign bond, and covering forward back into home currency.

If one side of the CIA relation is larger than the other, four markets simultaneously operate to restore equilibrium. Profit makers push the four markets so CIA holds as shown in Figure 12.4. The initial equilibrium is the one described in the example of CIA between ringgits and dollars.

Suppose the Fed lowers the discount and interest rate i. Asset holders notice that the return on covered foreign bonds has become higher. The first step in buying a foreign bond is to buy foreign currency. The demand for ringgits rises, pushing e above 2.26. The supply of loans in Malaysia rises, pushing below 4%. Finally, investors will want to cover their earnings back into dollars. Ringgits are sold forward, increasing the forward supply and pushing f below 0.27. All of these changes (higher e, higher i^*, and lower f) lower the right side of the CIA relation.

> *Covered interest arbitrage works through the spot exchange, international credit, and forward exchange markets. International interest rates are linked through the FX market.*

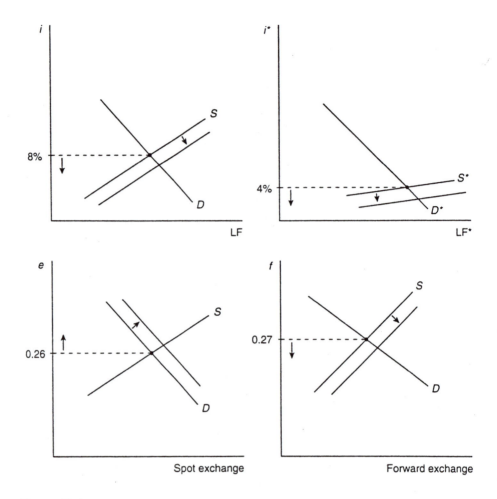

Figure 12.4
Market Links between Interest and Exchange Rates
This diagram illustrates how covered interest arbitrage equates the return to riskless
international investments. In the original equilibrium, $1 + i = (f/e)(1 + i^*)$. If i falls with
a credit expansion, the demand for spot exchange rises, the supply of foreign loanable funds
rises, and the supply of forward exchange falls. Every adjustment works to maintain covered
interest arbitrage.

EXAMPLE 12.10 *Inflation and Interest Rate Differences*

Differences in inflation π and interest rates i are similar across countries. High
nominal interest rates are deflated by high inflation making real interest rates
similar across countries. Inflation and interest rate differences compared to
the US in 1998 are reported below using data from the FRB St. Louis. A
larger inflation rate difference implies a larger nominal interest rate difference.
Currencies inflating rapidly depreciate in the foreign exchange market and sell
at a discount in the forward market due to covered interest arbitrage.

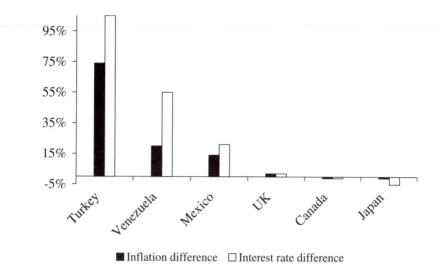

Inflation difference ☐ Interest rate difference

Problems for Section B

B1. With the perpetuity bond paying 100,000 pesos per year, suppose the dollar is expected to have an inflation rate of 2%. Find the dollar value of the peso bond. Do the same if expected inflation is 12%.

B2. Diagram and explain what happens in the FX market in Figure 12.3 when

- the domestic interest rate falls
- the foreign interest rate rises
- there is news of an expected expansion in the US economy
- political unrest breaks out in Korea.

B3. In the example of CIA, find the profitable position if the forward exchange rate is $/ringgit = 0.26. Do the same if the forward rate is 0.28.

EXAMPLE 12.11 *IRP, Not Quite*

Interest rate parity holds because investors watch interest rates. These figures from the FRB St. Louis illustrate the 1998 *effective real interest rate*, subtracting the rate of depreciation Δe from the rate of interest. A bond that pays over 100% in Turkey may sound like a rare find but inflation eats away at the return. Before the fact, investors know interest rates but not depreciation. Some investments are made on the basis of expectations about future exchange rates. The highest and lowest three countries are included along with the US. The high variation in the effective interest rate gives international investment high risk and return.

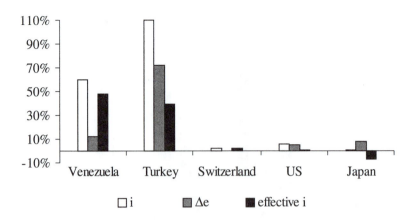

C.   INTERNATIONAL MONEY

This section examines the link between money supplies and price levels. *Inflation* occurs when the price level rises or the value of money falls. The *price level* is the average price of all products. International commerce depends on money and the exchange of monies through the exchange rates.

What is Money?

The *functions of money* are:

* *medium of exchange*
* *store of value*
* *unit of account*

Money as a *medium of exchange* makes commerce possible. *Barter* is direct trade of one product for another and only the most primitive societies are supported by barter as households trade hides for corn, meat for labor, and so on. Money allows people to specialize and trade. International commerce requires a mechanism for trading mediums of exchange, the foreign exchange market.

Money as a *store of value* allows consumers and firms to delay spending. If you are paid Friday, some money must be stored until the following Thursday and the held money represents potential purchases throughout the week. An inflating currency is a poor store of value. *Hyperinflation* is very high inflation forcing people to scramble to spend their cash before it loses value.

Money is also a *unit of account* for measuring relative values. This car is worth $20,000, that shirt $25, and a night on the town $50. In relative terms, the car is worth 800 shirts or 400 nights out. People become accustomed to valuing products in their currency and are ready to make and accept payments in their currency.

Only certain commodities can perform money's functions. Bricks would be a good store of value and unit of account but are too heavy to be a medium of exchange. Ice cream would be easier to carry than bricks but would not work as a store of value. Paper clips might be money if their supply could be limited.

Money is controlled by government central banks. Government *monetary policy* directly controls the *monetary base*. The banking system is made up of commercial *financial intermediaries* that accept deposits and make loans. Financial intermediation facilitates lending and borrowing, expanding the monetary base. The link between the money supply and the price level determines how well a currency performs its basic functions.

Money and Prices

The *demand for money* depends on the goods and services it can purchase. The price level P is the average price of all products, $P = \$/good$. The inverse of P, $1/P = goods/\$$, is the *purchasing power of money*.

As P rises, the purchasing power of money falls and less products can be bought with each dollar. When P rises, people want to hold less money and switch to other assets: stocks, bonds, gold, jewelry, real estate, or foreign currency. Money that loses its purchasing power with inflation is not demanded as a store of value.

The *money market* is in Figure 12.5. Along the vertical axis is the price of money, $1/P$. The demand for money slopes downward due to purchasing power. The *supply of money* is a vertical line at the current supply, $1 trillion. The government central bank controls the money supply and is assumed not to let the price level influence supply.

A money supply of $ 1 trillion and price level of 1.25 are roughly the US 1990 levels of $M1$ and consumer price index (1982 = 1). $M1$ is cash and demand deposits that can be withdrawn by check. The price index of 1.25 indicates prices were 25% higher in 1990 than in 1982. Where supply and demand meet, the value of money is $1/P = 1/1.25$ and the price level $P = 1.25$. Increasing the money supply to $1.2 trillion would lower the price of money to $1/1.5 = 0.667$ and raise P to 1.5. Lowering the money supply to $0.8 trillion would raise the price of money to 1 and lower P to 1.

Let M be the money supply and V is its velocity, the average number of times each dollar changes hands per year. The product MV is the value of all transactions in the economy. P is the price level and Q is the quantity of output. The product PQ is the value of output or GDP.

The money market illustrates the quantity theory of money based on the quantity equation, $MV = PQ$.

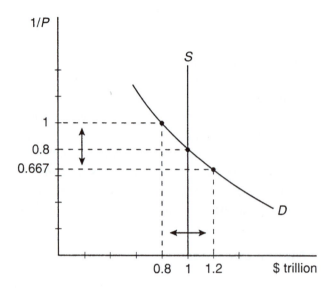

Figure 12.5
The Money Market
The demand for money slopes downward because a higher price level (P) means a lower price of money ($1/P$) and a higher quantity of money demanded for transactions. For given supply, the equilibrium price level of $1/1.25 = 0.8$ is determined. A higher supply raises the price level. If the money supply increases to $1.2 billion, the price of money drops to $1/1.50 = 0.667$. A lower supply of money lowers the price level. If the money supply falls to $80 billion, the price of money rises to 1.

If M increases by 20% to $1.2 trillion in Figure 12.5 and both V and Q are constants, P increases by 20% to 1.5. Velocity V is generally constant. Real output is not greatly affected by money growth as long as monetary policy is predictable. If M falls by 20% and Q is unchanged, P would then fall by roughly 20%.

The quantity equation shows the link between the money supply and the price level. Currencies whose supply is increasing rapidly will experience more inflation than currencies whose supply is stable.

Some of the demand for a currency is foreign since foreign wealth holders will want to hold the currency if they think it will perform well as a store of value.

Suppose investors expect the dollar to appreciate relative to the other currencies. The demand for dollars increases as in Figure 12.6. Increased demand drives the price of the dollar ($1/P$) to 0.9, lowering the price level P to $1/.9 = 1.11$. In the FX market, the demand for dollars is rising and the dollar appreciating.

A currency with relatively low inflation will appreciate on the FX market.

Central banks should have the monetary policy goal of a steady price level. Although there is popular political concern over "liquidity" and interest rates, a stable price level should be the only goal of monetary policy.

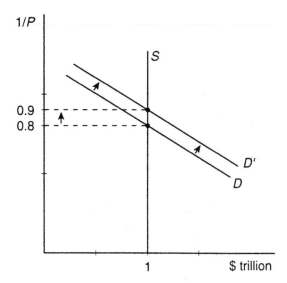

Figure 12.6
Increased Money Demand
With money supply constant, higher money demand will increase the price of money and lower the price level. The increase in the demand for money from D to D′ causes *P* to fall from 1.25 to 1.11. This increase in money demand can be foreign in origin.

Episodes of high inflation and the international instability of 1970s drove home the principle that erratic prices harm the economy. The US dollar has an important role on the international scene with about a quarter of international transactions are carried out in dollars. Governments and banks all over the world keep reserves of dollars and many countries peg the value of their currencies to the dollar. If the dollar loses value because of oversupply, global inflation is encouraged. The same can be said about the other two major international currencies, the euro and the yen.

The dollar has a record of inflation. Goods that cost $100 would have cost only $23 in 1970. Inflation eats away at the value of a currency. Most other currencies have had higher inflation and a few have had lower inflation.

EXAMPLE 12.12 *Money Growth and Inflation*

Inflation is fueled by high money supply growth. Relative prices of individual products may rise due to increased demand or decreased supply but for the average price of all products to rise the money supply must expand. These 1998 figures from the FRB St. Louis illustrate the link between money supply growth and inflation across countries.

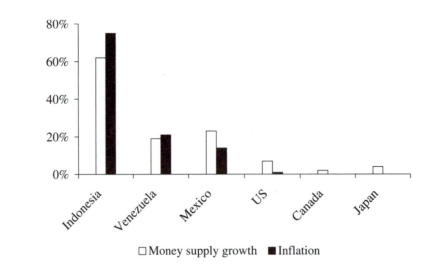

□ Money supply growth   ■ Inflation

Fiat Currencies versus Monetary Standards

Governments have devised different ways to control their money supplies and price levels, affecting the FX market and international commerce. The international monetary system is an extension of national monetary systems. A depreciating currency helps export industries but importing industries and consumers must pay higher prices. With depreciation, the currency loses value.

Fiat currency is paper money that is demanded simply because it has to be accepted by law as a medium of exchange. Central banks print money and create domestic credit. Fiat currencies are not backed by gold, silver, or any other commodity. The US government stopped redeeming dollars for gold in 1933 and defining the dollar in terms of gold in 1971. Money is demanded only because people accept it as payment for goods and services. The dollar carries its own endorsement "This note is legal tender for all debts, public and private".

Under the *gold standard* of the 1800s governments were willing to exchange gold for paper money, or vice versa. Currency notes were equivalent to a certain amount of gold. The US experimented with a *bimetal standard* for a period in the late 1890s with the dollar defined in terms of both gold and silver. The *Bretton Woods* fixed exchange rate system lasted from the end of World War II until the early 1970s and attempted to fix exchange rates at historically familiar levels. The international floating exchange rate system is compatible with flat currencies. Major currencies seek their market exchange rates although central banks intervene in the market.

EXAMPLE 12.13 *The Great Contraction*

The Great Depression resulted from poor monetary and trade policy, a disastrous decline in the US money supply and extremely high tariffs. Bennet McCallum

(1989) builds a historical model of the US economy and tests what would have happened with more steady growth in the money supply. With a rule linking money supply growth to past output, the US economy would have grown steadily throughout the Great Contraction. Output and employment would not have collapsed. A fixed money supply growth rule would take away the discretion of the Fed to control the money supply, providing greater price stability and smoother output growth. An equivalent policy is to target zero inflation.

The Gold Standard

The gold standard lasted from the late 1800s until World War I with the English pound as the major currency. The pound was worth 0.234 ounces of gold and the dollar 0.048 ounces, freezing the dollar/pound exchange rate at $2.234/0.048 = 4.87 = \$/\pounds$. Currencies were widely accepted all over the world because they were redeemable into gold and frozen relative to each other. There was no foreign exchange risk in international commerce, creating a favorable international atmosphere and high levels of economic growth.

The US had little gold relative to Europe during the late 1800s. Under the gold standard, growth in the money supply is limited by the supply of gold. Immigration and output growth in the US outpaced growth of the money supply, causing deflation. The demand for money grew faster than supply, the price of money ($1/P$) rose, and the price level (P) fell. There was political pressure to expand the money supply to facilitate commerce but gold was scarce.

The solution was a bimetal standard, with the dollar defined in terms of both gold and silver. If the official relative price of silver in terms of gold did not exactly match the market relative price, traders could make risk free arbitrage profit. If the official price of silver was too high, traders could buy cheap silver in the market and trade it to the government for gold. Bad money chased out good money and gold was hoarded.

The principle that bad money chases out good money is *Gresham's law*, named after a British banker of the 1500s. In those days, coins actually contained the metals worth the stamped value. Circulating coins were shaved around the edges. Gresham was suspected of shaving coins and hoarding the shavings. Anyone who found an unshaved coin (good money) would store it or shave it and only shaved money circulated.

EXAMPLE 12.14 *Causes of the Great Depression*

The Great Depression lasted for about ten years following the stock market crash of 1929. International trade virtually halted with the Hawley-Smoot tariff act and similar restrictive tariffs worldwide. The loss of imported intermediate and capital goods made the effects serious. Reduced trade lowered income and slowed recovery. The Great Contraction of the money supply slowed recovery.

Harold Cole and Lee Ohanian (1999) point out that the National Industrial Recovery Act (NIRA) of 1933 encouraged cartels that restrict output and raise prices, contributing to the length and depth of the depression. NIRA was designed to stimulate the economy but had the opposite effect.

Collapse of the Gold Standard

World War I stopped international commerce, disrupted foreign exchange markets, and destroyed the international monetary system. Following the war, countries tried to return to the gold standard but governments increased their money supplies to finance the war expenses. Inflation increased prices in Europe relative to the US.

Exchange rates from the gold standard era proved unworkable. The pound was worth more at the government's gold exchange window than in goods and services. The British gold supply dwindled as traders cashed in pounds for gold. The pound was overvalued making British exports uncompetitive. The UK dropped the gold standard in 1931. The dollar remained redeemable in terms of gold and became the standard international currency. Investors wanted the stability provided by gold and eagerly traded dollars for gold. US gold supplies dwindled and the US government stopped redeeming dollars for gold in 1933.

Governments devalued their currencies repeatedly to make their exports cheaper abroad. Inflation was high worldwide. German hyperinflation created the economic instability that allowed the Nazi party to take control. In misguided efforts to save jobs, high tariffs were imposed worldwide. The US passed the infamous Smoot-Hawley Tariff Act. International investment disappeared because of the high exchange risk. The Great Depression of the 1930s was an international event that led to World War II.

EXAMPLE 12.15 *Safe Haven*

The US is a safe haven in the eyes of many investors. The US has political stability relative to many countries. There is no imminent military threat and there are prospects for continued high growth. Higher defense spending makes the US appear a safer haven. Robert Ayanian (1988) and Vittrio Grilli and Andrea Beltratti (1989) show that defense spending raises the demand for US assets. When demand for US assets rises, demand for dollars also rises. Increased defense spending causes dollar appreciation.

The Bretton Woods System

The international monetary system fell into disarray during World War II. After the war everyone wanted stable monetary systems and prices. An international conference was held in Bretton Woods, New Hampshire to create a reliable international monetary system.

A *gold exchange standard* evolved. Currencies were defined in terms of gold but were not redeemable. The dollar was defined as $0.029 = 1/35$ ounces of gold and became the international standard. The US held more than half the world's gold stock. Other currencies were defined in terms of the dollar. The English pound was defined as $2.80, 360 Japanese yen were set equal to $1, and 4.2 German marks were defined as $1. The International Monetary Fund was created to ensure that governments kept their exchange rates close to these rates.

The fixed exchange rates of Bretton Woods operated under an *adjustable peg* system. A country with a trade deficit could leave its exchange rate fixed and borrow from the IMF to meet the cash shortage. If a country had a chronic trade deficit, the IMF might eventually allow it to depreciate.

During the 1950s international trade and investment grew at low but steady rates. Money supplies grew at low rates and price levels were stable worldwide. Europe and Japan rebuilt from the war. The US experienced BOT deficits, suggesting the dollar should depreciate. If the dollar lost value in terms of gold, anyone holding gold would enjoy a profit. In anticipation, the price of gold was bid up well beyond the official price of $35 an ounce. The Bretton Woods system nevertheless managed to hold together even through high US inflation during the Vietnam War.

The dollar had not been redeemable for gold since 1933 but the US government continued to redeem foreign government holdings of dollars for gold. The US gold stock steadily declined and other countries, notably France, built up their gold stocks. As the US gold stock declined, the credibility of the Bretton Woods system suffered. In 1971, President Nixon cut the dollar from its definition in terms of gold and the Bretton Woods fixed exchange rate system collapsed.

EXAMPLE 12.16 *Purchasing Power of the Dollar*

The inverse of consumer price index (CPI) since 1952 shows the dollar's decline in purchasing power. There had been a slight deflation during the 1920s and 1930s, but inflation during World War II and up to 1950. During the 1950s and 1960s there was low inflation. Starting in the late 1960s through the early 1980s, inflation rates were high and purchasing power fell dramatically. During the 1980s and 1990s inflation continued but declined. The Fed has the responsibility for controlling the money supply and inflation, and should target zero inflation. Government budget deficits are the cause of the high growth rates in the money supply, inflation, and loss of purchasing power. The dollar depreciates on the foreign exchange market relative to currencies with lower inflation.

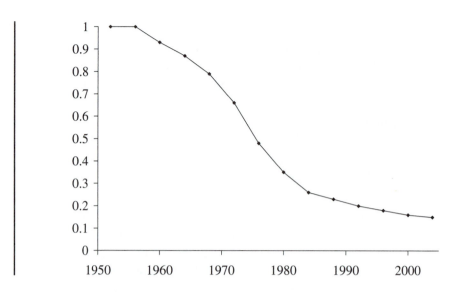

Market Exchange Rates

International differences in inflation rates, OPEC oil embargoes, and increased international commerce caused the Bretton Woods system to collapse. Fixed exchange rates failed, not for the first time. The price of gold was bid above $600 by investors who saw it as a safe haven. Countries tried to adjust their fixed exchange rates but by 1973 the world had adopted floating exchange rates. In the 1920s there had been a floating system and Canada floated its dollar during the 1970s.

With floating exchange rates, each government is free to determine its own money supply growth and inflation, and both increased during the 1970s. International banks increased their FX operations and established foreign branch operations. Brokers and traders set up shop. Speculators attempted to outguess the market and make profits trading exchange. Hedging and speculating in foreign exchange increased and FX markets grew into lively worldwide business.

The resulting floating exchange rate system has never had entirely free markets. Governments regularly intervene to influence the value of their currencies and many governments impose direct controls. The system is a *managed float*. The IMF acts like a bank for government central banks, making loans to deficit countries. It supplies its own money, the *special drawing right* (SDR) used for transactions between central banks. The SDR is part of each national monetary base.

The market system has worked through periods of upheaval: oil embargoes, debt crises, deficits and surpluses, emerging economic powers, banking failures, and increased international investment. The market exchange rate system is superior to any controlled or coordinated system.

Economic theory and history teach that wise governments let markets operate. Free foreign exchange markets have proven capable of facilitating international commerce. The positive role for government exchange rate policy is to target zero inflation with steady money supply growth.

Problems for Section C

C1. Explain how well each of the following used in various societies would perform each of the functions of money: beaver tails, tobacco, dried buffalo chips, beads, and very large boulders.

C2. Can the supply of money come from competing private banks? How would such a private money supply system, *free banking*, operate? Diagram the supply curve. How would the international monetary system operate?

C3. Any commodity standard of money ties the value of money to a certain quantity of some commodity. Explain which of these commodities would function better as money standards: gold, oil, wheat, a stock market price index.

D. MONEY AND INTERNATIONAL FINANCE

Money supplies and monetary policy affect international finance. The foreign exchange market transmits international monetary signals and reflects each country's monetary policy.

Government Bonds and the Money Supply

Governments create national debt with deficits by spending more than tax revenue. Governments can raise the money for deficit spending by selling *government bonds*, promises to pay the bondholder its face value on maturity. A government with a deficit then becomes a demander in the credit market.

When a government borrows the interest rate rises. The increased supply of bonds causes bond prices to fall. Higher interest rates and lower bond prices attract foreign investors. Demand for the domestic currency rises, causing it to appreciate. Currency appreciation can in turn lead to a current account deficit.

This link between the government deficit and the trade deficit is called the *twin deficit* but there is some controversy whether it exists. Government deficits in the US during the 1980s and 1990s were associated with current account deficits, but the dollar has appreciated and depreciated and the current account has risen and fallen.

Governments can also finance deficit spending by increasing the money supply. Monetary expansion is carried out predominantly by *open market operations.* The government prints new bonds, selling them to acquire cash to pay payroll and bills. The central bank buys the new bonds, paying for them with the newly printed money. If the supply of money grows faster than national output, there is inflation.

Government deficits can be financed by bond sales (which raise interest rates) or expanding the money supply (which may lead to inflation).

EXAMPLE 12.17 *Dollarization*

Imagine coins sent from heaven with stable value demanded by everyone. Any country would be better off with that currency. Prices would be stable. Investment and economic growth would be encouraged. The government could not print money to inflate its way out of fiscal deficits. Governments would have to rely on taxes and bond sales for spending. Some countries have adopted such coins, the US dollar. William Gruben and Sherry Kiser (1999) discuss dollarization that would allow Latin American countries to avoid their periodic currency collapses due to irresponsible fiscal policy.

International Money Supplies and Price Levels

In the 1700s, David Hume wrote about the long run relationship between money, prices, and trade in the *price specie flow mechanism.* When the money supply in one country increases, its price level increases. Higher prices cause the country to export less as its products become more expensive abroad. Imports increase because they become cheaper at home and the trade deficit creates an outflow of money. Through the influence of prices, specie or currency flows internationally.

The link between the money supply and inflation is illustrated by the quantity equation,

$$MV = PQ$$

Suppose the money supply M is $1 trillion and GDP or Q is $4 trillion. On average, each dollar in the money supply changes hands four times during the year and the $1 trillion of money supports $4 trillion of transactions. Money velocity V is equal to 4.

If the government increases M while output Q and velocity V remain constant, P must rise. If M rises to $1.1 trillion P will be 1.1, a 10% increase for both M and P.

Evidence of a positive relationship between the growth of the money supply and inflation is overwhelming.

Purchasing Power Parity and the Real Exchange Rate

There is a link between money supplies and exchange rates with prices linked by trade. Most products can be traded. Even haircuts in Iowa include an array of imported products, including clippers from Germany, a vacuum cleaner from Japan, a brush from Mexico, and so on.

Purchasing power parity (PPP) would hold if all goods and services were freely traded. PPP is stated

$$P = eP^*$$

P is the home price level, P^* is the foreign price level, and e is the exchange rate. PPP holds due to arbitrage since any price difference generates trade that eliminates it. When all goods are freely traded, PPP is the *law of one price* that arbitrage equalizes the price of the same good across locations.

There is empirical evidence supporting PPP, which says products cost the same across countries, over long time periods. Transport costs, protection, and *nontraded goods* weaken PPP.

Suppose $P = 1.25$ euro and $P^* = 125$ yen, hypothetical price indices between the EU and Japan. The *real exchange rate* comes from the PPP relation

$$e_R = P/P^*$$

The real exchange rate in €/¥ is $e_R = 1.25/125 = 0.01$. The real exchange rate is used by currency traders to anticipate the direction of change in exchange rates.

If the market exchange rate is €/¥ $= 0.02$, the yen is overvalued and can be expected to depreciate. Japanese products are overvalued by the market exchange rate, Japan would run a current account deficit, and the yen would depreciate. The Japanese government might try to delay this depreciation, and predicting the timing of the depreciation is difficult. Successfully predicting exchange rate movement would result in profits in the exchange market.

Deviations from PPP diminish over time. Kenneth Froot and Kenneth Rogoff (1995) show that deviations from PPP have a half life of 4 years with half of the deviation from PPP eroding after 4 years.

EXAMPLE 12.18 *Big Mac PPP*

Prices of Big Macs provide insight into currency values and are reliable indicators of price levels across countries. *The Economist* tracks the price of Big Macs and these prices anticipate exchange rate adjustment. Big Macs are produced locally with standardized products including a wide range of labor and capital as well as intermediate products. The average 1989 price of a Big Mac in the US was $2.02. Figures below show the Big Mac price in each country relative to the US (an implied exchange rate) and the value of the dollar in that currency, some rescaled for comparison. The dollar was undervalued against the won, yen, franc, mark, and pound, and overvalued against the Canadian dollar, Hong Kong dollar, Singapore dollar, and Yugoslav dinar. The Korean won was 44% overvalued relative to the dollar. In Singapore and Yugoslavia, the currencies were so overvalued that active black markets provided rates closer to the underlying market rates. The Yugoslav dinar was 160% (1.6) overvalued. In every instance, the currencies moved as predicted by the last column.

Country	Big Mac P^*	P/P^*	e	% Difference
South Korea	2400 won	1188	666	−44%
Japan	370 yen	183	133	−27%
France	17.7 francs	8.76	6.37	−27%
Germany	4.3 marks	2.13	1.89	−11%
Britain	1.26 pounds	0.62	0.59	−5%
Canada	2.15 C$	1.06	1.19	13%
Singapore	2.80 S$	1.39	1.96	41%
Yugoslavia	7000 dinar	3465	9001	160%

EXAMPLE 12.19   *1930s PPP*

In 1931, the UK gave up the gold standard. Speculation turned against the pound and it depreciated 30% versus the dollar, which remained on the gold standard and was perceived as a safe haven. The relative price of US goods rose 10% as described by S.N. Broadway (1987). PPP was 40% out of line between the US and the UK by 1933. The US then dropped the gold standard, the dollar depreciated, and P/P^* fell. By 1934, PPP had returned proving a reliable predictor of ultimate exchange rates.

EXAMPLE 12.20   *C$ and Prices*

The Canadian dollar declined 25% relative to the US dollar during the 1990s even though the price level in Canada rose by an annual average of 2% to 3% in the US. According to PPP with 1990 as the base year, dollar prices of products in Canada were too low at the end of the decade. Either the Canadian dollar would appreciate or prices in Canada rise. Charles Engel (1999) discusses why prices in Canada stayed out of line. Firms might *price to market* because of differences in demand in the two countries. If demand in Canada is lower or more elastic, firms will price discriminate and charge lower prices. Second, investors might expect the Canadian dollar to appreciate. Investors would be willing to hold discounted Canadian investments if they were expected to appreciate. If the Canadian dollar depreciated on speculation, the bubble could burst. As an example of a bursting bubble, the yen depreciated over 80% from May 1995 to August 1998. The Canadian dollar was overvalued in 1990 and shopping centers sprung up on the US side of the border.

Relative Money Supplies and the Real Exchange Rate

The relationship between relative money supplies M/M^* and the real exchange rate P/P^* is shown in Figure 12.7. If $M^* = 76$ billion Swiss fancs and $M = \$1000$ billion, $M/M^* = 13.2$ and $P/P^* = 1.12/1.07 = 1.05$, the 1989 money supplies and consumer price indices (1985 = 1) for Switzerland and the US. If M increases by 10% to \$1.1 trillion with all outputs and M^* constant, M/M^* rises to 1100/ 76 = 14.5, P rises by 10% to 1.232, and the real exchange e_R rises to 1.15. Figure 12.7 illustrates the relationships between money supplies, price levels, and the real exchange rate.

Countries with higher money supply growth rates experience inflation and depreciation.

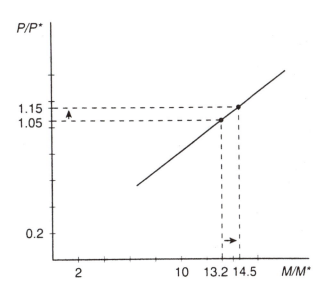

Figure 12.7
Relative Money Supplies and the Real Exchange Rate
This schedule shows the link between relative money supplies M/M^* and the real exchange rate P/P^*. PPP implies the relative price level P/P^* is the real exchange rate e_R. Increasing M relative to M^* causes e_R to rise, a depreciation of the home currency. The market exchange can be expected to fall.

The positive relationship in Figure 12.7 is well established. A few of the countries with higher inflation rates and faster depreciating currencies in recent history have been Mexico, Brazil, and Israel. Countries with the lowest rates of inflation and appreciation have been Germany, Switzerland, and Japan.

If inflation jumps, debtors paying off fixed term loans benefit but creditors are hurt. Unexpected deflation has the opposite effect, redistributing income to creditors. If lenders and borrowers anticipate inflation, its level has no real effect.

If inflation is predictable, exchange rates have little impact on international commerce.

Economic variables can be reduced to real terms and people learn to think in real terms. Businesses in countries with high inflation quote prices in stable currencies.

Central banks might temporarily support a currency that is rapidly inflating, but they cannot do so indefinitely. Inflating currencies depreciate. Inflation values currencies against goods and exchange rates value currencies against each other.

Controlling the Money Supply

A country chooses its money supply growth, price level, and exchange rate system. Money supply growth is the result of economic processes including central bank activity, commercial lending, and private spending.

The primary job of the central bank is to control the money supply, no trivial task. The Great Depression of the 1930s might be called the Great Contraction because the US money supply fell 25%, a monetary catastrophe. As a result, there was literally very little money. Add to this the Smoot-Hawley tariffs averaging 60% and the recipe for government induced economic disaster was complete.

Control of the money supply is a central issue of economic policy. A competitive banking system and efficient financial intermediation are essential for a successful economy. The link between government deficits and the money supply suggests that a government wanting to control inflation should control its spending.

EXAMPLE 12.21 *Big Banks*

The world's largest banks are multinational firms operating branches in different countries. The *Institutional Investor* lists the top ten banks by total capitalization in 1998.

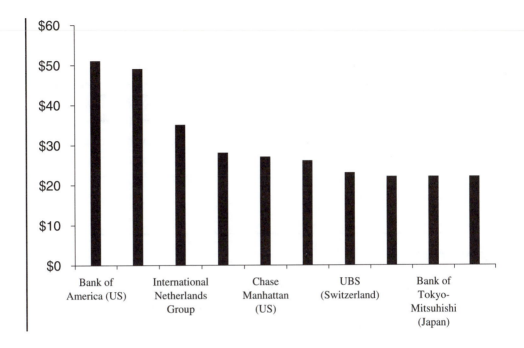

Problems for Section D

D1. What difference does it make whether a Japanese or a US citizen buys the US bonds issued to finance a government budget deficit?

D2. If $P = \$1.25$ and $P^* = 200$ pesos, find the real exchange rate in terms of $/peso and peso/$. If the market rate is peso/$ = 150, which currency is overvalued? Which currency should appreciate?

D3. Suppose in Figure 12.7 the foreign money supply M^* increases to 79.8 billion Swiss francs with M at $1 trillion. Find the relative money supply and the real exchange rate.

CONCLUSION

As international trade and finance become more integrated, there is more direct involvement with firms and consumers in other countries. In virtually every country, many domestic industries are involved in producing for export and imports are used in domestic production and consumption.

International finance is crucial for growth, economic production and countries are becoming increasingly interdependent. The gains from international finance are sizeable. The basic lesson of international economics is to reap the benefits of open international commerce. Free international financial markets are an important step toward specialization and a healthy international economy.

Terms

Adjustable peg	Hyperinflation
Bimetal standard	Open market operations
Covered interest arbitrage	Price specie flow mechanism
Fiat currency	Purchasing power parity (PPP)
Forward exchange rate	Real exchange rate
Gold exchange standard	Real interest rate
Gold standard	Special drawing rights (SDRs)
Gresham's law	

MAIN POINTS

- Credit markets match lenders and borrowers, determining interest rates and the quantity of loans. International credit markets cross borders.
- Exchange rates and international interest rates are linked through international financial transactions.
- A country's money supply relative to output determines its price level and inflation rate. Relative money supplies ultimately determine exchange rates.
- Price levels are linked across trading partners through exchange rates and purchasing power parity.

REVIEW PROBLEMS

1. Explain which group in a growing economy, borrowers or lenders, would favor restricting inflow of foreign investment.

2. Show what happens in Figure 12.2 if people in the home country start saving more because of tax reductions on income from savings. Explain the international adjustment.

3. If the home country decides to restrict the inflow of foreign capital in Figure 12.2 with an investment quota of $2 billion, show what happens to interest rates in both countries.

4. Some international loan occur through the sale of private and government bonds. Explain the difference when foreign investors in Figure 12.2 are buying private versus government bonds.

5. The Mexican government has historically limited foreign ownership of firms in Mexico to 49%. This restriction was lifted with NAFTA. Predict the long run term effects on the peso/$ exchange rate.

6. In the example of international inflation and CIA, suppose the ringgit interest rate is 4% and the spot exchange rate is $/ringgit = 0.30. Find the implied forward exchange rate. Which currency is selling at a discount?

7. Domestic auto firms in the US use as many foreign components as foreign automakers in their US plants. Would this influence a foreign firm's decision to build a plant in the US or a domestic firm's decision to build a plant in Mexico?

8. Suppose Nissan builds a new $10 billion automobile plant in the US raising 50% of the funds through the issue and sale of new stock in US. How will the new plant affect the US capital

account? How is the US balance of trade ultimately affected?

9. Suppose the supply of loans in the home country decreases in the international financial markets of Figure 12.4. Explain the effects on the credit and FX markets.

10. Starting with the money market in Figure 12.5, show and explain what happens if foreign investors expect the dollar to depreciate.

11. The following quote appeared in Wachovia's *Foreign Exchange Review* (January 22, 1990). Discuss using concepts from this chapter:

   News that the US trade deficit fell in November pushed dollar down against the German mark. The dollar later recovered in a technical correction of the mark which was overbought in the euphoria over events in Eastern Europe.

12. Suppose the dollar is put on a bimetal standard. The government defines the dollar as 0.0025 ounces of gold and 0.185 ounces of silver and stands ready to trade paper dollars for either gold or silver. In the market, the price of gold is $393.75 and the price of silver is $5.25/oz. What will arbitragers do? What will happen to government stocks of gold and silver? Which is the bad money?

13. Does a government surplus have to lead to a trade surplus? Describe the link between the government surplus and the trade surplus.

14. List three reasons why PPP may not hold.

15. Is a country with a relatively young population more or less likely to have unexpectedly high inflation? What about a country with a relatively wealthy population? Which country is more likely to have zero inflation?

READINGS

Gary Smith, *Money, Banking, and Financial Intermediation* (1991) Lexington. Introduction to monetary economics.

Symposia: New institutions for developing country debt (1990) *Journal of Economic Perspectives*. Proposals for dealing with LDC debt.

Ron Jones and Peter Kenen, eds. (1985) *Handbook of International Economics*, vol II, Amsterdam: North-Holland. Surveys of international monetary economics.

Central Bank Watch, the American Banker Newsletter Division. Periodical to keep international bankers abreast of central banks.

International Trade Finance Report, Morgan Williams Group, online articles and information on international finance.

Ronald McKinnon (1993) The rules of the game: International money in historical perspective, *The Journal of Economic Literature*. A look at the game played by central banks.

CHAPTER 13

Open Economy Macroeconomics

Preview

This chapter on open economy macroeconomics covers
- The microeconomic foundations of macroeconomics
- The closed macro economy
- The open macro economy
- Inflation and the exchange rate

INTRODUCTION

Macroeconomics paints a big picture of an economy and how it relates to the rest of the world. The major macroeconomic variables are national output, unemployment, the interest rate, inflation, the balance of payments, and the exchange rate. Macroeconomics focuses on the role of government policy influencing these variables as it attempts to manage aggregate production, employment, and income distribution. The government uses monetary and fiscal policies, and in an open economy uses international investment and exchange rate policies, to influence what is produced, how it is produced, and how income is distributed.

This chapter focuses on the fundamental models of the open macro economy. The foundations are an aggregate production function and the optimal decision making by households and firms. Saving and foreign investment feed into the capital stock for production. Output goes into consumption, investment, government spending, and net exports. The balance of trade and capital account are critical to the open macro economy.

A.   MICROECONOMIC FOUNDATIONS OF MACROECONOMICS

Macroeconomics searches for simple models to explain the behavior of aggregate economies, no simple task given the thousands of markets at work. The foundation of macroeconomics is based on microeconomics, the neoclassical production model, the overlapping generations (OLG) model of lifetime saving, and the optimal investment model.

The neoclassical production model shows the link between saving, the capital stock, and production. The OLG model explains saving as an optimal lifetime process. The optimal investment model explains investment spending by firms as optimal borrowing or bond holding. These microeconomic models provide a foundation for the open economy macro models that examine how national income, the interest rate, inflation, and the exchange rate are related to each other.

EXAMPLE 13.1 *US National Income Accounts, 2004*

National income in the US was $11 trillion in 2004. Consumption spending C went 60% for services and 40% for goods. About 2/3 of the $3 trillion investment spending I was by firms, the rest by households on residences. Government spending G was $2 trillion. The largest categories of federal government spending are Health & Human Services and Social Security, tax redistribution programs that account for about half of G. Unlike consumption, export revenue X and import spending M involve mostly goods. M is only 1/6 services but the share of services in X has grown to 1/3.

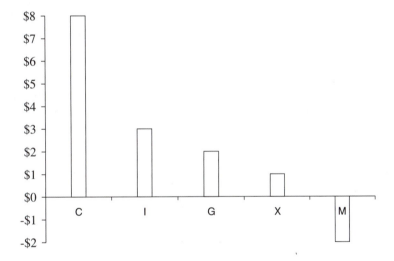

Production and Economic Growth

The story of macroeconomics begins with producing output. The macro economy produces the single aggregate output Y with inputs capital K and labor L in the *neoclassical macro production function*

$$Y = A f(K, L)$$

where A represents the level of technology. Increased inputs of K or L raise Y at diminishing rates due to *diminishing marginal productivity*. Holding labor constant, for instance, additional capital machinery and equipment raises output but contributes diminishing amounts given the fixed amount of labor in the economy.

There are also *positive cross productivity* effects with more of one input raising the other's productivity. An increase in the number of workers holding the capital stock constant raises capital productivity. An extra worker in the economy also raises national output by the worker's wage.

Improved technology A raises output holding levels K and L constant. Technology is difficult to gauge but if output rises with input constant, it must be increasing. In practice, capital input imbeds technology and separating the two is difficult. Macroeconomics focuses on changes in the economy over a few quarters or perhaps years. There is no doubt that technology improves over the decades, but across a few years it is safe to assume that technology at the aggregate level is constant.

The *Cobb-Douglas production function* scaled to the US economy is

$$Y = AK^{.3}L^{.7}.$$

With competitive input markets, capital and labor are paid their marginal products, $r = MP_K$ and $w = MP_L$ where r is the return to capital and w the wage.

Figure 13.1 shows this *per capita production function*

$$y = Ak^{.3}$$

where y is income per worker Y/L and k is the capital/labor ratio K/L. The scale is an approximation for the US economy in 2002 with $Y = \$10$ trillion, $L = 200$ million, and $y = \$50,000$. The labor share of national income is $wL/Y = 70\% = .70$ implying the wage $w = \$35,000$.

Suppose the real return to capital is $r = 5\% = .05$. The capital share of national income is then $rK/Y = 30\% = .30$. If a unit of capital input costs \$1 it follows that $K = \$60$ trillion and $k = \$300,000$. This k is higher than estimates because the labor force L is the base and "capital" is the residual of GDP after labor with other inputs such as natural resources excluded. The scaled production function drawn in Figure 13.1 is $y = 1137k^{.3}$.

Labor and capital generate *national income*, the sum of payments to the factors of production in $Y = wL + rK$. Dividing by L, per capita income is the wage plus capital income per capita

$$y = w + rk.$$

This linear equation breaks per capita income into its labor and capital sources. The slope of the tangent to the production function in Figure 13.1 is the capital return $r = .05$ and the intercept of its tangent with the y axis is the wage w. Higher k implies y and w rise while r falls as the tangent line flattens.

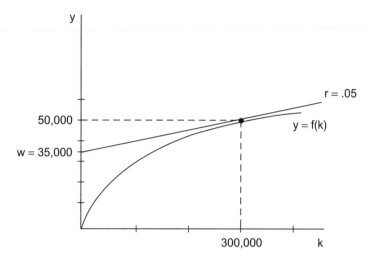

Figure 13.1
The Macro Production Function
This macro production function is scaled to the US economy with k = $300,000, y = $50,000, and w = $35,000. Income per capita y is an increasing function of the capital labor ratio k. The per capita production function is concave to the origin due to diminishing marginal returns to capital.

Moving up along the production function as the capital labor ratio k increases, one result is higher per capita income y. *Economic growth* is a long term process that involves moving up the production curve over time with k increasing due to saving. Economic growth redistributes income with r falling and w rising due to the higher capital/labor ratio and increased labor productivity.

Income per capita y is an increasing concave function of the capital/labor ratio k. Economic growth occurs over time as k increases due to saving with the wage rising and the return to capital falling.

EXAMPLE 13.2 *Production Function Plots*

Output per capita y is an increasing concave function of the capital labor ratio k as these plots illustrate. The first is the US economy from 1950 to 1990 in $1990 with real income per capita y and k from the World Bank. The theoretical production function assumes constant technology that changes over the decades but this plot illustrates the underlying production function. The second plot of k versus y across sample countries in 1990 also illustrates the increasing concave shape of the aggregate production function. Estimating production functions with econometric techniques, the challenge is to hold technology constant over time or across locations.

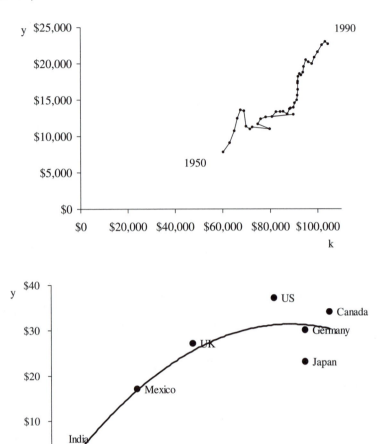

The Savings Rate and Growth

Income is spent or saved, and the stock of productive capital is the accumulated result of past saving. Capital equipment, machinery, structures, and infrastructure is accumulated over time by saving out of income to make resources available for the production of investment goods. Foreign investment can also add to (or subtract from) the capital stock but for the present keep the economy closed. Countries that save more income accumulate capital and move up along their production growth curve more quickly.

   If 20% of income is saved, the *saving rate* is $\sigma = S/Y = 0.2$. Capital accumulates according to $K' = .2Y$ where the ' refers to a change over time. Capital accumulation would increase k but K must grow faster than L for an increase in $k = K/L$. If the labor force L grows at a 2% rate, K must grow by more than 2% for economic growth. In the example, the growth rate of capital is $\sigma Y/K = .2Y/K = (.2 \times \$10 \text{ trillion})/K = \$2 \text{ trillion}/K$. With K equal to $\$60$ trillion, the growth rate of capital is 3.3% and k rises along the production function.

A higher saving rate implies faster growth and higher income per capita. Saving rates vary across countries. Asian countries have had the highest saving rates and fastest growth rates over the past 50 years. Saving more now implies consuming less, making the decision to save difficult.

The *steady state* occurs when K rises to the level that k becomes constant. In the example, the steady state occurs when capital grows at 2% along with labor. Per capita income y, wage w, the return to capital r, and k are all *stationary* in the steady state. Some of the wealthy countries in the world are in the steady state but most countries are moving up along the production function. Macroeconomics is more concerned with small nudges along the production function but the underlying economic growth remains more important in the long run.

EXAMPLE 13.3 *Economic Growth in DCs and LDCs*

This data shows the long term growth in per capita income y is constant $\$2000$ across some DCs and LDCs from Maddison (1991). The UK was the early leader among the DCs but grew more slowly during the 1900s. The US and Canada (CN) lead the DCs but Japan (JP) and Germany (GE) have closed the gap since 1950. The LDCs tells a different story with a lower y scale. Korea (KO) has been accelerating while India (IN) and China (CN) have progressed very little. Colombia (CL) has grown slowly but steadily. Argentina (AR) started high in 1870 but grew slowly and fell back due to socialism. These trends are different due to the capital/labor ratio paths as the countries move along the theoretical production function in Figure 13.1.

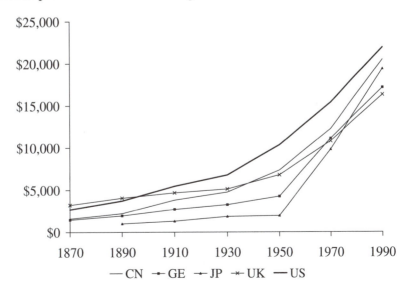

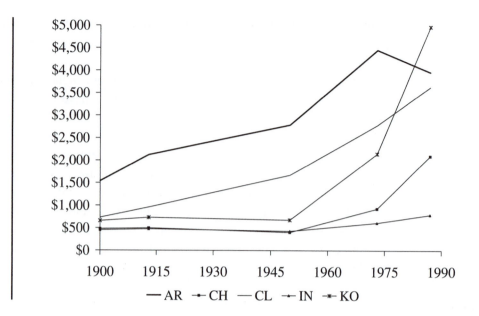

EXAMPLE 13.4 *Approaching the Steady State in Germany*

Following World War II, Germany began slow steady economic growth. High rates of saving and investment built the capital stock and the capital/labor ratio rose along with the real wage in the chart below (€1999). Over this time period, Germany has had a stable government with reliable property rights, relatively unobtrusive taxes, a balanced government budget, and low inflation. NICs and LDCs can learn from this example that economic growth based on reasonable government policy is slow but reliable.

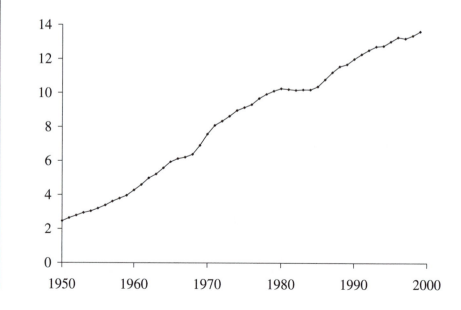

Endogenous Saving in the OLG Model

The decision of how much to save depends on the pattern of income, the interest rate, and preferences about consuming now or later. On average, households save out of income during their working years to retire on their savings. There are also social security schemes that tax workers to pay retirees directly, eroding the incentive to save. A few households inherit wealth and have a steady stream of income over their lifetime.

The *overlapping generations (OLG) model* provides a simple framework to study the saving decision. Suppose all households work when they are young, save a portion of their labor income, and then live off savings plus interest earnings when they retire. Suppose there is no inherited wealth or social security tax scheme. The simple interest rate applies across the two periods, working youth and retirement in old age.

When the current workers retire and the retirees die, the next young generation begins work. Each overlapping generation has young workers and retired capitalists. The capital stock must be purchased by the young workers from the old retirees during each *overlapping generation.*

Figure 13.2 illustrates the *optimal savings decision* for a young working household. Labor income during youth is the wage w along the horizontal axis.

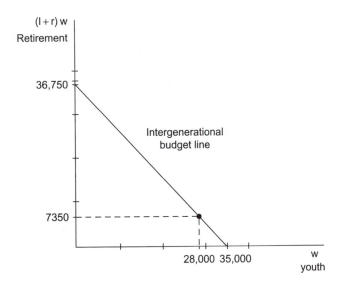

Figure 13.2
Optimal saving in the OLG Model
Labor income w is saved and transferred to retirement at the interest rate r. With $r = .05$, wages of $35,000 transfer to $1.05 \times \$35,000 = \$36,750$ potential retirement income. The typical household maximizes its *intertemporal utility* subject to this budget constraint, consuming $28,000 while working and $1.05 \times \$7,000 = \$7,350$ while retired.

The household can transform its labor income to retirement, earning interest rate r. With w wage in youth, potential retirement income is $(1 + r)w$. In the example $w = \$35,000$ and $r = 5\%$ making potential retirement income $\$36,750$. The figures are yearly income, and this simple example assumes people work as many years as they are retired.

The line connecting w with $(1 + r)w$ is the *intergenerational budget line*. The household can select any point along the line according to *time preferences*. In the example at the aggregate level, $\sigma = 0.2$ and saving is $0.2 \times \$35,000 = \$7,000$. Consumption in youth is $\$28,000$ and savings earns 5% interest making retirement consumption $\$7,350$. There are actually more years of work than retirement and people do not consume such low levels after retirement.

Social security provides retirement income by taxing young workers, an inefficient scheme that lowers the intergenerational budget line in Figure 13.2 making both workers and retirees worse off. Social security taxes reduce income in youth, lower total saving, and force households onto a lower budget line. The subsidy to retirees earns no interest, leaving both youth and retirees worse off. The interest rate also rises due to the reduced saving, lowering per capita income and economic growth.

A higher interest rate r raises the intergenerational budget line and would likely encourage saving by raising the opportunity cost of consuming during youth. Depending on preferences, consumption in both periods could rise. The increased saving S means a higher saving rate σ.

Preferences might change over time, and likely differ across countries. Households that are frugal and plan ahead have preferences biased more toward the future, save a larger share of income, and enjoy higher income in retirement. Countries with higher discount rates consume more out of income, save less, and grow slower.

EXAMPLE 13.5 *S/Y, I/Y and i in the US since 1950*

> Saving and investment both depend on the interest rate and are shown as percentages of GDP in the US since 1950 along with the real short term interest rate (the commercial interest rate less inflation). S/Y and I/Y generally move together and trended upward slightly since 1960. Negative real interest rates in the 1970s were due to high inflation. A falling interest rate should lower investment spending but since 1982 the opposite has been just as likely to occur. In the OLG model a falling interest rate would lower saving, but the opposite has typically occurred since 1982. These trends indicate other influences on investment and saving behavior. Estimating the interest rate effects on saving and investment requires a complete model and careful estimation.

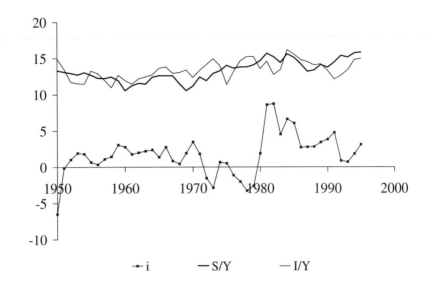

$-$ i $-$ S/Y $-$ I/Y

Problems for Section A

A1. Find per capita income y and the wage w in Figure 13.1 if $k = \$200,000$ and the interest rate $r = 6.6\%$. Explain the difference from the wage in the text example. Diagram this change in position on the production function.

A2. Find the capital labor ratio k that would be required for income per capita y to be \$60,000 in the economy of Figure 13.1. If $r = 3.3\%$ find the wage w. Diagram these two positions on the production function.

A3. Suppose the young households in the OLG model of Figure 13.2 save 30% of their income. Find their consumption levels in youth and retirement. Diagram this optimal saving behavior using an indifference curve for consumption across the two periods.

A4. Compare the indifference curve in Problem 3 with one that must lead to the optimal consumption in Figure 13.2. Suggest what might lead to the increased saving.

B.   CLOSED ECONOMY MACROECONOMICS

Every economy is open to some extent to international trade and finance but it is best to begin the study of macroeconomics with a closed economy. There are two sides to the macro economy, production and money. Interaction of product and money markets determines national output and the interest rate. Monetary and fiscal policies affect output, investment, and the interest rate, indirectly affecting unemployment, inflation, and economic growth.

Aggregate Production

A *closed economy* has no international trade or investment and all output goes to domestic consumption, investment, and government spending. The national income statement for a closed economy equates output Y with spending,

$$Y = C + I + G.$$

Consumption spending C is for current goods and services. *Investment spending I* by firms adds to the capital stock for future production. *Government spending G* goes to government employees and purchases that provide government services and goods. Continuing the example, $C = \$8$ trillion or 80% of $Y = \$10$ trillion, $I = \$2$ trillion, and $G = 0$. With the capital stock $K = \$60$ trillion, its growth rate due to domestic investment is $I/K = 2/60 = 3.33\%$ disregarding depreciation.

Lending and borrowing are critical to the macro economy. Some *economic agents* including consumers, firms, and the government have less cash than they want while others have more. In broad terms, lending and borrowing in the *credit market* allows households to save for retirement, firms to borrow for expanded production, and the government to spend beyond its ability to tax.

A *bond* is an agreement that promises to pay back a loan with interest. Assume bonds are risk free with agents trading freely in the *credit market*. The simplest example is a *perpetuity* paying a perpetual income stream. The price of a perpetuity bond securing a \$1 payment forever at an interest rate of $r_B = 5\% = .05$ is $p_B = 1/r_B = 1/.05 = \$20$. At the 5% interest rate, \$20 earns \$1 interest payment per year forever leaving the \$20 principle untouched. A lower interest rate implies a higher bond price with more money required to yield the same \$1 income stream. If r_B falls to 4%, p_B rises to \$25.

A firm considering an investment project will compare its projected rate of return to the interest rate. The opportunity cost of spending on an investment project is buying a bond, and firms short of cash but long on ideas can borrow at the interest rate and spend on projects with higher expected rates of return. A higher bond rate lowers investment spending with firms only pursuing investment projects with higher expected returns. At a lower interest rate, more investment projects become attractive and investment spending increases. Competition between bonds and investment spending I equalizes returns.

Continuing the example, suppose every decrease of the interest rate r by .01 raises investment spending I by \$0.4 trillion. The linear *investment function* in Figure 13.3 with $r = .05$ and $I = \$2$ trillion is then $I = 4 - 40r$.

Firms wanting cash for profitable investment projects can also sell stocks as *equity* promising the holder of the stock a share of future profit. *Stock dividends* depend on uncertain profits making the stock return riskier than the fixed interest rate on bonds. To compensate for the higher risk, stock returns are higher on average. Since the 1800s, stock returns in the US have averaged about 6% in

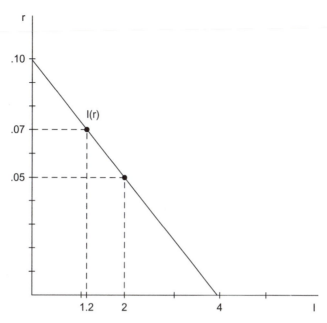

Figure 13.3
Investment Function
The investment function $I = 4 - 40r$ yields investment spending of 2 ($trillion) when $r = .05$. If r rises to $.07$, I falls to $4 - 2.4 = \$1.2$ trillion. If $r = 10\%$, $I = 0$, and $I = 4$ if $r = 0\%$. There is a negative relationship between r and I since firms have the option to spend on investment projects or buy bonds with return r.

real terms while real returns on bonds have been about 2%. Comparing assets, the higher return of stocks comes with higher risk or variation. A firm wanting to borrow can assume *debt* by selling bonds directly or borrowing from *financial intermediaries* or banks. Financial intermediaries match borrowers with lenders.

Economic agents save out of income for future spending. The rate of saving is σ and total saving is σY. National income less consumption is $Y - C = I + G$. Output not consumed equals saving S, equal to investment plus government spending in the closed economy,

$$S = \sigma Y = I + G.$$

In the example $\sigma = 0.2$ and $S = 0.2 \times \$10$ trillion $= \$2$ trillion. Assuming $G = 0$, $I = \$2$ trillion.

The *IS curve* in Figure 13.4 shows combinations of r and Y where $S = I + G$. Higher Y implies an increase in S and the interest rate r has to fall to increase I to return to product market equilibrium with investment equal to saving ($I = S$ or *IS*). The IS curve has a negative slope. In the example $S = .2Y$ and $I = 4 - 40r$ leading to the IS curve in Figure 13.4 with $G = 0$,

$$IS \ curve: r = .1 - .005Y.$$

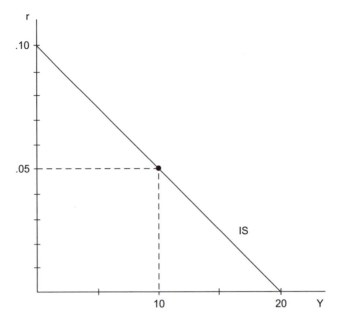

Figure 13.4
The IS Curve
To the right of the IS curve, saving is greater than investment. If $r = .05$ and $Y = 11$, there is excess saving $S = 0.2 \times 11 = \$2.2$ trillion with $I = 4 - 40 \times .05 = \$2$ trillion on the investment function in Fig. 13.3. The IS curve is the combinations of r and Y that satisfy $S = I + G$.

On the right side of the IS curve there is *excess saving* beyond what is invested and $S > I$. On the left side there is a *saving shortage* with $I > S$. Output Y adjusts so the economy is on its IS curve.

Moving down the IS curve, Y increases and r falls. The fall in r implies the economy moves to a higher capital/labor ratio k along its production function in Figure 13.1. More capital and perhaps more labor come into production. The wage w and per capita income y are higher with the higher k. There must have been available capital to produce the additional output, and this slack in the market for productive capital allows the economy to move down its IS curve. There is not enough time to produce new capital moving along the IS curve. If more labor is employed in the process, the *unemployment rate* falls.

> *Moving down along the IS curve, national income increases and the interest rate falls. There must be increased capital input, raising the wage and per capita income.*

EXAMPLE 13.6 *Macro Models*

Macroeconomics searches for simple relationships in aggregate data. Rates of output growth, unemployment U, inflation I, deficit spending relative to GDP, and the balance on goods and services relative to GDP are listed from the *Economic Report of the President*. High output growth might be expected to lower unemployment, but higher unemployment benefits increase the incentive to declare unemployment. Inflation is generally thought to stimulate growth, but the lower growth rate in the money supply since the 1990s led to lower inflation with no effect on output growth. Expansionary fiscal policy and higher government budget deficit is thought to stimulate output, but the link is not apparent. Unemployment and inflation appear to move in the same direction. Trade deficits have not lowered output growth, and are apparently not related to government budget deficits in $(T-G)/Y$. There may be no simple models to analyze what is happening in the underlying markets.

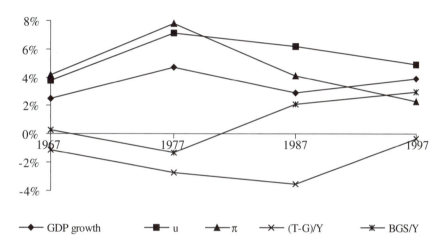

Capital and Labor Markets

The macro economy is based on its capital and labor markets. Demand determines input prices and levels, and the macro model assumes available inputs.

The *demand for productive capital* in Figure 13.5 is its marginal product, $MP_K = D_K$. Firms hire capital when its marginal productivity is greater than its price. The marginal product of capital from the production function is $MP_K = 341K^{-.7}L^{.7} = 341k^{-.7}$. If $r = .05$ capital utilization is $K = 60$ trillion given $L = 200$ million and $k = 300,000$. If r fell to .04, K would rise to 84 trillion along the capital demand curve D_K.

There must be idle capital for the economy to increase Y moving along the IS curve. There are practical reasons for idle capital. Firms rent capital from its owners who are ready to supply the machinery and equipment but it may have to be moved and installed where production takes place. Production schedules may leave capital occasionally idle. Labor has to be trained to operate machinery and equipment. Regular maintenance downtime may leave capital under utilized. To move down along the IS curve, idle capital must be put to work.

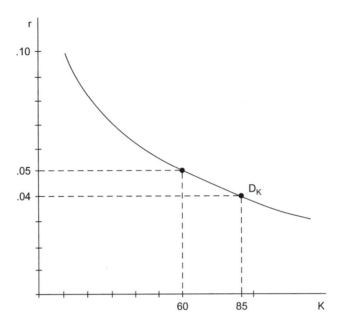

Figure 13.5
The Demand for Capital
The marginal product of capital $MP_K = 341k^{-.7}$ comes from the production function $Y = AK^{.3}L^{.7}$ or $y = 1137K^{.3}$. If r rises, K has to fall for an increase MP_K. The higher price of capital forces firms to reduce capital input so it becomes more productive on the margin.

Figure 13.6 shows the *labor market*. The demand for labor D_L is its marginal product $MP_L = 796k^{.3}$ from the example production function. Firms hire labor according to its marginal productivity, making MP_L the demand for labor D_L. In the example with $K = \$60$ trillion, firms employ 200 million workers at $w = \$35,000$. If w rose to $\$40,000$, the quantity of labor demanded would fall to 128 million along D_L.

Increasing Y on the IS curve, K input increases raising MP_L and w. Firms may want to hire more labor depending on the substitution between labor and capital. If so, there is an increase in labor demand and more labor is hired, increasing capital productivity in the adjustment process. Given the total amount of labor available L_{tot} the unemployment rate $u = (L_{tot} - L)/L_{tot}$ declines when L increases. Consistent with the declining r along the IS curve, there is an increase in k implying the percentage increase in K is larger than the percentage change in L.

Moving along the IS curve to higher output increases capital input and raises the capital/labor ratio. To increase output for the increased investment at the lower interest rate, there must be available inputs in the capital and labor markets.

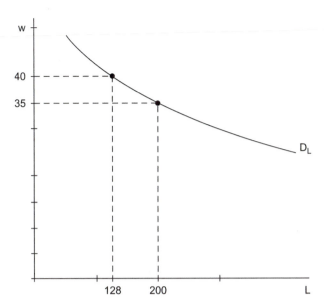

Figure 13.6
The Demand for Labor
Labor demand is its marginal product derived from the production function. Firms hire labor to adjust its marginal product MP_L to the wage w. In the example $MP_L = 796k^{.3} = \$35,000$ and $L = 200$ million. A fall in w implies k has to fall, and given the K input L must increase along the demand curve for labor.

EXAMPLE 13.7 *The Capital Stimulus of Free Trade*

One impact of free trade on the economy is through its effect on the return to capital. If a capital abundant DC opens to trade, the return to capital increases with exports of capital intensive products. The higher return to capital encourages saving shifting the economy to a higher production function with accelerated capital accumulation. Richard Baldwin (1992) estimates these dynamic gains from trade across a number of European countries and finds they range up to 8%, larger than estimated gains from trade. The flip side, however, is that trade would lower the return to capital, saving, capital accumulation, and growth in capital scarce LDCs. Foreign investment would counteract this negative trade effect in the LDCs, and free trade and investment are the total policy package.

The Macroeconomic Money Market

Money is a *liquid asset* required for transactions but holding money involves a lost opportunity to buy bonds and enjoy the future return. *Liquidity demand* is a function of income and the interest rate,

$$L = L(\overset{+}{Y}, \overset{-}{r}).$$

Spending requires liquidity for transactions leading to the positive effect of Y on the demand for money. A higher interest rate makes bonds more attractive lowering the demand for liquidity.

The government central bank indirectly controls the real money supply M_s through the commercial banking system. The central bank directly controls its credit C_{CB} in the reserves of commercial banks that generate revenue by lending deposits in excess of reserves. The total money supply M_s is a multiple of C_{CB}, $M_s = \mu C_{CB}$.

Money market equilibrium occurs along the LM (liquidity = money) curve,

$$LM \; curve\text{: } M_s = L(\overset{+}{Y}, \overset{-}{r}).$$

The LM curve is upward sloping since an increase in Y would have to offset by a higher r to keep the demand for cash L equal to a fixed supply M_s. The interest rate r adjusts to keep the economy on its LM curve.

The money supply M_S is a policy variable controlled by central bank credit. *Expansionary monetary policy* increases M_s shifting the LM curve to the right.

For the US in 2003, $M_s = \$1.3$ trillion with a ratio of cash to income of $\$1.3/\$10 = .13$. Given a constant cash/income ratio, $\$100$ of additional income

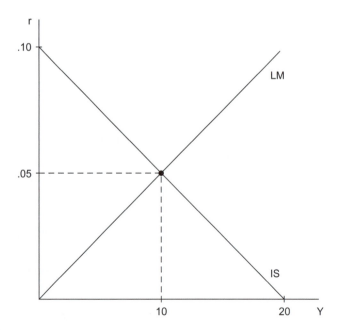

Figure 13.7
The ISLM Closed Economy
The LM curve $r = .005Y$ intersects the IS curve $r = .1 - .005Y$ at the closed economy ISLM macro equilibrium $r = .05$ and $Y = 10$. The product IS market and the money LM market are both in equilibrium. *Fiscal policy* shifts the IS curve and *monetary policy* shifts the LM curve.

increases the demand for liquidity by \$13. If the elasticity of liquidity demand with respect to the interest rate is -1, the marginal effect of r on L is $\$1.3/.05 = -26$. The *linear liquidity demand function* is then $L = 1.3 + .13Y - 26r$. With $M_S = 1.3$, the *LM curve* in Figure 13.7 is

$$LM\ curve: r = .005Y.$$

The closed economy ISLM model in Figure 13.7 has equilibrium in investment-saving and liquidity-money where the IS and LM curves intersect at $r = .05$ and $Y = 10$ trillion.

The ISLM model determines the interest rate and output that clear the product and money markets in the economy.

EXAMPLE 13.8 *Money supply growth, inflation, and the interest rate in the US*

An increase in the money supply lowers the real interest rate in the ILSM model but can also lead to inflation. This chart tracks the annual growth rate of the US money supply along with the inflation rate p and the short term real interest rate *i*. Rising money supply growth rates lead to inflation as seen from 1960 into the 1980s. The monetary growth rate then became more erratic but tended to fall as did inflation. The Fed does not specify an exact inflation target but does profess concern. The real interest rate fell during the 1970s with high inflation but jumped around 1980 as inflation began to fall. The true underlying relationships have to be estimated in a complete model but the time trends are suggestive.

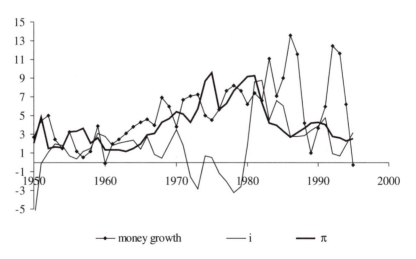

Monetary Policy

Macro policy aims to manage the macro economy targeting the interest rate and output. *Monetary policy* refers to control of the money supply M_s. *Expansionary*

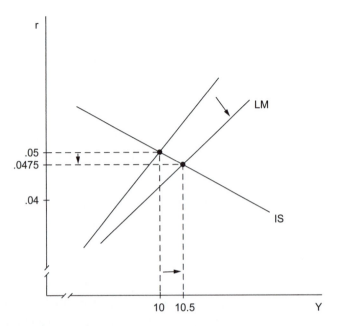

Figure 13.8
Expansionary Monetary Policy
An increase in the money supply shifts the LM curve to the right, lowering the interest
rate and raising output. There must be idle capital in the economy to be employed at the
lower interest rate. Labor productivity and the wage increase. While there is no inflation
in the ISLM model, inflation occurs if the output does not keep pace with money supply
growth.

monetary policy is an increase in M_s shifting the LM curve to the right as in
Figure 13.8.

An increase in the money supply moves the economy down the IS curve,
raising output Y and lowering the interest rate r. A 10% increase in M_S
from $1.3 to $1.43 trillion lowers r from 5% to 4.75% and raises Y from 10
to 10.5.

The falling r implies a higher bond price with investment spending increasing
to $2.1 trillion along the investment schedule $I(r)$ in Figure 13.3. With the shift
in Figure 13.8, the capital/labor ratio k in Figure 13.1 increases from $300 to
$327 thousand, output per capita y rises from $50,000 to $51,300, and the wage
w rises from $35,000 to $35,900. Expansionary monetary policy has real impacts
in this closed economy macro model.

One political motivation for expansionary monetary policy is unemployment
but any labor market stimulus is possible only if there is idle capital. Such
transitory stimulus occurs over the short time span of a quarter (3 months) to a
year.

Continued expansion of the money supply at a pace faster than output growth leads to *inflation* with no positive impact on the labor market. The ISLM model assumes zero inflation with the price level constant, but the effects of inflation can offset the positive transitory effects of the increased money supply. Further, there may be no positive transitory effects at all in an open economy.

Economic growth is a gradual process that results from saving, investment, and capital accumulation. Expansionary monetary policy does not stimulate economic growth.

> *A monetary expansion may stimulate output, raising the capital/labor ratio, per capita income, and the wage, but lowering the return to capital. The increased demand for labor may lower unemployment. Expansionary monetary policy, however, has no long term effect on production potential and may lead to inflation.*

EXAMPLE 13.9 *The Inflation Drag*

The ISLM model gives the impression that expansionary monetary policy leads to higher output. Over the short time span of the model, output can increase if there is idle capital and no inflation. Greece provides an example of the harmful effects of inflation on GDP growth. Beginning in the 1970s, Greece pursued expansionary government spending and industrial subsidies with unsustainable welfare and retirement programs causing government deficits financed by monetary expansion. Inflation rates of 25% and higher through the 1980s disrupted economic planning and were a drag on output. There were also high tariffs and tight restrictions on international investment and money flows. Percentage changes in GDP were low and sometimes negative. That all changed with Greece's entry into the EU and then the euro currency in 1992. As inflation fell with the euro, output growth began to rise steadily and has continued to rise since.

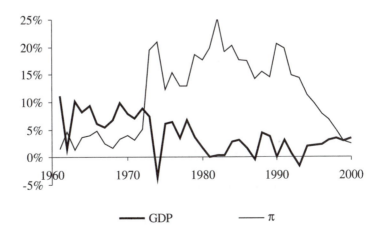

Macroeconomic Fiscal Policy

Fiscal policy refers to the program of government spending G and taxes T. Start with $G = T = 0$ and let G increase to examine the effects of *expansionary fiscal policy*. Lowering T has the same aggregate effect although there are issues of income redistribution. From the national income equation, saving equals investment plus government spending, $\sigma Y = I + G$. An increase in G shifts the IS curve to the right since more income Y is required to generate increased saving σY to match the increase in $I + G$.

Figure 13.9 shows the effects of an increase in government spending equal to 1% of GDP or $100 billion in the example. The IS curve shifts to $r = .1025 - .005Y$. Output Y rises from $10 to $10.25 trillion and the interest rate rises from 5% to 5.125% up along the LM curve. The higher return to capital reduces capital input and k falls along the production function in Figure 13.1. There is increased labor employment along the labor demand curve with a lower wage, and the unemployment rate u falls. There must be unemployment slack for the increase in G to raise Y as in Figure 13.9.

Capital owners are better off with the higher r but income per capita y falls to $49,600, w falls to $31,600, and k falls to $293,000 along the production function in Figure 13.1. The economy switches toward more labor intensive

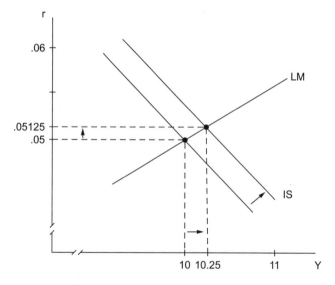

Figure 13.9
Expansionary Fiscal Policy
An increase in government spending G with taxes T constant, or a decrease in T with G constant, shifts the IS curve to the right. Output expands with increased labor employment but the wage falls. With full employment of labor, the LM curve is vertical and there is no increase in output due to expansionary fiscal policy.

production due to the lower relative price of labor. Investment spending drops from $2 to $1.95 trillion along the investment schedule in Figure 13.2, implying slower economic growth. This reduction in investment spending is the *crowding out* of government spending. The political saying that "government spending creates jobs" may be true, but it also eliminates other jobs due to crowding out.

Firms determine the level of employment according to labor demand. There must be available workers not employed at the present wage and willing to work for a lower wage to increase output as in Figure 13.9. This labor market condition is not generally sensible and expansionary fiscal policy is certainly not capable of increasing output indefinitely. Even though fiscal policy may succeed in stimulating short term employment around election time, it is an unattractive tool for active macro management.

Successful expansionary fiscal policy requires unemployment slack in the labor market. Wages and investment spending fall but employment increases. The declining investment and growth suggest it is wiser to address the problem of unemployment directly through the labor market.

Another issue is that the ISLM model disregards the effect of government deficits and debt implied by expansionary fiscal policy. If $G > T$, the government must either expand the money supply or borrow to pay for the excess spending. Expanding the money supply amounts to monetary policy and that can be pursued on its own merit with no change in government spending or taxes.

Government borrowing implies repayment and future taxes. According to *Ricardian equivalence*, taxpayers understand the future tax liability and increase their saving rate σ to pay the future tax. This increase in s lowers the IS curve back toward its original position in Figure 13.9 making the fiscal policy ineffective.

Taxes must finance government deficit spending due to expansionary fiscal policy, offsetting any positive effect on output or employment. Fiscal policy is not a viable tool to manage unemployment.

EXAMPLE 13.10 *Inflation, Unemployment, and Trade in Portugal*

One example of inflation and unemployment is Portugal, a small open economy that joined the EU in 1992. Unemployment did not respond to expansionary fiscal policy and associated government deficits and inflation in the 1970s and remained high during the early 1980s. As the economy became more active in international trade beginning in the 1980s, unemployment fell. A decline in unemployment began in 1985 and continued along with the low inflation of the euro starting in 1992. Portugal became more open to trade, with the trade index $(X + M)$/GDP rising from just over 0.5 in 1985 to over 1 by 2000. Portugal provides an example of the gains from international trade and investment.

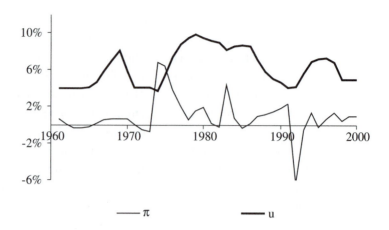

Problems for Section B

B1. Show and explain what happens in the capital and labor markets when the interest rate rises along the IS curve in Figure 13.4.

B2. Use input demands to explain how an increase in the interest rate r affects capital and labor employment.

B3. Show the effect of a decrease in the money supply in the ISLM model.

B4. Show the effect of an increase in taxes in the ISLM model.

C. THE OPEN MACRO ECONOMY

There are fundamental differences in how an economy open to international trade and investment behaves and how it responds to macro policy. The *exchange rate and international investment* play important roles in the open macro economy. Government policy makers have additional macro policy tools in the open economy, *fixed exchange rates* and *foreign investment controls*.

The Balance of Trade in Macroeconomics

The balance on goods and services *BGS* becomes part of the national income statement of an open economy,

$$Y = C + I + G + BGS$$

where $BGS = X - M$, export revenue X minus import spending M.

Total domestic spending $C + I + G$ is called *absorption A*. To derive national income Y from absorption A, add export revenue X since it is produced but not consumed, and subtract import spending M since it is consumed but not produced. A simple national income statement for the open economy is

$$Y = A + BGS.$$

Including the *BGS* and government spending *G* to the example of the 2002 US economy in \$trillion, $X = \$1$, $M = \$1.4$, and $BGS = -\$0.4$. Absorption $A = \$10.4$ is made up of $C = \$7$, $I = \$1.4$, and $G = \$2$. National income is $Y = A + BGS = \$10$ making the \$400 billion *BGS* deficit 4% of national income and 3.8% of domestic absorption.

The trade balance (BGS) depends partly on the exchange rate defined as the domestic currency price of foreign currency. In terms of the euro, $e = \$/\euro$. *Depreciation* $e\uparrow$ is a decrease in the relative price of domestic currency.

To isolate the effect of the exchange rate on the economy, it has to be adjusted by any change in price levels. The relative foreign price level P^*/P is called the *real exchange rate* e_R. For present purposes, assume P and P^* are constant and focus on the nominal *exchange rate e*.

Depreciation raises the *BGS* given the *Marshall-Lerner condition* of elastic export and import quantities. The adjustment in export plus import quantities must be elastic for depreciation to raise the *BGS*.

Higher foreign income Y^* raises X since the foreign country spends more on imports, and higher home income Y raises import spending M at home. The *BGS function* is summarized as

$$BGS = B(\overset{+}{e}, \overset{+}{Y^*}, \bar{Y}).$$

The *BGS* function is part of the open economy IS curve, $\sigma Y = I + G + BGS$. For a fixed level of saving $S = \sigma Y$ and government spending G, a trade deficit "crowds out" investment. The real story, however, is how these variables adjust together in the open economy.

EXAMPLE 13.11 *Prices and the BOT in Korea*

Prices of imports and exports are expected to affect the trade balance but the relationship depends on import elasticities as Korea illustrates. These series show price indices of imports and exports in Korea generally rose during the 1970s and 1980s with a bump during the oil embargo of the late 1970s. The *BOT* was negative with a dip due to the higher price of oil. Import prices then leveled out during the early 1990s falling slightly behind export prices, a improvement in the terms of trade for Korea. Nevertheless, the *BOT* became more negative. Starting about 1995, import prices began to outpace export prices with slightly falling terms of trade but the trade balance began a steady climb into surplus. The suggestion is that imports and exports are elastic but a closer look at the international markets is required to reach a conclusion. Economists use such *time series data* to gather empirical evidence on macroeconomic models, and adjustment varies across countries.

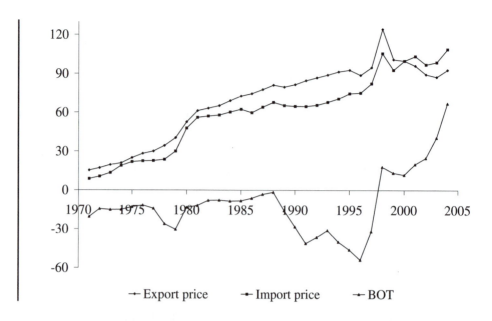

The Balance of Payments

The balance of payments *BOP* is the sum of the current account *CA* and the capital account *KA*, *BOP* = *CA* + *KA*. The *CA* includes the *BGS* and net investment income *NII*. A deficit in the *CA* implies a cash outflow for international transactions involving goods and services. The *KA* summarizes net international lending and borrowing. With a *CA* deficit, there must be offsetting international borrowing and a *KA* surplus.

In the example of the US in 2002, $CA = -KA = -\$0.4$ trillion with the US selling assets to generate cash inflow to offset the *CA* deficit. As a whole, the US is borrowing with the promise to pay in the future. The *CA* deficit lowers domestic investment *I* similar to the effect of an increase in government spending *G* but there is an increase in foreign investment *FI*. In the macro model, the US is selling bonds. Other countries such as China and Japan have *CA* surpluses and *KA* deficits, and are buying international bonds. Countries with *CA* surpluses lend to countries with *KA* surpluses.

A *small country* faces the interest rate r^* in the bond market of the rest of the world. If $r^* > r$ and the bonds are otherwise identical, domestic lenders would buy foreign bonds as the home country becomes an international lender. If $r > r^*$ domestic borrowers sell home bonds as the home country borrow internationally. For a *small country*, there is no change in r^* due to its lending and borrowing.

International lending and borrowing in a *large country* has an impact on international bond prices and interest rates. If $r^* > r$, the home country lends abroad increasing the supply of loans in the foreign country and lowering r^*. In the home country, the supply of loans decreases raising r and lowering the price of home bonds. International market forces push the home and foreign interest rates together. International lending and borrowing are not perfect and interest rates do not completely equalize but *arbitrage* tends toward international interest rates equalization.

Both r and r^* enter the capital account function

$$KA(\overset{+}{r}, \overset{-}{r^*}).$$

An increase in r^* creates an outflow of cash to buy foreign bonds. An increase in r creates an inflow of cash as foreign to buy home bonds.

The balance of payments is the sum of the current and capital accounts, leading to the *BOP function*

$$BP \text{ curve}: BOP = BP(\overset{+}{e}, \overset{+}{Y^*}, \overset{-}{Y}, \overset{-}{r^*}, \overset{+}{r}) = 0.$$

The BP curve in Figure 13.9 is the third part of the *open economy ISLMBP model* where the balance of payments equals zero, $BOP = 0$. It slopes upward since an increase in Y that lowers the BOP has to be offset by an increase in r. To the right of the BOP curve there is a deficit, and to the left a surplus.

The BP curve can be derived from the marginal propensity to import and the interest rate effect on the capital account. If the *marginal propensity to import* is constant at $M/Y = 0.14$, a \$100 increase in income increases import spending by \$14. If the elasticity of the KA with respect to r equals one, the marginal effect of r on KA equals 8 given the example of $KA = \$0.4$ trillion and $r = .05$. The scaled BP function in Figure 13.10 is then $BOP = 0 = 1 - .14Y + 8r$ or

$$BP \text{ curve}: r = -.125 + .0175Y.$$

This BP curve in Figure 13.10 shows combinations of r and Y where $BOP = 0$. To the right of the BP curve there is a BOP deficit and to the left a BOP surplus. The BP curve shifts right with depreciation or devaluation $e\uparrow$ higher foreign income Y^*, or a higher foreign interest rate r^*. A flatter BP curve indicates a higher degree of international capital mobility since less of an increase in r is required to offset an increase in Y. With *perfect international capital mobility*, the BP curve is flat at the international interest rate r^* and international capital is readily available to keep $BOP = 0$.

EXAMPLE 13.12   *The Ups and Downs of the US BOP*

During the 1800s the US was a growing debtor country with a capital account KA surplus and current account CA deficit. Foreign investment went into railroads, infrastructure, and agriculture. By the late 1800s output had climbed

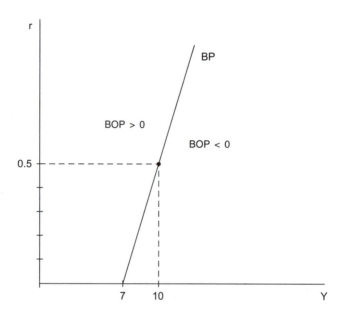

Figure 13.10
The BOP curve
The *BOP* curve shows combinations of *Y* and *r* where *BOP* = 0. To the right of the curve, *Y* is too high (*r* is too low) and *BOP* < 0. To the left of the *BP* curve, *BOP* > 0.

and there was a *CA* surplus. Following the Great Depression and two World Wars, there was a *KA* deficit as the US invested in reconstructing Europe and Japan. Investment income then led to a *CA* surplus up to 1980. Since that time, increased import spending on oil and consumer goods has outpaced exports of resource based production, high tech manufactures, and business services. The net result is a *CA* deficit and the associated *KA* surplus.

The Open ISLMBP Economy

The IS, LM, and BP curves jointly determine the interest rate *r*, national income *Y*, and either the exchange rate *e* or the money supply M_s in the open economy. If the exchange rate *e* is floating, it is market determined by the ISLMBP equilibrium. If it is "fixed" by the government, the money supply is forced to adjust in the macro equilibrium.

Figure 13.11 shows the open economy equilibrium at point A where the IS, LM, and BP curves intersect. If the economy is not at point A, adjustments lead *r*, *Y* and either *e* or M_S toward the macro equilibrium. There are various degrees of exchange rate fixing and market intervention, and to the extent that exchange rate *e* is not allowed to adjust the money supply M_s must.

There are automatic market adjustments toward the macro equilibrium in the product, money, and international markets. For instance, if *Y* = 10 but *r* = .04 at

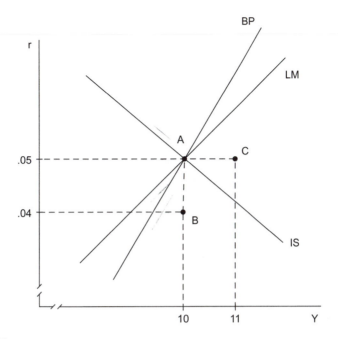

Figure 13.11
The ISLMBP macro model
The IS, LM, and BP curves combine into the ISLMBP model. At point A, the product, money, and international markets are in equilibrium.

point B in Figure 13.11, there is excess demand for output below the IS curve, excess demand for money to the right of the LM curve, and a *BOP* deficit to the right of the BP curve. A rising interest rate helps to resolve these imbalances, lowering the demand for money and raising the capital account. The excess demand for money at point B is equivalent to an excess supply of bonds, pushing the price of bonds down (the interest rate up). A higher interest rate attracts foreign investment raising the *BOP*. Market forces push the economy toward point A although the path may not be a straight one since the rising interest rate lowers investment spending and output.

Adjustment paths toward the macro equilibrium vary depending on how markets in the economy adjust. From point C where $Y = 11$ and $r = .05$, there is excess supply of output, excess demand for money, and a *BOP* deficit. The interest rate rises to eliminate both the excess demand for money and the *BOP* deficit, and output falls to eliminate the excess supply of output. The economy moves toward the macro equilibrium at point A. The *BOP* deficit also causes exchange rate depreciation with a market exchange rate. If the exchange rate is fixed, the *BOP* deficit causes the money supply to fall.

Adjustment paths and mechanisms depend on the *foreign exchange and international financial systems*. These macro adjustment processes are the essence of macro forecasting models used by financial firms, international agencies, and government officials. The track record of macro forecasting models is reasonably good. The more successful models are run by private firms in their financial advising. No model, however, can anticipate arbitrary changes in government policy.

EXAMPLE 13.13   *A Recent History of the Dollar and the BOT*

The history of the dollar exchange rate $1/e$ with a weighted 1973 index of 100 is shown below along with the *BOT* in $1992. During the 1950s the US generally had a *BOT* surplus. With its fixed Bretton Woods exchange rate, foreign exchange reserves and gold holding expanded. Starting in the late 1950s there was a growing *BOT* deficit through 1973, with foreign currencies, gold, and other assets depleting. When the dollar was cut loose from its price in gold, the fixed exchange rate system collapsed. The dollar depreciated and the *BOT* deficit began to shrink. After a brief turnaround in 1975 the dollar depreciated in the late 1970s and by 1980 there was a *BOT* surplus. Starting in 1981 the dollar appreciated sharply and the *BOT* fell into deficit. Then in 1986, these trends reversed with the dollar depreciating and the *BOT* climbing back toward zero. In the early 1990s the *BOT* deficit began to grow with increased spending on oil and cheap labor intensive imports in NAFTA and WTO. The subsequent depreciation up to 2004 was insufficient to reverse the growing *BOT* deficit.

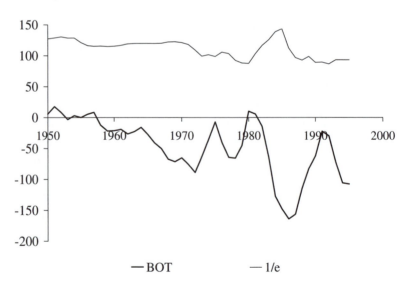

Monetary Policy with a Flexible Exchange Rate

Expansionary monetary policy shifts the LM curve out to the right, moving the economy from point A to B in Figure 13.12. In the new domestic equilibrium to

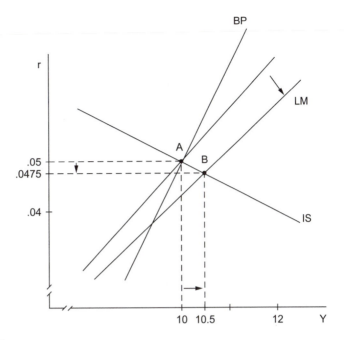

Figure 13.12
Expansionary monetary policy
An increase in the money supply shifts the LM curve right moving the economy from point A to B where there is a *BOP* deficit. With a flexible exchange rate the currency depreciates, shifting the BP curve out to point B. The monetary expansion has the same effects on r and Y with a flexible exchange rate as in a closed economy. With a fixed exchange rate the money supply diminishes, returning the economy to its original position at point A. The monetary expansion has no effect with a fixed exchange rate.

the right of the BP curve there is a *BOP* deficit. The domestic markets clear at point B but the international market is out of balance and there is subsequent adjustment.

The shift to point B is the same as in Figure 13.8. A 10% increase in M_S lowers r from .05 to .0475 and raises Y from 10 to 10.5. At point B there is a *BOP* deficit with the economy to the right of the BP curve. According to the *BOP* function at point B, $BOP = 1 - .14Y + 8r = -.09$ and there is a *BOP* deficit of $90 billion.

With a *flexible exchange rate*, depreciation $e\uparrow$ raises the *BGS* shifting the BP curve to point B. In the example, the *BGS* of −$400 billion has to rise by $90 billion to return the *BOP* to zero. In percentage terms, this is a 90/400 = 22.5% increase in the *BGS*. If the elasticity of the *BGS* with respect to the exchange rate equals one, depreciation of 22.5% returns the *BOP* to zero. At the new equilibrium, the *BGS* will be −$310 billion and there will be an associated *KA* surplus of $310 billion.

With a flexible exchange rate, the effects of the monetary expansion are a lower interest rate, increased investment spending, a lower capital account, higher output, exchange rate depreciation, a higher balance on goods and services, and a decrease in the capital account. Home investment increases relative to foreign investment. Capital and labor markets adjust exactly as in the closed economy.

Policy makers may be under pressure, however, not to let the currency depreciate. Import prices rise with depreciation. More expensive imported intermediate products put pressure on domestic producers, some of them exporters. Consumers do not like higher prices of imported consumer products. Import competing producers in other countries would complain about the increased competition due to the *appreciation* of their currency. Depreciation also discourages foreign investment since earnings are discounted when converted back to foreign currency.

Exchange market intervention is the rule following expansionary monetary policy. Governments would like to be able to increase the money supply with no depreciation but that is impossible. The possibility of government intervention in the foreign exchange market to support domestic currency leads to market uncertainty, unpredictable market reactions, and erratic exchange rate movements. Traders focus more on government policy than underlying market fundamentals. Unlike private traders, the government has no profit motive in the foreign exchange market making its moves difficult to predict.

With flexible exchange rates, monetary expansion leads to a lower interest rate and higher output exactly as in a closed economy. The currency depreciates causing an increase in the balance on goods and services. The capital account declines with the lower interest rate.

EXAMPLE 13.14 *Money Growth and the Exchange Rate*

No single variable will explain changes in the exchange rate but there is no doubt that over long periods of time money supply growth has a fundamental effect. The chart below tracks money supply growth and a trade weighted index of the dollar (1973 = 10). Exchange rates were fixed in the Bretton Woods system from 1950 to the early 1973 and little variation occurred in the exchange rate. With the advent of floating exchange rates, the rising money supply growth led to depreciation up to 1981. During the oil crises of the early 1980s the dollar was a safe haven and investors increased demand for dollars. Beginning in 1986 the dollar depreciating up to 1990 and has held constant since. Monetary policy should limit money supply growth to the proven rate of increase in real output in order to eliminate inflation. If trading partners followed suit, exchange rates would stabilize according to purchasing power parity. The erratic monetary policy illustrated by the high variation in money supply growth now leads to uncertainty regarding the exchange rate.

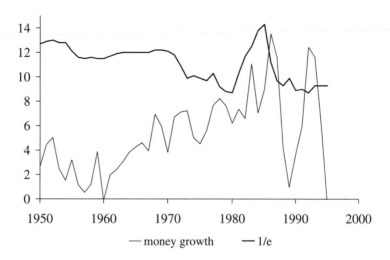

— money growth   — 1/e

Monetary Policy with a Fixed Exchange Rate

With a fixed exchange rate, the monetary expansion and *BOP* deficit at point B in Figure 13.12 lead to a decrease in the money supply. The economy spends more on imports than it makes on exports and its cash is depleted. With the money supply leakage, the LM curve shifts back to the left and the economy returns to its original point A. Monetary expansion is ineffective with a fixed exchange rate, creating a temporary *BOP* deficit and international cash outflow.

A government with a fixed exchange rate may not want to "play by the rules" of a fixed exchange rate system. It may instead increase the money supply to offset the cash outflow due to the *BOP* deficit at point B. Looking closer, M_S is a multiple μ of the sum of central bank credit C_{BC} and foreign exchange reserves FX_R,

$$M_S = \mu(C_{BC} + FX_R).$$

With a fixed exchange rate, the *BOP* deficit at point B drains FX_R lowering M_S. The offsetting increase in C_{BC} is called *sterilization* of the *BOP* deficit.

Another way to force expansionary monetary policy is to restrict the international cash flow. In many countries, domestic investors are not allowed to buy foreign bonds or other assets. These types of investment restrictions, however, discourage international investment and keep incomes low. With a fixed exchange rate the government has to accept that there is no independent monetary policy, an important lesson for hundreds of small countries.

In an open economy with a fixed exchange rate, expansionary monetary policy has no permanent effect on output or the interest rate. There is a temporary balance of payments deficit and international cash outflow. With a fixed exchange rate there is no independent monetary policy.

EXAMPLE 13.15 *Price Level Differences and Real Exchange Rates*

When price levels differ across countries, real exchange rates may be critical in the macro adjustment process. Price levels in fact vary quite a bit across countries, even for the countries in the OECD. High income and demand raise prices for nontraded goods and services, and also leads to price discrimination for traded products. These price indices range from over 104 to less than ¼ that level, and price levels in LDCs are much lower. Price level differences imply the real exchange rate eP^*/P differs from the nominal rate e.

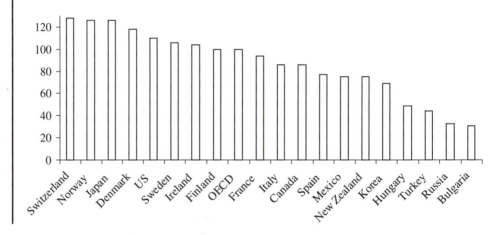

Fiscal Policy with a Flexible Exchange Rate

Expansionary fiscal policy expands the domestic economy but creates a balance of payments deficit. The IS curve shifts to the right leading to the *BOP* deficit pictured in Figure 13.13. For simplicity start with $G = T = 0$ and let G increase by 1% of GDP or $100 billion in the example. Output Y increases from $10 to $10.5 trillion and the interest rate r rises from 5% to 5.125% as in Figure 13.8. The shift in the IS curve moves the economy from its initial equilibrium at point A to the new domestic equilibrium at point B with a *BOP* deficit to the right of the BP curve.

The government deficit generated by the increased spending leads to a balance of payments deficit, called the *twin deficits*. Governments that run fiscal deficits generate *BOP* deficits. Decreasing taxes has the same effect of shifting the IS curve to the right and creating a *BOP* deficit. Subsequent adjustment depends on the exchange rate system.

With a *flexible exchange rate*, the *BOP* deficit at point B causes depreciation $e\uparrow$ and a shift of the BP schedule to point B. Fiscal policy works with a flexible exchange rate and the currency depreciates. In the BP curve $BOP = 1 - .14Y + 8r$, the *BOP* deficit at point B is −$60 billion. Depreciation raises the *BGS* from

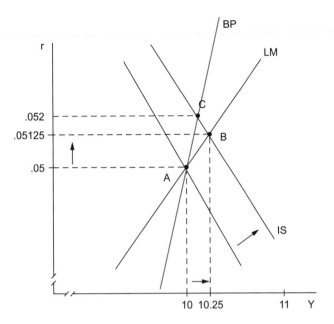

Figure 13.13
Expansionary Fiscal Policy
An increase in government spending or a decrease in taxes shifts the IS curve out moving the economy from point A to B where there is a trade deficit. With a flexible exchange rate, the currency depreciates shifting the BP curve out to point B, and the fiscal policy is effective. With a fixed exchange rate, the money supply falls shifting the LM curve in and moving the economy to point C. Fiscal policy has a larger effect on the interest rate but a smaller effect on output relative to a closed economy.

−$400 billion to −$340 billion, an increase of 60/400 = 15%, to return the *BOP* to zero. If the BGS elasticity of the exchange rate equals one, a depreciation of 15% returns the *BOP* to zero. The capital account increases by $60 billion with the higher interest rate.

> With a floating exchange rate, expansionary fiscal policy raises national income but has side effects. The interest rate rises, lowering investment, the capital/labor ratio, and the wage. There is a balance of payments deficit that has to be corrected by depreciation. The higher interest rate attracts foreign investment that displaces domestic investment.

EXAMPLE 13.16 *Dollar Depreciation, 2003*

The US trade deficit narrowed in November 2003 as civilian aircraft and capital good exports led a 3% jump in export revenue (*Reuters*, January 2004). Exports had been rising steadily with the dollar depreciation. Concern over the US government deficit is credited with causing the depreciation during 2003. EU policymakers meanwhile were concerned that the euro appreciation would stifle an export led recovery, expressing a desire to work with other central banks to appreciate the dollar. The dollar depreciation continued through 2004 but turned around by the summer of 2005 when the proposed EU constitution did not pass a popular vote.

Fiscal Policy with a Fixed Exchange Rate

With a fixed exchange rate, expansionary fiscal policy leads to a *BOP* deficit that cannot be corrected by depreciation. The fixed exchange rate can be *devalued* but that makes the currency floating but at government direction. At point B in Figure 13.13 there is a *BOP* deficit caused by the expansionary fiscal policy.

The macro solution is for the money supply M_S to decrease as the economy spends more than it makes internationally. The fall in the money supply shifts the LM curve left to point C. With a fixed exchange rate, the fiscal expansion leads to an offsetting monetary contraction.

In the example there is a *BOP* deficit of −$60 billion and M_S falls by this amount, from $1.3 to $1.24 trillion. In percentage terms, this is a money supply reduction of .06/1.3 = 4.6%. From point B to point C in Figure 13.13, r rises from 5.1% to 5.2% and Y falls from $10.2 to $10.1 trillion along the new IS curve. From the original equilibrium, the *BGS* falls $14 billion due to increased imports and the *KA* rises by that amount due to the higher domestic interest rate.

Relative to a closed economy, the fiscal expansion creates less of an increase in output but more of an increase in the interest rate. This higher interest rate implies more of a decrease in investment spending, a lower capital/labor ration, a lower wage, and slower economic growth. The higher domestic interest rate attracts more foreign investment.

Total investment, domestic plus foreign, falls due to a fiscal expansion with a fixed exchange rate. At point C with $r = 5.2\%$ in Figure 13.13, domestic investment falls to $1.92 trillion along the investment schedule in Figure 13.2. This decrease of $80 billion in domestic investment is less than completely offset by the $14 billion increase in foreign investment, and total investment falls by $64 billion. Foreign investment only partly replaces domestic investment and economic growth slows.

Expansionary fiscal policy may, however, temporarily lower unemployment. It is no accident that governments increase spending as election time approaches, part of the *political business cycle*. Investment, however, is the only proven path to higher income. Expansionary fiscal policy may increase output but it lowers investment and economic growth. There are also issues of government debt and future tax liabilities, making expansionary fiscal policy even less attractive.

With a fixed exchange rate, expansionary fiscal policy raises output but causes a temporary balance of payments deficit decreasing the money supply. The interest rate rises and domestic investment falls. Foreign investment increases but total investment, the wage, and income per capita fall.

EXAMPLE 13.17   *China's Fixed Exchange Rate*

China has begun a process of opening to the world economy as reflected by its growing export revenue and import spending relative to GDP. One indication of its potential role in the world economy is that the rising international price of oil due to increased demand in China. Foreign investment is funding the transition from state command and control to a more open country with free markets and more reasonable property rights, but the process is not quick or easy. As an example, in 2005 China still maintained a fixed exchange rate. If the currency is undervalued, Chinese products are cheaper abroad and export revenue is artificially high. The disadvantage of the fixed exchange rate is that China has no independent monetary policy and fiscal expansions have a magnified effect on the interest rate.

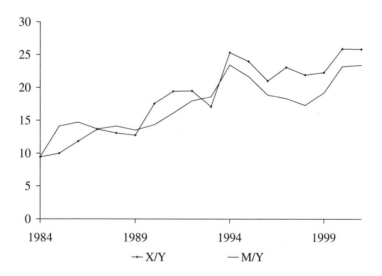

Competitive Devaluation

Competitive devaluation of a fixed exchange rate generates a trade surplus, raises national income, and lowers the interest rate but there are negative side effects. First of all, devaluation for the home country is *revaluation* for the foreign country with exactly the opposite effects, and *policy retaliation* can be expected.

Devaluation shifts the BP in Figure 13.14 to the right. The economy remains in domestic equilibrium at point A but there is a *BOP* surplus. The *BOP* surplus

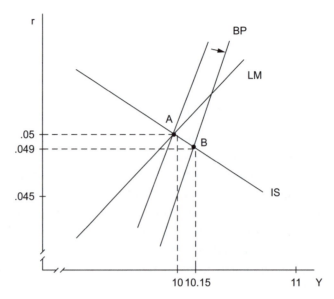

Figure 13.14
A Competitive Devaluation
A competitive devaluation shifts the BP curve out creating a trade surplus at point A. Foreign exchange reserves and the money supply increase, shifting the LM curve out to point B. The competitive devaluation stimulates output and lowers the interest rate but has the opposite effects on the foreign country.

increases the money supply sticking with the fixed exchange rate, leading to a subsequent outward shift in the LM curve and moving the economy to a new equilibrium at point B.

In the example with the exchange rate elasticity of the *BGS* equal to one, a 10% competitive depreciation generates a 10% increase in the *BGS*. The 10% devaluation raises the *BGS* from −$400 to −$360 billion. The money supply increases from $1.3 to $1.34 trillion given the money market equilibrium condition $M_S = 1.3 + .13Y - 26r$. At the resulting point B, national income Y increases from $10 to $10.15 trillion and the interest rate s falls from 5% to 4.9% along the IS curve.

The foreign country has a *revaluation* with exactly the opposite effects: a trade deficit, decreased money supply, lower national income, and a higher interest rate. Countries can become entangled in competitive devaluations and retaliations. If one country devalues and the other retaliates with a devaluation of its own, there is no change in the fixed exchange rate. Ultimately there is no effect except to create confusion that discourages international trade and investment. There are negative long term consequences if traders and investors pay more attention to government policy makers than market fundamentals.

Small open economies with fixed exchange rates may enjoy apparent success with competitive devaluations but market adjustments are disruptive, there is no prospect for continued success, and foreign retaliation can be expected.

Inflation typically occurs alongside devaluation. The increased output and lower real interest rate in Figure 13.14 assume there is no inflation. Price levels rise following competitive devaluation and inflation lessens its positive effects.

> *Competitive devaluation of a fixed exchange rate, holding the price level constant, increases output, investment, the money supply, and the trade balance. The effects are exactly the opposite in partner countries, however, and associated inflation lessens the positive effects.*

EXAMPLE 13.18 *The Exchange Rate in Korea*

Korea is an open economy that has developed rapidly over recent decades. This chart illustrates the history of its exchange rate *e*, balance of trade *BOT*, and *GDP*. The trade balance is in 1995 $billions and *GDP* in $10 billions for visual comparison, and the exchange rate is trade weighted. In the late 1970s, the won appreciated (a falling *e*) and the *BOT* fell. When the won depreciated in 1979 the *BOT* increased until 1986. The won then appreciated sharply and the *BOT* soon fell. In 1996 the won sharply depreciated with the Asian crisis and the *BOT* began a steady climb. This chart suggests the exchange rate has an effect of the *BOT* but through all of this, *GDP* rose fairly steadily with a blip during the Asian crisis. A complete model and statistical analysis are required to reach a conclusion but the exchange rate does not appear to have had an influence on *GDP* in Korea. The effects of devaluation or depreciation on *GDP* in Figure 13.14 are apparently small in Korea.

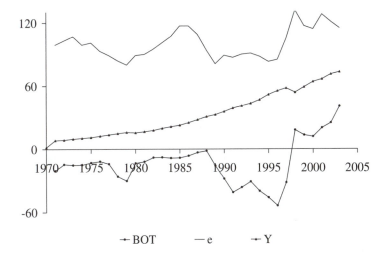

EXAMPLE 13.19 *Exchange Rate Risk and Asian Exports*

Depreciation should affect trade and raise export revenue, but the risk associated with increased exchange rate volatility can discourage trade. WenShwo Fang, YiHao Li, and Henry Thompson (2005) find evidence of negative risk effects in 3 of 8 Asian countries using monthly data during the years 1979–2002. The currencies all depreciated on average, from 1% to 5% on a yearly basis. Risk measured as the standard deviation of the monthly percentage changes ranges from 2% to 7%. The chart below shows that the small yearly effects of depreciation on export revenue in Singapore, Taiwan, and Japan were outweighed by large risk effects. The units are percent effect on export revenue per year. The Philippines, Thailand, and Indonesia gained about 2% export revenue per year due to depreciation. Risk had no impact in Malaysia, the Philippines, Thailand, and Indonesia in spite of their higher risk levels. Singapore and Taiwan had the lowest risk but the highest risk effects, almost 8% per year in Singapore. Traders who are not used to exchange volatility are apparently the most vulnerable to its effects. When present, risk effects dominate the positive effect of depreciation. In Korea, risk had a positive effect on export revenue.

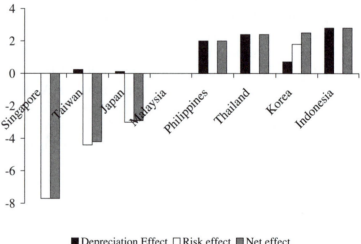

■ Depreciation Effect □ Risk effect ■ Net effect

Problems for Section C

C1. Suppose investment $I = 2$, government spending $G = 1$, absorption $A = 11$, export revenue $X = 6$, and national income $Y = 15$. Find consumption spending C, import spending M, and the BGS. Find the real exchange rate if the home price level $P = 1.1$ and foreign $P^* = 1.5$.

C2. Derive the open economy IS equation $\sigma Y = A - C + BGS$ from the national income equation.

C3. Show and explain the effect on the BP curve of
(a) an increase in foreign income Y^*
(b) an increase in the foreign interest rate r^*
(c) a revaluation of the domestic currency.
C4. Show and explain the effects of a decrease in the money supply in the open ISLMBP economy with
(a) a flexible exchange rate
(b) a fixed exchange rate.

EXAMPLE 13.20 *Dollar Depreciation and US Tourism*

The weak US dollar during the 2000s has made travel to the US a bargain but foreign tourists are not taking advantage (Barbara De Lollis, USA TODAY, 31 March 2005). "We should be doing better than we are, based on the sale that the US is having," says Roger Dow, CEO of the Travel Industry Association. The US share of international travelers declined from 8% in 1994 to 6% in 2004 but with a worldwide increase of 37%. There is increasing competition from new destinations such as Dubai, Budapest, and China. US foreign policy makes the US "less cool" for younger travelers says Cari Eggspuehler of Business for Diplomatic Action, and tight security discourages travelers. "As a country, we simply have not been out there promoting the US like Australia, New Zealand, and even Jamaica and Aruba," says James Rasulo, President of Disney's Parks and Resorts. The bottom line is that the demand for US tourism is declining, outpacing the effect of the falling price due to depreciation. Such declining demand for exports shifts the BP curve in Figure 13.14 to the left.

D. INFLATION, THE EXCHANGE RATE, AND MACRO POLICY

The ISLMBP model assumes the price level does not change but inflation is often the direct result of expansionary policy. Inflation is an increase in the price level P. In the open economy, inflation lowers the real money supply M_S/P and shifts the LM curve to the left. Inflation also depreciates the real exchange rate, raising the price of exports relative to imports. Inflation raises the nominal interest rate and discourages international investment. The present section examines the effects of inflation on the macro economy in a model of *aggregate supply and demand*.

The Monetary Model of the Exchange Rate

On the monetary side of the economy, the real money supply M_S/P equals demand for cash balances $L(Y, r)$. The nominal money supply M_S is deflated by the price level P to find the real money supply. If P rises with M_S constant, the real money supply decreases and currency loses its power to purchase products.

The *monetary model of the exchange rate* is based on this money market equilibrium. *Purchasing power parity* $P = eP^*$ holds with free trade and the same prices for nontraded products across countries, making the exchange rate the ratio of price levels $e = P/P^*$. Money market equilibrium holds at home and in the foreign country, $M_S^*/P^* = L^*(Y^*, r^*)$. Solving for the price levels, $P = M_S/L$ and $P^* = M_S^*/L^*$, making the exchange rate a ratio of money supplies and demands

$$e = M_S L^*/M_S^* L.$$

Money demands L and L^* depend on incomes and interest rates, making the exchange rate a function of relative home variables

$$e = e(\overset{+}{M_S/M_S^*},\ \overset{-}{Y/Y^*},\ \overset{+}{r/r^*}).$$

An increase in the supply of home money M_S relative to M_S^* depreciates the exchange rate, one of the most accepted principles in international economics. The effects of changes in Y and r, however, differ in this monetary model from the ISLMBP model.

In the ISLMBP model, an increase in Y raises import spending, leading to a *BOP* deficit and depreciation with a floating exchange rate. In the monetary model, an increase in Y raises the demand for cash and appreciates the currency. The two theories are both correct but they focus on different aspects of the economy and hold other things constant.

A complete macro model includes the influences of income on both import spending and money demand, and the net effect on the exchange rate depends on which is stronger. Empirical tests can determine which effect holds under which circumstances. Generally rising income and appreciation go together as in the monetary model of the exchange rate.

Another difference is the effect of a change in the interest rate r. In the ISLMBP model an increase in r raises the capital account, increases demand for home currency by foreign investors, and appreciates the currency. In the monetary model, an increase in r lowers the demand for domestic cash and depreciates the currency. The monetary model disregards international investment, and the ISLMBP model disregards domestic liquidity demand. The complete macro model allows both effects, and the stronger effect dominates.

In practice, the interest rate effects are weak or offsetting, and the interest rate has little effect on the exchange rate. Empirical evidence is difficult to accumulate for a number of reasons. The real interest rate r is not observed directly since it depends on expected inflation. Exchange rate reaction to real interest rates may not be immediate, making it difficult to uncover in the data. Also, both interest and exchange rates are continually adjusting to exogenous changes in the economy.

An increase in the relative domestic money supply depreciates the currency. The effects on income and the interest rate depend on the strengths of domestic liquidity demand versus international trade and investment. Higher income and appreciation go together over long time periods. The connection between interest and exchange rates is weak.

EXAMPLE 13.21 *Long Term US/UK PPP*

PPP has been tested numerous times using different techniques and data. PPP would hold if all goods were freely traded, countries produced and consumed similar products, and exchange rates were free. William Crowder (1996) presents evidence that a long run equilibrium relationship holds between US dollars and UK pounds from 1900 to 1991 and a weaker relationship holds between Canadian and US dollars. In the long run, P and eP^* tend to move together. The strict proposition that $P = eP^*$ does not hold due to variations in measuring price indices, nontraded goods, and managed exchange rates. The presence of the long run relationship, however, reflects the presence of PPP.

Aggregate Demand and Supply

The *aggregate supply and demand ASAD model* introduces the price level and inflation to the ISLMBP model. The *aggregate demand curve* shows combinations of the price level P and income Y where there is ISLM equilibrium.

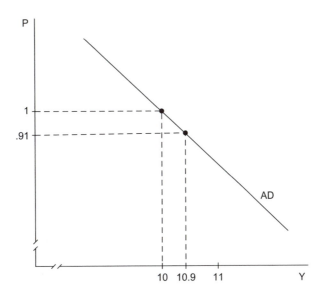

Figure 13.15
The Aggregate Demand Curve
The AD curve slopes down since a falling P raises the real money supply M_S/P increasing income Y in the ISLM model. Moving down the AD curve with a lower P, r rises in the ISLM model and w falls in the production function. Contractionary policy shifts the AD curve left, lowering output at the present price level.

A decrease in the price level P raises the real money supply M_S/P and shifts the LM curve to the right. A fall in the price level from $P = 1$ to 0.91 shifts the LM curve exactly as in Figure 13.8 with the real interest rate falling from 5% to 4.75% and Y rising from 10 to 10.5 along the IS curve.

The *aggregate demand curve* AD in Figure 13.15 shows the incomes Y that go with price levels P and the shifting LM curve. Along the AD curve there is ISLM equilibrium. The linear AD function in Figure 13.14 is $P = 2.8 - .18Y$ from the example. Moving up the AD curve, the LM curves shifts left, the real interest rate r increases, and the wage w falls along the production function. Expansionary fiscal and monetary policies shift the AD curve right, increasing output in the ISLM model.

The upward sloping *aggregate supply curve* in Figure 13.16 relies on price misperceptions among firms and workers. Multiply the price level P by real output Y to find nominal output $Y_N = PY$. An increase in P raises Y_N and the nominal revenue of firms. When P increases, firms do not notice associated cost increases and raise output perceiving an opportunity for profit. Given slack in the input markets, Y increases. Such an increase would be temporary but that is how higher P leads to a higher Y along the AS curve. The plotted AS curve $P = .1Y$ assumes a 1% increase in P results in a 1% increase in Y.

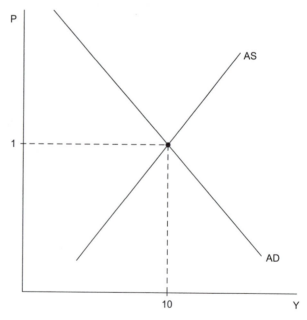

Figure 13.16
The ASAD Economy
The aggregate supply and demand ASAD model determines the price level P and national income Y. The AD curve captures the money and product markets in the ISLM model. The AS curve slopes upward if firms, workers, and investors misread changing prices of output and inputs. Approaching full employment, the AS curve becomes vertical.

There is also misperception of earning potential by workers and investors. Firms wanting to increase output offer higher wages, encouraging an increase in the quantity of labor supplied. Workers notice the higher wage but do not realize the price level is increasing and the real wage w/P is constant. Workers are tricked into working by the higher nominal wage. Similarly, investors are tricked into supplying too much capital.

The ASAD economy has an equilibrium at the intersection of the AS and AD curves, in the example at $P = 1$ and $Y = 10$. If the economy is near full employment, there is no slack in the input markets and the AS curve is vertical.

The Macroeconomics of Aggregate Supply and Demand in the Open Economy

The price level affects the balance of trade through the *price adjusted exchange rate* $e_p = eP^*/P$. The *BOP* function is then

$$BOP = B(\overset{+}{e_p}, \bar{Y}) = 0$$

with a positive effect for the price adjusted exchange rate $e_p = eP^*/P$ and a negative effect for Y. A higher price level P raises the relative price of

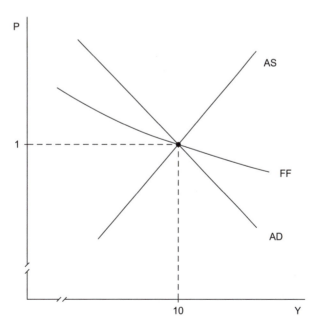

Figure 13.17
The ASADFF Model
The FF curve shows combinations of P and Y where $BOP = 0$. A higher P is offset by a lower Y to keep $BOP = 0$. The open economy P and Y are determined where the AS, AD, and FF curves intersect.

home products lowering *BOP*. A higher *Y* raises import spending *M* and lowers *BOP*.

The *FF curve* in Figure 13.17 shows combinations of *P* and *Y* with external balance where *BOP* = 0. It has negative slope since an increase in *P* lowers the *BOP* and requires a reduction in *Y* to return to external balance at *BOP* = 0.

With a constant *marginal propensity to import*, the additional import spending per dollar of income, the average propensity to import *M/Y* is constant. In the example, *M/Y* = 0.14. If $e = P^* = 1$ the FF curve is then $BOP = 1.4/P - .14Y = 0$. Figure 13.17 shows the internal and external equilibrium where the AS, AD, and FF curves intersect in the ASADFF model.

Expansionary fiscal or monetary policies shift the AD curve to the right as in Figure 13.18, raising output and the price level and causing a *BOP* deficit in the move from point A to B. The 10% increase in *Y* and 10% inflation in the example could be the result of either an increase in the money supply M_S or an increase in government spending *G*. The *BOP* deficit at point B requires adjustment either through depreciation with a flexible exchange rate or a decrease in the money supply with a fixed exchange rate.

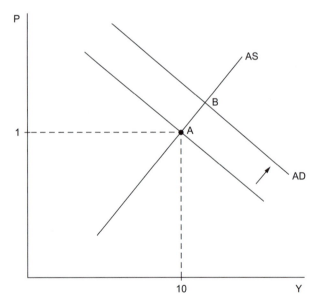

Figure 13.18
Expansionary Policy in the ASADFF Model
Expansionary monetary or fiscal policies shift the AD curve right, moving the economy from point A to B and raising the price level *P*. Output *Y* increases except near full employment with a vertical AS curve. With a flexible exchange rate, the currency depreciates due to the *BOP* deficit and the FF curve shifts out to point B. With a fixed exchange rate, the nominal money supply M_S decreases and the AD curve shifts back to point A.

With a flexible exchange rate, depreciation shifts the FF curve in Figure 13.18 out to point B. Expansionary fiscal policy raises the real interest rate r along the LM curve and the price level P along the AS curve. With inflation π, the Fisher equation $r = i - \pi$ implies the nominal interest rate i increases more than the real interest rate r. Expansionary monetary policy lowers the real interest rate r and the nominal interest rate i could increase but by less than inflation π.

With a fixed exchange rate, the *BOP* deficit at point B leads to a decrease in the money supply and a return toward the original macro equilibrium at point A. With expansionary monetary policy, the economy returns all the way to point A and there is no effect on Y or P exactly as in the ISLM model in Figure 13.12. Expansionary fiscal policy leads to a higher P shifting the FF curve right and raising Y and r, consistent with the ISLM model in Figure 13.13. The increase in Y is less than with expansionary monetary policy since government spending crowds out investment. Also, the increase in r is larger than with a flexible exchange rate.

Expansionary policy leads to inflation and a balance of payment deficit. With a flexible exchange rate, there is depreciation and higher output. With a fixed exchange rate, the external deficit reduces the money supply and there is no increase in output.

Macroeconomic Policy and Inflation in the Open Economy

Table 13.1 summarizes the macro effects of monetary and fiscal policy. The positive output effects assume the aggregate supply curve slopes upward. Near full employment, the Y effects are all close to zero.

There are sound reasons governments should shy away from fiscal and monetary policy to manage the macro economy:

- Nominal interest rates are sensitive to fiscal policy and changes disrupt investment and growth
- Inflation uncertainty disrupts commerce

Table 13.1 Macro Policy and Inflation

	e	Y	r	π	i
Monetary expansion					
Floating e	↑	↑*	↓	↑	↓ (or ↑ but less than π)
Fixed e	0	0	0	0	0
Fiscal expansion					
Floating e	↑	↑*	↑	↑	↑ (more than r ↑)
Fixed e	0	↑*	↑**	↑	↑ (more than r ↑)

*Close to zero near full employment

**Larger than with floating e

- Agents become preoccupied with government policy instead of economic conditions
- Policies with positive effects in one country have opposite effects on partner countries
- Positive impacts rely on slack in input markets and price misperceptions
- Near full employment output cannot increase

For many reasons, sound economic advice is to avoid active macroeconomic policy. The economy cannot be effectively "managed" by fiscal and monetary policy. Government spending projects should have to pass a benefit/cost test. Taxes should be set according to objective goals of income redistribution. Monetary policy should target zero inflation.

Problems for Section D

D1. Explain how an increase in the foreign money supply affects the exchange rate in the monetary model.

D2. Show the effects of expansionary policy on output and the price level in a closed economy with full employment.

D3. Show what happens in the ASADFF economy with a competitive devaluation.

D4. Show the effects of money supply contraction on output, the price level, and interest rates when with a floating exchange rate. Contrast these adjustments with a fixed exchange rate.

CONCLUSION

Macro policy is ineffective in influencing international trade, investment, and exchange rates. Similar to trade policy, macro policy is designed for the special interests influencing the political process and the policy makers themselves want to perpetuate their position. Governments can play a positive role by defining and enforcing property rights, redistributing income in a transparent political process, and supplying money with no inflation. The basic lesson of international economics is that competitive international markets are efficient and should be allowed to operate free of obtrusive government policy.

Terms

Absorption	ISLMBP open economy
Appreciation	Liquidity demand

ASAD closed economy	Monetary policy
ASADFF open economy	Monetary model of the exchange rate
BOP function	National income
Crowding out	Neoclassical macro production function
Depreciation	Overlapping generations model of saving
Devaluation	Perpetuity bond
Economic growth	Political business cycle
Fiscal policy	Real exchange rate
Fixed exchange rates	Ricardian equivalence
Floating exchange rates	Saving rate
Inflation	Sterilization
Investment function	Twin deficits
ISLM closed economy	

MAIN POINTS

- The microeconomic foundations of macroeconomics are the neoclassical aggregate production function and optimal saving in the overlapping generations model.
- The ISLM model includes the investment-saving IS product market and the liquidity-money LM market, and determines the interest rate and output consistent with the product and money markets. Holding the price level constant, the ISLM model shows the effects of fiscal and monetary policies.
- The open economy ISLMBP model adds the balance of payments and allows adjustment in the floating exchange rate or money supply with a fixed exchange rate. The effects of monetary and fiscal policies differ in an open economy compared to the closed ISLM economy.
- The monetary model of the exchange rate focuses on money markets across countries and the effects on the exchange rate through money demand and supply. The aggregate supply and demand ASADFF model includes the effects of inflation and shows that positive policy effects are dampened by inflation.

REVIEW PROBLEMS

1. Similar to Figure 13.1, diagram the production function $y = 10k^{.4}$ with $k = \$1000$. Indicate income per capita y and the wage w when $r = 6.3\% = .063$ and sketch the production function.

2. In the economy of Problem #1, suppose the growth rate of labor is 1% and the saving rate

is σ is 20%. What information is required to determine whether the economy is growing along its production function?

3. The economy of Problem #1 grows until the capital labor ratio k is constant at the steady state $k^* = 2188$. Find the steady state income

per capita y^*. Given the steady state interest rate $r^* = 4\% = .04$, find w^*.

4. Explain the labor and capital market changes in Problem #3. Use changes in supply and demand to illustrate what happens in the two markets as the economy grows.

5. Explain the changes in y, w, and r due to:
   (a) a decrease in the saving rate
   (b) improved technology
   (c) foreign investment
   (d) increased immigration

6. In the overlapping generations OLG model, suppose the wage in youth is $50,000 and the interest rate is 10%. Diagram the intertemporal budget line and find consumption in retirement if $40,000 is consumed in youth.

7. If the interest rate in Problem #6 falls from 10% to 5%, explain what will happen to the saving rate and consumption in both periods.

8. Find the level of saving that would equate consumption in youth and retirement in Problem #5 when $r = 10\%$.

9. Explain what happens in the capital and labor markets when the interest rate rises and the economy moves up along its IS curve.

10. Suppose there is a decrease in the money supply M_s in the ISLM model. Explain the underlying adjustments in the capital and labor markets.

11. Explain the labor and capital market effects of an increase in taxes T. Show the adjustment in the ISLM model along the production function and the IS curve.

12. Show and explain the effects of an increase in taxes in an open ISLMBP economy with
   (a) a flexible exchange rate
   (b) a fixed exchange rate

13. Show and explain the effects of a decrease in the money supply in an open ISLMBP economy with
   (a) a flexible exchange rate
   (b) a fixed exchange rate

14. Show how an increase in foreign income Y^* affects output and the price level in the ASADFF model. What happens to real and nominal interest rates?

15. Contrast the effects of a decrease in the money supply on output in the ISLMBP and ASADFF models.

16. Show the effects of expansionary policy on output and the price level in an open economy when there is full employment.

17. Explain the adjustment due to a sharp depreciation of the flexible exchange rate in the ASADFF model.

18. Explain why depreciation and inflation occur together in the ASADFF economy.

READINGS

Nelson Mark (2001) *International Macroeconomics and Finance*, Blackwell. A short advanced text on theory and application.

Robert Hall and David Papell (2005) *Macroeconomics: Economic Growth, Fluctuations, and Policy*, Norton. Macro text with an international slant.

Maurice Obsfeld and Kenneth Rogoff (1997) *Foundations of International Macroeconomics*, MIT Press. A thorough advanced text.

Gustav Cassel (1921) *The World's Monetary Problems*, Constable. A classic on money.

Francisco Rivera-Batiz and Luis Rivera Batiz (1994) *International Finance and Open Economy Macroeconomics*, Prentice-Hall. The complete source for the ISLMBP model with its many possibilities.

Hints and Partial Answers

Chapter 1

A2. Domestic supply rises.

A4. With identical supplies, the country with lower demand exports.

C2. XS increases.

D2. In the US, $S/M = 3/2$.

Review

2. Japanese XD rises.

4. Russian XD rises.

6. XD^* from ROW rises.

8. XD from US falls.

10. Venezuelan steel costs $450.

12. Avoid mercantilist arguments.

14. Consider resource availability, technology, and climate.

Chapter 2

A2. The PPF is $220 = 4S + 5M$, $M/S = 4/5$ and output of S is 27.5.

B2. $M/S = 5/4$ at home.

C2. Limits to tt are $.01 > tt > .004$.

C4. 114 on the A axis.

D2. The US is abundant in skilled labor.

Review

2. Delta is the intermediate country and might produce both goods.

4. F specializes, producing 60 S and exporting half.

6. Consumption with trade at home is worth 72.5 M and H gains more.

8. $ew^* = \$8.80$. $tt = 0.7$ and $w = \$12.32$.

10. $(3/5)(w/w^*) > e > \ldots$

12. $L^*/L = 5$ for good 2, and H exports it.

14. $\ldots > e > 0.0053$.

Chapter 3

A2. 105 on the M axis, 135 on the S axis, $MRT = 105/135 = 0.78$.
B2. The economy specializes in M.
C2. Producing S has higher opportunity cost with growth biased toward M.
D2. The cost of living is lower inside an FEZ.

Review

2. The 1986 PPF has the point $(M,S) = (625,2200)$.
4. See Figure 3.2.
6. $tt = M/S = 1.2$ and the gains from trade are 21%.
8. Growth biased toward exports means more trade and higher income.
10. Differences are created by local customs, laws, and input costs.
12. Agricultural output and exports drop.

Chapter 4

A2. Which industry can better influence politicians?
B2. Domestic quantity supplied is greater with a quota.
C2. There is no incentive to trade if prices are equal.
D2. Consider the increasing geographical areas.

Review

2. P rises to $1.5 \times \$30 = \$45$.
4. $D = 100 - P = S = -10 + P$ and $P = \$55$.
6. Price is $50 and total loss is $500.
8. Imports are $D - S = 30$ and $P = \$40$.
10. The economy specializes in M but the tariff reduces M output.
12. Less local interests imply less protection.

Chapter 5

A2. Offer curves collapse.
A4. Foreign offer curve falls toward its import axis.
B2. Similar to A2.
C2. H 4%, F 6%, H 5%, ...
D2. At 6%, the P series runs $20, $21.20, $22.47, ... , $35.82.

Review

2 and 4. Foreign offer curve falls toward import axis.
6. Tariff expands domestic production.
8. Foreign reaction function is horizontal at 4%.

10. Reaction functions lie along the axes.

12. A tariff on M pulls OPEC offer curve in toward its import axis.

Chapter 6

A2. MR for M is \$150. For the 5th unit of L, MRP = \$2.25.

B2. $K = L = 0.2$.

C2. Both countries employ 60 K and 30 L in S production.

D2. Unemployed L implies less production of labor intensive goods.

Review

2. Demand rises in the market for M capital.

4. Isocost line is $1 = $2L + $3K$ and $K = 0.2$.

6. $K = 0.1$.

8. H is labor abundant.

10. The endowment point lies between M' and S.

12. If $L^* = 100$, $(K,L) = (200,50)$

14. $(M,S) = (400,500)$ in H and $(300,600)$ in F, $tt = 1$

16. Strong factor intensity can generally be recognized.

Chapter 7

A2. Temporary losses can be offset by future profit.

A4. Foreign P would be lower than home P.

B2. Aggregation simplifies theory but hides information.

C2. Unspent income can be loaned to others.

D2. Protection is not productive activity.

Review

2. P rises to \$800 and X falls to \$800,000.

4. Foreign revenue is \$192 and home revenue \$187.50.

6. US: $wL/rK = \$209/\$134 = 1.56$, $w/r = 1.4$, and $L/K = 1.56/1.4 = 1.1$.

8. DF runs from \$10 to \$3 on the demand curve, FS starts at \$3.

10. Equilibrium high output for both, SA could pay Libya to remain.

12. PPF expands with bias toward M.

Chapter 8

A2. Emigration from F is 8 million.

B2. Incoming L raises K productivity.

C2. A 5% increase in skilled labor raises unskilled wages to \$8060.

D2. Production of high tech goods & business services fall.

Review

2. Consider other influences on supply and demand for each labor.
4. Immigration shifts labor intensive production.
6. US firms have comparative advantage in these activities.
8. Japan investment in US raises US wage.
10. The specific factor model can predict the effect of increased capital.
12. Mexico is abundant in unskilled labor and scarce in capital.
14. FTZs encourage foreign investment and trade.

Chapter 9

A2. Which industry uses standard techniques and which firms specific inputs?
B2. What happens to pollution tax revenue?
C2. North PPF is biased toward S and free trade raises southern wages.
D2. Do the same groups oppose free trade and free factor mobility?

Review

2. Each plant produces the same output.
4. Less TV output and higher prices.
6. Domestic firms would ask for the same favor.
8. North exports services to South in exchange for manufactures.
10. CU would be tough because it implies free migration.
12. US-Mexico agreement is different from US-Canada agreement.

Chapter 10

A2. Import elasticity is $15/17 = 0.88$.
B2. The *BOT*, *DI*, and *KA* increase, and *NII* falls in the future.
C2. Which country is growing? Which is stable and wealthy?
D2. *PI* and *KA* increase now.

Review

2. XD, P, q_{imp}, and M all move in the same direction.
4. $S/M = 5/12.50 = 0.4$.
6. $BOT = -\$744$, ...
8. Investment flows are US debits.
10. Some nations are in a recession while others are expanding.
12. There is no necessary link between income and BOT.
14. Export taxes would decrease production in the export industry.

Chapter 11

A2. $/DM, lower expected German prices cause demand to fall.
A4. *BGS* is positive during the contract period, negative during pass through.
B2. Idea is to limit exchange of foreign currency for DM.
D2. Real return drops to $97.

Review

2. Yen prices are 495 and 562.5, rice demanded is 4.050 and 3.375 million.
4. Supply of euro falls.
6. Change in export revenue is −5% + 7% = 2% and BOT rises.
8. Central bank is selling assets that should rise in value.
10. Central banks were buying marks, yen, and pounds.
12. Profit is $320.51. If won/$ falls to 750, she loses $512.82.

Chapter 12

A2. Interest payments are $160 million.
A4. *NII* is −$0.94 billion. A3 and A4 are *NII* of the US in 1989 and 1990.
B2. (a) and (b) $/won rises. (c) dollar rises. (d) $/won falls.
C2. Banks want to maintain value of their notes and supply slopes upward.
D2. $P/P^* = 0.000625$, $/peso = 1/1500.

Review

2. XD for loans from US falls.
4. Why buy a riskier private bond?
6. $f = 0.31$.
8. KA rises by $5 million and BOT will rise.
10. Demand for dollars falls.
12. Market relative price of gold = $393.75/$5.25 = 75, official price = 74.
14. Nontraded goods, protectionism, and fixed exchange rates hinder PPP.

Chapter 13

A2. Use production function $y = 1137k^{.3}$ to find k. Then use the statement of per capita national income.
A4. Consumer optimization requires that the optimal indifference curve is tangent to the budget line.
B2. There is a change in the quantity of capital demanded.
B4. Higher taxes shift the IS curve.
C2. Saving is the key.

C4. The decreased M_s shifts the LM curve left. The economy remains in domestic equilibrium and then adjusts.

D2. AS cannot ass full employment output Y_{full}.

D4. AD shifts with the reduction in Ms. Consider real and nominal interest rates.

Review

2. In the closed economy, capital growth equals total saving.

4. Diagram the labor market with wage w and the capital market with return r. Start with an original equilibrium in each market. Remember the labor force L grows.

6. To plot the intertemporal budget line, find total potential income in retirement if there is no consumption in youth.

8. Remember that what is not saved in youth is consumed.

10. The decrease in the money supply shifts the LM curve left.

12. The increase in T shifts the IS curve left. The economy remains in domestic equilibrium and then adjusts.

14. The higher Y^* shifts the FF curve.

16. Use the ASADFF model.

18. Consider changes in AD.

Acronyms

ASEAN	Association of Southeast Asian Nations
APEC	Asian-Pacific Economic Coordination
BEA	Bureau of Economic Analysis
BOP	Balance of payments
BOT	Balance of trade
BGS	Balance on goods and services
CA	Current account
CIA	Covered interest arbitrage
DI	Direct investment in the BOP
DC	Developed country
EU	European Union
FDI	Foreign direct investment
FRB	Federal Reserve Bank
FTAA	Free Trade Area of the Americas
FX	Foreign exchange
GATT	General Agreement on Tariffs & Trade
GDP	Gross domestic product
GSP	Generalized System of Preferences
IMF	International Monetary Fund
IRP	Interest rate parity
ITC	International Trade Commission
KA	Capital account
LDC	Less developed country
MFA	Multifiber Agreement
MNF	Multinational firm
NAFTA	North American Free Trade Agreement
NII	Net investment income
NBER	National Bureau of Economic Research
NIC	Newly industrialized country
NTB	Nontariff barrier
OECD	Organization for Economic Cooperation and Development
PI	Portfolio investment in the BOP
PPP	Purchasing power parity
SDR	Special Drawing Rights
TS	Trade in services in the BOP
UN	United Nations
US	United States
VER	Voluntary export restraint
WTO	World Trade Organization

References

Alavi, Jafar & Henry Thompson (1988) Toward a theory of free trade zones, *International Trade Journal*

Amaya, Naohiro (1988) The Japanese economy in transition: Optimistic about the short term, pessimistic about the long term, *Japan and the World Economy*

Amuedo-Dorantes, Catalina, Cynthia Bansak, & Susan Pozo (2005) On the remitting patterns of immigrants: Evidence from Mexican survey data, *Federal Reserve Bank of Atlanta Economic Review*

Anderson, Kym & Hege Norheim (1993) Is world trade becoming more regionalized? *Review of International Economics*

Arndt, Channing & Thomas Hertel (1997) Revisiting 'The fallacy of free trade', *Review of International Economics*

Aw, Bee Yan & Mark Roberts (1986) Estimating quality change in quota-constrained import markets: The case of US footwear, *Journal of International Economics*

Ayanian, Robert (1988) Political risk, national defense and the dollar, *Economic Inquiry*

Bahora, Alok, Kishore Gawande, & William Kaempfer (1998) The dynamics of tariff retaliation between the US and Canada: Theory and evidence, *Review of International Economics*

Bailey, Jessica & James Sood (1987) An export strategy for banana producing countries, *The International Trade Journal*

Baldwin, Richard (1992) Measurable Dynamic Gains from Trade, *Journal of Political Economy*

Baldwin, Robert (1971) Determinants of the commodity structure of US trade, *American Economic Review*

Baldwin, Robert & Craig Cain (1997) Shifts in US relative wages: The role of trade, technology, and factor endowments, *NBER Working Paper #5934*

Baldwin, Robert & Glen Cain (2000) Shifts in relative US wages: The role of trade, technology, and factor endowments, *Review of Economics and Statistics*

Ballie, Richard & William Osterberg (1997) Central bank intervention and risk in the forward market, *Journal of International Economics*

Barro, Robert (1989) The Ricardian approach to budget deficits, *Journal of Economic Perspectives*

Batra, Ravi (1992) The fallacy of free trade, *Review of International Economics*

Batra, Ravi & Daniel Slotje (1994) Trade policy and poverty in the United States: Theory and evidence, 1947–1990, *Review of International Economics*

Beard, T. Randolph & Henry Thompson (2003) Duopoly quotas and relative import quality, *International Review of Economics and Finance*

Beeson, Patricia & Michael Bryan (1986) Emerging service economy, *Economic Commentary*, FRB Cleveland

Ben-David, David (1993) Equalizing exchange: Trade liberalization and income convergence, *Quarterly Journal of Economics*

Ben-David, David & Alok Bohara (1997) Evidence on the contribution of trade reform towards international income equalization, *Review of International Economics*

Berman, Eli, John Bound, & Stephen Machin (1998) Implications of skill-biased technological change: International evidence, *Quarterly Journal of Economics*

Bernard, Andrew & Bradford Jensen (1998) Exceptional exporter performance: Cause, effect, or both? *Journal of International Economics*

Bernhofen, Daniel M. & John C. Brown (2005) Comparative advantage gains from trade: Evidence from Japan, *American Economic Review*

Bourgheas, Spiros, Panicios Demetrades, & Edgar Morgenroth (1999) Infrastructure, transport costs and trade, *Journal of International Economics*

Branson, William & Nikolaos Monoyios (1977) Factor inputs in US trade, *Journal of International Economics*

Broadberry, S.N. (1987) Purchasing power parity and the pound-dollar rate in the 1930s, *Economica*

Brook, Douglas A. (2005) "Meta-Strategic Lobbying: The 1998 Steel Imports Case", Business and Politics, Article 4. *http://www.bepress.com/bap/vol7/iss1/art4*

Brown, Lynn (1986) Taking in each other's laundry: The service economy, *New England Economic Review*, FRB Boston

Bryan, Michael & Susan Byrne (1990) Don't worry: We'll grow out of it, *Economic Commentary*, FRB Cleveland

Buluswar, Murli, Henry Thompson, & Kamal Upadhyaya (1996) Devaluation and the trade balance in India: Stationarity and cointegration, *Applied Economics*

Caprio, Gerard & Patrick Honohan (1999) Restoring banking stability: Beyond supervised capital requirements, *Journal of Economic Perspectives*

Casas, Francisco & Kwan Choi (1985) The Leontief paradox: Continued or resolved? *Journal of Political Economy*

Cha, Baekin & Daniel Himarios (1995) The internationalization of the US wage process, *Review of International Economics*

Chang, Tsangyao, Wehshwo Fang, Wenrong Liu, & Henry Thompson (2000) Exports, imports, and income in Taiwan: An examination of the export led growth hypothesis, *International Economic Journal*

Childs, Nathan & Michael Hammig (1987) An examination of the impact of real exchange rates on US exports of agricultural commodities, *The International Trade Journal*

Clerides, Sofronis (2005) Gains from trade in used goods: Evidence from the global market for automobiles, *CEPR Discussion Paper # 4859*

Cline, William (1997) *Trade and Income Distribution*, Washington: Institute for International Economics

Cole, Harold & Lee Ohanian (1999) The Great Depression in the United States from a neoclassical perspective, *Quarterly Review*, FRB of Minneapolis

Cross, Sam (1998) *All About the Foreign Exchange Markets in the United States*, FRB New York

Crowder, William (1996) A reexamination of long run PPP: The case of Canada, the UK, and the US, *Review of International Economics*

Cumby, Robert (1996) Forecasting exchange rates and relative prices with hamburger standards, *NBER Working Paper #5675*

Davis, Donald & David Weinstein (1995) Intra-industry trade: A Heckscher-Ohlin Ricardo Approach, *Journal of International Economics*

Davis, Donald & David Weinstein (1998) Economic geography and regional production structure: An empirical investigation, *Federal Reserve Bank of New York Staff Reports, #40*

Deardorff, Alan & Robert Stern (1984) The economic effect of complete elimination of post-Tokyo Round tariffs. In *Trade Policy for the 1980s*, William Cline, ed., Washington: Institute for International Economics

DeLong, Bradford & Larry Summers (1990) Equipment, investment and economic growth, *NBER Working Paper #3513*

Dinopoulos, Elias & Mordechai Kreinin (1988) Effects of the US-Japan auto VER on European prices and on US welfare, *The Review of Economics and Statistics*

Dollar, David & Edward Wolff (1988) Convergence of industry labor productivity among advanced economies, 1963–1982, *The Review of Economics and Statistics*

Dollar, David & Edward Wolff (1993) *Competitiveness, Convergence, and International Specialization*, Cambridge: MIT Press

Eckels, Alfred (1998) Smoot-Hawley and the stock market crash, 1929-1930, *The International Trade Journal*

Edwards, Sebastian (1999) How effective are capital controls? *Journal of Economic Perspectives*

Eichengreen, Barry (1991) Historical research on international lending and debt, *Journal of Economic Perspectives*

Eichengreen, Barry (1999) *Toward a New International Financial Architecture: A Practical Post-Asia Agenda*, Washington: Institute for International Economics

Eichengreen, Barry & Douglas Irwin (1994) Trade blocs, currency blocs, and the disintegration of world trade in the 1930s, *NBER Working Paper #4445*

Engel, Charles (1999) Are we globalized yet? *Economic Letter*, FRB San Francisco

Engel, Charles & John Rogers (1994) How wide is the US border? *NBER Working Paper #4829*

Falzoni, Anna, Giovanni Brunno, & Rosario Crino (2004) Foreign Direct Investment, Wage Inequality, and Skilled Labor Demand in EU Accession Countries, *Centro Studi Luca d'Agliano Development Studies Working Paper #188*

Fang, WehShwo, Yihao Lai, Henry Thompson (2005) Exchange rates, exchange risk, and Asian export revenue, *International Review of Economics & Finance*

Feenburg, Daniel, Andrew Mitushi, & James Poterba (1997) Distribution effects of adopting a national sales tax, *NBER Working Paper #5885*

Feenstra, Robert (1988) Gains from trade in differentiated products: Japanese compact trucks, in *Empirical Methods for International Trade*, Robert Feenstra, ed., Cambridge: MIT Press

Feenstra, Robert & Gordon Hanson (1997) Direct foreign investment and relative wages: Evidence from Mexico's Maquiladoras, *Journal of International Economics*

Feenstra, Robert & Gordon Hanson (1999) The Impact of outsourcing and high-technology capital on wages: Estimates for the United States, 1979–1990, *Quarterly Journal of Economics*

Fischer, Stanley (1999) On the need for an international lender of last resort, *Journal of Economic Perspectives*

Ford, Jon & Henry Thompson (1997) Global sensitivity of neoclassical and factor proportions models to production technology, *International Economic Journal*

Frenkel, Jeffrey & Kenneth Froot (1990) Exchange rate forecasting techniques, survey data, and implications for the foreign exchange market, *NBER Working Paper #3470*

Garten, Jeffrey (1998) In this economic chaos, a global central bank can help, *International Herald Tribune*, 25 September

Gartner, Bruce (1987) Causes of US farm commodity programs, *Journal of Political Economy*

General Agreement on Tariffs and Trade (various issues) *International Trade*, GATT

Glesjer, Herbert, K. Goosens, & Eede Vanden (1982) Inter industry versus intra industry specialization in exports and imports, 1959–1973, *Journal of International Economics*

Goldberg, Linda & Keith Crockett (1998) The dollar and US manufacturing, *Current Issues in Economics and Finance*, FRB of New York

Goldberg, Linda & Michael Klein (1999) International trade and factor mobility: An empirical investigation, *Staff Reports*, #81, FRB New York

Golub, Stephen (1995) Comparative and absolute advantage in the Asia Pacific region, Working paper, FRB San Francisco

Griffen, James & David Teece (1982) *OPEC Behavior and World Oil Prices*, London: Allen & Unwin

Grilli, Vittrio & Andrea Beltratti (1989) US military expenditure and the dollar, *Economic Inquiry*

Grossman, Gene & Jim Levinshon (1989) Import competition and the stock market return to capital, *American Economic Review*

Grubel, Herbert & Peter Lloyd (1975) *Intraindustry Trade*, London: MacMillan

Gruben, William & Sherry Kiser (1999) Hey, Mr. Greenspan, can you spare a dollar? *Southwest Economy*, FRB Dallas

Gylfason, Thorvaldur (2004) Natural resources and economic growth: From dependence to diversification, *CEPR Discussion Paper No. 4804*

Hakkio, Graig & Douglas Pearce (1985) The reaction of exchange rates to economic news, *Economic Inquiry*

Hanson, Gordon (1998) Regional adjustment to trade liberalization, *Regional Science and Urban Economics*, 419-44

Hansen, Wendy & Thomas Prusa (1997) The economics and politics of trade policy: An empirical analysis of ITC decision making, *Review of International Economics*

Harris, James & Michael Todaro (1970) Migration, unemployment and development: A two-sector analysis, *American Economic Review*

Haskel, Jonathan & Matthew Slaughter (2002) Does the sector bias of skill-biased technical change explain changing skill premia? *European Economic Review*

Hickock, Susan (1985) The consumer cost of US trade restraints, *Quarterly Review*, FRB New York

Hickock, Susan & James Orr (1989) Shifting patterns of US trade with selected developing Asian economies, *Quarterly Review*, FRB New York

Himarios, Daniel (1989) Do devaluations improve the trade balance? The evidence revisited, *Economic Inquiry*

Huber, Richard (1971) Effect on prices of Japan's entry into world commerce after 1858, *Journal of Political Economy*

Hufbauer, Gary, Diane Berliner, & Kimberly Elliott (1986) *Trade Protection in the United States: 31 Case Studies*, Washington: Institute for International Economics

Hunter, Linda (1990) US trade protection: Effects on the regional composition of employment, *Economic Review*, FRB Dallas

Hunter, Linda & James Markusen (1988) Per capita income as a determinant of trade, in *Empirical Methods for International Trade*, Robert Feenstra, ed., Cambridge: MIT Press

International Monetary Fund (various issues) *Direction of Trade Yearbook, IMF Survey, International Financial Statistics*, Washington: IMF

Irwin, Douglas (1998) Did late nineteenth century US tariffs promote infant industries? Evidence from the tinplate industry, *NBER Working Paper* #6835

Karrenbrock, Jeffrey (1990) The internationalization of the beer brewing industry, *Review*, FRB St Louis

Kasa, Kenneth (1997) Understanding trends in foreign exchange rates, *Weekly Letter*, FRB San Francisco

Kaufman, Henry (1998) Preventing the next global financial crisis, *Washington Post*, 28 January

Kelly, Kenneth & Morris Morker (1998) Do unfairly traded imports injure domestic industries? *Review of International Economics*

Knetter, Michael (1989) Price discrimination by US and German exporters, *American Economic Review*

Kouparitsas, Michael (1997) A dynamic macroeconomic analysis of NAFTA, *Economic Perspectives*, FRB of Chicago

Kreinin, Mordechai (1984) Wage competitiveness in steel and motor vehicles, *Economic Inquiry*

Kreinin, Mordechai (1985) Internal trade and possible restrictions in high-tech products, *Journal of Policy Modeling*

Krugman, Paul (1987) Is free trade passe? *The Journal of Economic Perspectives*

Krugman, Paul (1998) Saving Asia: It's time to get radical, *Fortune*, 7 September

Lawrence, Robert & Craig Evans (1996) Trade and wages: Insights fron the crystal ball, *NBER Working Paper #5633*

Leamer, Ed. (1980) The Leontief paradox reconsidered, *Journal of Political Economy*

Leamer, Ed. (1984) *Sources of International Comparative Advantage: Theory and Evidence*, Cambridge: MIT Press

Lee, Jong Wha (1994) Capital goods imports and long run growth, *NBER Working Paper #4725*

Lee, Jong Wha & Phillip Swagel (1994) Trade barriers and trade flows across countries and industries, *NBER Working Paper #4799*

Lewis, Ethan (2004) How did the Miami labor market absorb the Mariel immigrants? *FRB Philadelphia Working Paper 04-3*

Lipsey, Robert (2000) The role of foreign direct investment in international capital flows, *NBER Working Paper #7094*

Lucas, Robert (1993) Making a miracle, *Econometrica*, 251–72

MacDougall, G.D.A. (1951) British and American productivity and comparative costs in international trade, *Economic Journal*

Maddison, Angus (1991) *Dynamic Forces in Capitalist Development*, Oxford: Oxford University Press

Maneschi, Andrea (1992) Ricardo's international trade theory: Beyond the comparative cost example, *Cambridge Journal of Economics*

Marjit, Sugata (1994) The fallacy of free trade: Comment, *Review of International Economics*

Markusen, James & Randall Wigle (1989) Nash equilibrium tariffs for the United States and Canada: The roles of country size, scale economies, and capital mobility, *The Journal of Political Economy*

Marshall, Alfred (1926) *The Official Papers of Alfred Marshall*, London: McMillan

Marston, Richard (1998) Pricing to market in Japanese manufacturing, *Journal of International Economics*

Maskus, Keith (1985) A test of the Heckscher-Ohlin-Vanek theorem: The Leontief commonplace, *Journal of International Economics*

Maskus, Keith (1993) Intellectual property rights and the Uruguay Round, *Economic Review*, FRB of Kansas City

Maskus, Keith & Mohan Penubarti (1995) How trade related are intellectual property rights? *Journal of International Economics*

McCallum, Bennet (1989) Targets, indicators, and instruments of monetary policy, *NBER Working Paper #3234*

Mishkin, Frederic (1999) Global financial instability: Framework, events, issues, *Journal of Economic Perspectives*

Moran, Theodore, Edward Graham, & Magnus Blomström (2005) *Foreign Direct Investment Promote Development?* Washington: Institute for International Economics

Ott, Mack (1989) *International Economic Conditions*, FRB St Louis

Panagariya, Arvind, Shekhar Shah, & Deepak Mishra (2001) Demand elasticities in international trade: Are they really low? *Journal of Development Economics*

Polachek, Solomon (1997) Why democracies cooperated more and fight less: The relationship between international trade and cooperation, *Review of International Economics*

Rassekh, Farhad (1992) The role of international trade in the convergence of per capita GDP in the OECD: 1950–1985, *International Economic Journal*

Rassekh, Farhad (1994) An evaluation of Batra's "Fallacy of free trade" *Review of International Economics*

Rassekh, Farhad & Henry Thompson (1993) Factor price equalization: Theory and evidence, *Journal of Economic Integration*

Rassekh, Farhad & Henry Thompson (1997) Adjustment in general equilibrium: Some industrial evidence, *Review of International Economics*

Rassekh, Farhad & Henry Thompson (1998) Micro convergence and macro convergence: Factor price equalization and per capita income, *Pacific Economic Review*

Ray, Ed (1991) Foreign takeovers and new investments in the US, *Contemporary Policy Issues*

Reinert, Kenneth & David Roland-Holst (1998) North-south trade and occupational wages: Some evidence from North America, *Review of International Economics*

Revenga, Ana (1992) Exporting jobs? The impact of import competition on employment and wages in US manufacturing, *The Quarterly Journal of Economics*, 255-84

Richardson, David & Chi Zhang (1999) Revealing comparative advantage: Chaotic or coherent patterns across time and sector and U.S. trading partner? *NBER Working Paper #7212*

Rogoff, Kenneth (1999) International institutions for reducing global financial instability, *Journal of Economic Perspectives*

Romer, Paul (1994) New goods, old theory, and the welfare costs of trade restrictions, *Journal of Development Economics*

Rousslang, Donald & Theodore To (1993) Domestic trade and transport costs as barriers to international trade, *Canadian Journal of Economics*

Ruffin, Roy (1988) The missing link: The Ricardian approach to the factor endowments theory of trade, *American Economic Review*

Ruffin, Roy & Farhad Rassekh (1987) The role of foreign direct investment in US capital outflows, *American Economic Review*

Sachs, Jeffrey (1995) Do we need an international lender of last resort? Princeton University, Frank Graham Memorial Lecture

Seshan, Ganesh (2005) The impact of trade liberalization on household qelfare in Vietnam, *World Bank Policy Research Working Paper # 3541*

Shapiro, Matthew (1987) Are cyclical fluctuations in productivity due more to supply shocks or demand shocks? *NBER Working Paper #2147*

Smith, Adam (1776) *The Wealth of Nations*, Penguin Classics

Smith, Alasdair & Anthony Venables (1988) Completing the internal market in the European community, *European Economic Review*

Stern, Robert & Keith Maskus (1981) Determinants of the structure of US foreign trade, *Journal of International Economics*

Stiglitz, Joseph (1997) Dumping on free trade: The US import trade laws, *Southern Economic Journal*

Sweeney, George, T. Randolph Beard, & Henry Thompson (1997) Quotas and quality in international trade, *Journal of Economic Integration*

Tarr, David & Morris Morkre (1987) Aggregate costs to the United States of tariffs and quotas on imports, in *The New Protectionist Threat to World Welfare*, Dominick Salvatore ed., Amsterdam: North-Holland

Thompson, Henry (1986) Free trade and factor price polarization, *European Economic Review*

Thompson, Henry (1987) Do tariffs protect specific factors? *Canadian Journal of Economics*

Thompson, Henry (1991) Simulating a multifactor general equilibrium model of production and trade, *International Economic Journal*

Thompson, Henry (1994a) An investigation of the quantitative properties of the specific factors model of production and trade, *Japan and the World Economy*

Thompson, Henry (1994b) NAFTA and industrial adjustment: A specific factors model of production in Alabama, *Growth and Change*

Thompson, Henry (1995a) Factor intensity versus factor substitution in a specified general equilibrium model, *Journal of Economic Integration*

Thompson, Henry (1995b) Free trade and income redistribution in some developing and newly industrialized countries, *Open Economies Review*

Thompson, Henry (2001) International trade with three factors, goods, or countries, *Keio Economic Studies*

Toledo, Hugo (2005) Coca substitution and free trade in Bolivia: The pending crisis, *Review of Economic Development*

Toledo, Hugo & Henry Thompson (2001) Bolivia and South American free trade, *The International Trade Journal*

Trela, Irene & John Whalley (1995) Internal quota-allocation schemes and the costs of the MFA, *Review of International Economics*

Uctum, Mitch (1998) Why have corporate profits declined? An international comparison, *Review of International Economics*

United Nations (1989) *Foreign Direct Investment and Transnational Corporations in Services*, New York: UN

Upadhyaya, Kamal & Henry Thompson (1998) The impact of the exchange rate on local industry, *Economia Internazionale*

Wacziarg, Romain & Jessica Wallack (2004) Trade liberalization and inter-sectoral labor movements, *Journal of International Economics*, 411-39

Wall, Howard (1999) Using the gravity model to estimate the costs of protection, *Federal Reserve Bank of St. Louis Review*

Walter, Ingo (1983) Structural adjustment and trade policy in the international steel industry, in *Trade Policy in the 1980s*, William Cline ed., Washington: Institute for International Economics

Weidenbaum, Murray & Tracy Munger (1983) Protection at any price? *Regulation*, July

Williamson, Jeffrey (1996) Globalization, convergence, and history, *Journal of Economic History*

Xu, Zhenhui (1996) On the causality between export growth and GDP growth: An empirical reinvestigation, *Review of International Economics*

Xu, Zhenhui (2000) Effects of primary exports on industrial exports and GDP: Empirical evidence, *Review of Development Economics*, 307-25

Yeats, A.J. (1974) Effective tariff protection in the United States, the European Community, and Japan, *The Quarterly Review of Economics and Business*

Name Index

Subject Index